MAGIC
IN THE AIR

ALSO BY MIKE SIELSKI

THE RISE: *Kobe Bryant and the Pursuit of Immortality*

FADING ECHOES: *A True Story of Rivalry and Brotherhood from the Football Field to the Fields of Honor*

HOW TO BE LIKE JACKIE ROBINSON: *Life Lessons from Baseball's Greatest Hero* (with Pat Williams)

MAGIC
IN THE AIR

THE MYTH, THE MYSTERY, AND THE SOUL OF THE SLAM DUNK

MIKE SIELSKI

ST. MARTIN'S
PRESS
NEW YORK

First published in the United States by St. Martin's Press,
an imprint of St. Martin's Publishing Group

www.stmartins.com

Designed by Steven Seighman

The Library of Congress Cataloging-in-Publication Data
is available upon request.

ISBN 978-1-250-28752-6 (hardcover)
ISBN 978-1-250-28753-3 (ebook)

First Edition: 2025

10 9 8 7 6 5 4 3 2 1

For all the scribes who showed me the way,
and for the ones who still do . . .

CONTENTS

PREFACE

THE JOURNEY

The photograph has frozen and preserved the image of a famous man in a curious moment. In it, the man, who will soon become the most consequential athlete of the twentieth century, is clad in a basketball uniform: tank top, shorts three inches from the tops of his thighs, brilliant white socks climbing his shins from underneath black hightops. He is standing underneath a regulation hoop and stretching upward toward the rim, right hand open, fingers splayed, a ball at their tips. He is not close enough to the rim to dunk the ball. But it is obvious from the striations of muscle along his arms and legs that, if he were to jump, even from the flat-footed position he occupies in the photo, he could dunk the ball, because at the instant that the camera flashes he is twenty-seven years old, in his physical prime, not yet weighed down by his career in professional sports, by the burdens he will bear, by the pressures and pain he will have to withstand. There is a wooden wall to his right, and the angle of the lens and the lighting in the gymnasium combine to project his shadow against that wall, as if his ghost were mimicking him.

The editors of the *Arizona Republic* thought enough of the photograph to publish it on the cover of the newspaper's sports section, across two of the page's eight columns, on Sunday, January 12, 1947. Though they ran it without including a photo credit—neither readers nor, later, researchers would know who had snapped the shot—it was as prominent as any picture in the paper, and they had a news peg to justify playing it up. On Monday and Tuesday nights, at Phoenix Union High School, the Del E. Webb Construction Company Webbcos, a local semipro basketball club, would be hosting a professional team from the West Coast: the Los Angeles Red Devils. The Red Devils existed for just one season, 1946–47, but they made that season count. They went 13–3, a record that included a victory over the Chicago American Gears and their center, George Mikan, and two wins over the New York Rens, the Black barnstorming team that was the equal of, and sometimes superior to, the Harlem Globetrotters. Their lineup featured several college standouts from the West Coast, but the player with the biggest name was the player in the photograph: five feet, eleven inches tall; already renowned as a football, track, and basketball star at Pasadena Junior College and UCLA; poised to be the focal point of the American public. In three months and three days, on April 15, he would debut for the Brooklyn Dodgers, playing first base, batting second in their lineup, at Ebbets Field against the Boston Braves. It only made sense for the *Republic* to put Jackie Robinson above the fold.

Robinson had signed with the Red Devils in October 1946, not long after finishing his first and only season of minor-league baseball in the International League with the Montreal Royals. But he had never been one to settle on just one pastime, even the national one, and as terrific as he was on the ballfield, his athleticism had shone even more brightly in other sports. In 1938, for instance, Robinson had set the national junior college record in the broad jump, leaping 25 feet, 6½ inches. Two years later, he won both the Pacific Athletic Conference and the NCAA championships.

"It is a wonderful event," Robinson once said. "You toe the line and sprint forward with all your strength. Then you jump. You really try to jump off the earth, and your legs churn the air like you wanted to reach the moon."

He might as well have been speaking about another dynamic act in another sport. It had not occurred to many basketball players in the 1930s and 1940s to dunk, even though some did and even though plenty were capable. "All we wanted was the basket," former Rens player John Isaacs told the *New York Times* in 2004. But one of them wanted something more. One of them was a pioneer before he became a pioneer, a legend before he became a legend.

"Guys would talk, and people said that out in California," Isaacs said, "Jackie was the first one to elevate and go over the rim."

There are particular innovations in particular sports that turn out to be the most important and influential aspects of those sports. These inventions make the games more exciting and interesting, broaden and deepen the appreciation and love for them. They diversify the action, create fresh styles of play, expand the notions of what is possible on the field or the court. Athletes go from being widgets on an assembly line, all of them shaped to do the same thing in the same way in the same ol' game, to flourishing as four-leaf clovers and diamonds, no two the same, each unique and beautiful. The forward pass lifted football from the land into the air, transforming it over time from nothing but a succession of bloody, brutal scrums in the dirt to a form of performance art that was made for a television screen: part ballet, part high-wire act, part military-style strategy and attack. The end of the Deadball Era in Major League Baseball led to the beginning of the home run era, to outfield fences and ballparks with nooks and crannies and character, to Babe Ruth and Hank Aaron and Aaron Judge, to steroid scandals and the fixation on launch angles.

Basketball has followed its own trajectory. Throughout its early years, it was ground-bound, limited by decorum and humility and the self-discipline that the sport's inventor, Dr. James Naismith, sought to instill in its practitioners. And it stayed that way until, like the first human being to craft a weapon and hunt for food, a player found himself high enough in the atmosphere to extend the basketball above the rim and throw the ball down through the hoop. Until the first player dunked.

It's no exaggeration to say that the entire social, cultural, and athletic evolution of basketball can be traced through the slam dunk and that, in turn, America's entire social and cultural evolution can be traced through it. The dunk is more than just two points. It is basketball's consummate symbol of superiority—the act, more than any other, that represents domination of an opponent. A PhD candidate could write a dissertation on the psychology implicit and overt in the dunk: the masculinity that has long been associated with the act of dunking; the emasculation of being "posterized"; the stereotypes of whites, Blacks, men, and women that play into the dunk's physical and emotional power and resonance.

The dunk has been a revolutionary agent, an expression of Black culture, a tangible indication, amid the righteous upheaval of the Civil Rights Movement, of the threat that Blacks were considered to be to the establishment. The NCAA banned it for almost a full decade, from 1967 to 1976, ostensibly because the association wanted to curtail player injuries and prevent the game from deviating too far from its more modest origins. But the rule seemed first and foremost a way to squelch the individual expression and athleticism that characterized the sport throughout urban America and that was intrinsic to the manner in which Black athletes played it. One of the primary targets of the ban, arguably the primary target, was Kareem Abdul-Jabbar, who at the time went by the name Lew Alcindor and was the fulcrum of John Wooden's dynasty at UCLA. That individuality and flair would nevertheless creep into basketball's highest levels, bubbling up from the playgrounds and parks until those qualities defined the sport's most fascinating players: players such as Connie Hawkins, David Thompson, and, of course, Julius Erving, who ushered the NBA into the modern era. Dunking became so identified with Black culture, in fact, that by the early 1990s it became acceptable to assert—in the title of a major Hollywood movie—that white men could not do it.

The dunk has been a mechanism for growing the NBA into a global Goliath. Magic Johnson and Larry Bird carried the league back to the top of the public's consciousness with their arrivals in 1979, but it was Michael Jordan—a singular sensation for his acrobatics—who transformed the NBA into a billion-dollar leviathan. The dunk turned basketball into a sport of corporate America. The dunk sold sneakers. The dunk spread the gospel of JUST DO IT across the nation.

The dunk, finally, remains a door that, when opened, allows access to the most colorful figures and moments from the sport's past. It introduces even the most passionate fan to people and episodes long forgotten but full of drama and even humor, people and episodes whose significance resonates still. More than that, the dunk and the history around it are just plain fun. And in an age when every shot, every pass, every dribble, every foul, and every spot on the floor where a player has taken a shot or thrown a pass or dribbled the ball or committed a foul are recorded and dropped into algorithmic formulas to try to optimize performance and increase our understanding of what the hell is happening out there, when following basketball or any major sport can feel like a never-ending battle to keep your mental hard drive from crashing due to information overload, the sport could use more fun. Professional basketball has become so analytical, so soulless at times that a player whose game and fame are predicated on pulling off spectacular dunks—a player such as Ja Morant, the Memphis Grizzlies' incandescent and troubled guard—stands out like a beam of light. This wasn't always the case. Joy used to be the rule, not a secondary consideration. Maybe we can get back there again.

Each of the chapters in this book could stand on its own as an essay, a brief article or post, or a magazine-length piece. Taken together, they form an unbroken narrative that will give the reader, I hope, the impression of being a time traveler, zooming from one era to another and from place to place, meeting and learning about a select few men and women who have one thing in common: their lives are defined, to varying degrees, by the slam dunk.

Some of these stories will sound too wild to be true. That's to be expected. The journalism of the early twentieth century and the oral history of basketball are fraught with embellishment and mystery and myth, with the haze of memory and the shading of reality. Years pass.

Fact morphs into embellishment. Embellishment becomes accepted as fact. The process is inevitable and, really, unstoppable. Mostly, I wanted to tell the stories that I thought deserved telling, those that involve the most famous and accomplished athletes in the sport, and especially those that hadn't been told all that frequently before now. So no, you won't find *everything* about the slam dunk in this book. What I can assure you, though, is that you'll find something about the dunk or the sport that you didn't know before, something that might make you laugh or shake your head, something that might compel you to remember when or wonder what's ahead. It will be an entertaining journey, and it begins, of all places, in western Kentucky, with an athlete who once appeared to hold the world, like a basketball, in the palm of his hand.

I

RISE AND FALL

In the winter of 2023, there was one athlete whose flair for dunking distinguished him from every other player in the NBA. It was his trademark, his identity. He was a natural successor, maybe the only one at the time, to MJ, to Dr. J, to those stars of the past whose names are still known by shorthand. Their glory was there for him, close enough to touch. And he nearly lost it all.

One of the foundational courses for undergraduates at Murray State University in Murray, Kentucky, is Com 161, which is an abbreviation for its more cumbersome official name: *Communication 161: Introduction to Public Speaking*. The university offers it every semester, either in two 75-minute classes or a single three-hour gulp each week. No fewer than 15 full-time and part-time professors teach it each term. No more than 25 students can enroll in any one section. There were 15 to 20 in Zac Boardman's class, he remembered, all of them seated at tables arrayed in three long rows when, in January 2018, he showed up on the first day of the spring semester. The students had to introduce themselves, and Boardman, planted in his chair in the back of the room, didn't notice the shy Black kid sitting at the opposite end of his row until the kid stood up to speak.

My name is Ja, he said. *I'm a good player, and I hope to make it to the NBA.*

Boardman reacted with surprised skepticism. *Yeah, right.* After all, he was born in Murray, had lived there ever since, and had rooted for the Murray State men's basketball team for most of his life, and a player who possessed such high expectations for himself—and a willingness to reveal those expectations to a room full of peers and strangers—was an uncommon thing within the campus's culture. Boardman had heard of Ja Morant, had seen him play a couple of times, but nothing more than that. The Racers would finish with a 26–6 record that season and had a roster laden with upperclassmen, but most of the student body, Boardman included, hadn't caught on to how good the team and, eventually, its starting point guard would be. Most students left Murray for winter break, putting aside their basketball fandom until at least two weeks after the turn of the new year, so they hadn't seen much of Morant. He hadn't been around that long. He, like Boardman, was just a freshman. No one in the classroom knew much about him. No one anywhere did yet.

His lean and wiry body now loose and droopy in a courtside chair at the Wells Fargo Center in Philadelphia, Ja Morant arranged himself as if he were accessible and comfortable when in fact—and it took just a few seconds to recognize this—he was not. The Memphis Grizzlies had just finished a morning shootaround in late February 2023, their game against the 76ers that night still more than seven hours away, and Morant now had to fulfill what is, for an NBA superstar, one of the more exasperating and annoying obligations of being an NBA superstar: speaking to the media. In this instance, though, the one thing that Morant couldn't call the obligation was *exhausting*. There were just two reporters there. I was one. (In an indication of the cutbacks and tightened purse strings common among local media companies, no Grizzlies beat writers had made the trip from Memphis to Philadelphia.)

Ross Wooden, the team's public-relations director, lingered a couple of steps away, ready to pounce to ensure that Morant wasn't asked too many questions over too long a period of time, *too many* being more than half a dozen or so, *too long* being five minutes.

Ever since the 2018–19 college basketball season, when Morant had zoomed from relative obscurity to national stardom during his sophomore year at Murray State, a few particular qualities had come to define him, at least in the public eye. The most obvious and compelling was his ability, from his space-rocket vertical leap to his fearlessness in confronting taller, stronger players, to dunk the basketball. Another was the joy with which he played and generally seemed to carry himself. Neither of those qualities was on display as he sat there, staring straight ahead at his teammates, who were still moseying through the final minutes of their workout. Neither of those qualities had been on display in recent days, either, or would be over the weeks to come.

On February 5, The Athletic had broken a story that cast Morant and his associates in an unflattering, even threatening light: After the Grizzlies had beaten the Indiana Pacers at FedEx Forum in Memphis on January 29, Morant and several acquaintances had "confronted members of the Pacers' traveling party near the team's bus in the loading area. . . . Later someone in a slow-moving SUV—which Morant was riding in—trained a red laser on them." Though a Pacers security guard had believed the laser to be a gunsight and told The Athletic as much, an NBA spokesman said the league had investigated and "could not corroborate that any individual threatened others with a weapon." Of course, in professional sports, absolution and redemption for such alleged conduct are always just one goose-pimpling performance away, but Morant had passed up a chance to attain both. Five days before the Grizzlies' game in Philadelphia, the NBA had held its annual Slam Dunk Contest, which once had been the most popular event in the weekend of festivities accompanying the league's All-Star Game. But the contest had grown so bland and boring over time that Michael Levine, the NBA's senior vice president of entertainment and marketing, had paved the way for Mac McClung—a point guard with the G League's Delaware Blue Coats—to compete in it, even though

McClung wasn't an NBA player. What McClung was was a viral sensation; his dunks in high school and college had generated millions of views on social media. He was also six-foot-two and white, the ideal stereotype of a dunking underdog, the perfect lure, one might think, for casual basketball fans to get interested in the contest again. And when McClung won the contest, he became an instant and fleeting celebrity.

Had Morant—by consensus the NBA's best dunker—and other stars chosen to participate, the league wouldn't have had to rely on such gimmickry to juice interest in a prime-time showcase of its players' athleticism and charisma. In the 1980s and '90s, the era when the NBA was expanding its reach from the regional to the national to the global, several of the sport's luminaries looked forward to the dunk contest; they considered it another arena of competition to establish and defend one's bona fides. Julius Erving, Michael Jordan, Dominique Wilkins, Clyde Drexler, Kobe Bryant: all of them and more took part. Since entering the league four years earlier, though, Morant had never entered the contest. Not once. "It's so watered down," Ronnie "Tee" Morant, Ja's father, told me. "There's no fun in it." Ja had been asked the year before, after throwing down a reverse, two-handed jam in the 2022 All-Star Game, what it would take to persuade him to participate. "Nothing," he said. "If I want to, I will. . . . The goal isn't high enough." In other words: The dunk contest wasn't worth his time. It wasn't worth his risking an injury. It wasn't worth his risking the humiliation of missing a dunk. It wasn't even worth someone asking him about it.

What did he think of McClung's performance and victory?

"I didn't watch none of that," he said at the Wells Fargo Center.

What? He had been there, at Vivint Arena in Salt Lake City, when McClung had won. He wasn't watching? Come on. And why the sullen indifference? Why act like an annoyed teenager, so put out by an easy question? Wasn't the dunk contest supposed to be fun? Wasn't *Ja Morant* supposed to be fun? He was supposed to be, much like Stephen Curry, an accessible superstar: not so tall, not so muscled, big beaming smile, someone who looks a little ordinary yet does extraordinary things. His dunks were blazing moments of superhuman-ness from a guy whose physical appearance and, on the surface, image suggested he was a normal human being.

"He's like a trampoline, a rubber band," De'Anthony Melton, who was Morant's teammate in Memphis for three years, told me. "The way he's able to full-speed stop and explode out there is probably one of the best ever, honestly."

Even his aborted dunks were captivating. Even they enhanced his reputation. In a February 2020 game, Morant had tried to dunk over Anthony Davis, the Los Angeles Lakers' center, six foot ten and 253 pounds. He leaped into Davis and extended his left forearm into Davis's neck like he was hitting him with a billy, only to have the ball carom off the backboard as the two players crashed to the floor. That sequence had inspired a headline in the *New York Times* later that year, "Ja Morant's Dunks Are Amazing. His Misses Are Even Better," and it had inspired this line from the story by the *Times*'s Scott Cacciola: "Few players have ever made missed dunks look cooler." What could be cooler as a pro athlete than having your failures be as cool as your successes? And what could be cooler than Morant's explanation for the play? "Just a guy standing in my way. I don't care about a name or who it is," he had said, as if he were an Eastwood-movie gunslinger who had come to clean up town by dunking on all the bad guys. That was cool. Saying that he hadn't paid any attention to the dunk contest . . . denying reality . . . ducking the most insignificant of questions just because he could . . . not so cool at all. But then, he had reached the stage of his life and career where he could be uncool if he so chose and fans and, more importantly, his sponsors would still think he was cool. He had signed an endorsement deal with Nike, for a reported $12 million, ahead of the 2019 NBA draft. He had signed, in July 2022, a five-year contract extension with the Grizzlies that would guarantee him $191 million. And in December, Nike had announced that Morant was getting his first signature shoe, the Ja 1, which was scheduled to be released April 1 and would be worth, based on the dollar figures of similar deals with similar stars—the Dallas Maverickicks' Luka Doncic, the New Orleans Pelicans' Zion Williamson—in the neighborhood of $75 million. Maybe this was what that kind of wealth and celebrity really bought. It bought the right to be insolent.

The other writer there with me, from *SLAM* magazine, asked Morant about the upcoming release of his signature shoe. Morant's eyes brightened. That subject he was happy to discuss. His conversations with Nike officials about creating the Ja 1 had begun a year and a half earlier, he said, and he was pleased with the result—teal with black and white trim, a slash of red around the ankle, the Nike swoosh black—and the response to it. Already, his teammates were wearing the sneaker at the shootaround. "I had to earn it," he said. "It wasn't going to be just handed to me. My play—that's pretty much what I did. Had to earn it. . . . I know it's a life-changing moment."

He understood fully why his style of play attracted people. "It's pretty much my athleticism," he said, "the excitement I play with, the flair." It was that flair—in a sport that had been trending toward the cold and analytical for years, toward the corner three and the high-efficiency shot and away from the long two and the pull-up two and just about any two-point shot that wasn't a layup or a dunk—that set him apart. He was a throwback in that regard, a reminder of the days when players such as Bryant and Allen Iverson would shake and bake and shed a defender and launch a twenty-footer or embark on a twisting, improbable drive to the hoop that could be classified as a "good shot" only because they were the ones taking it, only because any shot they took was inherently better than any other shot just about any of their teammates might take. No, their style wasn't always efficient, but it sure was entertaining, and the NBA's plummeting ratings in the late 2010s and early 2020s suggested that the paying public was picking up on the reality that the former wasn't necessarily the latter. Morant could marry the two concepts. He could make every shot count, and he and everyone watching him could have a blast while he was doing it.

"I want to be the greatest player to ever do it," he said. "I feel like I was standing out when I came in the league. I saw people who'd bring up my name as 'electrifying.' That was pretty much it. People found out at Murray State."

A Grizzlies-Sixers matchup presented the optimal conditions for a memorable Morant dunk. While the Sixers were among the NBA's better teams, their two primary guards, James Harden and Tyrese Maxey, were subpar perimeter defenders. Morant could drive to the basket either with his left hand or his right, and Harden, for his relative lack of foot speed, and Maxey, for his relative lack of upper body strength, would have a difficult time staying in front of Morant and directing him away from the basket. And though Joel Embiid, the Sixers' seven-foot-two center, was at once nimble and hulking and the team's best defensive player, his presence would not deter Morant in the least. There would be plenty of opportunities, I figured, for Ja Morant to posterize someone.

"He's spectacular," Sixers coach Glenn "Doc" Rivers said ninety minutes before the game began. "You try to crowd the paint as a group as much as possible, and basically you try to get as physical as possible—as physical as they let you."

Rivers was making a not-so-veiled reference to the difference between the NBA of 2023 and the NBA of the mid-1980s and mid-1990s. A smart and steady point guard for 14 seasons, including eight with the Atlanta Hawks when they were perennially challenging the Boston Celtics and Detroit Pistons for supremacy in the Eastern Conference, Rivers had seen the shape of the sport shift from his playing days to his coaching days. Anyone with a rudimentary familiarity with basketball could see it, even if Rivers wasn't quite accurate in explaining that change.

"The game was way more physical," he said. "The forearm check was even greater than the hand check. Unfortunately, I'm old enough to have been in the era of both, and when they took the hand check away from me, I didn't really care. When they took the forearm away from me, I said, 'I've got to retire.' The forearm was huge. You could chuck guys all the time. When they took that away, and you had to move their feet, I was like, 'Forget this. I'm getting out of here.' It is way different."

Rivers was correct and incorrect at the very same time. In his era, the three-pointer wasn't nearly so popular as it eventually became. So if you watch a replay of a game from, say, 1987, it's customary to see defenders sloughing off guards and small forwards near the arc, giving them ample room to take a shot most of them weren't inclined to take. Once someone drove into the lane, though, he could expect to receive a measure of physical punishment that modern-day players rarely have to fear. Kevin McHale clotheslined Kurt Rambis in the 1984 NBA Finals. The Pistons had those "Jordan Rules" for harassing and trying to intimidate the best player on the planet. Morant, in this age, faced tighter and more tenacious defense 20 to 25 feet from the basket, because the threat that he or any other guard in the league might take and make a three-pointer was now ever-present. But once the NBA changed its rules to open up the game and make it easier to score, cutting down on hand-checking and other forms of defensive contact, Morant and players like him had freer rein and clearer minds. If Morant surged past the guy who was guarding him and lifted off for a dunk, it was less likely that a center or power forward would knock him on his ass, Bill Laimbeer–style. Instead, the defender in front of him would simply try to block the dunk, if he dared to try, because daring to try to block a dunk set that defender up for embarrassment and threatened to change the emotional complexion of a game.

Morant had done exactly that to Malik Beasley and the Minnesota Timberwolves in Game 5 of the 2022 Western Conference quarter-finals. With each team having won twice, the Timberwolves were threatening to beat the Grizzlies in Memphis and take control of the series. They led by 13 points with less than ten seconds remaining in the third quarter when Morant surged down the middle of the lane, cupped the ball in his right hand, jumped over Beasley—who, at six foot four, was two inches taller than Morant—and slammed down a dunk that ignited an eruption of screams and cheers inside FedEx Forum. On the TNT telecast, play-by-play man Ian Eagle shouted out a clever pun: "OH, A JA-BREAKER!" Morant finished the game with 30 points. The Grizzlies rallied in the fourth quarter to take Game 5, 111–109, then won Game 6 in Minneapolis to advance to the playoffs' second round. It was difficult not to conclude that Morant, with that single play, had saved the Grizzlies' season and ended the Timberwolves'.

"If you dunk on somebody," Beasley told me later, "it takes the soul away from the other team."

For most of the night at the Wells Fargo Center, Morant was a less compelling figure to track than his father was. Wearing a beige bucket hat, a beige hoodie, and black sunglasses, gripping a plastic cup of white wine in his right hand, Tee Morant sat courtside, not far from the Grizzlies' bench. That is, he sat there when he wasn't strutting up and down the first row of seats, chatting with and dapping up fans and security guards. "I love the game so much," he said. "I wanted to walk up and get my wine and watch everything else."

Growing up in South Carolina, Tee himself was an accomplished ballplayer, a six-foot-five forward with a steady shooting eye. At Hillcrest High School in Simpsonville, South Carolina, he scored 25 points, including the winning basket, in a playoff victory in March 1993. Hillcrest won the state championship. The team's top player, Ray Allen, went on to the University of Connecticut, an eighteen-year NBA career, and the Naismith Memorial Basketball Hall of Fame. Morant ended up at Claflin, a historically Black university in Orangeburg with what was at the time a National Association of Intercollegiate Athletics (NAIA) basketball program. His coach there, Gus Guydon, described him as "a student of the game. You can't say that about a lot of players. Many just let their athleticism take over, but . . . Ronnie's like another coach on the floor. He stays focused."

At Claflin, Tee earned the conference's player of the year award as a junior, averaging more than 18 points and nearly 10 rebounds, making 50 percent of his shots from the field and 77 percent of his free throws as a senior. He also met the woman who would be his wife and Ja's mother: Jamie Shanks, herself a standout basketball player in high school and a member of Claflin's softball team. Jamie graduated from Claflin with a degree in biology in 1999; that August, Ja was born. Offered a contract to play basketball overseas, Tee decided instead to remain in the United States with his young family. He did manage to play professionally, in the summer of 2002, in the XBA, a six-team developmental league. Tickets were five dollars apiece. Crowds rarely surpassed one hundred people. The high school gyms in which the games were held often weren't air-conditioned—hardly a minor inconvenience when it's July in the South. The XBA did have one interesting distinction: To encourage exciting plays, dunks were worth three points instead of two. But it was a humble rung for Tee Morant to reach to complete his climb through pro basketball, and there was no doubt that he now relished the vicarious life that he could live through his son.

"Ja plays every aspect of the game, and that's how he was raised," Tee said. "It's not about a highlight here or there. It's about playing the way you're supposed to play. That's all I'm about. That's why I'm here right now. That's why I follow every game he plays. I always told him, 'You can't play the game mad. This is a kids' sport. Dr. James Naismith made this game for kids.'"

What Naismith couldn't have imagined in 1891, of course, was the space-age spectacle that his invention would become after more than 125 years of athletic and economic evolution. Both the Sixers and Grizzlies were playing for the first time since the All-Star break, and because the game offered the promise of a duel between Embiid, who would be voted the league's most valuable player that season, and Morant, the Wells Fargo Center was full and humming all night, flamethrowers blasting from behind one of the baskets during pregame introductions, hip-hop samples bridging every change of possession to ensure there was never any absence of ambient sound in the arena, more than twenty-one thousand people engaged and on edge, especially as Memphis, even without Morant at his best, built a 17-point lead in the first half.

Embiid had been listed on the Sixers' injury list as "questionable," meaning it was possible that he would not play, because of a "non-COVID-related illness." But in recent years, as he had piled up gaudy statistics and the team had excelled during the regular season, as he struggled to reach that same level of play in the postseason and the Sixers failed to advance beyond the second round, Embiid grew more cognizant and attentive to the manner in which he was and would be viewed around the league. The facile cliché was that he was concerned about "his legacy," in that, unless he won the MVP award and propelled the Sixers into the conference finals at least once, people would think of and remember him as a great player who was nevertheless not as great as the true immortals of his era. In this game, the showdown of superstars between him and Morant had not materialized in full: Aside from a ho-hum breakaway dunk, Morant was shooting terribly from the field, and Embiid was no better, and it wasn't until just more than six minutes remained in regulation, with the Grizzlies holding an 11-point lead, that one of them awoke.

The one was Embiid. He dropped in a layup, blocked a dunk attempt by the Grizzlies' Xavier Tillman, sank two free throws, and swished an 18-foot jump shot to tie the score at 100 with three minutes to go. That stretch of assertiveness, though, was just a prelude to the game's pivotal moment. Morant sized up the defender in front of him, Tobias Harris, waited until Tillman set a pick on Harris, then knifed to the basket. He jumped, both of his hands wrapped around the ball to stuff it home. The Sixers' P. J. Tucker, rooted in the lane, thirty-seven years old, wise and experienced but never an aerial acrobat even when he was younger, jumped with him, a futile act. From Morant's right, though, Embiid took one step over and met Morant at the peak of his leap. Morant never saw him coming. With his right hand, Embiid blocked the dunk.

The Sixers scored seven of the game's final eight points, Embiid capping the rally with a breakaway jam himself. He had tended, over his career, to flavor his postgame commentary with dry humor and matter-of-fact egotism. He did again, after the Sixers' 110–105 victory. "I like to think I'm a great defender because I just know how to position myself," he said. "I just know to place myself on the court. I don't chase after blocks. Guys who chase blocks, those are not great defenders. Tonight, I could not make any shots, especially the ones I usually make. But defensively I thought I had to be Bill Russell tonight to kind of balance it out." In the visiting locker room, Morant was in no mood to discuss Embiid's block. He had thrown down so many big dunks over bigger players. What was it like for him to be on the opposite end of an astounding play at the rim? "I don't know. I don't worry about that too much," he said with a snicker that seemed a defense mechanism, for more than anyone, the best of dunkers knows when his and his team's soul has been stolen.

If that was all he was going to share, it was enough. He'd had an off night, and sometimes, when a writer is searching and probing for detail and self-reflection, the source who provides the least insight is the subject himself. Besides, there was much more to Morant and his story than his brief career in the NBA. Anyone who wanted to find out how Morant had become maybe the most thrilling basketball player in the United States had to hightail it to western Kentucky, to the campus of 236 acres and eleven thousand students and one kid who, as far as everyone in town was concerned, walked on water because he walked on air. Ja and his dunks? Ja and his rise? Ja and the stardom that, a few days after I spent those few minutes talking with him in Philadelphia, appeared to be in jeopardy? To get to the bottom of all of that, you had to get to Murray State. The Sixers-Grizzlies game was on a Thursday night. I boarded a plane on Saturday afternoon.

No one just happens upon Murray. One makes a point of going there. One has to. If you're an East Coaster, the fastest and easiest way to travel to the place where Ja Morant revealed himself fully to the basketball world is to fly into Nashville International Airport, rent a car, and drive 120 miles northwest along I-24, through thousands of acres of fields and farmland, to CSFB Arena, the home of the Murray State Racers. Its interior bathed in gold and royal blue, the arena functions as a cozy community center for the university and the town. With a seating capacity of 8,600, it accommodates, when it's full, a crowd roughly half the size of Murray's total population. "It's a homey feel," Boardman said. "A lot of people who aren't from here come to school here and end up staying here." For Friday and Saturday night fun, students might hit a couple of frat parties, a couple of pubs and restaurants, and the local bowling alley. "Lil' old Murray—can't get in no trouble here," Morant once said. "Keeps you focused."

Word had gotten out around town about my reporting trip there, and when I arrived, I was a curiosity, a visitor from a vast, exotic land far away. On press row at a Sunday afternoon Murray State–Valparaiso basketball game, a couple of university administrators and basketball boosters sought me out to say hello, and John Wright, the sports editor of the local newspaper, the *Murray Ledger*, introduced himself, promptly slipped a digital voice recorder out of his pocket, and began interviewing me for a story on the (supposedly) big-time writer who was working on a book about Ja. "I couldn't live in a city as big as Philadelphia," another editor at the paper told me, her eyes wide. More than one resident mentioned that, in 2012, *USA Today* and the publishing company Rand McNally had named Murray "The Friendliest Small Town in America." That recognition was a point of pride for the community, but it didn't compare to being The Place Where Ja Morant Went to College.

Morant had happened upon Murray, too. Actually, Murray State happened upon him. He grew up in Dalzell, South Carolina, which has a population of fewer than 3,200 people. Though he averaged 27 points, eight rebounds, and eight assists over his final two seasons for Crestwood High School in Sumter, though Tee had his son leaping from one tractor tire to another to strengthen his legs and increase his vertical leap—"Jumpers jump," Tee said, "so I had him jumping on tires"—Ja drew little Division I interest, perhaps because he was as skinny as a licorice strip. His official height and weight, with the benefits of elite-level strength training through his first four years with the Grizzlies, were six foot three and 173 pounds, so one can only imagine how wispy he was as a seventeen-year-old. It took a remarkable bit of serendipity for Murray State to learn of and land him: James Kane, one of the program's assistant coaches, was at a summer AAU camp in Spartanburg to scout another player, Tevin Brown, already a Murray State recruit. Hungry, Kane ducked into a smaller gymnasium to try to find a vending machine. In that gym, Morant, so late an invitee to the camp that he wasn't on its official roster, was playing in a three-on-three scrimmage. Kane caught a few flashes of him, then called Matt McMahon, the Racers' head coach, and told McMahon that Morant was a surefire pro prospect. Within twenty-four hours, Morant had a scholarship offer from Murray State.

It took until Morant's sophomore year before Boardman and the rest of the Racers' fan base learned what kind of player he was and would be. He'd had an excellent freshman season, starting all 32 games, scoring nearly 15 points and handing out more than seven assists a game, and during the following summer he'd participated in the prestigious Chris Paul Elite Camp in Winston-Salem, North Carolina; he was the first Murray State player to have been invited to it. Optimistic scuttlebutt about him spread in the aftermath, especially once a video of Morant cutting toward the basket from the left corner, soaring above the rim, and throwing down a two-handed alley-oop dunk surfaced on social media. His true coming-out party, though, at least in Murray, was in the late fall of 2018 at "Racer Mania," the late-night campus pep rally that kicks off each basketball season. The team held a dunk contest, and Neal Bradley, the radio play-by-play voice of the Racers since 1993, was courtside watching as Morant had a teammate stand in front of the hoop, then jumped over that teammate and dunked. *That's good*, Bradley thought, *but I've seen that before.* Then Morant did it over two teammates. Then, three. Then, he brought out another teammate and positioned him in line. Four. He was going to jump and dunk over four teammates.

"Here's what I'm thinking," Bradley said. "It's not, 'Oh, gosh, this is Ja Morant, future NBA star.' I'm thinking, 'He's our only point guard. If he breaks his foot, we're screwed.'"

Sitting next to Bradley was his radio partner: analyst and former Murray State assistant coach Kenny Roth. *They can't let him do this, Kenny*, Bradley said to him. *They can't.* They did. "I've never seen anything like that in my life," Bradley said. "I just never had. I don't follow the NBA closely. Maybe that's done pregame, preseason. I don't know. I was just stunned."

He would, as the season progressed, cease to be stunned. There was Morant's 38-point, nine-rebound night in a six-point loss to Alabama—"Unbelievable, athletic plays at the rim," Roth said— and an assessment by Chris Stewart, the Crimson Tide's play-by-play man, who told Roth: "Kenny, that's the single best performance by an opposing player that I've seen in this building." There was the 98–77 victory over the University of Tennessee–Martin, when Morant caught a bounce pass on a backdoor cut and jammed the ball over six-foot-seven forward Quintin Dove. In the bleachers, a section's worth of UTM football players reacted by whooping and hollering and sprinting up and down a flight of stairs. "Who gets that kind of reaction from opposing fans?" Bradley said. "It was crazy." On the forty-five-mile ride back to campus from that game, someone turned the televisions on the team bus to ESPN, and every member of the Racers stopped to see that Morant's dunk was one of the "top plays" on *SportsCenter.*

There was the four-point will-tester at Tennessee Tech two weeks later, a game that drew more than 5,200 fans to the Eblen Center in Cookeville, Tennessee, an arena that usually doesn't need to accommodate more than 2,500 or so for a men's basketball game. Two hundred people lined up at midcourt afterward, all of them waiting for Morant to give them his autograph. He obliged them. After home games, he'd join in the kids' halfcourt games at CSFB Arena, playing tricks with the ball to get them laughing. "Ja always had boundaries in his life," Roth said. "When he got here, he had boundaries. He had fun, but he knew right from wrong and never would get out of that. Believe me, we've had plenty of guys who found a way to embarrass the program. His almost Globetrotter-like approach to the game from a fan-interaction perspective was inviting."

There was the Racers' next game, an 86–75 victory over Eastern Illinois, when Morant, leading a fastbreak, took off from just inside the foul line for a one-handed slam. That was the one that stuck with Lindy Suiter. Suiter is a chipper, gray-haired man in his mid-sixties, an insurance executive in Murray, the publisher of a newsletter called *The Racer Insider,* and by consensus the basketball program's most loyal and generous booster. "I was seeing stars," he told me. "That's what his dunks did to you." Suiter would sit next to Tee Morant during games, and every time Ja would spring up from the court, like a child's toy popping out of a box, and land in a heap among the bramble of bodies in the lane, Suiter would grab Tee's knee. *Tee, my God. I can't look.* They weren't the only ones flinching in those moments and sending good thoughts Ja's way, as if a town's collective desire to protect him would, like magic, keep him safe. "You get worried watching him," Wright said. "He's got to calm down about hitting the floor. He's got to be a little less violent. He's going to shorten his career." But Ja would bounce back up, apparently indestructible even if everyone knew, deep down, that he wasn't. Every time, he would bounce back up.

The season picked up the momentum of a runaway train because of him. Autograph-seekers—not the parents and children who just wanted a second with a budding superstar but the sketchy ones who sold signatures, genuine or phony, as their number-one hustle—clustered at the team hotel whenever the Racers were on the road, so they started traveling with a security detail. "Everywhere he went," Wright said, "it was like the president was here." They carried an 11-game winning streak into the NCAA Tournament, where, as a No. 12 seed, they upset No. 5 Marquette, 83–64, at the XL Center in Hartford, Morant punctuating the rout with a two-hand dunk early in the second half. "From there forward, we ran them out of the gym," Roth said. "The dunk itself, having someone like that with that weapon, with that particular play, it eats into the confidence of the opponent. They see what they're up against, and they just lose confidence, and that's what happened with Marquette."

Murray State lost in the second round, to Florida State, and Morant—the first college player in nearly thirty years to average at least 20 points and 10 assists in a season—withdrew from school to enter the NBA draft; Memphis selected him with the No. 2 overall pick. But he's never far away from Murray in mind or spirit. The Walmart in town is always stocked with Grizzlies gear. Through a career-networking agency, students at the university sit at tables on the CFSB Arena's concourse during home games, passing out Grizzlies stickers and Grizzlies pens and selling other Grizzlies paraphernalia. "He pops up everywhere," said Aubree Keeling, a junior at Murray State, who was staffing one such table at the Valparaiso game. "Anything that happens with him, everyone will share it on Instagram. Everyone loves him. He definitely put Murray on the map." Whenever Morant has a big game, Wright writes it up for the *Ledger*, just a couple of hundred words to let people know how their hero did, always including a dateline from wherever the game happened to be (MEMPHIS—, LOS ANGELES—, TORONTO—), even though he files the stories from his desk in the newsroom.

Suiter invited me to lunch at the Big Apple Grill & Bar, a local landmark and the host site, every Monday, of Murray State coach Steve Prohm's radio show. A hundred or so boosters and alumni gathered in a modest banquet room and, over quesadillas and wings and salads with bacon bits and fat chunks of tomato, listened to Prohm review the victory over Valparaiso the day before and kibitzed with one another. At my table, Suiter and Dave Ramey, who had been Murray State's sports-information director in the '90s, told Morant stories.

"The stardom didn't get to him," Suiter said. "The first game of his sophomore year, his dad came, and the first thing out of his mouth as he looked at me was, 'This year, you're fixin' to see Crestwood High's Ja.' What he meant was, 'We're fixin' to see Ja Morant take over. He's the man now.' Boy, he did not disappoint."

"We had the Big Ten regional package when I was growing up," Ramey said, "and the only comparison I could make was Magic. It reminded me of watching Magic at Michigan State. He was toying with people."

Suiter nodded. "I told his dad, 'It's a damn shame. I know he's gonna be rich, but we could be in the Final Four in two years.' We really could have, if he stuck out his career. But there was no way. He was just too good."

"I always thought the thing missing in our résumé was that we had never been to the Sweet Sixteen," Ramey said. "But Ja has given us the publicity that we would have gotten by going to the Sweet Sixteen."

"Which one," Suiter asked, "do you think is his most spectacular dunk?"

They batted the question back and forth.

"The one at Eastern Illinois—he takes off from the foul line, with the ball back here," Suiter finally said, cocking his right arm behind his head. "I really almost passed out on that dunk. That's a pass-out dunk. He'll make you pass out."

Since 1988, Murray State had labored through just one losing season, had won 23 regular-season conference championships, and had qualified for the NCAA Tournament roughly every other year. Yet for all the success that the program had enjoyed, Suiter had spent years trying to get the word out about the Racers, trying, in a pre-social-media world, to coax more publicity and attention from local and national newspapers and media outlets. Once in a while, a reporter from the Louisville *Courier-Journal* might pop in to cover a game or two and write a *Hey, wee little Murray State's not bad* feature story. But that was pretty much it until Ja came along. Popeye Jones, Isaiah Canaan, Cameron Payne: those Murray guys had gone on to the NBA, too, but they never started the sports-cultural needle quivering the way Morant had.

"That got me thinking," Suiter said. "Ja Morant is a hell of a player, probably the most entertaining player in the world. But would he have gotten the same attention if you took the dunk away from his game and he played a regular game? Would ESPN and everybody else have come here and seen what kind of all-around game he had without the slam dunk? It's the dunk. It's the dunk. The whole world knows about Murray State, all because of the slam dunk."

We finished lunch, and the next morning I drove to Nashville to board a plane back to Philadelphia. Just those three days in Murray were enough to understand: It was impossible for anyone to spend any time there and overstate how much Ja Morant meant to the people who lived in the town, who were connected to the program, and who loved both. It was also impossible for anyone to spend any time in

Murray without wondering how everyone there would react if Ja Morant were guilty of a colossal fuckup. Which, based on accusations and developments that surfaced not long after I returned home, he was.

I had made most of the arrangements for my trip to Murray with the help of Dave Winder, the university's associate athletic director for communications. When I met Winder, I told him about Morant's standoffishness during my interactions with him before and after the Sixers' loss.

"Fourth-year Ja," Winder said, "is not the same as first-year Ja."

That was February 26. He had no idea at the time how right he would turn out to be. On March 1, the *Washington Post* reported that in the summer of 2022, Morant had allegedly threatened the head of security of a Memphis mall and punched a seventeen-year-old boy during a pickup basketball game, knocking him to the ground and causing a "large knot" to swell on the side of the boy's head. Following the fight, according to police records that the *Post* had obtained, "Morant went into his house and re-emerged with a gun visible in the waistband of his pants and his hand on the weapon."

That afternoon, through a direct message on Twitter, I sent Lindy Suiter a link to the *Post*'s story. "I got a feeling he's being targeted," Suiter wrote back, still wanting, clearly, to think the best of Morant. That instinct became harder to justify come the early hours of Saturday, March 4, when Morant broadcast a live Instagram video of himself, shirtless in a strip club, brandishing a handgun. The NBA suspended him for eight games for, in the vague and all-encompassing term that professional sports institutions use in such situations, "conduct detrimental to the league," and across the media who covered and commented on the NBA there was little condemnation of Morant's actions but plenty of admonition for him: Ja could be pro basketball's next torchbearer. Ja had put himself and that precious (and lucrative) possibility at risk. Ja needed to wise up before he threw it all away. "Ja Morant's Support System Needs to Step Up Now," the headline of a March 5 column in The Athletic by longtime league insider David

Aldridge, was typical of the overall tone and messaging. Fox Sports's Nick Wright even suggested that, because so many of the NBA's players, and so many of its very best players, were born outside the United States, there was a "special marketing lane" into which Morant could slot himself—a once-in-a-generation opportunity that he would cost himself if he wasn't careful. "He has a real, real chance at making a billion dollars playing basketball," Wright said. "In a few years, could Ja Morant be the best American-born player in the league? I think so."

Unsurprisingly, Nike, as Morant's primary sponsor, was gentle in its public statement: "We appreciate Ja's accountability and that he is taking time to get the help he needs. We support his prioritization of his well-being." Morant in turn followed the steps of modern athletic media rehabilitation, granting an interview to a sympathetic interrogator, ESPN analyst Jalen Rose, a former college and pro star himself, born of a hard childhood in Detroit. "I needed my time away," he told Rose, "to better myself and become a more healthy Ja." The Grizzlies won his first game back, over the lowly Houston Rockets. He hammered down a big dunk in the second quarter. It was easy to think everything was and would be fine, if one were inclined to think that way.

"His recent behavior has come out of nowhere," Winder said. "I pray that he can get it turned to the direction he was going before. He can come back from this. I'm in his corner."

The Grizzlies, with a 51–31 record, were the second seed in the Western Conference postseason tournament. In Game 1 of the first round, they trailed the Lakers by four points with less than six minutes left in regulation when Morant, from the right side of the court, 35 feet from the basket, used a left-handed dribble to drive past Jarred Vanderbilt, a six-foot-eight forward. He lifted off the floor just inside the foul line as the Lakers' center, Anthony Davis, slid over in front of him.

Only Davis could know for certain whether that previous miss by Morant over him was on his mind, but a trend throughout the sport made what he did next predictable. Incentivized to draw a foul against the opposing team's star player—a generation of coaches at all levels of basketball demanding that their players *take the charge* had conditioned those players to look for the charge and for officials to call it—Davis insinuated himself into Morant's path to the basket, then shrank himself. Instead of leaping with Morant, as Embiid had done two months earlier, Davis crossed his arms against his chest, braced himself against the contact he knew was coming, and tried to draw an offensive foul on Morant. It was a ridiculous play by Davis, who was eight inches taller than Morant and who could have blocked Morant's shot—and, given the two men's size disparity, probably should have tried to block it.

Morant soared over Davis, who undercut him, lowering his head and shoulders enough that, when they collided, Davis first made contact with Morant's waist, upending him. As he tumbled to the court, Morant extended his right hand to break his fall. The microphones on ESPN's telecast picked up Morant's letting out an "Ow" as he hit Davis, then another "Ow" as he slammed, hand-first, to the floor. Davis went down with him. The referees called a charge on Morant; Davis's passive play had reaped its intended benefit. The sequence was a microcosm of the shift in the sport from boldness and chance-taking to pure efficiency. There was Anthony Davis, all eighty-two inches of skill and strength and hand-eye coordination, not playing Morant straight up, not bothering, really, to accept a challenge presented by a smaller, skinnier adversary. When a player like Davis either is choosing or has been coached to minimize the very attributes that make him special, something has gone quite wrong with the sport.

Morant lay supine on the court, his body and face twisting in pain.

"He's hurting," play-by-play man Mike Breen said. "He's running back to the locker room. Wow."

Morant missed the rest of that game and all of Game 2 with what the Grizzlies officially called a bruised right hand. He came back for Game 3, scoring 45 points in a spectacular performance . . . and in a 10-point Memphis loss. The Lakers won the series, eliminating the Grizzlies in embarrassing fashion with a 125–85 victory in Game 6. Morant missed 13 of his 16 shots from the field that night. In the loss's aftermath, ESPN's Tim McMahon wrote that, while the Grizzlies believed that Morant would be receptive to any guidance and support that the franchise might offer, "the struggles of Morant and his inner circle to adapt to the fame, celebrity, and potential for excess that come along with his rapid ascent to becoming one of the NBA's most popular players had to be addressed." For his part, Morant acknowledged as much. "I've just got to be better with my decision-making," he said. "Just [need] more discipline." That moment of self-examination turned out to be fleeting. Two and a half weeks later, Morant again flashed a gun during an Instagram Live video, and again, Lindy Suiter was puzzled. "I've had no contact with [the Morant] family in quite a while so I have no idea," he said in a text message. "Very disturbing! Very strange!" The NBA then announced, on June 16, that Morant would be suspended for the first 25 games of the 2023–24 season.

The irony of all that questionable judgment, and of all the resulting stigma and punishment, was that, more than a century before Morant was born, Dr. James Naismith had invented basketball for the expressed purpose of teaching the value of structure and rigorousness to those young men who played it. Quaint though the concept might be, basketball, its inventor believed, was supposed to build character. Yes, Ja was still just twenty-three years old. And yes, as Tee Morant had noted, Naismith had made basketball for kids, and one of his most devoted apprentices would be responsible for a strategic innovation that eventually would make it easier for its greatest athletes—the famous like Morant, the obscure and mythical from America's thorny past, the ones yet to come—to slip the bounds of gravity. But it's safe to say that Naismith would have looked at Ja Morant, flying so high above the court, so close to a fall away from it, and wondered what had become of the sport he'd created.

2

THE SOUL OF INNOVATION

Before anyone could dunk a basketball, before anyone could even conceive of such a thing, someone had to conceive of basketball itself, and someone else had to unlock the possibility for majesty within what was still a new sport.

The young man's father had warned him: *Your journey will be difficult. You are going off to college, to a land that you don't know and where no one knows you. You are Black. Just about everyone at the school is white. But there is one man there who can help you. Find him. Find that wise and generous man.*

In 1933, the undergraduate population of the University of Kansas comprised four thousand students. Of those four thousand, about sixty—1.5 percent—were Black. The restrictions placed on those select few marked them as lesser in their privileges, in their access to the instruction and knowledge and relationships that are held up as the hallmark of a college education, and in their humanity. No dorms, no dining hall, no dances: they were banned from all of them. Their ostracism was so pervasive, was embedded so deeply in the university's culture and daily life, that they could not even dip their feet into the university's swimming pool. That last regulation, in particular, would gall John McLendon.

McLendon had planned, all his life, to go to Springfield College in western Massachusetts, where Dr. James Naismith—there on a one-year faculty stint, training to be a physical-education director at a YMCA—just happened to invent basketball. On a field trip when he was twelve years old, McClendon had entered the gymnasium at Northeast Junior High School in Kansas City, Kansas, ninety miles southeast of his hometown, Hiawatha. He had never been in a gym before. "It was at this time that I made a decision about my future," he once said. "I was just entranced, because in the middle of the floor was a man shooting a basketball. I just couldn't believe how a person could stand that far away from the basket and toss a ball into a cylinder." It didn't matter that McLendon would grow to be just five foot eight and weigh 160 pounds, as thin and sinewy as rawhide but hardly built to be a dominant basketball player. He knew then, even so young, that he wanted to make the sport his occupation and vocation: learn it, play it, coach it, teach it. Naismith's reputation as a man of faith and integrity, progressive on race, color blind at a time when color blind-ness was rare and brave, stretched to the Midwest and the Great Plains during the Great Depression as basketball spread like kudzu across the country. "He was not," Rob Rains, one of Naismith's biographers, told me, "in favor of segregation."

McLendon's father, John Sr., a college professor, had encouraged him never to feel or flash any anger over the prejudice that he had encountered and that he was sure to encounter yet. Racism, John Sr. told John Jr., was a reality that had to be overcome by sound judg-ment, not by irrational emotion. He also encouraged his son to seek out Naismith. If John Jr. loved basketball that much, there was only one college for him: the University of Kansas, forty miles away from the McLendons' home, where Naismith was a faculty member in the physical education department. John Jr. would be the first and only Black student in that course of study at the university. So what? *You are entitled to be there*, John Sr. said—and drove him there himself.

McLendon followed his father's advice and, upon arriving on cam-pus, sought out Naismith at his office in Robinson Gymnasium. There are only so many human encounters and interactions that can, without exaggeration, be called *transformational*, not just for the people in-volved but for the direction of American society and history. Here was a white man in his early seventies, bespectacled and mustached and appropriately professorial in his comportment, not a native of the United States—Naismith was born in Almonte, Ontario—but now an esteemed national figure, a kind of celebrity. Here was someone asking for his help, someone who had just entered manhood, eighteen years old and Black and dreaming dreams that, had he been raised in a differ-ent family, had he possessed a personality that wasn't so optimistic and hopeful, would have had no chance of coming true. The older man had created a sport, had diversified American culture, made it richer and more rewarding. The younger man would improve that creation, offer a new interpretation of it that would make it more entertaining and accessible, that would initiate its transformation from a mere pas-time to an institution, an industry, a vessel to explore the limits of hu-man strength and vigor and will. The most striking expression of those limits would be, of course, the ability to transcend them, to rise higher than what appeared possible for an ordinary mortal, to defy both grav-ity and the unspoken humility that kept basketball players anchored to the ground and unadorned in their movements. To dunk.

That word, of course, had no purchase in their minds and on their tongues. There was nothing so grand and sweeping in their conversa-tion. The little things that change lives are always simple and invisible. According to the story that the young man, once his face had gone webbed with wrinkles, loved to share, McLendon introduced himself to Naismith and told him he thought Naismith would be his adviser and mentor.

Who told you this? Naismith asked him.

My father, McLendon said.

Come in, Naismith replied. *Fathers are always right.*

The most famous and important number in basketball is, of course, ten. Ten, as in feet. Ten feet, as in the distance from the ground or the floor to the rim. Ten is the number that even those who know next to nothing about basketball know about basketball. A lot of people know that Wilt Chamberlain once scored 100 points in a game. Fewer people probably know that the dimensions of an NBA court and a college court are identical: 94 feet by 50 feet. Fewer still know that the three-point arc stretches as far as 23 feet, 9 inches in the NBA but just 20 feet, 9 inches in men's college basketball; 20 feet, 6 inches in international play and in the WNBA; and 19 feet, 9 inches in high school and women's college play. And even if a fair number of people know that Kareem Abdul-Jabbar is the second-leading scorer in NBA history, behind LeBron James, how many of them can recite, off the top of their heads, that Jabbar racked up 38,387 points in his career? But pretty much everyone knows that a regulation basket is ten feet high. Not nine and a half feet. Not ten feet and a quarter inch. Ten, exactly. Ten is the number, really, that defines the dunk. Dunk on a shorter basket . . . big deal. Dunk on a higher basket . . . we'll get to that notion later. No, ten is it. Ten is perfect. Ten is the number that, really, defines basketball.

It was also, at the sport's birth, a completely arbitrary number.

It was understandable that it was arbitrary, because in the summer of 1891, James Naismith was up against a deadline for an unusual assignment. He had been on track to becoming a minister until, while studying theology and philosophy and competing in three sports at McGill University in Montreal, he impressed an opponent, during a rough football game, by playing hard and, at the same time, refraining from using any profanity. It was a revelation, he said, that "there might be other effective ways of doing good besides preaching." This view, which he adopted as a core conviction, placed him squarely within the Muscular Christianity movement, the belief, popular in the late nineteenth and early twentieth centuries, that robust physical activity served to give glory to God and enhance the spiritual well-being of its practitioners. Organized sports as salvation: the notion was the basis of the Young Men's Christian Association, and soon after their debut in Great Britain in 1844, YMCAs opened throughout the United States. When Naismith, at Springfield, toured YMCA chapters in Massachusetts, he "found that there was a possibility of building and developing the character of the individual through physical activities." His sister and uncle could not forgive him for eschewing a life and career as a minister, but he "never regretted it. . . . I am not sorry, and I have found [athletics] is a tremendously fine thing for the building of character."

Founded by an educator named Luther Gulick to be a YMCA training school, Springfield College was a hotbed for Muscular Christianity. One class, though, of what Naismith called "secretarial men"—in their early to mid-twenties, slender and broad-shouldered and grim-faced—grew unsatisfied with the available athletic options. They were restless, surly, unruly. So Gulick and another faculty member, Dr. R. A. Clark, assigned Naismith to find the class "recreative work: something that will please them and something they will want to do." He tried indoor football (". . . broke the arms and legs of the players"). He tried soccer (". . . broke all the windows"). He tried lacrosse (". . . broke the apparatus," whatever the apparatus may have been). Two weeks went by. Naismith had another twenty-four to forty-eight hours before he would have to report back to the faculty whether he had succeeded or failed, and all his attempts had been failures. Then, he remembered a game he had played as a boy in Canada: "Duck on a Rock." A player would set a small stone on top of a larger rock; the rock Naismith and his friends used had been two feet high and two feet wide. The other players would line up and throw their stones to try to knock off their friend's. The concept started Naismith thinking. What if all the players used the same stone, and what if that stone were a ball . . .

I think I have it! Instead of throwing the ball straight for the goal, let us throw it in a curve and we cannot throw it hard. You must take your time and use skill instead of power and speed. Then I thought of putting a mark on the floor; just a circle, and use that for the goal, but the goal keeper [sic] would stand in it and we could not make the goal. Put it above his head and no one can stand in it and you would have a chance of making a goal once in a while. It would be horizontal and high in the air.

The original rules of basketball—thirteen of them; he would tack them on a wall at the college—unfurled from there. When it came time to test-drive his new sport, Naismith noticed there were peach baskets nailed to the railing of Springfield's track. Perfect. They would be the goals. The railing from which the baskets were hanging just happened to be ten feet high.

Rick Cox, the husband of Naismith's great-granddaughter Celeste Carpenter-Cox, has devoted much of his life to studying the man's life and legacy. "The game that is played today," he told me, "is just so far from what he envisioned." Cox has studied well. Basketball "is not a game intended merely for amusement," Naismith once wrote. It had a deeper, more profound purpose: to hone and mold the character of men, to provide them opportunities to test "how I shall act under unforeseen circumstances." To Naismith, there was a direct and unbroken line between how players reacted to difficult situations in a game—a referee's error, the final minutes of a tight contest, a bad shooting night—and how they reacted to difficult situations in everyday life. Basketball was at once a great apprenticeship and a great revealer. "He never viewed it," Rob Rains, who authored a biography of Naismith, told me, "as a showmanship event." He also didn't view it as an enterprise defined by the final score of any game, even one in which a championship was at stake. It was another of his protégés—Forrest Claire "Phog" Allen, who forged his legend at Kansas by beginning his second stint as head coach there in 1919 and winning 766 games over the next thirty-seven years—who helped shift the aims of the sport. Allen prioritized winning and losing more than he did educating and developing subsequent generations of men and women and making sure that Christian values guided them in their endeavors. "Phog Allen," Rick Cox said, "pushed more to win at any cost rather than grow up the next generation." But victory, to Allen, had to be achieved in the appropriate manner—he never did completely shed the residue of Naismith's philosophies—and when it came to the proper way to play basketball and the dunk's place in it, he was as pure a disciple of Naismith as one could have been. The dunk was showy.

The dunk was ostentatious. The dunk was an unnecessary blemish on the intrinsic beauty of the game.

"Dunking does not display basketball skill—only height advantage," Allen wrote in *Better Basketball: Technique, Tactics, and Tales*, his 490-page tome, published in 1937, in which he lays out his thoughts and philosophies on how to coach, teach, and change the sport. "Even the tallest player should not be able to jump up and touch the rim or the ball on the rim."

McLendon had wanted to play for the university's varsity team once he got to campus, only to learn that the "open" tryouts that Allen, who was also Kansas's athletic director, held were open in name only. As part of an agreement among the schools in the Big Six Conference, Blacks weren't permitted on any varsity team at Kansas in the 1930s. What's more, every phys-ed major at the university had to pass a water-and-safety test, but Blacks weren't permitted to use the Robinson Gymnasium pool . . . which wasn't a problem, as far as the KU administration was concerned, until McLendon came along. A former lifeguard, he rejected an offer to waive the test. When he attempted to swim one day, school officials drained the pool. He tried again. They drained it again. "One of the authorities said to us that the pool isn't really restricted because of your color," McLendon once said. "It's restricted because we have some students here who don't know any better who might hurt you or harm you if you go in." Naismith had two football players stand guard by the pool so McLendon could complete his test. If that measure seems meager, given Naismith's power and esteem at Kansas, McLendon never thought so. "One thing he taught in the adjustment to adversity," McLendon once wrote, "is that no matter what kind of problem you had, never let it defeat you. Even though you may not think something is fair or just, you can't let that stop you. You just try to get around it. Dr. Naismith's attitude may not be viewed as modern by today's standards; people have learned the method of protest to bring pressure on those who make the rules. . . . His philosophy was that adversity was just another opportunity. That may sound naive, but it worked for me then, and it still applies today."

McLendon began seeing and collecting signs around campus that said: DO NOT SWIM WITH THE N——R. The situation went from simmer to boil. So McLendon and Allen bargained for and agreed to a solution: if Allen opened up the pool to all KU students for two weeks and if there were no racially related incidents during those fourteen days, the pool would remain open to everyone. McLendon then called a meeting of sixty Black students, telling them to stay away from the pool. Two weeks passed. No incidents. Allen called McLendon "a smart aleck," but at Naismith's insistence, he acceded to allow integrated swimming. McLendon had faced off against one of the powerful men in college sports. And won.

In light of that episode, it might sound like Allen, in *Better Basketball*, was practicing a kind of preemptive dismissal of the dunk based on the race of the athletes who eventually would popularize it. *Those Blacks don't have any real basketball skill.* Make no mistake: Allen shared plenty of the prejudice endemic to that age. As scholar Aram Goudsouzian has pointed out, Allen as Kansas's athletic director excluded Blacks from varsity athletics, and he went along with the Big Six's unspoken ban on Blacks. There's some mitigating context, though. One, Allen hadn't coached a Black player before writing *Better Basketball*; LaVannes Squires, the first Black player in KU history, didn't suit up for the Jayhawks until the early 1950s. So Allen's broadside against the dunk would have been based on his watching white players do it most of the time. He hated the shot no matter the race of the player perpetrating it. Two, author Scott Ellsworth noted that Allen's adherence to Kansas's and the Big Six's policies belied many of his personal views and actions on race. His next-door neighbors in Lawrence, for instance, were descendants of a man who had been born a slave before serving as a private in the Civil War, and that Black family was not the only one Allen befriended. "I don't know anything about him negative," Arthur Lloyd Johnson, a member of one of those families, told Ellsworth. "When they started integrating, he was ready to coach Blacks. I wouldn't scratch him up to a racist." Finally, McLendon himself regarded Allen as a victim of a system that, even with his stature, he was powerless to change. "If he tried . . . ," McLendon once said, "he'd have lost his job, as great a coach as he was." Yes, Allen's distaste for the dunk might have been an offshoot of the contemptible limits of his tolerance and forbearance, but it was as much or more a reflection of the limits of his, and each of his predecessors and contemporaries', imagination.

"A team of giants who are smart and fast have been both the prayer and the dream of the basketball coach," he wrote in *Better Basketball*. "These dream men whose heads just graze the rim of the baskets and who with one hand dunk the balls through the hoops, like children inserting pennies in gum machines, may yet have to see another sport in which to excel."

Allen turned out to be wrong, of course. He and those who thought like him were familiar with basketball as it was then: If a player was dunking, it was because he was tall enough to dunk without having to jump all that high. And if he was that tall, he probably wasn't all that athletic and graceful, at least not compared to the players who would follow him. Those giants did exist, and through the 1920s and 1930s, they would establish the dunk as a fixture in basketball. Still, it took the vision of that former freshman who didn't possess the right skin tone to play in the Big Six Conference to free those later eagles to fly.

Naismith spared McLendon none of his testimonies about the connection between spiritual grace and athletics, and McLendon, for his part, embraced their give-and-take on those matters, for he recognized how much they meant to his mentor. During a career in which he coached for five college programs over a thirty-year period, won 496 games and lost just 179, won three National Association of Intercollegiate Athletics championships at Tennessee A&I in Nashville, arranged and won "The Secret Game"—North Carolina College of Negroes' 1944 victory over Duke Medical School, in what is believed to be the first integrated basketball contest—was the first Black head coach at Cleveland State University, was the first Black head coach in the American Basketball Association, and was a member of two US Olympic coaching staffs, McLendon carried his love for and loyalty to his adviser long after Naismith's death in 1939. When the NBA expanded into Canada in 1995, adding the Toronto Raptors and the Vancouver Grizzlies, McLendon commemorated the dawn of those franchises by traveling to Almonte to see and touch the schoolyard rock where Naismith, as a child, had played "Duck on a Rock." Roy MacGregor, a sportswriter for the *Ottawa Citizen*, accompanied McLendon on the trip, and when he asked what Naismith would think of present-day basketball, McLendon told him, "I don't think he'd like it very much. He'd like certain aspects of it, but I know he wouldn't care for the pro game very much—not the way they violate the rules. There's traveling all the time. They take those extra steps when they dunk. They run over picks. All that trash talk—it doesn't have any place in the game." Three years earlier, in a letter dated January 28, 1992, to Naismith's great-granddaughter Laurie, McLendon had handwritten the following in blue ink on Cleveland State University stationery:

> *I have been so very fortunate in life to have the benefits of Dr. Naismith's teachings and guidance. He was so much to so many young people. . . . Providence placed us together. The circumstances surrounding our eventually meeting and time together defies the experience as being mere coincidence. I know better. . . .*
>
> *I still remember clearly his discourse on "Immortality" and what it means to various doctrines (religions). I will share some of these thoughts with you at a future time. Suffice it to say, he was a real minister and would insert his views on morality and ethicality (gently) into our preparation for being Physical Educators and young adults.*

By no means did Naismith limit his discussions with McLendon to the ecclesiastical and the sentimental. No basketball-related subject stimulated Naismith more than the fast break, and he and McLendon traded thoughts about it often. Mind you, it took Naismith a while to understand and appreciate how to tweak the sport to accent fluidity and a faster pace. At first, he wanted to use boxes as the goals, wanted to call it not "basketball" but "box ball," and he waited more than a decade after he had invented the game to figure out that he should remove the bottoms from the baskets. "When I asked him why he didn't take the bottoms out," McLendon once said, "he gave me one of the worst looks he ever gave me." Once he took out the basket bottoms, though, Naismith imagined basketball being played in the same manner that volleyball has generally been throughout the country—as a fun time-passer, a staple of barbecues and picnics and family gatherings, a couple of dozen people on each side, as loose and chaotic as the "dogfight beach football" that Tom Cruise and his understudy fighter pilots play in *Top Gun: Maverick*. That vision informed his instructions and guidance to anyone who took it up. He was cautious not to overcoach players, and after McLendon had finished classes one day at Kansas, he and Naismith, as they walked through the gym, came upon a large group of children playing basketball. Naismith asked them for the ball, and once they handed it over to him, he told them: *Whenever on the court you have it, that's where your offense begins. And whenever the other team has the ball, that's where your defense begins.*

"I took that to mean that you played basketball on the entire court," McLendon once said. "Your offense started off the boards or whenever you got possession. That's when your offense begins. You don't come down the court, stop, and decide, 'OK, now I'm going to run and play this and that.' The same on defense: If you get the ball anywhere on the court, you don't retreat. You attack. So that's where I got the press-and-run game from."

There was a difference, though: what Naismith saw as basketball's ideal state, free-flowing and unfettered, a river over rocks, McLendon saw as a structured method that he could design and refine and teach, as if he were simplifying a complex math problem so that any student could solve it. By writing *Fast Break Basketball* in 1964, while he was coaching at Kentucky State College, he became the first Black coach to author a book about basketball, and it is a lasting testament to the way he considered and analyzed the game. The book is loaded with diagrams, 154 in all, showing how players ought to align themselves on the court and embark on a break, like birds flying in a V formation, with synchronicity to fill every lane and give themselves plenty of passing and shooting options. McLendon viewed the fast break as the quintessential representation of cohesive, unselfish basketball, and because he trusted that the system would give his teams such an advantage when they executed it well, he demanded that his athletes condition themselves mentally and physically to handle playing at such a frenetic pace. Fatigue, he believed, was purely psychological; if a competitor wanted to win badly enough, there was no way he or she would feel tired at any point during a game. "It is nonexistent," he wrote, "as long as the desire to excel is uppermost in the player's mind." He required all the men who aspired to play for him to prove, during tryouts, that they could run three miles in less than twenty minutes for twenty-one days. He was Nolan Richardson and Forty Minutes of Hell, Paul Westhead and The System, before either man was coaching and either stratagem existed. "Our conditioning objective," he wrote, "is to have each player on the squad in such a state of physical readiness that he can play forty minutes of full-court offense, combined with a full-court defense." Winning basketball, at its essence, came down to a group of players running faster and longer than their opponents. A true team would be united in that willingness to endure.

"You have to have a team that doesn't care who scores," McLendon once said. "It's not a star-centered offense. It's a team game, and everybody has to do their part. And not only that, they have to do it all the time. I usually say it's not a game of skill as much as it is a game of will. It's not 'Can you do it?' but 'Will you?'"

Few, if any, of these principles and beliefs would seem to link themselves to the nature of the dunk. Not at first, anyway. The dunk is nothing if not individually centered. It requires little teamwork at all, unless you're talking about an alley-oop. It features the sort of showmanship that both Naismith and McLendon abhorred. They taught that basketball was to be played with varying degrees of courtliness. But without McLendon's innovation, without the fast break, the dunk's full power and elegance might never have manifested themselves. No Magic-to-Worthy for the Showtime Lakers in the 1980s. No Charles Barkley—part-Caterpillar, part-Harley—off-roading down the court and hammering down a two-handed slam. No Grant Hill soaring over Naismith and McLendon's Jayhawks in the 1991 NCAA championship game. No Julius. No Jordan. No Ja. The fast break turned a basketball court into a runway. The game went from being stationary and stuck on land to being a breathtaking display of swiftness and motion and flight. It's easy to say that the sport's evolution was inevitable, and maybe it was. In that case, the only conclusion to draw is that Naismith and McLendon's meeting, as the latter suggested in his letter, was fate.

That McLendon, who died in October 1999 at age eighty-four, received little credit at the time for his influence on basketball should not be surprising, given the racial dynamics in the sport and in the country then. The notion that a Black coach could—to put it bluntly—outthink his white counterparts, could devise a new strategy that would take the game to places it hadn't been before, was too outlandish and unsettling for too many sports fans at the time to contemplate. They, and the rest of America, were only beginning to reckon with having Blacks compete as athletes, as equals, as superiors, in the most mainstream of team sports: baseball and football. As basketball's popularity grew, as it spread from one YMCA to another, one high school to another, one college or university to another, one club team to another club team into larger professional leagues, as it challenged those sports for the public's attention, the portion of the public with the most cultural power could accept only incremental progress—and only on its terms. If, as Allen had argued, dunking wasn't basketball, what was the fast break? Ben Jobe, a mentee of McLendon's who went on to coach for twelve years at Southern University, boiled down the difference between how particular teams and coaches were regarded when he blanched at the praise heaped on the Duke Blue Devils in the late 1970s for their high-tempo offense. "Duke did it; it was genius," Jobe said. "We did it; it's jungle ball."

Jobe spoke from experience. More than a terrific coach himself—he went 208–142 at Southern—he was a witness, in 1955, when McLendon was coaching at Tennessee A&I (now Tennessee State), to the consummate example of the prestige that white coaches enjoyed, even as they stood on the shoulders of their lesser-known peers. Visiting McLendon at his office, Jobe opened the door to find a white man standing in the room, his back turned to McLendon. The man, Jobe could tell, had chalk in his hand, though Jobe couldn't see his face. McLendon told Jobe to go kill some time in the cafeteria: "Give me about an hour."

When Jobe returned, he asked McLendon who the man was. McLendon whispered to him, "I'm going to tell you this, but you must never, ever mention it."

The white man was Adolph Rupp: fifty-four years old, a quarter century into his forty-two-year tenure as the head coach at the University of Kentucky. The Wildcats happened to be in Nashville to play Vanderbilt, and Rupp had taken time to visit McLendon and pick his brain.

"He had some questions about my philosophy of the game," McLendon told Jobe. "But he wouldn't want anyone to know that he was getting this knowledge from a Black coach. So don't you mention it."

Nine years later, in 1964, McLendon encountered Rupp again, this time on a recruiting trip to Louisville, when the two of them dueled to try to entice a standout center from Seneca High School, Wes Unseld, to one of their programs. In fact, the coaches' paths crossed literally on the doorstep of the Unseld home: McLendon was on his way in to visit with Wes and his family. Rupp was on his way out, and he was not pleased. He had, McLendon later remembered, "a very, very grim look on his face," and when McLendon greeted him, he didn't respond, so engrossed was he in reviewing what had just transpired. Unseld's mother then met McLendon at the door.

"Come on in and talk to Wes," she told him. "I don't think he's going there."

Unseld didn't go to Kentucky State, either. He stayed local, picked Louisville, and became a Hall of Famer, one of the toughest and smartest centers in the NBA, and perhaps the best outlet passer the game has ever known. The significance of that moment was not that both Rupp and McLendon had courted one of basketball's great dunkers, for they hadn't. Unseld was not that kind of player. As his hometown paper, the *Courier Journal*, noted in 2020, in the second paragraph of Unseld's obituary: "He didn't dunk much." No, the moment's significance was in its timing and its symbolism. One couldn't ask for a more fitting metaphor than the scene at the Unseld house: Rupp and his restrictive, authoritative manner on the way out; McLendon and his refreshing new approach—the tactical pad from which so many dunks would be launched—on the way in. That crackling between those two wires, between a coach who represented what basketball was becoming and a coach who represented what basketball would no longer be, happened just as a revolution was raging throughout the sport. It was a revolution that McLendon had helped to unleash. It was a revolution that Rupp and other power brokers and decision-makers in basketball would in three years' time do their damnedest to stop.

3

KING OF THE CAGERS

So . . . who was the first player to dunk a basketball? When did it happen? Where? These are natural questions to ask here . . . except those questions lead to another: How can we know for sure?

et's say it's the year 2023. Let's say you're a basketball fan. And let's say, in flipping through TV channels or scrolling through videos on YouTube, you come upon one or more of what can loosely be called "debate shows": shoutfests over contrived controversies and barroom-style topics. Among the most popular (and tiresome) of those topics is an obvious one: Who is the greatest basketball player of all time? It makes for an easy segment. A Baby Boomer or Gen Xer says "Michael Jordan" in a manner that implies disagreement is inconceivable. A millennial-aged pundit makes the case for LeBron James. Someone mentions Bill Russell or Kareem Abdul-Jabbar in a quick gesture of t-crossing, i-dotting respect. And off they go, loudly, into intellectual oblivion.

Before the advent of ESPN and Fox Sports, of course, there was no such daytime discourse to be had. Information and opinions swirled through only so many funnels before reaching the masses. If a newspaper columnist or radio voice declared that a particular athlete was the finest in his or her respective sport, what choice did readers or listeners have but to regard that assertion as gospel? They had seen little live sports, if any. They hadn't heard much more. They had to believe what they read.

So, for instance, if S. O. Grauley, who became the sports editor of the *Philadelphia Inquirer* in 1926 and who had been, according to one description, "watching the sports parade since before the turn of the century," had some thoughts about who the best athletes in America were, those thoughts would be considered newsworthy. And, to his credit, Grauley wasn't the sort to offer a hot take just for hot take's sake. Were he still alive today, he'd be no click-chaser. He considered Babe Ruth the greatest baseball player of all time, Jim Thorpe the greatest football player, Joe Louis the greatest boxer.

And the greatest basketball player?

Jack Inglis.

Jack Inglis?

Yes. Jack Inglis.

How could it be anyone else?

"From 1909 until his untimely death . . . ," Grauley once wrote, "Jack Inglis was the talk of the cages."

You think Grauley was an outlier with that opinion? He was not an outlier with that opinion. Here was the *Wilkes-Barre Record* in 1923:

"Jack Inglis's name will never die so long as basket balls [*sic*] are being thrown at iron hoops."

And here was the Carbondale (PA) *Leader* in 1918:

"As a basketball player, Inglis was at his zenith in this city, and his wonderful work on the court attained for him the reputation of being one of the greatest stars of the game."

Better yet, what about Nat Holman—the famous barnstorming player of the 1920s who earned even more renown, and eventually an induction into the Naismith Memorial Basketball Hall of Fame, as the longtime head coach at City College of New York? In his eyes, Inglis was one of the six top players he ever encountered, "a master of the art of dribbling, a great shooter, aggressive, steady, and a fine team man."

So why catalog all this praise for a long-gone giant of the game's distant past? Why bring up Jack Inglis here at all? What the hell did he have to do with the slam dunk? As it turns out, Holman holds the answer.

To understand the praise heaped on Inglis in the early years of the twentieth century, one first has to understand the early years of professional basketball. There was no single pro league. How could there be? *De jure* segregation was in place. Travel was a burden. Costs could be prohibitive. Instead, through the century's first two to three decades, there was the Black barnstorming circuit, and there were a dozen or more white leagues, most of them sprouting in the northeast areas of the country, some of them so close in geography and nomenclature that you have to wonder whether it was too difficult to consolidate some of them into bigger leagues or whether the people in charge simply couldn't be bothered. The Western Massachusetts League was a stone's throw from the Central Massachusetts League, and both would have seemed perfectly positioned within the New England League, which could have included the Connecticut State League and competed against the Hudson River League, the New York State League, and the Pennsylvania State League, all of which could have settled under the umbrella of the Eastern League. But hey, hindsight always has a fighter pilot's eyes.

Sports historian Robert W. Peterson pinpointed Trenton, New Jersey, as the birthplace of pro ball; in 1896 and 1897, the Trenton Basketball Team started paying its players to take on YMCA and college clubs. More relevant here, though, was that the team transformed the high-ceilinged social hall on the third floor of the city's Mason Temple into an indoor basketball court. Ringing and enmeshing that court, along the sidelines and baselines, was a twelve-foot-high wire fence that, the thinking went, would prevent the ball—the lumpy, leather, stitched-up ball—from bounding into the stands . . . and keep the people in the stands from bounding onto the court or otherwise interfering with play. Soon enough, as more and more courts popped up on the East Coast, more and more of them were wrapped in fencing. Because of that trend—and because it was easier to fit one word with six letters into a headline than it was to fit two words with seventeen— the use of the term "cagers" to describe "basketball players" became common in newspapers.

Inglis was the king of those cagers, at least in the minds of many sportswriters in many of those newspapers. He had the classic look of an athletic hero from that age: blond hair, full lips, sad eyes. In his two collegiate years at Rensselaer Polytechnic Institute, located in his home-town of Troy, New York, Inglis was the captain of the football team, helped the basketball team rip off a 15-game winning streak—he made 20 shots from the field in one of those victories—played baseball, and ran track. After he graduated from RPI in 1910, his transition to the pros was cake; Troy had a club in the New York State League. Inglis helped Troy win three league championships, flashing a spark of creativity that few players possessed: he would rush toward the basket, jump, and loft the ball on an arc—a technique that was an antecedent of the modern jump shot. Once the New York State League folded, he moved on to Carbon-dale of the Pennsylvania State League. There, he was "the best drawing card . . . a splendid specimen of physical manhood, and his speed and cunning in mastering the fine points of the game made him a great favorite among the fans not only in this city but where he played." His renown stretched thirty miles south of Carbondale to Pittston, where he "was widely known . . . as a stalwart athlete and a manly young fellow."

In 1918, with the United States having entered World War I the year before, Inglis enlisted in the Navy. He was a machinist's mate, second class, stationed at Pelham Bay, when he returned home to Troy on furlough. On Tuesday, October 1, he contracted the strain of in-fluenza that at the time was called the "Spanish flu." On Sunday, October 6, he died, at age thirty-one, one of 675,000 casualties of the flu in the United States, one of more than 50 million across the globe.

Let's say it's the year 1918. Jack Inglis's death is a thunderbolt of break-ing news. It's not just that people recognize his name and read about his accomplishments. It's that newspapers are telling people that they should recognize his name and encouraging them to read about his accomplishments. Again, a different time, a different way of consuming mass media. It wasn't until another eighty-seven years passed, though, that Inglis's most significant contribution to basketball lore was revealed.

Let's say you're a writer. Let's say you're a prolific writer. You don't have to be Stephen King or Danielle Steel or James Patterson; you don't have to be a successful prolific writer. You just have to write a lot. You probably haven't written and won't write as much as Bill Gutman does. He has written about basketball and baseball and football and tennis and cycling and figure skating and track and field. He has written nonfiction books and biographies and novels. He has written books for kids, and he has written books for grown-ups. He has written more than two hundred books, and he began one of them, *Tales from the 1969–70 New York Knicks*, published in 2005, with a brief survey of basketball history.

"These early games were marked by some strange plays," Gutman wrote. "When there was a net around the court, a player could be trapped if he dribbled into the corner. The defender could grab the net on both sides and literally pull it around him."

It's comical to picture a team employing this strategy in the modern era of pro basketball. There's Kobe Bryant or Jimmy Butler, probing the baseline for an opening to shoot or pass, and from the sideline, a couple of bench guys on the opposing team, like they're trolling for tuna, throw a gill net over him. Illegal defense? Only in international waters.

Anyway, in the same paragraph, Gutman provided a delicious tidbit.

"In a game played with a cage around the court and no backboard," he wrote, "an early pro named Jack Inglis jumped up alongside the basket, grabbed the cage, and pulled himself up alongside the basket. While the defenders looked up at him helplessly, a teammate passed him the ball. Inglis caught it while hanging onto the cage with one hand and dropped it through the basket. An early version of the slam dunk. It was a perfectly legal play, because no one had ever seen it done before."

This was a remarkable moment: the consensus best basketball player in the country refusing to be constrained by the strictures of expectations or unwritten rules or even a physical enclosure. This was a spontaneous display of imagination and creativity that would lead, necessarily, to the expansion of that imagination and creativity—to all the forms of the dunk that would follow. Jack Inglis just happened to be the first . . . assuming that he had done what Gutman said he had done. Gutman, who was eighty years old and living in the Hudson Valley at the time I was researching this book, did not attribute that anecdote to any source within the text of *Tales*, and he did not include any footnotes or endnotes. So I emailed him to ask where he had uncovered the remarkable scene of Inglis swinging like a spider monkey above the court. He responded promptly.

"I had a big book on the history of basketball, which I no longer have, and might have gotten the reference there," he wrote. "I also interviewed Nat Holman many years ago, and he might have been the one who told me the story. Apparently, Inglis was a very strong man and certainly capable of doing what is described. I certainly would not have made the story up. My gut tells me that I heard the story from Holman, but we're going back some fifty years."

In a follow-up email, Gutman was more certain on his sourcing: "I know that there are writers who, shall we say, tend to embellish some of the old stories, and I wanted to assure you that if I used that quote, it was something I got legitimately. The more I think about it and stretch my memory, which is still very good, I'm almost sure that Holman told me the story." Nat Holman died in 1995, ten months shy of his ninety-ninth birthday. If he did in fact witness Jack Inglis, king of the cagers, drop in the first slam dunk and set the stage for the sport's gradual metamorphosis into an astounding display of human flight, he told no one other than Bill Gutman, and he took that sight of a seminal moment in basketball with him to his grave.

4

LIONHEART

Accounts of the early days of organized basketball, at all its levels, are often skeletal and fragmented at best. Go digging for anecdotes and episodes of players' introducing the dunk to the sport, and you can spend hours fruitlessly scanning through online archives and thumbing through old books whose pages browned long ago. When you find such a story, especially one like this, one that has so many delicious details and that demonstrates how the dunk was becoming more common in and important to the sport, you savor it.

Before graduating from **Placer Union** High School in Auburn, California, in 1930, Bernard Dobbas selected an excerpt from an obscure nineteenth-century poem to be the quote alongside his senior yearbook photograph. The excerpt was from "The Jester's Plea" by Frederick Locker-Lampson.

The World! Was jester ever in
A viler than the present? . . .
Yet if it ugly be—as sin,
It almost is—as pleasant.

Dobbas's world, for the eighty-three years he was alive, was at times one and then the other. It was ugly—in the brutal, primal meaning of the word, particularly in one flabbergasting encounter—and it was pleasant. Let's begin with the pleasant.

He was a two-sport standout at Placer Union High in track and basketball, six feet, five inches tall, wavy dark hair. Placer County is in the Sacramento Valley. Placer County was gold country, and Dobbas's descendants, who were Swiss, immigrated to the area before the Rush. The land was life, still, once he came around; he was the secretary of Placer Union's chapter of Future Farmers. While studying agriculture at the University of California, Davis, he was the basketball team's captain, starting center, and best player. In one 1934 game, a loss to San Francisco, Dobbas scored 12 of the Aggies' 28 total points. A year later, they scored 44 points in a victory, and he had 20 of them. The *Placer Herald* ran an assertive headline on Saturday, January 12, 1935: "Bernard Dobbas Is Star." On the same day, though, the Woodland *Daily Democrat* published a story that made Dobbas part of basketball history from then on.

In describing Dobbas's 27-point performance in a 42–32 Davis win over Sacramento Junior College, the story's author, "J. S.," noted that, in high school, Dobbas "could cup the casaba from all angles, and he showed a lot of general all-around basketball ability." Against Sacramento, he was especially dominant in leading a Davis comeback from a late five-point deficit:

"Dobbas broke loose. Unerringly accurate, he converted three field goals, then a tip-in. . . . [He] busted through again and dribble[d] down court for another 'dunk' shot."

Both *SLAM* magazine and *MEL Magazine*, in Los Angeles, cited this as the first documented mention of a slam dunk. And, based on J. S.'s phrasing and reporting, Dobbas apparently dunked more than once in that game. But this seminal moment in the sport was barely noticed then or remarked upon thereafter, a tiny-type footnote in a life that included a long career as a rancher in Northern California, a service stint in World War II, and the opportunity while in college to spar with Max Baer, who at the time was the world heavyweight champion.

"Everybody from school kept urging me to knock out Baer," Dobbas, whom one writer called "a clever boxer," once said. "So one day, I belted him on the jaw with all my might. He just stood there, looked angry, and started coming at me. I got out of that ring in a hurry and never went back."

Dobbas wasn't so quick to retreat a few years later, in a more threatening situation. In the fall of 1939, he and his cattle dog were hiking in El Dorado County when, in a remote wooded area, they came upon a mountain lion. The cat tried to climb a tree to escape, but Dobbas's dog seized it, only to have the lion gain the upper hand in an *Animal Planet*–style battle and start mauling and clawing the dog. To save his companion, Dobbas picked up a heavy tree limb and whacked the lion with it about the head until it was dead. He then toted the body back to his home, where, from time to time, he would show it off to his friends.

"Mr. Dobbas always chuckled at—but never denied—subsequent reports that he had killed the mountain lion with his bare hands," Joe Carroll, a journalist from Auburn, California, Dobbas's hometown, once said.

The tale spread across the country, wire services and newspapers collaborating to bring it piping hot to families' breakfast tables (e.g., *CATTLEMAN KILLS LION WITH CLUB*). Dobbas "became a national celebrity," his obituarist, Jon Engellenner of the *Sacramento Bee*, wrote in July 1996. But Engellenner's piece never so much as hinted at Dobbas's singular distinction in basketball, his contribution to advancing the usefulness and popularity of the game's burgeoning innovation. The word *dunk* didn't appear in the obit, which is a shame. Barney Dobbas had proved himself capable of cupping a casaba and clubbing a cougar, and it's rare to see that kind of versatility in the sport anymore.

5

THE FARM BOY AND THE FÜHRER

Today, basketball is rightly seen as an international game, and the 1992 US men's Olympic team—with Michael Jordan having just won his second NBA championship with the Chicago Bulls that spring, with an assemblage of talent on its roster that has yet to be equaled—was so superb and such a fascination that it accelerated the spread of the sport around the world. But those Summer Games, in Barcelona, were not the first to feature a US team whose best player was best known for his ability to dunk. Jordan had a historical forerunner, in function if not style, who took the dunk to places it had never been.

ts sheened black hull 705 feet long and 100 feet high, its white super-structure blazing and brilliant whenever sunlight struck it, its average speed on its trial voyage more than 22 knots—the usual cruise ship today hums along the water at 20—the S.S. *Manhattan* was a swift and mighty thing, the largest ocean liner ever constructed in the United States. On July 15, 1936, its commander and crew launched it on its most important assignment: making off from Pier 60 in New York for Hamburg, Germany, to shepherd the 334 men and women who made

up the US Olympic team across the Atlantic Ocean to the Summer
Games in Berlin.

These would be the Games of Jesse Owens, of Adolf Hitler, of
Leni Riefenstahl, of the world order about to topple out of its delicate
balance and sports serving as a symbol of good, in the end, triumph-
ing over evil. Germany had been awarded the Games in 1931. Hitler
had become chancellor two years later, and his campaign against the
country's Jewish people was already underway, his broader and darker
aims already apparent to any geopolitical leader with eyes to see. The
Amateur Athletic Union (AAU), at the time the world's largest sports
governing body, had voted in November 1933 to boycott the 1936
Berlin Olympics unless, the *New York Times* wrote, "there is a change
in the attitude of the Hitler government toward Jews in sport." There
was, of course, no such change, but there was also no international
appetite for forgoing the Olympics. Not a single country refused, on
principle, to send its athletes to Berlin. In December 1935, the AAU
voted again, this time in favor of participation. Publicly silent on the
question of whether the United States ought to boycott, President
Franklin Roosevelt did not bid the team farewell. Olympic officials
told the athletes that Roosevelt was opposed to their going; if he'd
had his way, the US wouldn't have sent a team to Berlin at all. But he
didn't stop any of those athletes from boarding the *Manhattan*, even
after March 7, when Hitler ordered German troops, in violation of
the Treaty of Versailles, to enter and remilitarize the Rhineland—the
gambit that set the stage for worldwide war.

The ship itself, in all its magnitude, betrayed none of that global
tension, outrage, and uncertainty. It was, by one expert account, the
"latest, largest, and finest" vessel born of America's shipyards over
the previous decade. It weighed more than thirty thousand tons, accommodated 1,239 passengers, and cost (together with its sister ship,
the *Washington*) $21 million to build. The first page of the passenger
manifest was a message from United States Lines, the corporation for
whom the New York Shipbuilding Company constructed the *Manhattan*: "We feel honored in being the link that bears you on your journey
across the Atlantic. We will make every effort while you are aboard to

help keep you fit and happy and ready for this greatest of sports events. You are the chosen youth of the world who will cement new friendships by your *esprit de corps* and by your moral and physical courage in the stadium." Its dining saloon seated 396 people and had two stories, and though the athletes were consigned to steerage while International Olympic Committee president and Hitler sympathizer Avery Brundage and his lackeys enjoyed first-class accommodations, the nightly dinner menu was a testament to the pounds that the competitors packed on during their nine days at sea: five kinds of cheeses, chicken liver *sauté*, risotto *à la creole*, prime rib, baba *au chocolat*, more.

Among those chosen youth were athletes who, in Berlin, would establish themselves as some of the most accomplished and memorable in American Olympic history. There was sprinter Helen Stephens, who won the 100 meters and was one leg of the US's 4 × 100 gold-medal quartet. There was the men's eight-oar rowing team, whose humble backstory and unlikely victory over Germany became the basis for Daniel James Brown's bestselling book *The Boys in the Boat*. There was, of course, Owens, the walking, talking thumb in the eye of Hitler, the everlasting rebuke to any filth-ridden philosophies about a master race, the winner of four gold medals: in the 100 meters, the 200 meters, the long jump, and the 4 × 100.

And there was a six-foot-eight native of Happy, Texas—present-day population: 678—with a cherubic face and gigantic hands, with fingers so thick that he wore a size-15 ring, with a background as modest as that of anyone aboard the *Manhattan*. There was Joe Fortenberry, one of the thirteen players on the US men's basketball team, its starting center. He was already a pioneer in his sport, and in a small corner of the country, he would grow to be famous for it.

I was off-roading in a rented RAV4, trundling over anthills and bouncing over tractor tracks cut into the firm soil of a six-hundred-acre stretch of farmland, high and hot winds buffeting the vehicle, for the sake of seeing exactly where Joe Fortenberry first dunked a basketball. It was mid-May 2023—springtime in West Texas, scorching summer conditions anywhere else. Fortenberry's son, Oliver, bald and bearded and seventy-three years old, sat in the front passenger seat next to me. He knew exactly where, on this vast expanse of browned earth and tall, patchy grass, the barn where his father grew up and taught himself to play basketball stood. Oliver directed me to pull over near a mound of sand-colored dirt. This was the place. Before we got out of the RAV4, though, he gave me a warning.

"Watch out for rattlesnakes," he said. "Truly."

I shot him a look of alarm—raised eyebrows, gaping mouth— unsure whether he was being serious or having fun with a naive Yankee. But Oliver seemed guileless, so I opened my door, surveyed the soil for rattlers, and, finding none, stepped out for what I would make sure was a quick reporting stop. There wasn't much to see anyway, just an azure sky and land that seemed without end. There was a house on the property. It was a gray blob in the distance.

"Imagine a gangly, tall kid," Oliver said, "playing basketball in the middle of nowhere."

Joe Fortenberry was fourteen years old and six-foot-three when his family, farmers all, settled in Happy in 1925. It was an upgrade in living conditions for them. The Fortenberrys had resided in even smaller hamlets before that. Even the towns' names were miniscule— Leo and Joy—and their homes weren't houses but prairie shacks that didn't have electricity or running water, that did have kerosene lamps and outhouses. "This is bleak now," Oliver said. "Just think how bleak that was then."

Joe was a self-taught dunker. Nailed to a side of the family barn in Happy was a barrel hoop. It made for a fine basketball goal. There was a loose board above it, and when Joe tried to bank the ball off the barn and through the hoop, that loose board would prevent a true carom. He kept missing. So he started jumping high enough to shove the ball through the hoop. It's unknown—even by Oliver and his sisters, Sally and Trish—whether Joe dunked during any of his varsity games at Happy High School. But in the foyer just beyond the doors to its modest gymnasium—a dead ringer, with its tight sidelines and four rows of cherrywood bleachers, for the Hickory Huskers' home court in *Hoosiers*—Happy High memorializes him on a shelf in a trophy case with a black-and-white headshot and a brief biography that refers to him as Happy's "most renowned high school athlete" and "the greatest offensive center in basketball."

By the time he turned eighteen, Fortenberry had sprouted five inches and possessed the kind of country-raised strength that a weight room can never provide. His growth in high school, both as a player and in his height, was profound enough that Sam Burton, the head coach at West Texas State Teachers College in Canyon, seventeen miles north of Happy, recruited him. There, Fortenberry's day-to-day life was a spare, frontier-like existence. Forget the idea of basketball consuming his life, as any sport does for any Division I athlete today. Basketball was Joe's refuge. Forget a dorm room. He lived in a shack on the edge of Canyon. Forget a meal plan. He was a deadeye shot with a rifle, even from horseback, and rabbits were always plentiful. Forget any NCAA gobbledygook about amateurism or any name-image-likeness opportunities. He earned pocket money fighting bare-knuckle boxing matches against the toughest guys from other towns. Once, before a bout in Clayton, New Mexico, a fighter sucker-punched him before Fortenberry could step out of his Model T. Still in the driver's seat, Fortenberry returned fire and then some, knocking the guy out with a straight left before pulling away.

Twice at West Texas, he was an All-American, in 1931 and 1932, the Buffaloes winning 20 games in each of those seasons, and their star center's repertoire of post moves apparently included the dunk shot. "He did it in a game," Oliver said as we sat together in the living room of his home in Amarillo, the same rancher that Joe and Bobbie Fortenberry bought in 1956, the same house in which Oliver grew up. "He told me he did. I don't know what team it was against. And his coach told him, 'Joe, that's not elegant. That's not part of the game. Don't do it again.' So I'm sure he didn't do that, but he did it in practice when no one was around." It wouldn't be the last time Joe would dunk in practice. It would be one of the last

times he did so without anyone taking particular note of what he
had done.

Texas kids become Texas men, and Texas men work in the oil industry. That truth is everlasting, at any time, in any era, even during the
Great Depression. The difference for Joe Fortenberry was that he had
to leave Texas to find that work. He was twenty-five when he took
a job with the Globe Refining Company in McPherson, Kansas—a
city, with a population now of roughly thirty thousand, that rests
pretty much in the center of the state and, in turn, in the center of the
United States. For Joe, one of the primary benefits of working there
was that in 1933, the company, for marketing purposes, had formed
a basketball team: the Globe Refiners. (The team was also called the
Oilers, giving the name some sports-tied cachet before Wayne Gretzky
came along.) It was common practice at that time for a city, a town,
or a large company or corporation to sponsor a team, a piece of oft-
forgotten history that puts complaints from fans and media these days
about advertising patches on uniform sleeves and hilariously awkward
bowl-game names (for example, the 2022 Union Home Mortgage
Gasparillo Bowl) in some perspective.

Frequently, those teams would compete at what was then considered the highest level of basketball in the country: the national AAU
circuit. Joe himself had played for such a club—the Ogden Boosters, in Utah—for a couple of years before Gene Johnson, Globe Oil's
coach, coaxed him to Kansas. Johnson, in fact, set about compiling a
team of relative giants, recruiting, among others, a six-foot-six player
named Harry Dowd and a center, Willard Schmidt, who had led
Creighton University to a Missouri Valley Conference championship
and who, at six-foot-nine an inch up on Fortenberry, could lay claim
to being the tallest man on what headline writers routinely called "the
tallest basketball team in the world." A hooper/refinery worker like
Fortenberry or Schmidt would earn a cool $400, total, for spending
four months of the year, December to March, practicing, traveling,
and playing games for the Oilers. But the more valuable compensation

was the status that accompanied playing for the team—and the opportunity to be selected to the US Olympic team.

"Boy," Fortenberry once said, "I want to make that trip."

Basketball had never been included in the Olympics before 1936, and it had taken relentless lobbying and behind-the-scenes efforts from another Kansas-based figure, Phog Allen, for the International Olympic Committee to adopt the sport for the Berlin Games. To select a roster, Allen would oversee a tournament, made up of eight teams from the AAU, NCAA, and YMCA, at Madison Square Garden in April. The Olympic team would then be compiled from the tournament's champion and runner-up: seven players and the head coach from the former, six players from the latter.

The Garden would be familiar territory for the Refiners. They had traveled there already, in March, for an exhibition game against a college all-star team. The day before that game, which McPherson won, 45–43, several reporters on hand observed the team practice at the West Side YMCA. One of them summarized what they saw and how they reacted in the third paragraph of a story headlined, "Awesome Kansas Giants Reverse Basketball Lay-Up Shot Process," in the March 10, 1936, edition of the *New York Times*.

> The McPherson version of a lay-up shot left observers flabbergasted. Joe Fortenberry, 6-foot 8-inch center, and Willard Schmidt, 6-foot 9-inch forward, did not use an ordinary curling toss. Not those giants. They left the floor, reached up, and pitched the ball downward into the hoop, much like a cafeteria customer dunking a roll in coffee.

Jack Inglis was scaling cages in the 1910s, and Barney Dobbas was jamming regularly in the 1920s per the daily newspapers in northern California, and one can only guess how many Black players were dunking in their barnstorming leagues over those same decades. But a mention in the *Times*, with the paper's reach and prestige, quick-dried and solidified any event's pedestal in history's display room. So it was for Fortenberry and his dunk. Sally Fortenberry Nibbelink, one of his daughters, acknowledged as much. "It would be really hard to prove beyond a shadow of a doubt that he was the first guy to dunk a basketball," she told me. "But we do have the article from the reporter from the *New York Times* who saw him at Madison Square Garden."

The reporter turned out to be more than a reporter. The reporter was Arthur J. Daley, whom the *Times* promoted to sports columnist on Christmas Eve 1942; who, in 1956, became the first journalist to win the Pulitzer Prize for full-time sports coverage; and who was a contemporary, colleague, and rival of another sportswriting legend. "Mr. Daley was a gentle, diffident man whose shyness made him uncomfortable in unfamiliar surroundings," Red Smith wrote in his *Times* obituary for Daley, who died of a heart attack on Jan. 3, 1974, at age sixty-nine. "He was never altogether at ease around racetracks because he felt unsure of his authority in the sport." The tartness of those lines shouldn't be surprising. Smith didn't think much of Daley as a wordsmith—he considered him "a pedestrian writer," according to Smith's biographer, Ira Berkow—and was hurt that the Pulitzer committee gave Daley the award before it honored him.

There's no small measure of irony, then, at least from Smith's perspective, in Daley being the writer who introduced the term *dunk* to a national audience. Nearly two weeks after Daley's story appeared in the *Times*, in fact, the March 21, 1936, edition of *Newsweek*—its cover art a photograph of Hitler shaking hands with one of his apologists, former British prime minister David Lloyd George—included a non-bylined story about the US Olympic basketball team. Fortenberry and Schmidt, according to the story, "drop balls down through the hoop as effortlessly as the average man deposits a lump of sugar in his coffee." The similarity between the *Times* and *Newsweek* stories was a testament to the banality of Daley's metaphor, perhaps the plagiaristic instincts of the unknown *Newsweek* scribe, and sportswriters' timeless fondness for a good cup of joe. It also showed the degree to which Fortenberry's ability to dunk fascinated those who saw him do it, even if none of them saw him do it in a game. To Fortenberry, there was a difference between dunking during practice and dunking during games. As his college coach had taught him, he considered the latter to be bad form.

"We thought it was kind of showing off," Fortenberry once said after he had stopped playing competitive basketball. "And I still think it is."

Despite winning the national AAU tournament later that month in Denver, in April the Refiners lost the championship game of the Olympic Trials tournament, 44–43, to a club out of Hollywood that was sponsored by Universal Pictures and appropriately called the Universals. The upshot of the outcome was that the Universals would have more of their players on the Olympic roster than the Refiners. Fortenberry, who had 17 points in the loss, making him responsible for nearly 40 percent of the Refiners' offensive output, had nothing to fear. He was one of the six McPherson players to make the cut. No, the worry for Fortenberry, or for any of the other men on the Olympic roster, was whether any of them could afford to go. With the Depression raging and offering an excuse for even America's largest and most profitable companies to pinch pennies, neither Universal Pictures nor McPherson Globe would pay to send the players to the Games. The players got there only with help. Some Universal actors— Boris Karloff and John Boles, the stars of the 1931 film *Frankenstein*, for instance—donated money toward the cause, and the Refiners raised the $1,000 for the journey themselves, through door-to-door soliciting throughout Kansas.

The last weeks before the Games brought more problems, all of them injuries. Schmidt lacerated his left heel when, during a workday shower at McPherson Globe, he stepped on a piece of tin. The wound was long and deep enough that it required eight stitches. Then, on July 3, Fortenberry and teammate Tex Gibbons were passengers in a 1936 Chevrolet, a local car dealer behind the wheel, the Chevy, according to one report, "a prize car that the [Refiners] were using to raise money for the Olympic trip." The dealer drove the Chevy into a ditch, the vehicle flipping several times. Fortenberry had bruises to his head. The accounts have Gibbons's injuries covering seemingly most parts of his upper body: a left arm in a sling, a six-inch gash along his right forearm, a severe cut to his right ear. What was certain was that the two were fortunate to be alive. The reasons given for the accident varied, as well: either the driver was run off the highway by a truck or the men in the Chevy had been drinking, or both. When I asked Oliver Fortenberry what his father had been up to that night, he said: "Something untoward." The US men, the favorites to win the gold medal, were not entering the Olympics on an upbeat, optimistic note.

When the *Manhattan* docked in Hamburg on July 24, 1936, the disembarking athletes were greeted by a wide white banner affixed to a shipyard wall: WELCOME TO GERMANY. To either side of the banner hung a flag: on the right side, American; on the left, Nazi. German boys as young as thirteen were clad in Hitler Youth uniforms: deep tan shirt jackets, black patches on the shoulders, a red-and-black band around the left arm with a swastika flaring in the middle. On a motorcade to the Olympic Village, which after the Games would be converted into officers' quarters for the German army, Francis Johnson, a guard on the US basketball team, saw Nazi soldiers standing shoulder to shoulder for nine miles. One day during the Games, a giant zeppelin—its length 803 feet, its diameter 131 feet, the Olympics' symbol of five interlocking rings painted on its sides, its journey powered by more than seven million cubic feet of hydrogen, a highly flammable gas—trundled across the clouds above the competitors. That flight of the *Hindenburg* LZ129 was intended to be another garish display of German technological superiority. Just nine months later, on May 6, 1937, above Lakehurst, New Jersey, another of its flights would end in fiery catastrophe.

In *Games of Deception*, his chronicle of the '36 Olympics, author Andrew Maraniss describes a scene that took place at a lodge in the city of Dessau, where the American basketball team was living during the Games. There, "players were relaxing on lounge chairs when . . . Hitler and his girlfriend, Eva Braun, appeared before them." While standing on the patio, Hitler and Braun exchanged pleasantries and small talk with the players before he "snapped up his right arm in a familiar Nazi salute," Maraniss writes, "and was gone."

Joe Fortenberry was there, three feet away from the dictator and his mistress. "He said, 'If I'd known what was going to happen, I'd have jumped him right there,'" Oliver told me. "Maybe he would have. Maybe he wouldn't have. If he had, he would have torn him apart." For his part, Joe was neither frightened of nor impressed by Hitler, who at five-foot-eight was a foot shorter than Fortenberry, but amused by him and the Svengali-like sway he held over the country. "When I saw him," Fortenberry once said, "I thought, 'How could a little guy like that have so much control over these people?' It was a comedy to us Americans. We laughed about it. They treated him like he was their god."

The breadth and significance of those Olympics—the lengths to which Hitler went to transform the event into a propagandic show-case of Nazi strength, Owens's tangible and symbolic repudiation of the wickedness underpinning that campaign, the Games' subtext of horrors and battles yet to come—have reduced Joe Fortenberry and the details of the basketball competition in Berlin to a relative af-terthought. And understandably so. Adjust the focal length of your historical lens to zoom in on them, however, and you uncover a fasci-nating story in its own right.

The Olympic basketball tournament and its quality of play were as far from the cold, flawless efficiency for which the Germans were striving as could be. The International Basketball Federation (FIBA), according to the official report of the '36 Games, "expressed the wish that the tournament should not take place indoors, but in the open air." As if the twenty-one participating nations were playing pickup games on courts near Venice Beach or on West Fourth Street in Greenwich Village, the tournament would be held outdoors. Unlike those more basketball-appropriate sites, though, the Olympic courts were not made of asphalt. Once it acquiesced to the IOC's request, the German Organizing Committee tried to transform five of the Reich Sport Field's lawn tennis courts into basketball courts, hardening the surfaces with clay and sand and suspending hoops from padded posts.

The makeshift nature of the courts might have seemed an equalizer for the United States' opponents, given that so many of those coun-tries had just taken up basketball and none of their teams featured any players who could match up size-wise against Fortenberry and Willard Schmidt. But those nations weren't taking any chances: Not long after the US team's arrival in Berlin, several coaches successfully lobbied FIBA to pass a resolution that set a height limit of six foot one for the Games. They'd be damned if Fortenberry or Willard would dunk on them. Only a fierce protest from the Americans got the rule overturned just before the tournament's first round. Otherwise, the player who most represented the leap into modernity that the sport was poised to take never would have played a minute.

Schmidt was a valuable backup on the US team, but Fortenberry proved to be head and shoulders above him (figuratively) and everyone else in the tournament (literally), scoring 20 points in a 56–23 victory over the Philippines in the fourth round. The Americans then handled Mexico, 25–10, in the semifinals, setting up a game against Canada for the gold medal.

Thousands of people had attended the early-round games of the tournament, and for the championship game on August 14, the Germans had erected a small brick wall enclosing the main court. The wall might have been aesthetically pleasing, but once a storm settled overhead, it was, practically speaking, a nightmare, trapping rainwater and turning the court into a pool of more than a foot of standing water and the basketball—which, with its weight and slick surface, was more like a medicine ball—into a child's bathtub toy. "A dribble wasn't really a dribble," the US's Sam Balter once said. "The ball didn't bounce back up. It splashed and floated away." Fortenberry, true to his farming roots, said the court was "as muddy as a hog pen." Spectators were few, and they pulled up their cars close to the court, or took shelter under trees, or used newspapers as umbrellas, the black print leaking down their arms. The players didn't run up and down the court. They slogged through a mire. Once they forged a nine-point lead in the first half, the Americans could no longer function on offense. The ball was too wet and heavy to pass with accuracy and force. The good news for them was, the Canadians fared even worse. Twice, they managed to get off clean shots at the basket, only to have Fortenberry leap up and snatch the ball out of the air as it descended toward the rim—a play that would be offensive goaltending today but was perfectly legal then. The final score, 19–5, seemed something out of a slow-pitch softball game, not a duel between presumably the two best basketball teams in the world. But the United States had won the first gold medal in basketball in Olympic history, and Fortenberry, with those two blocks and a game-high eight points, had been as responsible as anyone for the victory.

"During the national anthem," Fortenberry said, "I couldn't wipe all the tears away. It was wonderful."

Perhaps the only person in Berlin happier with the outcome of the tournament—and especially with the opponents in the tournament's final game—was Dr. James Naismith: citizen of Canada, citizen of the United States. A nationwide fundraiser within the basketball community covered Naismith's travel costs to Germany, yet somehow the AAU initially had left his name off the list of those officials who should receive complimentary passes to the Games. Once the error was corrected, Naismith was feted in Berlin with the appropriate amount of reverence and respect for his standing in the sport. He tossed the basketball in the air for the opening tap of the opening game, between Estonia and France, and each of the participating teams lowered its national flag when Naismith strode past. The spectacle was beyond anything that he had envisioned for basketball, as was the manner in which the world's best players played. The idea of dunking had never occurred to him. The sight of someone dropping the ball through the hoop—even as Fortenberry and Schmidt made sure to limit their aerial exploits to practice and warm-ups—was a revelation.

"Son," Naismith told Fortenberry, "if I had known how high you guys could jump to dunk the ball, I'd have nailed the peach basket higher."

Upon their return from Berlin, the United States' Olympians were greeted with a ticker-tape parade through the streets of Manhattan, and Mayor Fiorello La Guardia gave them personalized medals from the city of New York. Oliver Fortenberry still has his father's, keeping it buried at the bottom of one of many cardboard boxes and plastic tubs where he preserves Joe's memorabilia.

In a way, Joe's life was only just beginning after the Games. He accepted a job with the Phillips Petroleum Company as a land man, acquiring and writing drilling leases. During World War II, he served in the 36th Infantry Regiment, and in 1947, he married his wife, Bobbie, who herself had been a Navy gunnery instructor. After Joe, Bobbie, and their three children settled in Amarillo, she served as the librarian at the local newspaper, the *Globe-News*, for twenty years. It was a neat contradiction: Bobbie as a keeper of the historical flame, working for the institution whose purpose was to inform the community, married to Joe, who was the town's most famous resident and, at the same time, did little or nothing to advertise his fame and accomplishments. He kept his Olympic gold medal in a shoebox on the top shelf of a hall closet. He acknowledged it only if someone wanted to see it. "He never, ever brought it out to show anybody. Ever," Oliver said. "He just wasn't that kind of guy." A distant cousin and close friend of Joe's daughters, Beth Fortenberry, once watched him reach up into that closet—"Not on his tippy toes or anything," she said— and remove that shoebox. Once. It was the only time he spoke about the Olympics with her.

His legend grew as legends grow in towns and small cities, by word of mouth, through personal interactions that morphed into anecdotes that morphed into tales that seemed too tall to be true. Joe Fortenberry could pick up a John Deere plow. Joe Fortenberry could body-slam a 350-pound calf. When Joe Fortenberry shook a woman's hand, he extended just his index and middle fingers, lest he crush her delicate hamate and metacarpals into a fine powder. "When you're the biggest guy anybody's ever seen," his nephew Ed Wright told me, "it sticks with you." In 1966, when Joe was fifty-five years old, he came home from work one day, still dressed in his business hat and suit and overcoat, pens and business cards overflowing from his shirt's lapel pocket. Oliver, who was on Tascosa High School's varsity basketball team then, was outside, trying to dunk on the family's driveway hoop. Joe hadn't suited up for the Oilers in years.

I wonder, Joe said, *if I can still do that.*

He took off his hat and his coat. Oliver tossed him the ball. Joe jumped up and stuffed it, pens and cards flying out of his pocket and spilling all over the driveway. He grinned.

I don't think I'll do that again, he said.

Once in a while, a reporter might call the Fortenberry house to chat with Joe for a story. One did, for instance, ahead of the 1992 Summer Olympics in Barcelona, when the United States loaded its men's basketball team with the best of the NBA's best. Joe's was a natural number to dial. A player who had altered basketball by drawing attention—intentionally, unintentionally, didn't matter—to himself and this singular act, this move that few of his peers, if any, could pull off, that seemed to lift the sport into a higher dimension? Sorry, Wilt. Sorry, Doc. Sorry, Michael. Joe was doing that before any of you were even born. A US Olympic team that had thrust hoops to the forefront of the international sports scene through an overwhelming performance? Sorry, Dream Team. Joe and his guys had done that in Berlin half a century earlier. In the Fortenberry house, in one man's personal history, the past truly was prologue. Hell, yes, you call *that* guy. "I think the Dream Team will slaughter everybody," Joe told the reporter. "They will win by whatever they want to. That's kind of the way we were when we were there." In 2015, Michael McKnight—in writing an essay for *Sports Illustrated* about his quest, as a six-foot-one, forty-two-year-old man, to dunk—mentioned Joe in his first sentence and referred to him throughout the piece. The article reignited hope, among Oliver and other members of the Fortenberry family, that Joe and the rest of the 1936 Olympic team might earn induction into the Naismith Basketball Hall of Fame. That hope, as of this book's publication, remains unfulfilled.

Having contracted shingles and cancer, Joe Fortenberry died in 1993, at eighty-two. His Olympic gold medal is embossed on his tombstone. Bobbie died in 2022, when she was ninety-two. Oliver has left much of his parents' home as it was when Joe and Bobbie were alive: wood paneling, dozens of photographs whose frames resemble gold crown molding, glassware and decor that have long turned retro. Retired, he had worked in the petroleum industry, too, as a land man, just like his father; Joe taught him the business. He never married, and when Joe first got sick, Oliver moved home to care for him. He laments the changes in his neighborhood, just as any man in his seventies might. Amarillo is a place of ennui, of supermarket parking lots made of dingy concrete and endless as gray deserts, its crime rate higher than 95 percent of US cities. Maybe things would be better, and he would be happier, if more people remembered his father.

"Everybody knew who he was," Oliver told me. "Now nobody does, hardly. These young people don't know. He's passing out of reality."

At West Texas A&M University, Joe's uniform No. 8 hangs from the rafters of First United Bank Center, a maroon banner steady and motionless high above the court, but it's another alumnus—former NBA point guard and head coach Maurice Cheeks, a member of the Naismith Memorial Hall of Fame—who has been honored with a statue outside the entrance to the arena. Joe's nephew Ed Wright, an enthusiastic West Texas booster, points out the banner to the men's and women's basketball and volleyball teams, which is more talking up of Joe Fortenberry than Ed's uncle ever did. In 2021, just to find out how much Joe's gold medal was worth, Oliver appeared on PBS's *Antiques Roadshow*. An appraiser estimated its value to be between $150,000 and $175,000. Oliver has stored it in a safety deposit box ever since, afraid that he'd be setting himself up for a burglary if he kept it in his house. But two days before I arrived in Amarillo, he withdrew it, because someone wanted to talk about his father, and he wanted that someone to see and touch the medal.

Out on the farm in Happy, Oliver glanced around. The wind was kicking up, rippling the pages of my notebook, whistling in our ears, and he remarked that if Joe had learned to shoot and dribble and play and dunk outside, in this kind of weather, then the rain and quasi-flooding and the waterlogged basketballs in Berlin couldn't have bothered him much.

"Give that ball to LeBron," Oliver said, "and see how many points he scores."

It was, at its most basic and literal, a ludicrous statement. LeBron James, against those athletes? With his athleticism? With theirs? With his experience in basketball? With theirs? Rain, no rain, regular basketball, shitty basketball, mini basketball, no basketball: The results would be predictable and laughable. There was more going on in what Oliver said and meant, though. Here was a son whose father had achieved great things. A son whose father had made and been an integral part of American and Olympic history. A son who had watched for years as his father's name faded out of the public's consciousness everywhere outside of his family and a few quarters of a town no one thought of much. Joe Fortenberry had won a gold medal in the 1936 Olympics. Joe Fortenberry had helped stick it to *Der Führer*. Joe Fortenberry had dunked a basketball before just about anyone else had.

"He started it," Oliver said. "Somebody had to hit the first home run. Somebody had to throw the first perfect game. You can say, 'Aw, somebody else would have done it.' Yeah, but he did it first."

OK, but you can also say that, as remarkable as Joe Fortenberry's story is and life was, there really is no way to know for certain whether he was the first man to dunk. There were those more obscure players from previous years—Inglis and Dobbas and who knows how many other undocumented dunks and dunkers. No one *really* knows, right? And no one will ever know, right?

Joe Fortenberry's son shook his head, a little gesture with a lifetime's worth of defiance and loyalty and love behind it.

"I do," he said.

6

THE GLANDULAR GOON

"I know Kurland. There's some writing that he did the first dunk in a college game. And he didn't. I don't want to get in an argument with them. But I only know what my dad told me, that he did it in 1929 or '30 at West Texas. All I have is his word. His word is better than anybody else's word. Period."

—OLIVER FORTENBERRY

He's fortunate. Yep, **Oliver Fortenberry** is a lucky man. Here's why: Bob Kurland's family members didn't want to get into an argument, either. And there was no need for one, no need for a who-dunked-first debate, because the two men at the center of that debate would be put off by it more than anyone.

Joe Fortenberry would be heartened, I suspect, by the qualities that he shared with Kurland, the man who is credited—wrongly, in Oliver's mind—with being the first player to dunk during a college basketball game. The similarities between Fortenberry and Kurland are quite profound, actually, and the idea of setting one of them against the other in any regard, of having a duel of legacies here, just doesn't feel right.

It's possible, maybe more than possible, that Joe Fortenberry can stake a claim to the distinction that has been one of Bob Kurland's basketball birthmarks. Bob Kurland, who was the starting center for and star of the 1945 and 1946 Oklahoma A&M Aggies—the university wasn't called Oklahoma State yet—the first team to win consecutive NCAA championships. Bob Kurland, who—before the Dream Team and the Redeem Team, before Kobe Bryant and Carmelo Anthony were restoring America's dominance over international basketball— was the first player to win two Olympic gold medals, at the 1948 and 1952 Summer Games. Bob Kurland, who—in front of nine thousand people in a packed Convention Hall in Philadelphia in December 1944, in a game against Temple University—dunked. Their lives and athletic careers echo each other, Fortenberry's a kind of fairy tale, Kurland's remarkable in its own right. Would being the lone answer to a trivia question matter that much to either of them?

"I'll just tell you like it is," Ross "Rocky" Kurland, the younger of Bob's two sons, told me. "My dad was very humble. It didn't matter to him if he was the first guy to dunk."

If you know the full breadth of Bob Kurland's story, you know that his son is right. You also know that he's wrong. In one way, dunking a basketball meant nothing to Bob Kurland. In another way, nothing meant more.

Born in St. Louis two days before Christmas 1924, Kurland was the son of immigrants, one from Germany, one from Poland. The family lived meagerly. Kurland's parents, Albert and Adele, purchased their house from the Sears, Roebuck & Co. catalog—one of the 70,000–75,000 homes that the company sold from 1908 to 1940 through its Modern Homes program—and Albert built it himself. Come the Great Depression, though, the Kurlands, unable to afford their mortgage, had to rent out the house and move into the chicken coop behind it, bearing up through the kinds of conditions that were common in the early 1930s: no electricity, no running water.

Even if he didn't have the ideal diet for someone who would sprout to close to seven feet tall, Bob had genetics on his side. His father was six foot two. His mother was five foot nine. His paternal grandfather was six foot four. He had an uncle, on his mother's side, who was six foot six. He grew out of his clothes faster than his parents could buy him new ones. He grew to be six foot six by the time he had turned thirteen. He grew to the point that he couldn't play with other children: He was too self-conscious, and they were too . . . what? Repelled? Frightened? Impatient and immature? He didn't go to the movies because the ticket agents couldn't gauge how old he really was. "It was an embarrassing, difficult time, and I didn't like it," Kurland once said. "I was a big, gangly kid, and height at that time was not looked upon in the same way as it is today. I had to carry my birth certificate to the show because the show was ten cents for a kid under twelve and fifteen or twenty cents for a guy over twelve. I'd have to show them my birth certificate."

He spent much of his childhood by himself, fishing in the Mississippi, hunting in the woods near the river's banks, or shooting his dilapidated basketball through a tire rim he had nailed to a telephone pole. The pole was spiked atop a steep hill. If Kurland missed a shot, he'd have to run down the hill to retrieve the ball, then trudge back up again, as if he were a six-foot-seven Sisyphus.

At Jennings High School, Kurland walked into the office of Walter Rulon, the school's boys' basketball coach, and told him that he wanted to play for him. *He might have possibilities*, Rulon thought, but it took just a few workouts for the coach to see that Kurland, already so tall and still growing, wasn't well coordinated. "He would fall almost constantly," Rulon once said, and that clumsiness sapped what little confidence Kurland had. To counteract Kurland's low self-esteem, Rulon gave him pep talks, encouraging him to stop stooping over, to throw his shoulders back and stand up straight, and to use his height as a means to an end. He had been given a gift, not a handicap, and through basketball, he could make the most of that gift.

Through Kurland's freshman year, Rulon never played him more than five or six minutes a game. His true progress came during and after practice; Kurland remained in the gym for hours after his teammates had left, working on his shooting, dribbling, and hand-eye coordination, particularly when it came to the timing and dexterity necessary to rebound, block shots, and defend the rim. By his junior year, he could exploit his physical advantage over opposing centers and forwards and, while hardly graceful yet, was coordinated enough that he could join Jennings's track team as a high jumper. Like any seventeen-year-old, Kurland wanted to be different and, at the same time, to fit in. When he at last understood that his height would never allow him to conform, that his social development had been affected by his size, he channeled the time and energy that he would have spent making friends and forming relationships into sports. Sports made it OK to be different. Sports made it OK to stand apart from, and above, everyone else.

"It was a way out," he said, "a way out of being seven feet tall. I wanted to prove I was average."

He proved better than average. On a rainy afternoon when he was a senior, wearing baseball cleats to get a decent foothold on a muddy track, Kurland cleared five feet, ten and a half inches to set the state high jump record. His daughter Barbara Rintala explained that it was important to Kurland to note that he wore special shoes—and that his competitors didn't—that day. "He could just fall over the bar, but he had to have a 'reason' he succeeded," she told me. "That was his humility." As for his basketball career at Jennings, he led the team to a 42–6 record over his final two seasons, and in one game, he scored 33 points . . . in little more than a half. For college, he preferred to stay local; his top choice was the University of Missouri. But Don Faurot, Mizzou's athletic director, didn't think Kurland could play college ball because he was too tall—and told him so. "I wanted to go to my state university," Kurland once said, "but all he would offer me was a job waiting tables for twenty-five cents an hour, and I had to pay for my tuition, room, and board."

There was one hope for him: Rulon had attended Maryville State Teachers College, and one of his classmates and friends there was Henry Iba, who by 1935 had become the athletic director and men's basketball coach at Oklahoma A&M and who had elevated the Aggies among the premier teams in the country. Rulon wrote and mailed a note to Iba, who, according to one account, "blinked slowly" as he read a passage of the letter "in which Rulon said he had a seven-footer who might turn out to be a pretty fair country player." Iba offered Kurland a scholarship; he was the only coach to do so. Oklahoma A&M had a strong engineering program, which interested Kurland, and through the basketball scholarship, the university would cover the cost of his tuition, room, board, and books, plus pay him ten dollars a week to sweep the gym and lock up its doors and windows once the floor sparkled. Iba made no promises about playing time—or even about Kurland's place on the roster. He liked Kurland's attitude, enthusiasm, and effort, but he had never coached a player as tall as Kurland, who stood six feet, ten and a half inches in bare feet when he entered college. *I don't know if you'll be a good basketball player or not,* Iba told him, *but I'll tell you what I'll do: if you come here, go to class, and stay eligible, I'll see you get a college education.* Kurland accepted the offer. In the late summer of 1942, he took a bus to Stillwater, toting all his belongings in one small tin suitcase.

"For my father," Rocky Kurland told me, "the education was a big deal, not the basketball. Basketball was a way for him to see the world."

His dark, pomaded hair combed straight back in a severe slick, his demeanor so stoic that it seemed his face might split in half if he smiled, Henry Iba was the embodiment, in appearance and demeanor, of a sports authority figure in that era. Players did not question his coaching philosophy or methods of discipline, and they did not become close, intimate friends with him while they were undergraduates. He was fond of telling them: *You can call me "Coach," or you can call me "Mr. Iba." But you don't know me well enough to call me "Henry." I'll be your friend after you finish school.* "But," Kurland once said, "you had great confidence that if you ever had a problem that required some counsel and guidance, you could go to him." Kurland needed that counsel and guidance. He had not yet overcome the insecurities that had plagued him throughout high school. Iba looked and acted in the manner a coach was supposed to look and act, but Kurland looked and acted like few basketball players, if any, before him—and certainly none at Oklahoma A&M. Still just 212 pounds as a sophomore, with a 33-inch waist and a 42-inch inseam, he had a long, drawn face with a rectangular jaw and a shock of red hair that he parted from left to right, a physical trait that carried its own set of socially constructed stereotypes: he had to be strange, or hot-tempered, or wimpy, or unable to stay outside too long on a sunny day, or someone who considered himself intellectually superior to his peers—or all of the aforementioned. (A 1997 study by researchers at Syracuse University and Ithaca College found that "redheads typically receive negative treatment as children, and, as a consequence, experience lowered self-esteem, feelings of differentness, and a sense of being the center of attention." This was a perfect description of Kurland's adolescence and young adulthood.)

His embarrassment over his size had not abated, and it only intensified after, for publicity reasons, Otis White, Oklahoma A&M's sports-information director, added an inch and a half to Kurland's height on the Aggies' roster, making him officially (and inaccurately) seven feet tall. Later in his life, Kurland could and would joke about the embellishment. "I'm like steel," he once said. "You elongate with heat." Not at the time, though. "If I was six-eleven and three quarters," he said early in his college career, "it wouldn't matter so much. But because I'm seven feet, everybody looks at me as though I were a freak." He struggled to lounge comfortably on the large davenport in Iba's office. Even with his head propped up with pillows on one side, his legs dangled over the other, his calves resting atop an armrest. The Aggies would travel by train, and Kurland was too long to sleep in one of the berths. So Iba had him sleep on a bench in the men's lavatory. Kurland could stretch out there, but every time the train hugged a curve, he fell to the floor. Teammates and opponents alike regarded him as an exotic creature who belonged behind glass.

"They ridiculed him a lot," Iba said. "It took a strong man to stand up to it."

Kurland intensified his routine of putting himself through post-practice drills, and Iba was only too happy to encourage him. One afternoon, Iba had him try six hundred left-handed hook shots. The first hundred touched neither the rim nor the backboard. He missed the next hundred. "After that," Iba said, "he started to connect." The primitive nature of his training regimen, of any Division I basketball player's training regimen in the early to mid-1940s, extended beyond the lines of the court. Oklahoma A&M's athletic department had no strength-and-conditioning coach, of course. No athletic departments did then, and Kurland's list of equipment was brief: sneakers, shirt, shorts, a jockstrap, tape, and a jar of vitamin pills. To strengthen Kurland's legs and increase his lateral mobility—the Aggies played mostly man-to-man defense, and Kurland would have to guard shorter, quicker players—Iba handed him eight feet worth of rope and made him jump it. To strengthen Kurland's upper body . . . never mind. Weight lifting? Push-ups? Forget it. No one gave such exercises any thought.

It is difficult to comprehend now how much of an anomaly Kurland was. The ten players who had started in the 1940 national championship game—between Kansas, coached by Phog Allen, and Indiana—averaged just more than six feet tall, and it would take decades before the sport, at the collegiate and professional levels, would become so closely associated with men who towered over the rest of the population. The average NBA player's height, for instance, didn't reach six foot six until 1975. But Kurland wasn't the only college player in the country who stood out for his size, and he wasn't, at first, even the best or most productive. George Mikan entered DePaul University at the same time Kurland began at Oklahoma A&M, and Mikan, at six foot ten, contributed significantly to coach Ray Meyer's team right away, scoring 11.3 points a game as a freshman as the Blue Demons reached the regional finals of the NCAA Tournament. Yes, basketball was changing, but the question of whether it was evolving or devolving depended on whom you asked.

"Fans held conflicting views of the big man," Michael Schumacher wrote in his biography of Mikan, *Mr. Basketball*. "They hated what they perceived to be his unfair advantage over shorter players—unless, of course, the big man was on their team—but they were nevertheless excited by the domination."

One man, perhaps the most powerful man in college basketball, wasn't so conflicted. After Kansas edged Fordham by a point at Madison Square Garden one night in December 1942, Allen combined a rant about the state of the sport with a radical proposal to change it forever. Kansas and Oklahoma A&M hadn't yet faced each other that season and wouldn't for another two weeks. Kurland hadn't yet begun to reach his potential as a player, and Allen never mentioned him by name. But Kurland's presence was enough to set him off, and Jack Cuddy, a reporter for the Associated Press, was there at the Garden to preserve Allen's tirade for posterity.

Someone, Allen said, needed to protect basketball's integrity from the "freaks and glandular goons," like Kurland, who threatened to take over the game. To that end, Allen said, the rims should be raised from ten feet to twelve feet, "and those skyscraper players will be swept off the court because they'll be expected to play the game—instead of merely standing beneath the baskets as tall towers of defense." These "circus giants" and "glandular giants" would be forced to play a more refined style of basketball, and Allen didn't believe they could, and besides, the sport's inventor had offered no decree that it couldn't evolve. "When Dr. Naismith hung his peach basket ten feet from the floor a half century ago," Allen said, "he didn't mean that this height would prevail down through the ages."

Unsurprisingly, Allen's language stung Kurland, and Kurland never forgot it. One day in March 1991, he and Glenn Miller, a sportswriter for the Fort Myers News-Press, sat in lounge chairs on the back patio of Kurland's Sanibel Island home—Kurland's boat dangling above the Gulf of Mexico from a davits system, waterbirds chirping and singing, a nearby canal still and quiet. Miller brought up Allen. Kurland, sixty-six years old then, made it clear that those insults still cut him. "When I was a kid . . . and I was, as Phog called me, a 'glandular goon,' how tall was he at thirteen or fourteen? I really didn't like being different. I was really a screwed-up kid, but that game was the way I was going to excel, the same way some people drive sports cars or have fancy clothes or big houses. The game of basketball was the way I was going to satisfy the drive for my own personal ego and pride. Probably for that reason, I worked very hard.

"There was a time when I didn't like to be as tall as I am."

There's no indication that Allen paid any mind to that possibility—that Kurland would be so uncomfortable in his own skin that he'd carry the pain of that ridicule with him for the rest of his life. Allen had begun his drumbeat about raising the rim years earlier—remember his condemnation of the dunk in *Better Basketball*—and kept it up thereafter. He wasn't content to neutralize the effectiveness of Kurland and players similar to him. He wanted the game kept where he believed it belonged: below the rim. He wanted goaltending and its corollary, dunking, eliminated from basketball entirely. That way, Cuddy wrote in his dispatch, "the 'giants' would become useless, and the hoop sport would revert to the fast, strategic game that Dr. Naismith had in mind." Early in his tenure at Kansas, Allen wrote an essay for the magazine *Country Gentleman*. Its title: "Dunking Isn't Basketball."

No one could have disputed that, at his core, Allen was correct in one aspect of his foresight: the effect that Kurland, Mikan, and players like them were having and would have on basketball was too profound to ignore. Because defensive goaltending was still permissible during Kurland's first two seasons at Oklahoma A&M, Iba sometimes had him root himself under the basket and swat away any shot that came anywhere near the rim. After Kurland blocked 17 shots in the Aggies' 59–40 upset of Oklahoma on January 12, 1944, Allen taunted Sooners coach Bruce Drake: "I bet [he] would have welcomed twelve-foot baskets Wednesday night. Bob Kurland caused the Sooner hot shots . . . to change shooting tactics, and in trying to arch shots over the Cowboy giant, they overshot the goal. With twelve-foot baskets, Kurland would have been unable to knock the ball away from the goal. This ridiculous situation will continue on courts until baskets have been raised out of reach of these defensive skyscrapers." Drake was not only the head coach of the Aggies' primary rival but a member of the NCAA coaches' rules committee. If Allen intended his gibes to spur Drake and the committee into action, his strategy worked. Sure enough, the NCAA banned goaltending for good in 1944.

While Allen had shifted the sport a bit in his preferred direction, he comes off in the light of modernity as obsessive, as a control freak who demanded that the game be played a certain way, a way that he could manipulate. Kurland's and Mikan's height and the nimbleness they could and would develop threatened to strip him of that power, and those were just the first rumbles of the ground shifting under Allen's feet. In 1952, he still didn't have a player on Kansas's roster taller than six foot ten. He couldn't conceive that basketball might retain the tactics and fluidity that he so treasured even while its practitioners grew taller and taller, and in light of his recruitment of one player—a native of West Philadelphia, a big kid from a big family—less than a decade later, Allen's position on the issue would prove to be laughable in its irony.

Iba spun the ban as a net positive for Kurland, positing that Kurland wouldn't have to jump as much during games and, as a result, wouldn't tire out as quickly. "Assuming he will improve each year as he has the two seasons he's been with me so far," Iba said in January 1944, "I don't see how he can miss becoming basketball's greatest center." Oklahoma A&M finished 27–6 in Kurland's sophomore year, and as he and Mikan established themselves as the nation's two best and best-known players, the perception that big men didn't belong in basketball morphed into the belief that big men were essential to basketball. Stanley Frank, who covered World War II for the *New York Post*, profiled Kurland for *Collier's* magazine, heralding him as a revolutionary force. "As informed clients know too well," Frank wrote, "the emphasis on height in basketball has exposed the public to freaks, misrepresented as athletes, who have nothing to recommend them but size. Not so with Kurland." Frank even went so far as to condemn the goaltending ban as gigantasophobic. "There are ranker injustices abroad in the world," he wrote, an assertion that, based on his experiences as a foreign correspondent, he knew to be true, "but the rule was a flagrant piece of discrimination aimed at a kid who happened to grow up good and large—but good. By the same reasoning, Joe Louis could be restrained from striking a muscular meatball with his right fist because he hits too hard with it."

The money quote in the piece, the truest indication of how far Kurland had come, was from St. John's coach Joe Lapchick. "The kid is great on sheer ability," said Lapchick, whose coaching careers at St. John's and with the New York Knicks earned him entry into the Naismith Memorial Hall of Fame in 1966. "What amazes me is the way he has improved. I was out of town with my team when he first played in 1942. When I asked about Kurland, everyone laughed and said he was just an overgrown clown. I saw him the next year, and I saw a boy who knew the game and could run and shoot and handle himself. He has another year to go, and he'll still be better. But right now, I've got to rank him with all the big men who have played."

Long before Purdue's Zach Edey transformed himself from a seven-foot-four Tin Man into college basketball's most dominant player, leading the Boilermakers to the 2024 Final Four, Kurland established himself as the prototype for the clunky, robotic center who sharpens his skills and streamlines his movements. Once so clumsy that he could barely run up and down the court without tripping over his own feet, Kurland at times brought the ball up for Oklahoma A&M, dropping it to a guard just inside the halfcourt stripe. He'd then slide into the high post to catch a return pass, put the ball on the floor again, and score on a sweeping hook or scoop shot. When the Aggies ran a dribble-handoff offense at the top of the key, Kurland didn't have to be content with standing several feet away, waiting to grab a rebound; he could be part of the swirl, coming off a screen to loft a one-handed runner from ten to fifteen feet out. In a tight game against NYU on December 13, 1944, he chased down a loose ball from halfway across the court, swan-dived to grab it, and tossed it over his shoulder to a teammate, who scored and was fouled—the three-point play the difference in Oklahoma A&M's 44–41 victory. Kurland had 14 points himself, but what impressed John Cody—the head coach of Temple University, the Aggies' next opponent—was his fluidity and coordination. He had become everything that Phog Allen had said big men weren't. The dunk was no longer Kurland's sole way to score and never would be again; it made him the precursor to Hakeem Olajuwon and Kobe Bryant, players for whom dunking was merely the finishing touch on a lovely and unpredictable pattern of shot fakes and impeccable footwork. "He has learned to use his left hand," Cody said. "The goaltending rule has not handicapped him at all."

Two days after that NYU game, the Aggies were in Philadelphia on Friday, December 15, practicing at Weightman Hall on the campus of the University of Pennsylvania. They were to face Temple—a matchup of unbeaten teams—the next night in the second game of a Saturday doubleheader. The *Philadelphia Inquirer* hyped the game in its Saturday morning edition, touting the chance for city basketball fans to see Kurland, "the Nation's [sic] tallest player," and the contest presented him with an opportunity for some redemption. Oklahoma A&M had beaten the Owls the previous season, but Kurland, still just a sophomore then, still haunted by outsiders' derision and his internal doubts, had fouled out, tears flooding his face as he left the court and headed to the bench.

That Kurland—that younger, less poised Kurland—might have been flustered by a quirky set of circumstances that forced the Aggies to adjust their itinerary. They had been originally scheduled to work out not at Weightman but at Convention Hall, where they would play Temple, all the better to get accustomed to an unfamiliar arena. But on Thursday, December 14, the Orquesta Típica of Mexico—Mexico City's official orchestra—had held a concert at the hall, and the maintenance staff hadn't laid the basketball court back down in time for the Oklahoma A&M practice. Convention Hall would be ready to go for Saturday, though, and the musicians remained in town to attend the doubleheader.

It happened so quickly that one would have understood if the Convention Hall crowd had barely taken notice. Hell, Kurland himself didn't think much of it. Besides, it simply just wasn't done in those days. "Not in a game," Mikan once said. Perhaps once in a great while a spectator might be fortunate enough to be on hand when a center might cast humility aside for a moment during pregame warm-ups. But not in a game. Not until Kurland wrapped his hands around a loose ball while he was standing under the basket.

"I got it up and stuffed it in," he once said. "That started it, I guess. . . . It wasn't planned, just a spontaneous play in Philadelphia. . . . I wasn't trying to jump over an automobile. That wasn't my bag."

Was this truly the first dunk in college basketball history? Officially, no, because it didn't count. Iba gave an interview in 1991, at age eighty-seven, in which he asserted that Kurland was the first college player to dunk in a game, but he added an important caveat: "The referee disallowed it." Per the rules at the time, Kurland technically had interfered with the ball while it was in the cylinder, and because rims at that time were so fragile—the breakaway rim hadn't been invented yet—such interference couldn't be permitted. "If you held the rim," Kurland once said, "you had to get a janitor with a ladder to straighten it." Yet if you dump "first college dunk" into Google, Kurland is the first name that pops up, thanks to a 2021 article on NCAA.com— headline: "The Story Behind the First Known Dunk in College Basketball History"—which was based largely on a 2012 article in the *Orlando Sentinel*, which called Kurland "the granddaddy of the dunk" and was based on an interview with Kurland in which he talked about the Temple dunk, which Iba said was the first known dunk in college basketball history. And 'round and 'round we go.

And that endless loop of circular history is fine. There's nothing wrong with it. To address another assertion, the one Rocky Kurland made about his father, the distinction of being the first person to dunk in college basketball, whether it was rightfully his or not, probably didn't matter at all to Bob Kurland. (He missed 18 of his 27 shots from the field in the game, by the way, and Oklahoma A&M lost, 46–44.) What did matter to him was this: that dunk was a necessary validation of his journey, of the confidence that he developed over time, the confidence that basketball gave him. Dunking became a regular part of his repertoire—in a 62–37 victory over Utah in the quarterfinal round of the 1945 NCAA Tournament, Kurland made 14 shots from the field, scoring repeatedly by using what one writer called "a duffer," a common term at the time for a dunk, "in which he leaped into the air and pushed the ball downward through the netting with a terrific swish." Dunking moved him one step away from being a freak, unsure of himself, sensing the hot stare of every person who shared a room with him. Dunking told him, reassured him, that he was supposed to be that tall, that there was a reason for the condition that he considered, for so long, a deformity. Later in that Temple game, the Owls' David Fox was whistled for a foul and complained about the call, and Kurland, towering over him, towering over everyone else in Convention Hall, patted him on the head and said, "Take it easy, son." The people in the stands laughed. With Kurland. Not at him.

The 2022–23 Oklahoma State men's basketball media guide comprises 246 pages. Bob Kurland's name appears in it eighty-four times, but there is no mention of his dunk against Temple. Everything he did after that dunk overshadowed that dunk, even if everything he did after that dunk was, directly or indirectly, because of that dunk.

The 1945 NCAA Tournament was his coming-out party, and that duffer-laden win over Utah was just the introduction to the introduction. He scored more than 21 points a game in the tournament, and after the Aggies routed Arkansas in the semifinals, association officials handed him the Western Regional Final trophy, only to have Kurland hand it back so he could rush to the locker room to celebrate with his teammates. The Aggies traveled by train over two days from Kansas City (where they had beaten Arkansas) through Chicago to New York, where their opponent in the championship game would be NYU. There, Kurland took in the unique atmosphere at Madison Square Garden: the seats practically on top of the floor, the men puffing on Pall Malls and Rigolettos, that thick smoke hovering over the court like a nimbostratus and obscuring the view of the ceiling. Dolph Schayes, eventually a Naismith Hall of Famer, a freshman for NYU then, noticed that, during time-outs, the A&M players "would lie on the floor in a circle around the coach spaced the proper number of degrees. And the big guy with red, red hair—he seemed to be bigger than anybody, so much more than seven feet." That night, he was bigger than anybody: Oklahoma A&M 49, NYU 45, Kurland 22. Two nights later, again at the Garden, he was bigger than Mikan. Oklahoma A&M and DePaul—the winner of the National Invitational Tournament (NIT)—met for the "mythical national championship" in a charity game to raise money (more than $50,000, as it turned out) for the American Red Cross. Kurland had 14 points. Mikan had nine, fouling out in the first half. The Aggies won, 52–44, giving their home state a glimmer of happy light as the depressive daily casualty reports from World War II rolled in, as the number of Oklahomans killed in battle surpassed thirteen thousand by the end of March 1945.

While Kurland's height made him ineligible to serve in the armed forces, several other Aggies already had completed tours in the war. "We had guys who had been in the infantry," he said. "These weren't little boys playing. They were playing a boys' game for the joy of playing. These guys didn't rattle." No one on the 1945–46 Aggies did. They went 31–2, including a 12–0 record in the Missouri Valley Conference, and edged North Carolina, 43–40, to win their second consecutive national title. Kurland, who scored 19.5 points per game that season, put up 23 in that championship game, dunking twice. And his 58-point performance in February 1946, on an array of layups and tap-ins in an 86–33 victory over St. Louis University, so humiliated the six-foot-eight freshman who guarded him that night—future Hall of Famer Ed Macauley—that Macauley carried a newspaper clipping of the game with him throughout his ten-year career in the NBA. "Every time I thought I needed to be humble," he said, "I would look at that box score and remember I was the guy who held Bob Kurland to 58 points."

Had sports-talk radio been the institution in the mid-1940s that it would become in the 1980s, the phone lines would have been lit up from coast to coast over a single question: Mikan or Kurland? Who was the better player? Who will be the better pro? The two of them had gone head-to-head five times, and DePaul had won three of those games. Mikan had slightly better statistics and an NIT championship. Kurland had two NCAA championships and had come further in his development as a player—maybe there was more talent within him that was as yet untapped. *Bernie from the Bronx . . . you're on. . . . Who ya got? What's your take?*

Different time. Different landscape. Different priorities. In the mid-1940s, professional basketball teams traveled by buses and touring cars and paid their players in cash out of paper bags. There were no television contracts. There was little stability or reliability. Kurland said that he and Mikan were offered between $15,000 and $18,000 a year to play pro ball, a gargantuan sum that Kurland, cautious by nature, turned down. "I asked him about that one time," Rocky Kurland told me. "My dad was like, 'Rock, I didn't want to take the money. I didn't think the NBA was going to last, especially if they started paying people like me that much money.'"

In 1946, Mikan signed with the Chicago American Gears of the National Basketball League, embarking on a career that marked him forever as a trailblazer in the sport. Like Joe Fortenberry before him, Kurland took a job with Phillips 66, then worked in various roles for the company for more than forty years. He was president of a fertilizer subsidiary, marketed the company's first self-serve gas stations, was a general sales manager and the president of its plastics division. Like Joe Fortenberry before him, Kurland played for Phillips's AAU team, winning three national championships. Like Joe Fortenberry before him, Kurland was an Olympian who could dunk and had dunked but didn't dunk during the Games. During the '48 Olympics in London, the United States beat Czechoslovakia, 53–28, in round-robin play. Kurland had just six points, but by then, his dunking was renowned enough that the Associated Press noted: "The Americans' mastery was so complete that the Phillips Oilers' seven-foot Bob Kurland, who can dunk the ball in the basket with the mildest sort of leap, never once indulged in this advantage." He retired from basketball in 1952, at twenty-seven, and though he was inducted into the Naismith Hall of

Fame in 1961 and served as its president in the early 1990s, he never achieved the same measure of public recognition that Mikan did.

"I've never regretted it," he said.

His life in the sport framed his life outside it and his views about it. He never shed his relative discomfort with his height, not fully, not before his death in 2013 at age eighty-eight, but whenever he'd be among his peers in Springfield for the annual Hall of Fame induction ceremony, he'd relax, be lighter on his feet. Basketball, he would tell his wife, Barbara, and their four children, was a means to a good life, not an end unto itself. He assumed people were honest and hardworking and friendly unless and until they proved otherwise. "Because of his size, he was probably one of the least race-conscious people," his daughter Barbara told me. "I think he knew that because he was different—maybe not different socially, but different physically. He always had something that stood out. Imagine going someplace and knowing that every time you walk in that room, you get noticed. Whether you want to or not, you can't fade away. That's an interesting way to go through life."

In December 1982, ahead of the first game between the dominant college centers of that time, Georgetown's Patrick Ewing and Virginia's Ralph Sampson, Kurland compared that matchup to his and Mikan's: "It was like this Sampson-Ewing game that way, with a really big buildup." Kurland saw their excellence for what it was: the natural next step, once the powers that be had cast aside their fears about letting big men dunk, in basketball's progression and improvement. At a time when opposing fans held up signs and bedsheets that said, EWING IS AN APE and EWING KANT READ DIS and chucked bananas on the court, Kurland told the *Washington Post* that he saw Ewing as "a player completely immersed with the idea he's going to win a game. He's so physically strong. He's overwhelming. And yet I see a gentleness in him that tells me he enjoys playing. I think, against Sampson, that Ewing will be so involved that he'll make something unexpected happen. He's explosive, whereas Sampson seems to work from a game plan. They're both phenomenal. . . .

"If you take pride in anything, it's not the physical. It's not the mechanics of learning how to play. It's in having the guts to stay in there and prove that you could play when Phog Allen called you a 'glandular goon.' Until George and I came along, the whole psychology of it was that big boys couldn't do much. It hadn't been proven otherwise until then. Now you see those two play today—Sampson and Ewing—and they just have phenomenal ability. George and I had pretty good mechanics, but these guys have such foot speed and such jumping. Hell, it's a different world now."

It was. It would be. Bob Kurland had done so much to make it so. The dunk had done, and would do, so much to make it so. No one could argue with that.

7

1955

Two of the sport's immortals, in the year that each of them sailed out from under any remaining shade of obscurity. Basketball became fully airborne because of them.

In a Southwest Philadelphia row house, Carl Lacy listened closely to the staticky fizz of sounds flickering from the small radio plugged into his bedroom wall, his disbelief growing as most everything he once knew to be true about the sport he adored was rendered obsolete. It was March 19, 1955, and at Municipal Auditorium in Kansas City, Missouri, the racial, stylistic, and substantive axis on which basketball revolved was shifting. The La Salle Explorers—the defending NCAA champions, from Lacy's hometown—were losing to the San Francisco Dons. But Lacy was too young, just seventeen years old, to understand fully what was really going on in that game, how nothing would be the same again. Had Lacy been able to watch it, the action might have looked familiar and the outcome easier to reconcile. But watching was impossible for him. "If you had a TV back then," Lacy told me, "you were rich," and his family was not rich. All he knew was that La Salle's Tom Gola—the best player in the country, as far as Lacy and much of the rest of the country were concerned—was getting his ass kicked . . . and that someone Lacy had barely heard of before was doing the kicking. Someone named Bill Russell.

Just fifteen days earlier, in front of 8,500 people on a Friday night at the Palestra, Lacy had taken part in the Philadelphia Public League championship. A five-foot-eleven junior at West Philadelphia High, Lacy played guard for the varsity team, but because he could jump so high, he had often played forward or center throughout his years of organized hoops. In those instances, though, he never had occasion to dunk the ball—not because he couldn't, but because the manner in which basketball was coached and played didn't afford him the opportunity to dunk. If he was playing center and leaped to grab a rebound, he had to pass the ball immediately to a guard. If he was playing guard and bringing the ball up court, he had to pass the ball immediately to a center or forward near the basket. "You had to slow the game down," Lacy told me. Of course, the star player on Overbrook High School, the team that had beaten Lacy and West Philly, 78–60, to win the Public League title, had no such restrictions. Even as a teenager, Wilt Chamberlain was *sui generis*. He dunked whenever, however, on whomever he wished.

Despite the one-sided outcome, West Philly had done well to limit Chamberlain, who averaged more than 47 points that season, to just 33. "We double-teamed him," Lacy told me. "It didn't work." That victory would be the penultimate game of Chamberlain's high school career; six days later, he and Overbrook routed West Catholic, 83–42, for the city championship. None of those three schools—Overbrook, West Philly, West Catholic—was located more than three miles from the other. They were aligned in a triangle that was, in the mid-1950s, the nexus of basketball power in the city.

Lacy was eighty-five years old on the September 2023 day that I visited him at his home to talk about all of this. His memories of those times, of those games and athletes, were as fresh and meant as much to him that morning as they ever had. So much had changed, and so little. He was still trim, with a throaty voice and a quick, high laugh. He still lived in a row house in West Philadelphia. Covering a wall in a nook of his living room were photos and newspaper clippings from his playing days in high school. His favorite of those photos had captured a mysterious moment in a high school game: Lacy and Chamberlain, both in the air at the same time, at the same height, at the rim. Was Chamberlain blocking Lacy's shot? Was Lacy somehow blocking Chamberlain's? He relished the ambiguity of it. It made for a fun conversation piece, a chance to kid around. *You're darn right I blocked Wilt. (Wink, wink . . .)* Why spoil it with certainty? "People like to talk to him because he remembers everything," his wife, Rosalie, told me. Everything, including the traits that, in his mind, made Wilt Chamberlain the greatest basketball player of all.

"He was bigger and stronger than anybody," Lacy said. "When his teammates went down, he could just pick them up like this." Sitting on his couch, Lacy reached down to the floor, his index finger and thumb outstretched, as if he were picking up a used tissue. "That's how strong he was. He was fast. He could jump, not just because he was seven feet. He could *jump*. I feel that even today, he would dominate because he was so much faster and stronger than anybody."

As wondrous as Chamberlain was, however, and as renowned as he was nationwide—surely the most famous high school athlete in the United States—Lacy admired most his accessibility and friendliness. His quirky and silly-sounding nickname alone, "Dippy," a shortened version of "Big Dipper," implied that he possessed those qualities. (Later, once he had earned his riches in pro basketball, he had the more formal and elegant version of the term, Ursa Major, put on his boat and house. "It has a special ring to it," he once wrote, "a certain beauty and power and grace and majesty.") During and after his time at Overbrook, Chamberlain would show up at Haddington Recreation Center, where guys from neighborhoods in and around West Philadelphia, even from outside the city limits, would wait for the chance to play against him. They'd wait and wait as one team after another lost to Chamberlain's, and some stayed all day without ever taking the court because the line of teams ahead of them was so long.

"They'd have to leave, and he would apologize," Lacy, who coached at the rec center for years, said. "He knew they wanted to play against him. 'Come back next week. I'll make it a point to play against you.' He was a nice guy. Wilt was a *nice guy*. He recognized everybody. No matter who was there, he would take time. He was still just a neighborhood guy to everybody. He was still Dippy."

Tom Gola was not as much a man of the people. At La Salle High School, he had set the Philadelphia scholastic career scoring record—which Chamberlain subsequently broke—and at La Salle College, he had led the Explorers to the 1952 NIT Championship as a freshman and to the 1954 national championship as a junior. Six foot six and positionless, the son of a Philly cop, Gola was, according to one basketball historian, "Magic Johnson without the flair." So widespread was his fame that he had appeared on *The Ed Sullivan Show*, and he carried himself with a regal comportment, an air that commanded respect and deference from every teammate and competitor, Black or white, who encountered him.

Except that guy on the radio, that guy from the West Coast playing for San Francisco, that guy Lacy knew nothing about, wasn't showing Gola any respect, and as the world would come to understand soon enough, Bill Russell would be damned if he'd defer to anyone, on or off a basketball court. The ass-kicking went on and on: USF 77, La Salle 63. *Man,* Lacy thought, *as good as Tom Gola is, somebody's better than him?* From his competing against Chamberlain to his discovery and newfound admiration for Russell, Carl Lacy connected the two figures who in that year, 1955, would introduce the dunk to a wider and vaster audience than it had ever known, and how many other people could say the same? How many other teenagers and men listening to that game were thinking the same things he was? How many of them appreciated that, even if they couldn't see what was happening in Kansas City that night, they were bearing witness to the rarest kind of earthquake, an impossible kind of earthquake, the kind that disrupts and destroys what has been established for so long, yes, but also leaves the landscape better and more beautiful and on a firmer foundation than it had ever been before?

Reams of words have been written in books, in magazine profiles, and in newspaper articles about Bill Russell and Wilt Chamberlain, about

Russell's eleven championships with the Celtics and his activism, about Chamberlain's 100-point game and his lamentations about the lack of love given to Goliath, about Russell's wives and Chamberlain's women (twenty thousand by his own estimate, give or take), about their basketball careers, their styles of play, their personalities and friendships and championships, their influence on basketball and their influence apart from basketball, their similarities and differences, their rivalry. John Taylor, who wrote one of the best of those books, his chronicle of Russell's career with the Boston Celtics and Chamberlain's with the Warriors and 76ers and Lakers, titled it exactly that: *The Rivalry*. Here, though, it's helpful to focus on one significant year, 1955, the year in which Russell and Chamberlain, each still in the nascent stage of his manhood, entered the nation's collective consciousness. The former turned twenty-one. The latter turned eighteen. They had not yet met. But already they were on a collision course, Russell the ultimate winner versus Chamberlain the singular force, and the timing of each one's emergence—within the context of the tumult around them, upheaval that they both symbolized and inspired—was hardly coincidental.

The culmination of Chamberlain's high school career and the first national acknowledgment of Russell's greatness took place at the calendar midpoint between two of the most consequential events of the Civil Rights Movement: the Supreme Court's decision in *Brown v. Board of Education* on May 17, 1954, and Rosa Parks's refusal to sit in the "colored section" of an Alabama bus on December 1, 1955. Ten months after *Brown*, nine months before the Montgomery boycott, Russell and Chamberlain were letting America know what was going on and what was coming. More than 60 percent of Black Americans in the 1950s lived in urban areas, and from those tenements and terraces, from those concrete courts and unforgiving double rims and chain-mesh nets, bubbled up the creativity and arrogance and elegance and showmanship, the whole fierce ethos of playground basketball, that transformed the sport at the same time that Thurgood Marshall, Parks, Martin Luther King Jr., and a wave of righteous souls like them were transforming America. When Russell joined the Celtics in 1956, he was the lone Black player on their roster and one of just fifteen in the entire NBA. Within ten years, nearly half the league's players were Black, and he and Chamberlain were simply older, savvier, more accomplished versions of the people and players they had been back in '55, when they raised basketball to an altitude it has not fallen below since. It was who they were and how they played, high above everyone else.

Bill Russell's paternal grandfather, Jake, was a sharecropper who once stood on his porch and fired a shotgun into the dead-ass darkness of the Louisiana night to chase away a group of Ku Klux Klan members who were creeping toward his house. Bill Russell's father, Charlie, worked in a paper bag factory and was a champion logroller and could scoop up Bill under one arm and Bill's older brother, Charlie, under the other and carry them like stacks of two-by-fours, and he owned a nine-hundred-pound mule named Kate—he used Kate to plow his garden—and he had hands like giant leather shovels and built his own trucking business. Bill Russell's mother, Katie, got him a library card one day—a seminal moment in Bill's life—and insisted that he go to college, and she fought him, with her fists, five times in the name of teaching him how to be a man, and she died of kidney failure when she was thirty-two and he was twelve, at which time Charlie abandoned the trucking business, which was profitable, to raise his two sons. Know that about Bill Russell, know all that about Bill Russell's childhood, and you'll be a long way toward understanding Bill Russell, as an athlete and as a man.

Not long before Katie died, the Russell family had moved from Louisiana to Oakland. There, at McClymonds High School, Bill met George Powles, the school's basketball coach, who would prove to have as positive and profound an influence on him as any in his early life. Powles coaxed Russell to try out for the team, kept him on the roster as the last man on the junior-varsity bench despite Russell's inexperience and undeveloped skills, and encouraged other players on the team to foul, bump, and antagonize him in any way they could in the name of stirring Russell to be more aggressive. To call Russell a project then was to be kind. "He couldn't even put the ball in the basket when he dunked," the Hall of Fame baseball player Frank Robinson, who played basketball at McClymonds, once said. It took Russell until his senior year to become the starting center for McClymonds's varsity squad, but he soaked up the advice that Powles, who was white, gave to his players, most of whom were Black. He insisted that they remain stoic and gentlemanly on the court at all times, no matter how biased, unfair, or inappropriate the officiating or the conduct of their opponents might be. He told them that, if they complained about bad calls or if there was a fight of any kind, they would never be given the benefit of the doubt and would be assigned all the blame because "you are a Negro team." The best retaliation, he advised them, was to play harder than their opponents and embarrass them by beating them. "For the first time," Russell once said, "I came in contact with a white person who brought things down front, who talked to us realistically."

No college recruiters showed any interest in Russell until his final high school game. On a tip from a player on his team who happened to play against Russell—and have Russell block several of his shots—in a pickup game, Phil Woolpert, the head coach at the University of San Francisco, dispatched scout Hal DeJulio to McClymonds to determine if Russell was indeed an unearthed diamond. Russell's timing couldn't have been better; he played his best game at McClymonds, scoring a career-high 14 points, and wowed DeJulio.

"I saw Russell's head rise above the multitudes," DeJulio once said. "I couldn't believe it." He was confident that, once Woolpert saw Russell run and jump, "he'd see he had a man from Mars, something he'd never seen." Russell "had incredible timing, speed, and he was intelligent right from the start."

He was also still raw as hell. It's not how anyone is accustomed to thinking of Russell, not as a basketball player or in any other regard.

Proud? Yes. Angry? Yes. Disciplined? Absolutely. We're talking about a player who, whenever he blocked an opposing player's shot, tried to keep the ball in bounds or, even better, direct the ball toward a teammate. No one pictures Russell in need of training or refinement, but he did, in fact, need it. And he received it once he was selected to play for the California High School All-Stars, a barnstorming team of seniors that was funded by a consortium of businessmen in Contra Costa County and that traveled by Greyhound bus up and down the West Coast, the Pacific Northwest, and western Canada. As a "splitter," a senior whose school year began in January and ended the following January—and he was the only splitter on McClymonds's varsity— Russell was eligible for the All-Stars, unlike any of his teammates. "The man who ran the tour was trying to build up his program," he wrote in *Second Wind: The Memoirs of an Opinionated Man*, "and he badly wanted to have a player from McClymonds, which had had the best team in Northern California that year. . . . Getting to go on the tour was luck. What would happen along the way was magic."

The tour kicked off in February 1952. The roster had ten players, and though Russell wrote in *Second Wind* that the All-Stars had just two Black members, contemporaneous coverage of the team indicates there were as many as three: Russell; Eural McKelvey, a six-foot-five forward; and another forward named Fred Jacobs. McKelvey and Russell became and remained friends for the rest of their lives. They were so close that, after Russell's father retired at sixty-five, McKelvey, who played for the Harlem Globetrotters for seven years before becoming the foreman of a fruit-canning plant, hired Charlie to work part-time. "There are some people who are reclusive, but once they get to know somebody, they really open up to a select few people," McKelvey's son Greg told me. "I think that's the way Bill was with my dad."

At first, Russell did not stand out much on the All-Stars, his basketball skills still too rudimentary, his height and natural athleticism his most beneficial attributes to the team. He scored four points in one game, against a high school team from Blaine, Washington, and eight points in another. One observer did note that even based on that limited exposure to Russell's game, Russell "was a stuff-'em-in guy who pounded in his shots from above the basket's rim." But when the club routed the Vancouver All-Stars, 144–41, on Wednesday, February 6, 1952, Russell and McKelvey received the kind of condescending media treatment reserved for Black players. Each of them had 18 points in the game, but their scoring totals went unmentioned in Ron Gray's account in the *Vancouver Sun*. Instead, Gray wrote that the two of them "kept the crowd of 600 amused with their antics." What those antics were, one can make only an educated guess. S. L. "Brick" Swegle, the All-Stars' coach, had them play what Russell called "Negro basketball" at a time when most coaches told their players not to leave their feet unless they were going after a rebound. "He allowed us to do just about anything we wanted on the court," Russell wrote. "It was a holiday for our white players, who loved jump shots like everybody else but had been anchored to the floor by their coaches. We ran and jumped on that tour, and we wore out most teams."

McKelvey was his most influential teacher on the team. Russell began practicing a form of visualization that he relied on throughout his career. He'd watch one of his teammates, often McKelvey, do something on the court—snatch an offensive rebound, make a quick move to the basket, and drop in two points—then close his eyes and go over the sequence again and again in his mind. "I'd try," he wrote, "to create an instant replay on the inside of my eyelids." McKelvey supplemented Russell's mental reps by tutoring him in the science of rebounding and shot-blocking: reading angles, understanding the importance of positioning.

"They saw how athletic he was," Greg McKelvey told me. "If they could teach him to rebound, there would be more shots for everybody. My dad would tell him when a shot went off, if it missed, 'This is where it is likely to come off the rim. See if you can beat your man to that spot.' Russell was so athletic. He jumped really well. He had the long arms. They figured that if they could maximize his talents, it would be better for everybody."

The several weeks that Russell spent with the California All-Stars would be a turning point for his basketball career. It marked the moment that he began to develop into the defensive force that he would be at San Francisco and throughout his years with the Celtics. He could dunk, and he could stop opponents from dunking or scoring, and that combination of intelligence and athleticism set him apart. "My first dose of athletic confidence was coming to me when I was eighteen years old," he wrote in *Second Wind*. "On that tour I was in the first glow both of jumping and discovering new moves. They reinforced each other: I jumped higher because the moves in my mind were beginning to work on the court, and some of the moves worked better because I was jumping so high. I was learning to jump with a purpose." He had not been the high school prodigy that Chamberlain was, not even close, but he would catch up to him, in fame and as a prospective foil, soon enough.

To look at the house at 401 North Salford Street, in the Haddington neighborhood of West Philadelphia, is to wonder how it could have accommodated Wilt Chamberlain, let alone the rest of his family. It was one of forty-two homes that builder Thomas Marshall constructed on a plot of land he purchased in 1896, all of them featuring Pompeian brick fronts and porches. It was later owned, for a time, by the retailer who sold Mme. French's Whooping Cough Syrup. Wilt's parents, William and Olivia, bought it on September 23, 1939; in that home of less than 1,300 square feet, in that home with arched window openings and brick painted dark green, they and their eleven children (two of whom died of pneumonia early in their lives) resided for twenty-four years. William worked as a janitor and later as a porter at a Sears, Roebuck & Co. location in the northeast section of the city. Olivia was a homemaker. As far as the Chamberlains were concerned, they were better off than most of their relatives because they owned a house with a garage.

Olivia's father had been seven-foot-two, and she herself stood five foot nine, a half inch taller than her husband. So there was little doubt that at least one of the children would sprout to an unusual height. It turned out to be the seventh eldest of the eleven. "Right away, we knew Wilt was going to be tall," Selina Gross, one of his sisters, once said. "Even at five years old, he looked like he was twelve years old." Chamberlain's parents had relocated to Philadelphia during the Great Migration—William from Virginia, Olivia from North Carolina—and William would send Wilt to Virginia each summer to stay with relatives, tend animals on a farm, and work in cotton fields. "He'd come back from Virginia," Selina said, "and be another two inches or so taller." Those inches kept adding up until he was six foot five before he was out of elementary school. He, and everyone close to him, knew he would grow to be a giant.

What he didn't know was how to dunk, not really, not yet.

Recruiters for St. Thomas More, a Catholic high school in the Chamberlains' neighborhood, tempted him with offers of free subway tokens and lunches. He spurned their overtures. His siblings had gone to Overbrook High School, and so would he. Chamberlain wouldn't enter Overbrook until the fall of 1952, when he was a tenth grader. But Sam Cozen, the school's varsity basketball coach, had heard about him and his exploits at Shoemaker Junior High School and wanted to give him a head start in getting acclimated to his new surroundings and a more advanced level of basketball, especially since Cozen wouldn't be coaching him for long. Cozen had accepted the head coaching job at nearby Drexel University. For a season, he would coach both teams at the same time, then resign and hand over the Overbrook job to some-one else. That *someone else* turned out to be Cecil Mosenson, a West Philadelphia native, Overbrook alumnus, and former varsity basket-ball player who was just twenty-two when he returned to the school as an English teacher and Cozen's successor. First things first, though: Cozen invited Wilt to Overbrook one day to meet the players, most of whom would become Chamberlain's teammates the following year. Mel Brodsky, a sophomore guard on the team, told me that, when Chamberlain walked into the gym, "all of us sort of froze a little bit."

Gothic in its architecture, a hundred years old as of 2024, twin brick turrets flanking its main entrance, Overbrook has long been nicknamed "The Castle on the Hill." In the early 1950s, its basketball gymnasium was a closet inside that castle, so small that it seated just three hundred people, so small that whenever the Panthers had a game that promised to bring in a large crowd, they'd play it at a nearby junior high school. There were just ten to fifteen rows of bleachers along each of the lengthwise sides of the court, and its baselines and baskets were so close to the building's walls that a player driving to the hoop risked slamming face-first into one of them if he didn't or couldn't stop himself in time. It was awkward enough for the upperclassmen who were used to the court's cumbersome alignment. "I'm six-two, and I could dunk," said Brodsky, who, after graduating from Overbrook, was part of two Final Four teams at Temple under coach Harry Litwack. "You took a step on the wall, and you went up and dunked." But it took Brodsky hours in the gym to teach himself that maneuver. If Chamberlain tried to jam on one of those hoops, he might crash through the wall. He was still growing into his body, still prone to getting his feet tangled up, still learning how to stretch his leap higher and farther into the air, still learning how high and far he was capable of leaping.

"Did Wilt know how to dunk? Yeah, a little bit," Brodsky said. "He knew how to put the ball in the basket. Hal Lear showed him how to dunk the ball."

A six-foot senior shooting guard, Lear was bound for marvelous careers at Temple, in the Eastern League, and in the NBA. He was Overbrook's most graceful player, and he needed all of ten minutes to demonstrate to Chamberlain how to take two steps before lifting off of one foot, how to time his jump to arrive at the rim at the top of his jump, and how to add flair and a snarl whenever he hammered the ball through the hoop. "Hal was unbelievable," Brodsky said, "and he showed Wilt how to dunk with enthusiasm. That was the first time we saw that. We were stunned at how athletic Wilt was."

Their astonishment, predictably, would wane. (As a member of Overbrook's track-and-field team, Chamberlain would run the 440 meters in 49 seconds and high-jump six feet, six inches, and the "running and high-jumping and putting the shot in high school," he said, "helped immeasurably with the timing and coordination and judgment necessary to be a good playmaker or shooter or rebounder.") But it took time.

Like Bob Kurland, Chamberlain had his own set of insecurities born of his height—understandable for someone who was six foot eleven by his fifteenth birthday and who had stuttered as a child—though he in time would shed many of them. His "long, spindly shanks," as Mosenson described him, and the scars that slashed across his legs at haphazard angles from cotton bushes and bolls made him self-conscious. He donned knee-high socks to hide them. He didn't feel normal, didn't look normal, wasn't regarded as normal. How could he be? Nine-and-a-half-inch hands, seven-foot-two wingspan, his body, his athleticism, the praise that he received—all of it was so outsized. "You just have to see him once to know that there's no high school player in the country who can touch him," said North Carolina State guard Phil DiNardo, who, as a standout at Southern High in Philly, had played against Chamberlain once . . . when Chamberlain was a *sophomore*.

Slowly, it dawned on teenaged Wilt that the qualities that made him strange also made him something close to superhuman, and he relished it. Mosenson, for instance, once was sitting in his office with Overbrook football coach Ed Veith, who was a beefy 220 pounds, when Chamberlain came in, scooped up Veith, tucked him under his arm, and toted him down a hallway. "When he first started," Brodsky told me, "he was very humble and withdrawn a little bit. By mid-season, he wasn't so humble anymore. And by my senior season"—Chamberlain's junior season—"he had an attitude already: that he was Wilt and the rest of the world had to watch and pray."

Chamberlain's teammates were under no illusions about their meal ticket or his importance to them. There was little jealousy among them about him, and there were few, if any, accusations of selfishness or complaints that he was the alpha and omega of their offense. "We always wanted to feed him," Brodsky said, but Mosenson, reluctant to allow Chamberlain to turn every Overbrook game into a celebration of himself, tamped down that desire and insisted that the Panthers share the ball and play a more team-oriented style. Chamberlain, his ego already swollen, bristled at that approach and acted out in response, believing that Mosenson didn't understand him and had no idea what to make of him and his talent. "You should have seen the look on his face," Chamberlain wrote in his 1973 autobiography, *Wilt*, "the first time I dunked the ball. . . . Hardly anyone was dunking then. It wasn't the status thing it is now." And it was a strange thing to Mosenson. Wilt's first dunk in a game for Overbrook was accidental; on a fastbreak, he got too close to the basket and left himself with no choice but to jam it home. The spectators erupted in cheers. Mosenson didn't. "The old coach," Chamberlain remembered, "looked like I'd just jumped through the basket myself, feet first."

For a game against Frankford during his junior season, Chamberlain showed up, as Mosenson put it, having "adorned himself with a golf cap, a shimmering white silk scarf, and dark sunglasses," an outfit that today would be *de rigueur* for any baller at any level—high school, college, professional—but that put his head coach on edge. Mosenson told him to de-accessorize, a stern, show-of-force order from a young coach with a whiskerless face, rosy cheeks, and a fondness for wearing bow ties. Chamberlain then ignored Mosenson in the pregame huddle and refused to shoot for the game's opening three minutes, angering him so much that he benched Chamberlain twice in the second half and reamed him out in a one-on-one meeting afterward.

Mosenson's fury at Chamberlain's insolence, though, didn't last beyond the five-mile bus ride to Overbrook's next game, at Roxborough High School on Thursday, January 15, 1954. When the Panthers arrived, Roxborough's administrators made them dress for the game in a classroom, not a locker room. *Guys*, an angry Mosenson told his players, *today's the day. Feed Wilt*. They did, and Wilt ate. Overbrook won, 114–51, and Chamberlain scored 71 points, making 29 field goals and 13 of his 17 free-throw attempts (so much for Wilt's terrible foul-shooting habits), dropping in a layup to break the previous city single-game scoring record of 55 with one minute and forty-seven seconds left in the third quarter. He even put up 13 points in the fourth quarter, which suggests that Mosenson felt no guilt about letting his dogs chew on Roxborough's bones.

The vivid *71* in the box score tied the unofficial Pennsylvania high school high mark, a noteworthy enough accomplishment that the

Associated Press filed and wired a brief story to hundreds of newspapers. "The Negro," it read, "who now has 161 points in four league games, tied the state standard set February 22, 1951, by Joe Holup of Swoyersville, against Wilkes-Barre Township High." The legend had breached Philadelphia's border. The world would be made aware of Wilt Chamberlain, then and forevermore.

"Everybody knew how important he was," Barry Galman, one of Chamberlain's classmates, told me. "He was a celebrity then, but nobody knew the heights. You couldn't foretell what was going to happen."

Under Phil Woolpert, the University of San Francisco Dons had gone 10–11 in 1952–53, the season before Bill Russell could play for them. The arrival of a six-foot-ten center, especially one with Russell's leaping ability and speed, would have seemed an ideal opportunity for any coach to innovate, to tailor his offensive and defensive systems to the strengths of such a special talent. Russell had averaged more than 20 points a game for the freshman team and, when practicing against the varsity, had routinely snuffed the shots of Frank Evangelho, the Dons' starting center. During an offseason workout while he was an underclassman, some of his friends were curious how high he could jump from a running start. "I left chalk dust from my fingertips at a point fourteen feet above the floor," he said, "four feet above the basket and a foot above the top of the backboard." But Woolpert retained the conservative thinking common among coaches then: A player who left his feet for any reason, no matter how high he could jump or how quickly he could spring from the court, exposed himself to pump fakes and fouls. The writer John Edgar Wideman felt those strictures and limitations on his game even into the 1960s, when he was an undergraduate at Penn and the Quakers' team captain and top scorer. "College basketball lacked the spontaneity, the free-form improvisation and electricity of the playground game," he wrote in *Brothers and Keepers*, one of his memoirs. "Most coaches designed offenses more

suitable for corn-fed, Big Ten linemen than for the high-flying whip-
pets and greyhounds the city game was beginning to breed. 'Playground move' was synonymous with bad move. Not *bad* move, but
something undisciplined, selfish, possibly immoral."

Russell and Woolpert clashed initially over their disparate views on
how Russell ought to play. "I admit that, at the time I was coaching
him, I was kind of old school," Woolpert once said. "The coach had
to run the show, but not through intimidation—through persuasion.
Sometimes, I just couldn't persuade Bill." To Russell, the dunk wasn't
just an easier way to score, and a blocked shot wasn't just an inge-
nious and awe-inspiring way of preventing his opponents from scoring. They were reaffirmations of *him*, of the singularity of being Bill
Russell. He possessed a self-assurance that his coach did not. Without
a winning season in his first three years at San Francisco, naturally
tense as he was, Woolpert was thin, chain-smoked, and shook with
nervousness at all times, as if he were a freshly struck tuning fork. Of
course he and Russell came into conflict. Woolpert was the kind of
person who wished others would make things easier for him because
he made things so much harder for himself, and Russell wasn't going
to make anything easier for anyone.

So Woolpert adjusted. Already inclined to prioritize defense over
offense, he had the Dons run a system in which they hounded opponents in the halfcourt and overplayed passing lanes, the logic being
that they could afford to take chances since Russell was looming in
the lane to protect the rim. "They practiced 75 percent of their time
on defense," Paul Woolpert, Phil's son, told me. "He talked about the
fact that he wanted his teams to let their opponents know very early
in the game that scoring would be extremely difficult. He didn't use
the word 'intimidation,' but I think that's what he meant." The Dons
went 14–7 in '53–54, Russell's first season, but they were missing a
key player, point guard K. C. Jones, who, stricken with appendicitis,
appeared in just one game. Jones was a relentless perimeter defender,
a one-man full-court press, the perfect complement to Russell. There
was every reason to think the Dons would be better with him and

Russell together. There were few people, if any, who recognized at the time just how much better they would be . . . and how different they would be from every college basketball team that had come before them.

Here's what happened: Wilt Chamberlain became a phenomenon. He had all the elements, checked all the boxes, reached all the people—all the basketball nuts throughout Philadelphia and the white sportswriters throughout Philadelphia and the white, blue-collar, barely interested-in-basketball sports fans throughout Philadelphia and the white, old-money, look-at-this-interesting-story-darling newspaper readers through-out Philadelphia and the Black men and the Black women and the Black kids in the Black basketball turfs throughout Philadelphia—North Phil-adelphia, West Philadelphia, South Philadelphia. He was too good to be true in too many ways.

"The dunk shot was scarcely known until Wilt came along," Mo-senson wrote in his memoir. "With his ability to go two and a half feet higher than the rim, and with his great strength, he could ram the ball down into the net with such force that sometimes he ripped the net."

Was he a troubled youth? He was not a troubled youth. He was a good student, keeping a B average, and his family was large and loving: two parents, a dad working difficult jobs for his kids, a mom working to keep those kids in line. He was neither sullen nor defiant in public, and he did not play dirty or go out of his way to bully smaller and weaker opponents (they were *all* smaller and weaker), and he did not do anything to make anyone who might be inclined to think the worst of him—or of someone who shared Wilt's skin tone—to think the worst of him. "He never raised his arm to hit another player," Mosenson once said. His shoulders seemed chipless. The New York *Daily News* ran a full-page story about Chamberlain in its Sunday, March 20, 1955, edition, and the reporter who wrote the profile, Pete Coutros, took care to note that Chamberlain "is not what has been commonly accepted as a 'goon.'" Like Carl Lacy said, he was a *nice guy*. And once he started reaching people beyond Philadelphia, people in New York, people beyond New York . . .

"There had never been a high school athlete," the writer Bob Ryan once said, "who had gotten the attention that Wilt Chamberlain did."

No one saw what those close to Chamberlain saw. "Wilt was complicated with his shifting moods," Mosenson wrote. "He was facing social pressures generated by his conspicuous height, his early fame, his life amid the racial tensions of the big city, and his adolescence." Walking down the street with his buddy from Northeast High School, Sonny Hill—Sonny Hill, who at five foot nine could dunk flat-footed, who eventually tore up the Eastern League and founded Philly's two premier summer leagues and remains the town's unofficial basketball mayor/spokesman/historian/raconteur to this day, in his late eighties—Wilt couldn't help but notice the passersby stopping to gawk at him . . . and he'd try to curl himself into the biggest ball of shame you'd ever seen. He'd try to hide. "When you grow to be seven-one," Hill said, "you can't hide." When you score 71 points in a game as a junior . . . when you score 74 points in a game as a senior . . . again against Roxborough; those poor, poor kids . . . you have no hope of hiding the rest of your life.

And how much better could he have been? And how much worse could it have been for those Philly Public League players tasked with guarding him? "Nobody was really dunking in those days," Hill told me. "The person who really brought the dunk into consistency in basketball was Wilt." But Chamberlain relied exclusively on those mushroom-cloud slams and a passive, one-handed fadeaway jumper to score. Mosenson tried to impress upon him that he would need a more varied array of moves and options as he advanced to college and the NBA. But it was so easy for him to pile up points with those two elementary shots—what high school player was blocking that fadeaway?—that he felt no need to diversify his game. A hook shot. A simple hook shot. Mosenson couldn't get him to learn even that. In February 1955, as Overbrook was preparing to play Roxborough for the second time that season, Mosenson warned his players not to embarrass their opponents, not to rub it in and run it up. Chamberlain reacted in a manner—eye rolls and deep sighs and defiance—that Mosenson couldn't ignore or let slide. He threw Wilt out of practice, telling him, "If you don't like the way I'm running the team, get out of the gym and don't come back." At the Panthers' next practice, though, Mosenson entered the gym to find Chamberlain, who stopped shooting baskets, shuffled sheepishly over to the coach, and asked him to work with him on his hook shot. He was back. All was forgiven. He would play against Roxborough. Mosenson told Overbrook's athletic director: *Be prepared. Against this team, Wilt might set a state record for points.*

Roxborough's coaches and players prepared, too. Or tried. They stalled throughout the first half, holding the ball, passing it around the perimeter, playing keep-away from Chamberlain. Mosenson was irate. First making his players get changed in a classroom, now this? He turned Chamberlain loose at halftime, told him to take whatever shot was available to him. The state record was his if he wanted it.

Watching from the stands was Joe Goldenberg, West Philadelphia High's star player, who had suffered an injury that was keeping him out of the lineup. So instead of having Goldenberg sit on the bench with his teammates at West Philly's next game, coach Doug Connelly sent him to scout Overbrook-Roxborough. Goldenberg returned with a report that beggared belief: Overbrook had won, 123–21. Chamberlain had scored 90 points, 26 in the first half, 64 in the second, 15 in one minute, and he had sat out more than four minutes of action, including the game's final two minutes and fifteen seconds. Ninety points. Ninety. In less than twenty-eight minutes.

"Where does he shoot from?" Connelly asked.

"Coach," Goldenberg said, "anywhere he wants."

Russell's individuality (and his teammates', to a lesser extent) was the enzyme for the Dons' excellence, and it yielded a level of collective performance that surpassed that of any college team before them and any after them save one. After losing to UCLA, 47–40, on December 11, 1954, San Francisco won 60 consecutive games—and two national championships—over the subsequent twenty-four months. It was the longest winning streak in college basketball history and has since been surpassed only by John Wooden's UCLA teams of the early 1970s, who won 88 in a row. There was no doubt some alchemy in the Dons' formula for greatness: Working at a small Catholic institution that did not have a gymnasium—the Dons played at Kezar Pavilion, a four-thousand-seat arena three-quarters of a mile from campus— Phil Woolpert had to recruit players who had not already committed to programs with better pedigrees and facilities. The result, in '54–55, was a roster that was the first in the country to start three Black players: Russell, Jones, and guard Hal Perry. The good fortune was that, in Russell, Woolpert had unearthed the rarest of gems in sports: an athlete so advanced, so distinct, that he made his teammates better simply by being himself.

"I remember my dad telling a story about Bill getting a steal," Paul Woolpert, himself a pro scout and coach for more than thirty years, told me. "At halfcourt, he dribbled once and dunked it, and the referee called a travel. At halftime, the ref came up to my dad and said, 'I blew that call. I've just never seen anyone do that before.' You think about changing the sport in terms of athleticism. This was a six-nine guy who could do everything. Think about it. There's not many guys who could do that: dribble one time, not travel, and dunk the ball. Obviously, Bill played *well* above the rim."

They even pioneered a tactic that has since become prevalent throughout the sport, though they never gave it a name.

"Before anyone came up with the term 'alley-oop,' that was one of their major deals: just get it up near the rim, and Bill would clean it up," Paul Woolpert said. "I also remember watching hundreds and hundreds of NBA games and college games with my dad, and he would just be amazed at how these guys would block shots and think it was cool to block it out of bounds. Bill wasn't just ahead of his time. He was basically the only one who blocked it and kept it in play, kept it to himself. If you think about someone who gets four or five blocked shots a game, that's four or five possessions. In most games, that's going to win or lose the game for you."

Russell posed a dual threat of intimidation: On one end of the court, he might go up to block a shot and pin the ball against the

backboard. On the other end, he might take advantage of the lack
of any rules against offensive goaltending, catch the ball when it was
just above the rim, and stuff it down. Either way, the other players
cowered beneath him. So once the 1954 NCAA Tournament began,
San Francisco's opponents began resorting to rough-and-tumble tactics to try to stop him. In the Dons' first-round game—at the Cow
Palace, nine miles south of USF—Russell rose for a dunk less than
thirty seconds after the opening tip-off, only to have West Texas State's
Ray Burris undercut him. Russell fell to the floor, landing flat on his
back. Silence dropped like a dark curtain over the partisan Cow Palace crowd of 11,002. Russell lay on the court for twenty seconds, then
wobbled to his feet and stayed in the game, only to have Burris knock
him down again a minute later and draw a flagrant foul. After the
game, Russell said he didn't think Burris's fouls were intentional, but
Jerry Mullen, the Dons' captain, was certain that the Buffaloes were
trying to scare Russell. "And he didn't scare," Mullen said. No, he did
not. San Francisco won, 89–66, and despite sitting out the final nine
minutes because the Dons' lead was so large, Russell finished with 29
points, including 20 in the first half.

Three more victories put the Dons in the championship game against
La Salle and Tom Gola: a more heralded team than San Francisco with
a more heralded player than Russell. An aficionado of basketball trivia
might remember that Gola remains the NCAA record holder for rebounds in a career, with 2,201, but that statistic alone does little to lend
the proper measure of perspective to his effect on the sport. When Gola
entered La Salle in 1951, New York City was the capital of college basketball, and college basketball was in the midst of an existential crisis.
The National Invitation Tournament, held at Madison Square Garden,
was the crown jewel of the postseason, more highly regarded than the
NCAA Tournament. But the infamous series of point-shaving scandals earlier that year involving City College of New York, Long Island
University, and NYU had crushed the sport's credibility, fostering the
perception that it was run by gamblers, gangsters, and thieves. Enter
Gola, who averaged 17.4 points and 17.1 rebounds as a freshman and

captivated the sporting press. When La Salle beat Dayton, 75–64, to win the NIT, he emerged as the tangible symbol for college basketball's rebirth—upright of character, unstained by any kind of disgrace, perfect for the media myth-making so common to that period. As one example, a magazine profile played up the fact that his father, Isidore, was a police officer, accenting the danger and blue-collar honorability of the job and its role in Gola's upbringing. "Poppa's all right," Gola's mother reportedly told her children one night. "He hit the robber three times with five shots." The possibility that Gola and the Explorers might lose to San Francisco seemed as remote as Ali flattening Liston or the 1980 United States Olympic hockey team beating the Soviets. Hell, few people had even heard of Bill Russell, let alone seen him play.

"The West Coast was not a prominent factor in NCAA basketball," Gola said in 1989. "People aren't going to believe me, but Bill Russell was not a big name on the East Coast. . . . Russell didn't know me, and I didn't know him. In fact, I had never seen Bill Russell until we met in the lobby."

That meeting took place on Saturday, March 19, 1955, the day of the national title game, at the hotel in Kansas City where the La Salle and San Francisco teams were both staying. That morning, Russell and assistant coach Ross Giudice passed Gola and La Salle head coach Ken Loeffler.

"Well, we're honored," Russell said to Giudice. "Here comes Mr. Gola."

"You'll be seeing a lot of him tonight, fellas," Loeffler said.

Nope. It was the other way around. Gola was La Salle's *de facto* point guard; the Explorers funneled their entire offense through him. Woolpert wanted to limit the amount of time that Russell spent guarding him, for fear that Gola would pull Russell away from the lane and the basket. So Woolpert assigned Jones to cover Gola and turned Russell loose to roam, to come off his man and double-team Gola if necessary. Loeffler and his team were unprepared for this wrinkle. San Francisco took an early lead and kept La Salle at arm's length the rest of the game. Finishing with just 18 points, more than six below his season average, Gola missed nine of his 15 shots from the field. Russell sank nine of his 22 shots, dunking twice and scoring many of his 23 points on tip-ins near the rim. He also had 25 rebounds. "All you can do against him," Gola said, "is to leap as high as you can—and hope."

Home in West Philadelphia, Carl Lacy wasn't the only Gola fan surprised and puzzled by Russell's dominance. Billy Packer, who spent more than thirty years as a college basketball analyst, was fifteen years old then and a Gola devotee. He, like Lacy, listened to the game on the radio and couldn't believe what he was hearing.

"The guy doing the game kept talking about this guy Russell who kept blocking Tom Gola's shots," Packer told John Feinstein for Feinstein's book *Last Dance: Behind the Scenes at the Final Four.* "I'm thinking, 'That's impossible. No one can do that to Gola. Who is this guy Russell?'"

The shockwaves from San Francisco's 14-point win and the ease with which Russell and the Dons shut down Gola, the golden boy of college basketball, were immediate and seismic. Less than twenty-four hours after the national championship game, the NCAA coaches' rules committee met in Kansas City and fielded no fewer than thirty-nine recommendations for changes to mute the influence of Russell and players like him. An exasperated Hank Iba, having coached Bob Kurland, stood up and told the group: "If it's gotten to the point where we have to legislate to win, we'd better quit." But the outcry was overwhelming. "The weakness in our game is that seven-footers like Russell of San Francisco have an unfair advantage," Xavier University's Ned W. Wulk said. "Require the great big fellow like Russell to score in the same legitimate way as the smaller player. Oblige him to shoot the ball. The tip-in or tap-in is not a legitimate field goal. . . . That smacks too much of volleyball to suit me." The committee widened the lane from six feet to twelve, instituted the three-second rule, and banned offensive goaltending. Russell reacted to the changes with a snicker: "If the big man can't move, the rule kills him. But the rule didn't get the tall ones like me. It nailed the fat ones."

Not everyone viewed him as a menace bent on ruining basketball. His performance in the tournament—he averaged 23.6 points and 12 rebounds over the five games—had been so awesome that it forced coaches to reconsider not only how to play and coach the sport but what people found entertaining about it. "You wouldn't believe it unless you'd seen it," Columbia coach Lou Rossini said. "Russell does things on offense that could revolutionize the game. A lot of us coaches came away with a new concept of basketball and with mental notes on how to coach our own big men to play as nearly like Russell as they can." East Texas State's Bob Rogers picked up on what his peers refused to acknowledge: the reaction inside Municipal Auditorium whenever Russell violated the code that his predecessors and competitors held sacred. "The crowd at Kansas City loved it when Bill Russell of San Francisco dunked the ball, especially when he did it back over his head," Rogers said. "What do the crowds cheer in the warm-up practice before a game? The dunk. We've legislated against fans' wishes."

As for neutralizing Russell, the measures were of course abject failures: the Dons went 29–0 in 1955–56, and he was just as dominant. "They aren't going to stop him with puny things like a twelve-foot lane," Phil Woolpert said. "The only way they'll beat him is to pass legislation that will keep him from lifting his arms." That December, legendary sportswriter Dick Young took in a 67–51 Dons victory over Holy Cross—and over Russell's future friend and Celtics teammate Tommy Heinsohn. The eighteen thousand people in a sold-out Madison Square Garden, Young wrote in the New York *Daily News*, "enjoyed the big guy's typical exhibition of dunking, funneling, tapping, and shot-blocking." Nothing had changed. Everything had changed. "The Dons were forerunners for the modern game," *Sports Illustrated*'s Kelli Anderson wrote in 2006. "In two short years, they shifted college basketball's balance of power from white to Black, from offense to defense, and, thanks to the backboard-clearing, shot-blocking, backward-dunking Russell, from horizontal to vertical." Forget two years. Try one night in the Midwest. Tom Gola had helped rebuild the sport. Russell helped redefine it. Gola had represented where the sport was. Russell represented where the sport would be.

It was fruitless to find the college or university that wasn't chasing after Chamberlain in the spring of '55, that wasn't sending him letters and phoning his house at all hours and sending swarms of alumni and donors to Philadelphia and buttering up Wilt and his family. Every time he walked through the front door, there were another five telegrams on his dresser and another smooth-talking salesman in the kitchen, and he could barely process the possibilities. Stay local? Play at La Salle or Temple or some other Philly school? Nah. He was ready to leave Philadelphia, strike out on his own far from the safe space of his neighborhood. Head north or west or maybe even south? No, no way he was heading south. "I didn't want the Ku Klux Klan burning any crosses in my chest," he wrote in *Wilt*. "No, thanks. I wasn't about to be a big, brave—dead—pioneer." No matter. Chamberlain had more options and suitors than any high school player ever, more than any high school player could have conceived or contemplated, because everyone believed he was playing this new sport in a new way, newer and better than anyone else, better even than Bill Russell. "Chamberlain," Tom Gola said, "would kill Russell." Jesus, right around the time Russell and San Francisco were dispatching Gola and La Salle, *Sport* magazine ran a story about Chamberlain in which Irv Goodman wrote that Wilt "might just be the best basketball player there is. 'Just might be' is the cautious phrasing of a reporter seeking an editorial hedge." Wilt didn't just have more options and suitors than anyone else; he had *endless* options and suitors. And out of all those options and all those suitors, of all the schools, all the programs, all the coaches, Wilt Chamberlain—the target of targets, the recruit of recruits, the colossus of the few teenaged colossi in the country—chose . . . the guy who hated the thing that Wilt did best? The coach who hated what basketball was becoming, who hated the evolution that Russell and Chamberlain were accelerating? The coach who hated the dunk?

Hell, yes, he chose Phog Allen and Kansas. Phog had his opinions about the dunk and the direction of the sport, to be sure, but he was no dummy. "I could win games," he once said, "with two sorority girls, two Phi Beta Kappas, and Wilt Chamberlain." So Phog unleashed a full-court press on Wilt. Phog flew to Philadelphia in January '55 to speak at a banquet honoring Wilt. Phog had KU alumni and officials mail more than five hundred letters to the Chamberlains, and he arranged to have three prominent Black alumni meet with Wilt and his parents and extoll the benefits of a KU education: newspaper editor and publisher Dowdal Davis, singer Etta Motten, and businessman Lloyd Kerford. Phog could charm Olivia Chamberlain with his courtliness and his accent on academics. "I'm a mama's guy," he once said. Phog could tout the spanking new campus basketball arena named after him—Allen Fieldhouse, dedicated on March 1, 1955, built for a cool $2.65 million. Phog could say nothing while the wealthiest Kansas graduates pooled $20,000 to make sure Wilt wanted for nothing while he was in Lawrence. Reporters went wild over those rumors; the term *name-image-likeness* wasn't in their lexicon then, but the term *amateurism* was. So what? Phog didn't care. Phog had other priorities. Chamberlain and Russell were changing the game, and Phog, just as he'd been with the big men before them, was bent on changing it back.

"I wanted to get this boy," he once said, "and I wanted him to stuff that basket full of basketballs. I'd show the rules committee how ridiculous that ten-foot basket was."

What about winning games and national championships with Chamberlain? Surely Allen wanted that, too, right? Funny. He never got the chance. He turned seventy on November 18, 1955, the mandatory retirement age for Kansas state employees, and the university's athletic board recommended that KU's regents deny Allen's request to continue coaching, which they did. (As John McLendon had rightly perceived years earlier, Allen was an influential figure at the university, but he was not all-powerful.) Phog Allen never coached Wilt Chamberlain in an official college basketball game. His successor, Dick Harp, did.

As far as Phog's peers were concerned, though, he had already in-flicted plenty of damage on the sport simply by coaxing Chamberlain to Lawrence. "I told Phog that he was trying to kill basketball by bringing that kid into school," said North Carolina coach Frank McGuire, whose Tar Heels would beat Wilt and the Jayhawks, 54–53 in triple overtime, in the 1957 national-title game. "Chamberlain will score about 130 points one night, and the other coach will lose his job. There might be somebody in the penitentiary who can handle him, but I guarantee you there is nobody in college." In November 1955, KU held its annual scrimmage between the varsity and the freshman team. Nebraska's Jerry Bush, among other coaches from the Big Seven Conference, attended the game. Sitting next to Bush, with the other fourteen thousand spec-tators in the stands, was Jimmy Breslin, gathering string for a profile of Chamberlain for the *Saturday Evening Post*. Since only a fool would try to paraphrase Jimmy Breslin, here is, word for word, how he de-scribed the scene in his piece:

> It didn't take Bush long to decide that this was only a sample of what was going to happen when Chamberlain became a varsity player. In fact, a single characteristic play was enough to shape his opinion. The Stilt drove to the top of the keyhole—or four circle—and went up for what appeared to be a one-handed jump shot. But he didn't come down. He kept floating through the air, did a complete twist, so that his back was to the basket, shoved his arm behind him, rotated it in helicopter style, and dunked the ball in the net. He landed somewhere behind the basket.

Then, Bush looked at Breslin.

"I feel sick," he said.

He wasn't the only one. The freshmen won the scrimmage. Cham-berlain scored 42 points, including one when, with a running start, he dunked a foul shot, a trick that he had unveiled from time to time while practicing at Overbrook. Contrary to the apocrypha surround-ing Wilt's ability to dunk from the free-throw line, he likely never pulled it off during an official game. Brodsky never saw him do it in high school, and author Robert Cherry, in researching his book *Wilt: Larger Than Life*, never uncovered any evidence that Chamberlain had done it during his college or NBA careers.

There was a reason Cherry never found that evidence. Kansas State coach Tex Winter—the brain behind the "Triangle Offense" that helped Phil Jackson win eleven NBA championships with the Chicago Bulls and Los Angeles Lakers—attended the KU scrimmage, saw the dunk, and decided he had to stop Chamberlain from showing up K-State and other teams in a similar manner. And since Winter was the chairman of the association's rules committee that year, he could clip Chamberlain's wings. Through Winter's influence, the committee, at the 1956 NCAA convention, banned dunking from the foul line and implemented a rule against offensive goaltending. The headline of Breslin's story, published in the *Post* nine months later, in December '56, was *Can Basketball Survive Chamberlain?* The notion that basketball might thrive because of Chamberlain and Russell was too radical and blasphemous to be entertained. It had to be squelched. It could not be permitted to flourish. Flourish, though, it would, through athletes with names that have never been forgotten, with games so dazzling that they stir souls and memories even now. So many would follow Russell and Chamberlain into the sunlight. So many would never fully emerge from the shadows of the city.

8

JUMPIN' JACKIE

The dunk was everywhere now, and a basketball fan didn't have to buy a ticket to Madison Square Garden or sneak into a college gym to find a court where a player, a true player, had the ball in his mitts and a plan on his mind to take everyone's breath away. Any city or town or neighborhood whose beating heart was the bounce of a basketball had someone like that. To see him was to remember him always, even if so many others never got the chance.

The most passionate basketball writer in the history of both basketball and writing was curling his bony body around me inside Madison Square Garden, then leaping toward a rim only he could see, then hammering down a dunk that had shaken him to his core when he was barely beyond childhood. This was March 2023, during the Big East Men's Basketball Tournament. I was there to cover Villanova, who would make a quick exit from the four-day event—a victory over Georgetown in the first round, a loss to Creighton in the quarterfinals. But Bob Ryan was there for the duration, once more having made the familiar 215-mile journey from Boston to New York to sit courtside at the Garden and share in the joy of the best week of hoops on the East Coast or anywhere else. Sorry, if you want to dispute the assertion that the Big East Tournament is better than anything else about March Madness, go ahead. You'll be shouting into the wind. The games are great. The Garden is packed and alive. There's no other way to say it: when it comes to the Big East Tournament, you have to be there.

But Ryan wasn't thinking or talking about Patrick Ewing or Providence College or the good ol' days of the 1980s Big East. He wasn't dunking, either, not actually, not anywhere but in his own mind. There we were, in the bowels of the arena, not far from the media dining area, not far from tables stacked with stale turkey sandwiches and tureens of terrible coffee. And Bob Ryan—four-time National Sportswriter of the Year, Celtics beat writer and columnist at the *Boston Globe* for nearly fifty-five years, biographer of John Havlichek and Bob Cousy and Larry Bird—was describing the instant that a long-forgotten showman of the sport made certain that at least someone would always remember him.

Jumpin' Jackie Jackson was twenty-two years old and six feet, five inches tall during the 1961–62 Eastern League season, a rookie for the Trenton Colonials making one hundred dollars a game. Ryan was fifteen, a student at Lawrenceville School, just seven miles outside the city limits, and he was likely the most enthusiastic fan of Eastern League basketball in the greater Trenton area. The caption quote beside his senior yearbook headshot was "What do you mean 'study?' The Colonials played last night." With NBA teams still slow to draft and sign Black players, with unwritten quotas still a fact of life for most NBA franchises, the Eastern League—its games held on weekends, featuring clubs in towns such as Allentown, Williamsport, Wilkes-Barre, and Camden—was in some ways a preferable alternative in that hoops-mad region of the country. Tickets were cheap, and the basketball was terrific, unusual, flashier for the talent its teams were willing to mine and acquire. Jackson added to that flash. There were rumors that he had leaped high enough to grab a quarter off the top of a backboard. But those stories were nothing compared to what Jackson did during the Colonials' pregame warm-ups one night at Trenton High School.

"I'm watching the layup drill," Ryan told me at the Garden, his hands moving in a martial-arts–like flurry in front of him, "and I was aware of his notoriety at the time. He had plucked the dime off the backboard, whatever. Fine. He goes on the right-hand side. He goes past the basket. Way past. Way fucking past it. He's still got the ball. I'm thinking, 'Where's he going, the men's room?' It was the longest reverse dunk from the distance from the basket."

Ryan started acting out Jackson's dunk, cupping his hands, raising them and lowering them. He slid ten to fifteen feet away from me, sort of sputtering as he spoke, his voice rising. People in the dining area started to look at us. His enthusiasm only intensified when I let him in on a secret: I had gotten my hands on a copy of Jackson's unpublished memoir, and I planned to weave excerpts of it into my chapter about him.

"I don't know if he propelled himself backwards. And it was so quick. It was like, 'Boom.' Seamless if it were here. I've never seen anything like that."

In other words: With Jackie Jackson, you had to be there.

I was born January 25, 1940, on a tobacco farm in New Bern, North Carolina. New Bern is a small town on the east coast of the state, about 100 miles from Raleigh-Durham. My father, Nathaniel Jackson, was a tobacco farmer who owned his own land. He used to live in New York, but he moved to North Carolina to open up the farm and work his tobacco business. My mother, Mary, was a housewife who took great care of us.

I was the youngest of seven children. New Bern was a segregated town, but that was the way of life then. When we played basketball, we had to play on dirt playgrounds. The school had outhouses. My older brothers introduced me to basketball. All of the neighborhood kids would come by our house to play ball with us. A lot of times, we would play right there in the backyard. The hoops would be made out of bicycle rims.

Having contracted high blood pressure, Nathaniel moved his family back to New York in 1950, figuring that he would receive better medical treatment there than in a tiny North Carolina town. His daughter Lovey, Jackie's eldest sister, was already living there, in Brooklyn. The family stayed with her for a week, then settled into their own apartment in the Bedford-Stuyvesant section of the borough, on Quincy Street.

I was thrilled to move to New York City. I was 10 years old and experiencing a lot of new things. Unfortunately, my dad died before I turned 11.

The cops in Brooklyn would always harass the neighborhood kids, so I joined the Police Athletic League and stayed active in sports so I could stay out of trouble. There was a playground on Sumner Avenue next to PS 44—the legendary "Soul In the Hole," where they still play tournaments to this day. This park and the tournament are the Brooklyn version of the famous Rucker Playground in Harlem.

When it was time for me to choose a high school, I wanted to go to Alexander Hamilton High School in Crown Heights with my friends, but my mother wanted me to go to Boys High, which was closer to my house, because my brothers went there.

Though, by his twelfth birthday, he had grown to five foot nine and could dunk, Jackie didn't make Boys High School's varsity roster as either a freshman or a sophomore. No wonder. Among the players already on the team were Lenny Wilkens and future Dodgers outfielder Tommy Davis. But before the 1957–58 season, his senior season, Jackson established himself as one of Boys' starters, and a friend of his whom he had gotten to know on the Brooklyn playgrounds—Connie Hawkins—entered the school in tenth grade and joined the team. The two of them were part of what had to be the most dazzling sight in any high school basketball gym anywhere in America: the Boys High pregame layup line. It was "legendary," David Wolf wrote in his essential biography of Hawkins, *Foul!* "The sight of thirteen players, some as short as five foot eight, dunking the ball in succession—from the side, down the middle, one-handed, two-handed, backhanded—convinced most young opponents that Boys was invincible." The display was almost as imposing as the Boys building itself, which was encircled by a black iron fence and seemed more a military headquarters than an educational institution.

Boys High was a racially mixed school in the 1950s. The Black athletes were encouraged to play basketball, but we were not selected for other sports. Tommy Davis was so good at baseball that they had to put him on the team. However, the most talented Black athletes in school either played basketball or ran track. It didn't hit me until I grew older that the Black ballplayers were steered toward Black colleges during the '50s and '60s.

The top basketball schools in New York at the time—St. John's University, NYU, and Long Island University—didn't recruit me. I was a good high school player, but I really developed my skills and leaping ability during my first year in college. If I had been a year younger and improved that much during my senior season at Boys High, I would have had all kinds of colleges knocking down my door.

Boys High had won 17 straight games and 37 of its previous 38 before losing to DeWitt Clinton High School, 52–41, in the 1958 New York Public Schools Athletic League championship game. It was the final game of Jackson's high school career, and it was memorable for all the wrong reasons: He scored just one point and was outshined by DeWitt's Jerry Harkness, who had 14 points that night and who, five years later, led Loyola of Chicago to the 1963 NCAA championship.

Jackson was named Honorable Mention All-City. It was a nice distinction, but hardly one that indicated he would do anything memorable after leaving Boys High. The school that recruited him most fiercely was Virginia Union in Richmond, a historically Black university known for its strong theology curriculum. He had two allies in the school's basketball program already. Howard Jones, the head coach, had been a legendary player at Boys High, and the team's starting point guard, also a Boys High alumnus and one of the most dazzling ball-handlers on the New York playground scene, was Ed "Czar" Simmons.

The first time I checked out Virginia Union was in July 1958. I went to the Port Authority in Manhattan to take the Greyhound bus down to Richmond. I was returning to the South for the first time since I left when I was 10.

After the eight-hour ride, the first thing I saw when we arrived in Richmond was the segregated waiting room at the bus depot there. Since I was born and raised in North Carolina, I knew about Jim Crow laws.

I caught a cab to campus. The driver dropped me off at the library, where I was supposed to meet Coach Jones. Instead, Czar was there. He introduced me to two of my teammates, Bruce Spraggins and Wellford "Bubba Cakes" Lewis, who were there to take summer classes.

Coach Jones set up a scrimmage for me and the current players on the team. The gym was packed to see "Ed's boy from high school." Ed was already talking smack around campus about how good I was. I dunked the ball five times in a row, and the whole gym was oohing and aahing. Ed hadn't seen me play in a year, not since he had gone to college, and he was amazed at how much my basketball skills and leaping ability had improved. On top of that, Coach Jones was really impressed.

I scrimmaged with the team for the next couple of days and had my way with everybody on the basketball court. When I got back to Brooklyn, I told my mother that I wanted to attend Virginia Union. Later that week, the school sent me a letter, and I accepted.

Virginia Union was, and is, a Division II program and a member of the Central Intercollegiate Athletic Conference. The CIAA's schools, the majority of which are historically Black colleges and universities, now number thirteen, and upon its formation in 1912, the league left no doubt about its mission. Its original name was the Colored Intercollegiate Athletic Conference—that remained its official nomenclature until 1950—and it provided an enticing alternative to those major programs whose coaches might have been less than enthusiastic about recruiting Black players. When Jackson got to Virginia Union, Clarence "Big House" Gaines was more than a decade into his forty-seven-year coaching tenure at Winston-Salem State, and one of his contemporaries was a star guard at Johnson C. Smith University in Charlotte: Fred "Curly" Neal, the future Harlem Globetrotter.

It's not fully accurate to paint the CIAA and conferences like it as some kind of underground civilization or parallel dimension where Black athletes were playing a Bizarro version of basketball, unobserved by mainstream culture. None of those programs or coaches or players was hiding. Only so many people cared to look.

In 1960, Jackson and three of his Virginia Union teammates—Czar Simmons, Bruce Spraggins, and Robert Moore—traveled to Spraggins's hometown, Williamsburg, to scrimmage against several players from William & Mary. The Tribe does not have what anyone would consider a rich basketball tradition. William & Mary has never qualified for the NCAA Tournament. But in January of that year, the Tribe had beaten West Virginia—a West Virginia team with Jerry West—on its way to a 15–11 season. Its best player was Jeff Cohen, a six-foot-seven thumper who scored more than 2,000 points in his college career, including a 49-point, 31-rebound outing his senior year, and who played professionally in the American Basketball League and for the Globetrotters' hostile partners in performance, the Washington Generals.

Every CIAA team had a good player, and all of those players either made the NBA or could have. What a lot of people do not realize is that in that era, in the early '60s, there were not a lot of options for Black ballplayers like there are today.

William & Mary was an all-white team. We played a few games that day in the gym against their starting five. We ran them out of the gym. They were no competition for us. This showed that we could have matched up against any team in Division I. Their coach said that he wished that he could have had us on his team, but because of segregation, that would never have happened at that time. There were secret scrimmages with all-Black teams playing against all-white teams all the time throughout the South. Some teams in the ACC would play against teams from the CIAA under the cover of darkness. Then you would see the white teams use our offensive plays on TV later that year.

Jackson led the nation in rebounding twice for Virginia Union, in 1959–60 and 1960–61, pulling down more than 24 a game, and averaging 19 points, in each of those seasons. He and Neal would reconnect later in their careers, and he and Cohen remained friends until Cohen's death in 1978, so close that one day, Jackson handed him a business card. It read: HAVE CONVERSE, WILL JUMP.

I came off the bench in my first game at Virginia Union. I dunked the ball the first four times I ever touched it, and I started every game after that, playing center and power forward because of my leaping ability. I could easily match up against a seven-footer and was quick enough to cause problems for any big man. And I always drove to the basket because of my speed.

When we traveled to North Carolina for a road game, the players and coaches piled into two station wagons. In a game against Johnson C. Smith, I came down on the fastbreak after a rebound, and Curly Neal posted up to try to draw a foul. I leaped over his head from the free-throw line and dunked the ball with ease. The crowd—their crowd—went wild.

I especially loved to play defense because I liked to stop the other team's best player, block shots, and rebound. And of course, I liked the roar of the crowd when I dunked.

After Jackson's freshman year, Howard Jones resigned and returned to Boys High School to coach.

My next coach was Tom "Tricky" Harris, who was the football and basketball coach for Virginia Union. He was the closest to a father figure that I'd had since

my own father died. He was an excellent recruiter who would get a pipeline of
players from churches throughout the country. I never forgot that when I grad-
uated from Virginia Union, he said one thing to me: "The next time you put
on a jock strap, make sure it's for pay."

Jackson's New York roots made it natural for him, when he returned
to the city in the summer, to take part in the Rucker Tournament, the
event that—even in its infancy, as it was then—defined urban hoops
in America. A playground director, a civic leader and social custodian
within the city's Black community, Holcombe Rucker became one
of the game's greatest grass-roots influences, not merely by founding
several youth leagues but, beginning in the mid-1950s, by coaxing
professional players to Harlem to take on those playground stars who
hadn't, and might never, get their shot in the NBA. That tournament,
the Rucker Pro League, held in those days at a park on Seventh Avenue between 128th and 129th Streets, showcased so many players and
so much of the talent and trash talk that was transforming basketball
that its influence and importance would seep into every crevice of the
sport's landscape.

    "A vicious slam or a breathtaking block," Jesse Washington wrote
for The Undefeated in 2015, "meant more at the Rucker than anywhere else."

My first time at the Rucker Tournament was in 1960, after summer school.
I played for a New York team against an All-Star team from Philadelphia.
We had Tony Jackson and Willie Hall from St. John's University, Czar, and
Spraggins. I matched up against Wayne Hightower, who went to Overbrook
High and the University of Kansas, just like Wilt Chamberlain had. The first
time I touched the ball, I blew past him and dunked. I had to hang on to the
rim because everyone ran past me and hit the wall. Tony and I were the co-MVPs
of the tournament.
    Those two All-Star teams would rotate where the games would play each

year between Harlem and Philadelphia. I would make my mark on the game during these years.

Jackson was back in Harlem, back at Rucker, in '61, this time with a team that would have been the equal, at least, of any in the NBA. The starting five were Jackson, Simmons, Spraggins, Walt Bellamy, and Connie Hawkins. Bellamy had just finished up at Indiana University and was about to begin his first NBA season with the Chicago Packers. Hawkins had just been expelled from the University of Iowa for his alleged involvement in a now-infamous (for his innocence) point-shaving scandal. Jackson was as captivating to the crowd as any of them.

"With his Genghis Khan mustache and a shaved head," Kareem Abdul-Jabbar once wrote, "he knew that the meaning of life hung on the rim."

Czar ran the Brooklyn squad at the Rucker. He was the coach and the captain. We would hang out all night and kill our opponents the next day.

As good as Brooklyn was, its primary competition—a team representing Manhattan—might have been even better: Satch Sanders of the Celtics; Cal Ramsey and Russ Cunningham from NYU; and Carl Green and Wally Choice, both of whom had been playing with the Globetrotters and in the Eastern League. Choice, in fact, would be Jackson's teammate with the Trenton Colonials.

Oh, and Wilt Chamberlain. The Manhattan team had Wilt Chamberlain.

The squad was named Big Wilt's Smalls Paradise, after the legendary Harlem nightclub. Playing for the Philadelphia Warriors but enamored with New York's nightlife, Chamberlain had purchased an ownership share of the club earlier in the year, when he was just two seasons into his NBA career and not yet twenty-five years old. It was an indication of the already strong connection between basketball and pop culture, particularly Black culture—a connection that would only grow stronger over time—and it was a reaffirmation of Chamberlain's standing in the sport. But the game would reveal a few timeless truths: that competition is unpredictable, that sports can be a great leveler, that one remarkable act from an unlikely source—in this case, a moment so stunning and electrifying that no one there to see it forgot it, furnished by an athlete mostly lost to history—can cut even the most powerful and imposing figure down to size.

Wilt would always fade away when he shot the ball. I told Connie to go up high when he defended Wilt. Once, when Wilt took a fadeaway, I pinned the ball to the top of the backboard, then I took it off the backboard while I was still in the air and threw it to Connie to start the fastbreak. Let me say that again: In that tournament, I pinned Wilt's shot to the top of the backboard.

Connie had the ball and took off on a fastbreak. He threw the ball to me to his left from the free-throw line. I ran across the backboard to go up for the dunk, but Wilt was right there. I snatched the ball down and went under the backboard to shield myself from Wilt, came up on the other side of the backboard while still in the air, and did a reverse dunk on Wilt.

The crowd went wild.

The game had to stop for fifteen minutes as the fans in the bleachers streamed onto the court to celebrate my move. People were screaming. Little kids were running all over the place. It was the craziest dunk that anyone ever saw.

"I didn't even know he could jump that great," Hawkins said later. "Four thousand people were yelling and hollering and dancing around. Then I looked at Dipper. He was staring down at Jackie. I got a feeling maybe we made a mistake."

Angry, Chamberlain dunked the next five times he got the

ball. His team won the game by 10 points. Did it matter what team won or lost? Did anyone give a damn about the final score? Only insofar as the outcome related to bragging rights, and by that standard, Jackson had flattened Goliath. Wilt had won the game. Jackie had won the crowd—and Chamberlain's admiration. "He's only six-three," Wilt once said, "but he can dunk every way imaginable. He's so beautiful—so much grace and style and power, so much perfection." Nobody remembered the final score. Everyone remembered Jumpin' Jackie Jackson and the dunk that shook Harlem.

My legend grew across the city . . . and across the country. It wasn't a big deal to me. I used to block everybody's shots. Not only would I block a shot, I would catch the ball and throw it to the guard to start a fastbreak . . . all while I was still in midair.

Later that summer, Jackson and Simmons played in a tournament in Rockville Center on Long Island. In the tournament's championship game, they faced a team with a point guard from Long Beach High School who was running the show for the North Carolina Tar Heels. The point guard's name was Larry Brown.

Rockville Center was a very white area back then. The tournament's organizers saw how good we were when we did our warmups. We were dunking and laying the ball up all over the place. Our speed was unmatched.

After we won, they didn't give us the five-foot-tall winners' trophy. They gave us the one-foot-tall consolation prize. The organizers couldn't stand to see these Black guys from the city take home that big trophy. I stayed pissed about that switcharoo the rest of my life.

I met Larry Brown at a Philadelphia 76ers game when he was their head coach. They were honoring the Harlem Globetrotters that night. Larry mentioned that game to me as if it were yesterday. He remembered that I blocked all of his and his teammates' shots.

I wish he could have gotten me that five-foot trophy.

In 1992, just after graduating from Syracuse University, Carl Agard chose, for his first full-time job, to work as a youth counselor at a non-profit community center in Bed-Stuy. Spike Lee had filmed *Do the Right Thing* in the neighborhood four years earlier. Just a mile and a quarter to the south, during the summer of 1991, race riots had left Crown Heights a smoking wreck of smashed storefront windows, with streets whose only cobblestones were chipped bricks and shattered beer bottles. Agard's primary role was to provide college-prep training and after-school programming—sports, especially pickup basketball, was a substantial part of that programming—but in that neighborhood, at that time, the job was more than just that of a glorified gym teacher. A counselor at the center had to reach kids. He had to command attention and respect. He had to have a story. Which is why the stories that the center's leaders told about one of the counselors, a man in his early fifties who was well over six feet tall, with muttonchops snaking toward his chin and a thick mustache, intrigued him so much.

That's Jackie Jackson, they'd tell Agard, as if the name were supposed to mean something to him. Agard had never heard of Jackie Jackson. *What's the big deal about him?* he'd ask.

At Syracuse, Agard had befriended several members of the university's basketball team, including stars Derrick Coleman, Rony Seikaly, and Billy Owens. He knew basketball and basketball history. He thought he did, anyway. But he knew nothing about anyone named Jackie Jackson, even though his bosses told him that Jackie Jackson had been a Harlem Globetrotter, that he had been a legend, that he had done something on a basketball court that . . . well, you had to be there to believe it.

As word spread about my leaping ability, more and more people wanted to see how high I could jump. At the corner of Putnam and Ralph Avenues in Brook-

lyn, there was a drugstore sign that was more than twelve feet off the ground. It said nothing but DRUGS. I could jump and touch it with no problem. I did it throughout high school like it was nothing, and my friends were always bragging about how high I could get.

One night, while we were drinking at a local bar, Czar bet a guy that I could take a quarter off the top of the backboard—not the rim, which is ten feet high, but the top of the backboard, which is thirteen feet high. We were all broke, so the bartender put up the money. You know the rest.

Agard and Jackson counseled the same group of kids. The two of them ate lunch together every day, chatting about their work and their shared love of the New York Yankees. "We would pull each other's tails," Agard told me, and he pulled Jackson's by expressing doubt about Jackson's basketball exploits.

"He'd say, 'Oh, yeah, I was a Harlem Globetrotter,'" Agard said. "Back then, there was no Google or anything. So I went to him, 'You ain't no legend, man. Curly and Meadowlark Lemon are legends. You ain't no legend, man.' He's like, 'I'm a legend. I'm a legend.'"

So Agard decided to try to confirm Jackson's stories. He went to the library, filed through old newspapers, and discovered that Jackson was telling him the truth. The Warriors had even picked him in the 1962 NBA draft, 43rd overall.

"He was real cocky," Agard told me. "He said, 'When I tell you I'm the shit, I'm the shit.'"

Opportunities were limited for the Black ballplayer in the early 1960s. There were only eight NBA teams with an unwritten quota of two Blacks per team. The only team that had more than two was the Celtics. I guess that's why they won so many championships.

In 1962, I tried out for the Pittsburgh Rens of the American Basketball League, but they cut me in training camp. The team folded later that year, but it hadn't taken me long to learn about the politics of professional sports. I was a lot better than the guys they kept on the team, but Connie Hawkins didn't speak up for me. He was the star of the team.

Hawkins was the star of the entire ABL, having led the league in scoring and rebounding. He was also, at the time, a shy teenager, and he spent that '61–'62 season hampered by various illnesses, including a vitamin deficiency that caused him to lose 27 pounds, from 195 to 168. He had more on his mind than his friend's future.

Besides, a kind word from Hawkins on Jackson's behalf might not have made any difference. Despite his obvious strengths, Jackson had the sorts of weaknesses that make it difficult for any player, even one who could sky over the rim like he could, to maintain any staying power in the pros. His jump shot was inconsistent at best. He was much better driving to the basket with his right hand, his dominant hand, than he was with his left. And though he was listed as being 195 pounds at Virginia Union, he appeared too frail to hold up over a full NBA season. "I've always played the game the same way," he once said. "If I could get my points by shooting from midcourt, I would." He was, at least, a man who recognized his own limitations.

After I got cut by the Rens, the Wilkes-Barre Barons of the Eastern League picked me up. We went all the way to the championship that year but lost to the Allentown Jets.

If you were a great Black player, your best option after the NBA was to play for the Harlem Globetrotters. Remember, the NBA had its limits, the ABL had folded, and the Eastern League was only a weekend league. Abe Saperstein, the owner of the Globetrotters back then, had a monopoly on Black ballplayers for years.

No, Saperstein didn't quite have a monopoly, but the Globetrotters offered three benefits that were hard for those ballplayers to turn down: stability, a decent salary, and public adoration, especially among children who perceived them as invincible wizards for so rarely losing a game. By the mid-1970s, a Globetrotter's average annual paycheck was $30,000, which, when adjusted for inflation, would exceed $186,000 in 2023 dollars. The difficult decision for any prospective Trotter was whether that salary was worth being what author Ben Green, in *Spinning the Globe*, his history of the Trotters, called "the Stepin Fetchit of the hardwood" and playing into rank racial stereotypes through the Trotters' clowning comedy.

"The slapstick antics, falsetto voices, rubbery-limb motions, toothy grins, and yelping dialogue are as modern American as Aunt Jemima and Little Black Sambo," Lacy J. Banks, a longtime sports columnist for the *Chicago Sun-Times*, once wrote, "and equally defaming to many Blacks."

The criticism wasn't universal. The players themselves "do not feel they are degrading their race," Frank Deford wrote for *Sports Illustrated* in 1973, and when Deford raised the question of whether the Globetrotters were Uncle Toms, Meadowlark Lemon, the team's most famous member, told him: "Look, if I'm Tomming by making people laugh, then all comedians, white or Black, are Uncle Toms." Jackson, who either had struck out in those other leagues or had those leagues strike out on him, made his choice.

Even though Sweetwater Clifton was one of the first Black ballplayers in the NBA, he was a Globetrotter first. Marques Haynes, a longtime Globetrotter, was one of the greatest basketball players of his era. He could even outplay Bob Cousy. If you wanted to continue to make money playing basketball, you had to play with the Trotters.

Jackson tried out for the Globetrotters, and made the roster, in November 1963. After his first season with the team, though, he was drafted into the army, serving for two years before rejoining the Trotters in 1966. "I had to get some kinks out of my playing form and never felt entirely loose," he said after his first season back. "I feel as frisky as a two-year-old colt now."

He stayed that frisky for fifteen years, traveling with and playing for the Globetrotters all that time, building a family—he and his wife, Jean, had two children, Robert and Christy—while keeping up with the club's grueling schedule, 389 games in one nine-month stretch. More than a decade into his career, he was a draw, maybe *the* draw, for the same reason he'd always been. The rookies who showed up at training camp every year would sneak looks at him, and Lemon would chuckle. "These highflying kids come in, and then J. J. starts smokin'," Lemon once said. "Sometimes you think a few eyes are going to roll from a few heads." They weren't the only ones. "No part of the Globetrotter game is more exciting than the slam dunk," Stan Greeson, the Trotters' president, said in 1977. "And Jackie Jackson is still the best there is."

How many more like him were there back then? How many more were there of those highflying kids who didn't quite have the stuff to make it to *the league* but who kept and still keep the dunk alive and electric and cool, always cool, through the ban in the 1960s and '70s to the three-point craze of the 2010s and '20s, through their reps in the parks and on the playgrounds, through semipro leagues in small cities and dead-main-drag towns, through the show teams that toss alley-oop passes between their legs and dunk with their eyes closed during nonstop tours of festivals and state fairs and suburban middle schools from coast to coast, in the professional leagues of Mexico and Eastern Europe and Western Asia? Jackie Jackson was just one of them, but really, he represented all of them and still does, just by living on in the memories of those lucky enough to have seen him or heard someone tell a story about him. Carl Agard, before and after he married Christy, heard all those Jumpin' Jackie stories and more, shook his head as people reacted to his father-in-law with a combination of glee and wonder and wistfulness. Jackie would never bring up those stories and the old days himself, Agard told me, but if a group of basketball fans started talking about dunkers and high leapers, he would stand his ground, insist that they mention him among the all-timers. If he had regrets that he wasn't more famous, that he never played in the NBA for even a minute, he didn't show them.

"On the one hand," Agard said, "he wanted to know how he would have done against the best of the best. On the other hand, he realized that those were the times. What can you do? Those were the times."

They tried to collaborate on an autobiography—the unfinished, unpublished manuscript that I mentioned to Bob Ryan, a copy of which Agard gave to me. They put a few thousand words' worth of Jackson's life and reflections down but didn't have the time or opportunity to finish the book. Before Jackson died in 2019, he and Agard would attend Globetrotters games—he had free tickets usually—and people would look at him and notice a six-foot-five man with a slight swagger to his stride. And they'd stop him and Agard to point and ask: *Who is he?* And Agard would tell them, and Jackson would keep several little cards in his pocket, wallet-sized photographs of him in his Globetrotters jersey, and he would autograph them and give them to those people, and then they would remember who he was or learn who he was, and either way they would never forget.

That's Jackie Jackson, from Virginia Union and the Globetrotters. He was the one who had the muttonchop sideburns. Who'd jump over guys to dunk on them when he was in college. Who threw it down over Wilt at Rucker. Who would dunk in the layup line before a game just to scare the dudes on the other team. That's him. That's Jumpin' Jackie. You should've seen him, man. You had to be there.

9

THE GOAT

Some players, from the fissured concrete courts of New York and LA and Indianapolis and elsewhere, were more than memories. They were the heroes and idols of those who came after them, those who emulated them, those who surpassed them. They were heroes and idols even when they themselves, as time passed, receded into nothing more than names whispered during conversations on street corners and in barrooms. *Is that . . . ? Couldn't he . . . ? What the hell happened to him?*

Earl Manigault's youth was already leaking out of him. He was nearly twenty. He had been expelled from Benjamin Franklin High School in East Harlem. Marijuana. They booted a kid for that then, even a basketball supernova like The Goat. Earl was OK with it. School was never his thing. To him, a classroom was a cage. Always would be. You could make a good case, based on the evidence of Earl's life, that he preferred prison—not a metaphorical prison, but the real goddamn thing—to a classroom, to living under those rules, having to make those grades, with those responsibilities. Still, what choice did he have if he wanted to get beyond the playground, beyond the neighborhood? Summer of '64, and in a few weeks he was bound for a prep school in North Carolina, the Laurinburg Institute. There, just like at Ben Franklin, attending an academic exercise would be just a box to check to make sure he could play ball, maybe catch a scout's eye, maybe get the break that everyone who had seen him play—and there were only so many people who had seen him play—thought he ought to get. But he wouldn't last long there. He had to know it. Earl was never one to play the long game, think big picture. He chased the beautiful moment. Even if the pursuit might kill him. Which, essentially, eventually, it did.

So he was in a park in Harlem, on 143rd Street. Not just any park—Jumpin' Jackie Jackson's park. And it wasn't just Jackie's park because he had been playing there for years. It was Jackie's park because Jackie was . . . *working there*. Summer of '64, and Jackie had been with the Globetrotters for less than a year, and he was about to head into the army, and he didn't exactly have millions of dollars socked away from two seasons in the Eastern League. So he took a job as a supervisor in the city parks department, wearing a green uniform and living in a red house right inside the boundaries of this particular playground. Hell, he was spending most of his time in one or another of them anyway, playing pickup, surfing on the rippling waves of his Rucker dunk over Wilt Chamberlain. And Earl had been there. Earl had seen it.

Now he and Jackie were crossing paths at the park, Earl making a point to walk toward him, to catch his eye, and they looked at each other, and Jackie nodded at Earl. That was it. A nod. Earl would hold on to that nod for more than a quarter century as not just a moment but *the* moment of his basketball life. "I was just a kid," he said in 1990. "He was a man. He was the Park Man." The nod said that Jackie had heard of Earl. The nod said that Jackie had seen Earl play. The nod said that Jackie was familiar with Earl, with the "double dunk," maybe the best and most legendary of Earl's moves, an array of moves that no teenager who stood just six feet, one inch should be capable of, an array of moves that would blow your mind and rock your world if you happened to see one of them. And all of Harlem had seen all of Earl's moves, at the Rucker, at the parks. The nod said that Jackie had heard of those moves and seen those moves, too, and the nod said that

Earl had Jackie's approval and respect, that the torch would be passed from Jackie to Earl . . . King of the Courts . . . King of Harlem . . . if the kid could just manage not to set himself ablaze.

The kid could not.

The skeletal details of Earl Manigault's life would not seem to warrant the *New York Times* publishing his obituary on May 16, 1998, following his death two days earlier, at fifty-three, from congenital heart failure. He had a fleeting but memorable basketball career at Benjamin Franklin High. He spent two and a half years at Laurinburg that were not as memorable. He spent less than a year at Johnson C. Smith College that was even less memorable than his year at Laurinburg. He served sixteen months at Green Haven Prison in New York for drug possession. He held a few nondescript jobs later in his life: painting houses, mowing lawns, and—just like his idol, Jumpin' Jackie—working for a recreation department.

But publish an obit the *Times* did. For Manigault wasn't the average flameout. Kareem Abdul-Jabbar once referred to him as "the best ballplayer his size in the history of New York," the two of them teaming up and squaring off on courts throughout Harlem when Jabbar was named Lew Alcindor. Same with Connie Hawkins—The Goat went up with and against him and all the other flashy names with flashier games around the five boroughs: Herman "Helicopter" Knowings, Joe "The Destroyer" Hammond, Richard "Pee Wee" Kirkland, streetball royalty, dunkers and dazzlers and captivating contortionists who never got a shot in the NBA or never gave themselves a shot in the NBA because of bad luck or addiction or another tragic flaw. "When I was playing," Manigault once said, "there wasn't anyone who could stop me. I could go right or go left, and when I couldn't go right or left, I'd go over them." The neighborhood team for which he played, Young Life, dominated the city's other rec- and youth-center teams and ruled the pickup circuit at the parks and playgrounds. He received seventy-three college scholarship offers. The institutions might as well have set the stationery on fire. At Johnson C. Smith, he got his girlfriend pregnant, flunked his classes, returned to Harlem . . . and tried heroin. He sniffed it. He shot it. He used it and got off it and had to have it again. His habit cost him somewhere between $90 and $150 a day. "I'm a rich man," he once said. "Just look at my arms. All of my money is in my veins." By the time he said that, he was an old man at just forty-four, and his basketball career was long gone.

His unfulfilled promise and the frequency with which he talked publicly about it earned him a particular kind of fame. The fame on the flip side of sports celebrity. The fame that is intense within a particular sport's particular community—among the historians and the long-timers and the all-time greats who crossed paths with him years earlier, who still have a moving picture of him flickering in their minds, who mention him in passing if someone happens to ask them to remember when—but tepid among the general population. The fame born not of prime-time games and TV highlights and postgame interviews and endorsement deals, but of books and documentaries and newspaper and magazine articles and, in Manigault's case, a 1996 HBO television movie based on his life, with Don Cheadle playing him. *Oh, right, right, right. Yeah, I've heard of that guy.* The kind of fame that lends itself to replenishing and needs replenishing to persist.

Earl Manigault's life had enough depth, enough significance, and enough accessibility that he was a perfect muse for any journalist looking for a subject that took a sports story outside the arena. From the mid-1970s to the early 1990s, through basketball's rise alongside and in some ways beyond football and baseball into the mainstream of American pop culture, through the spike in urban crime and the crack epidemic and the "War on Drugs" and the decimation of the nation's cities, he could be the consummate cautionary tale, the wispy, soulful might-have-been who never made it because the system and his own weakness conspired against him. Go ahead. Pull up a chair or knock on his door, if you could pin down where he lived. He would tell you all about it, be genuinely wistful about his missed opportunities, open up and give you the goods. No athlete was in the passenger's seat for more reporter ride-alongs than The Goat. Peter Goldman caught up with him for *Sport* magazine in 1978—back when that periodical could go longform-for-longform with *Sports Illustrated*—writing that "the dunk was Earl's art form and his weapon. . . . The dunk was his flight from terrestrial life, as well—a split-second's freedom skying high over the mean streets and daring them to bring him back down." At least two writers not only told The Goat's story but volunteered to be part of it . . . by taking him into their homes. In 1997, Mark Bradley of *The Atlanta Journal-Constitution* called Manigault "the greatest basketball player you never saw," which was pretty much on the money for his readers, because how many people south of Baltimore ever caught a glimpse of The Goat? Ian O'Connor— the biographer of Bill Belichick, Mike Krzyzewski, and Derek Jeter—got his big break in sportswriting when he was a lowly, coffee-fetching clerk at the *New York Times* by profiling Manigault. The story ran without a byline—*Times* clerks were afforded that recognition only in rare instances—but Frank Deford read it, contacted the paper to find out who wrote it, and later offered O'Connor a job at *The National* because of it. "After I'd become a columnist at the New York *Daily News*," O'Connor told me, "Earl was still telling people that he made my career. He was not wrong."

In 1991, four years before he won the Pulitzer Prize for Commentary, *Newsday*'s Jim Dwyer shadowed Manigault for a day, driving him along Morningside Avenue through the Upper West Side and Harlem, noticing men on park benches waving and shouting at him as the car rolled by.

"Everyone, you see, loves a failure," Dwyer wrote.

It is difficult to believe that Manigault didn't relish at least a little of the attention. No one wanted to frame him or his day-to-day life that way, of course. Everyone always wants to think the best of a sports hero, and if Manigault could not be called "a nice guy," given some of the things he did and was alleged to have done in his life, he could at least be called an accommodating guy. And he was so accommodating to those who put his exploits to paper, who saw him on the court, who described what it was like when a basketball was in his hands and he was in the air, that there isn't much else to do but find the best of the best of those works, listen to the people who produced them, and, as much as you can, get out of the way.

On the playgrounds, he was a powerful magnetic figure who carried the dreams and ideals of every kid around him as he spun and twisted and sailed over all obstacles. When he fell, he carried those aspirations down with him. . . . He has symbolized all that was sublime and terrible about the city game.
—PETE AXTHELM, *THE CITY GAME*, 1970

A prodigy himself, plucked out of Yale in 1965 to join Tom Wolfe and Jimmy Breslin on the staff of the *New York Herald Tribune* as the paper's horse racing reporter, Axthelm was a feature writer and columnist at *Newsweek* when he began gathering string for *The City Game*. There was never a better match of writer and subject. Axthelm was a raconteur with insatiable appetites for drinking and gambling who—like the streetball legend he would introduce to the world—died young. Eleven months older than Manigault, Axthelm went at forty-seven. Liver failure. The Goat outlived him by nearly seven years. Their stars burned so bright, then burned out so fast.

Peter Vecsey regarded Axthelm as a contemporary. Before he became the *New York Post*'s NBA columnist, before he followed Axthelm's example in parlaying a print career into a television career, Vecsey lived in the Stuyvesant Town section of Manhattan, which is where Axthelm was living when he wrote *The City Game*. Both men drank at the same bar. There, Axthelm filled in Vecsey on the project. His narrative would volley between vignettes on the Knicks of that period—the Clyde Frazier, Willis Reed, Bill Bradley Knicks— and stories about New York's hoops culture. Vecsey wasn't yet as immersed in that culture as he soon would be.

"I wanted to know, who the fuck was Manigault?" Vecsey told me. "Who's Helicopter? Who are these people? We'd talk about it."

So they'd talk about The Goat. About the circular, off-white scar in the middle of his chest—the scar he gave himself when, after shooting up, he fell asleep with a cigarette in his hands. About his nickname, which he got not because people thought he was the Greatest of All Time but because people mispronounced his last name. About a kid who wore weights on his ankles to play pickup and still dunked the damn ball. About The Goat being at Ben Franklin High and Alcindor being at Power Memorial High at the same time—the similar stories about their talent, the disparate directions of their lives. About his standout games at Laurinburg: 35 points in one game, 28 points in another, a writeup in the *Charlotte Observer* that touted him as part of the "new talent" at Johnson C. Smith. About JCS's coach, Bill Mc-Cullough, who loved fundamental basketball and hated dunking and wouldn't let Goat be Goat. About trying heroin for the first time, after a pickup game and before a party, and his preferred location for shooting it: Frederick Douglass Boulevard at 115th Street. About a guy who understood why others were drawn to him. "There weren't too many little guys back then soaring to the hoop and dunking and blocking the shots of guys six-nine and six-ten," he once said. "I was a pioneer in that sense. That's why I became so popular." About a guy who, even in understanding his appeal, couldn't preserve the magic that inspired it.

Vecsey started heading up to Rucker Park every weekend, chatting up guys, playing ball himself. In all his hours there, he couldn't miss The Goat. "Just gravitated to each other," he said. "I'm guarding him and talking to him. That's when we became boys. That day. I said, 'Just don't dunk on my dome.' He was laughing." Separated from his wife, Vecsey offered to have Manigault stay in his apartment with him. They were roommates for two weeks. Manigault could have periods like that, when he could keep himself clean for a spell, fill everyone with hope. Fill himself with it, too. Only to find himself empty again before too long.

Manigault was released, on parole, from Green Haven on December 14, 1970. Eight months later, after reading about The Goat in *The City Game*, Bill Daniels, the owner of the ABA's Utah Stars, flew to New York, rode around Harlem in a black Cadillac limousine to track down Manigault, and offered him a tryout. A cult figure like The Goat, with his kind of backstory, might boost the Stars' ticket sales, and Daniels, a cable-TV magnate and self-described "Taft Republican," seemed to have something of a savior complex: he had hired or placed roughly twenty-five former inmates in jobs before extending a hand to Manigault. The tryout lasted a week. Three days before The Goat's twenty-seventh birthday, he and seven other rookies were cut.

"I was too far gone," he said. "Drugs and prison had really screwed me up. I couldn't play defense. My timing was off. My game needed a lot of time to get itself back together."

His game needed more time than he could ever give. Daniels offered to pay for Manigault's college education; he even arranged for him to get a basketball scholarship to Snow College in Ephraim, Utah. Manigault told Daniels that he had to return to Harlem to take care of some personal matters. He never came back to Utah.

A year after the tryout, at eleven o'clock one night in February, Leonard Shapiro of the *Washington Post* called the Pennington Hotel, near 125th Street, on a tip that Manigault was living there. The desk clerk answered.

"Excuse me," Shapiro said, "is Earl Manigault there?"

"Earl who?"

"Earl Manigault. He's supposed to be living in your hotel."

"Ain't no Earl living here, man. You must have the wrong number."

"Wait a minute. Earl Manigault lives there. You probably heard of him, you know. He's a basketball player."

"Oh yeah, yeah," the clerk said. "*That* Earl. Why didn't you say you wanted Earl? He's in Room 124. Wait a minute. I'll go see if he's in."

He wasn't. Shapiro went up to Harlem to find him. He found out that Manigault didn't have a job. He found out that Manigault's brother Rickie was supporting him. Then he found Manigault.

"Oh," he told Shapiro, chuckling, "I was just on my way to rob somebody."

Shapiro hoped he was kidding. But was he? With The Goat, one never knew. He was always providing another reason to be skeptical or cynical about his chances for redemption.

For instance: Around 4 a.m. on July 7, 1977, Manigault was in the Bronx, sitting inside a brand-new Lincoln Continental as the car lingered on the street near an older Pontiac. When two patrolmen spotted the cars and became suspicious, someone inside the Lincoln pointed a sawed-off shotgun at them. The police pursued the vehicles until the Lincoln pulled over at 187th Street and Bathgate, in the Belmont section of the borough. While the other men in the Lincoln fled, Manigault stepped out of the car and fought with the two cops. After Manigault was subdued, police tracked his accomplices to an apartment in Kingsbridge Heights, where one of the investigating officers conned his way through the front door by asking to use the bathroom. Inside, he found a few pounds of marijuana, blueprints to seventeen floors of the Plaza Hotel, and a cache of at least a dozen guns . . . all in the bathtub. Manigault was one of six men arrested and charged with resisting arrest and weapons and drug possession. The Plaza apparently had been the next planned target for him and his crew. When Goldman's piece about him in *Sport* magazine came out in '78, the timing was bitter and fitting: The Goat had just been behind bars.

One day, Vecsey shared the story of the incident and Manigault's arrest with Connie Hawkins.

"What's the big deal?" Hawkins said. "He was cleaning his guns."

It was a sharp, funny line by the Hawk. It was so freaking sad, as sad as anything Axthelm had written in *The City Game*, in what it said about The Goat.

At eighteen, he had such control on a basketball court that observers said only one other New York youth showed as much promise, a giant by the name of Lew Alcindor. . . . Though he could dazzle any crowd with his speed and moves, nothing tore people up as much as when he leaped, dunked the ball, caught it with the other hand, and dunked it again, all in the same floating vault.
—RICK TELANDER, *HEAVEN IS A PLAYGROUND*, 1976

That was it. That was The Goat's signature move. That was the double dunk—jam, catch, jam—and that was what Rick Telander had come to Brooklyn to see. Just thirty and already a correspondent for *Sports Illustrated*, he'd arrived in May 1974, intending to write a piece for the magazine on "the court wizards of Foster Park." Growing up in

Peoria, Illinois, not far from Bradley University, he had been lucky enough to see some of college basketball's best Black ballplayers up close: Bradley's Chet Walker, Wichita State's Dave Stallworth, Louisville's Wes Unseld, Cincinnati's Oscar Robertson. His father would take him to games at Robinson Memorial Fieldhouse.

"When we would see these dunks," he told me, "I knew I was seeing something that was utterly transcendent. I mean, the crowds went crazy. It was like, 'Are you kidding me?' I was always enamored of the dunk and the magic of it. You just didn't see it with white basketball. You were taught how to use the backboard. I was fascinated by the jumping ability that came with the great Black athletes, the sudden appearance of the culture and the very effective part of the game—to see any game suddenly change. It was like the forward pass coming to football."

He met The Goat one day at Rucker Park, after he'd decided that he would stay in Brooklyn most of the summer, after he'd decided to write a book—a book that turned out to be a classic. Goat was working at a playground, his playground, at Ninety-Ninth and Amsterdam, counseling and coaching kids, planning as usual to stay clean. Goat told Telander about a dream he'd had when he was fourteen years old and five foot nine, a dream about dunking the ball, and then the next day—"Can you dig?" he asked Telander in the retelling—he *did it*. He showed up at 129th and Seventh Avenue and threw one down two-handed. Fourteen. Five foot nine. *Can you dig?*

"He's an urban legend," Telander told me. "I compare him to Babe the Blue Ox, Paul Bunyan, Mike Fink, Daniel Boone, people you never saw but you heard about, the things they could do, John Henry the Steel Driving Man. We live on mythology, and the mythology of Earl Manigault and the tragic never-realized potential—we were suckers for that. It is sad, and it's something we can all identify with. The oral spoken history of it—each tale is embellished.

"That was part of it, because nobody ever filmed Earl Manigault playing. He never played, as far as I know, on an official team. He played in high school, but nobody was filming high school games then, so there was no video of him playing. I was thrilled just to meet him. I really liked Earl, a very thoughtful guy. He told me stuff that was so insightful. He had that kind of sad, wise attitude to him, and he knew what he had lost and could never regain. I remember him saying, 'You can always fall back on the hard times. I can always go back to being a nobody.'"

Of course he could, because in due time, someone else would come around, someone with a notepad and a pen and curiosity. And for a little while, The Goat wouldn't have to be a nobody anymore.

What is it about the dunk shot that puts basketball on a different level? Why is the shot so special? Rising is one thing. Getting off the ground higher than anybody expects you at six feet, one inch; leaving the sidewalk with its chalk marks and painted signs (ROBERT LOVES GINA, BOYS HIGH FULL OF PUNKS, PUSSY IS GOOD) and tiny pieces of glass from soda and beer bottles. Off that cement that even has blood stains and piss spots; the same cement or gravel or whatever kind of sidewalk they call it technically, the cement you have skinned your knees on as a child; off of it and away from it and into the air. Rising, flying, taking off above all of this, moving away from it at least temporarily . . .

Slamming it down. It is a climax, a release, a statement somehow of yourself. Your self. I am The Goat. Move, please. I am in flight. This is me, SLAM.
— BARRY BECKHAM, *DOUBLE DUNK: THE STORY OF EARL "THE GOAT" MANIGAULT*, 1980

Sometime in 1978, or maybe 1979—it has been a long time, and he was seventy-eight years old when we spoke about it—Barry Beckham was sitting in his office at Brown University, where he taught in the English department, when his phone rang. On the line was an acquaintance of Beckham's, an editor in the publishing industry.

"How would you like," the editor asked him, "to write a book about Earl Manigault?"

A native of Atlantic City, New Jersey, Beckham would visit family every summer in West Philadelphia when he was a nine-, ten-, eleven-year-old kid. He was close with one of his cousins, and around the corner from his cousin's home was Haddington Recreation Center, a frequent hangout for a teenaged Wilt Chamberlain. "I would see him there," Beckham told me. "I had always been fascinated with basketball." As he grew up, words became his world. After graduating from Brown himself, he had written two novels, but he wasn't familiar with New York's hoops scene and its phenoms.

"Who," Beckham asked, "is Earl Manigault?"

The editor filled him in.

Oh, man, Beckham thought. *A basketball player. I can do this.*

He went down to the city, signed a contract, and before he knew it, he was following The Goat around the streets of Harlem. Every few feet, The Goat would see someone who knew him—in Harlem, everyone knew The Goat. And every few feet, The Goat would tell that someone, *This guy is writing a book about me. Tell him some stories.*

Once he collected as many of those stories as he could, Beckham suggested that Manigault relocate to Providence, if he could, so that they could conduct several tape-recorded interviews. They ended up sharing Beckham's apartment. When the Brown University students learned Manigault was on campus, several of them, including some on the basketball team, would take him to the gymnasium. "They were just fascinated," Beckham said—by the man, not by his game. "Nothing spectacular happened. He just moved very gracefully, passing the ball, but no dunks. He had graceful movement, but by then, he was pretty much finished playing."

Beckham wrote the first draft of *Double Dunk* in the third person . . . and hated it. He re-wrote the entire thing in the second person (*Mad as you are, you'd like to knock somebody on his ass . . .*), giving it an intimacy and urgency fit for Manigault's roller-coaster life, a firsthand feel whenever Beckham described one of The Goat's dunks. Someone asked Beckham: What was it? What tripped him up? So Beckham asked Manigault.

No discipline, Manigault told him. *I didn't have any discipline.*

"He was very open, very humble," Beckham said. "I'm trying to think of another word for 'sad.'"

> Goat tales were growing tall: Playground historians told of a
> junior-high-school kid who could throw it in, backwards, from a
> flat-footed position anywhere inside the paint; of a 15-year-old
> who took quarters off the tops of backboards and "made
> change on the way down"; of a six-foot junkie who NBA centers
> begged, in the halfcourt circle before Rucker Senior League
> games, not to slam on them while their wives were looking. One
> dunk, executed on a Friday evening in 1963 in the packed gym
> of P.S. 113 on 113th Street, has become truly mythic. Various in-
> cantations have Earl beginning his leap against six-five Vaughn
> Harper and six-nine Val Reed anywhere from the foul line to the
> top of the key, and executing one or two 360-degree rotations
> in midair before slamming it in—backwards, forwards, one- or
> two-handed, Around the World, depends who you ask.
> —IVAN SOLOTAROFF, "SITTING ON THE RIM WITH EARL
>   MANIGAULT," *THE VILLAGE VOICE*, OCTOBER 1990

It was Solotaroff who uncovered the nod. It was Solotaroff who coaxed that story out of The Goat, who solidified the link between Earl and Jumpin' Jackie.

"There was nobody The Goat loved more than Jackie Jackson," he told me. "That's all Earl needed, was one inchoate nod from this guy. That's so much of it. It's the inchoate that Earl manifested. He became the living embodiment of it."

From *Esquire* to *Philadelphia* magazine, from his two books to his essays and journalism for the *Village Voice*, Solotaroff had the résumé and sensibility to make him and The Goat an ideal match of writer and subject. The inner city was his favorite tableau.

"All I ever wrote about for the *Village Voice*," he said, "were Black people."

By the time Solotaroff took him on, The Goat was missing his two front teeth, and his arms were a nasty web of needle tracks. "I hear people say, 'There goes Goat. He used to be the baddest man in the world. Drugs brought him down,'" Manigault said in a 1986 interview. "People tried to show me the way. I didn't listen." Solotaroff hung out with him for six months. They hit the courts a dozen times in that span, and each time, Solotaroff contemplated the circumstances and sympathies that had led to The Goat's fate—the people who wanted the best for him, who took pity on him, who cut corners for him.

"Think about how many judges let Earl slide," he told me. "I thought about this unsatiated love of their own basketball games as kids. He just appealed to so many people who thought, 'If things had gone a different way, I wouldn't be this fucking lawyer. I wouldn't be this judge. I wouldn't be a sportswriter. I'd be The Goat.' There was just something about him that was every man."

The Rucker enhanced and promulgated the gospel. Jumpin' Jackie, Connie Hawkins, Kareem Abdul-Jabbar—they spread it, too. Told the stories of the guys in New York who were better than they were. Hell, Jabbar was the greatest player of his era, and even he was saying that the dunk really belonged to The Goat, to this guy in New York who was just six-one and could never save himself from himself. Once, as he reported his *Village Voice* piece on The Goat, Solotaroff took him out to a bar somewhere on Columbus or Amsterdam. A Freddie Hubbard tune was playing throughout the place, a plaintive trumpet, the soundtrack of looking back. And Manigault said, *This guy's looking for his note, and he's not going to stop until he gets there. Look at all the beautiful things he's doing while he fails to find the note. And that's what my life was.*

That image is the one that lingers when I think of The Goat. I think of the dunks first, of what it must have been like to be there to see one of them, knowing what was inevitably ahead for him, knowing that everything he did on a basketball court was so splendid and that none of it could last. That is The Goat's legacy—whatever legacy he has, that is. He could have been, should have been, the star before the other stars, the dunker before the famous and remembered dunkers, before Doc and Michael and David Thompson and Vince Carter, the man who rose from darkness to unveil the double dunk and open the imaginations of everyone who came after him . . . only he could never handle the spotlight himself, not for any lengthy stretch of time, not even as long as the time it took for him to come down from his last hit of heroin. I imagine The Goat down, The Goat struggling, The Goat teetering again. Then The Goat gets it together for a while, again, and I imagine another writer, brilliant and willing and wondering how in the hell Earl Manigault threw it all away and still lived to tell so many about it, and that writer comes along to ask him questions and tell the world about him. Again. By the end, reliving the past was just about all he had, and in those moments and memories, in the familiar anecdotes and the worn-out one-liners, in the looking back at the dunks that were and even the dunks that should have been, I imagine The Goat happy.

10

THE HAWK'S HIGHEST FLIGHT

Were it not for a professional basketball league created on a whim . . . were it not for that league's first star . . . were that star not an all-time great player and an all-time influential dunker . . . would basketball be where it is today?

Inside a glass case, on the second floor of the Western Pennsylvania Sports Museum in the Strip District of downtown Pittsburgh, a priceless piece of Connie Hawkins's past was hidden from anyone who wasn't searching for it. The museum, twenty thousand square feet in all, houses altars to virtually every sacramental individual and institution in the city's sports history. The place is awash in black and gold, the colors of Pittsburgh's three major professional sports franchises: the Steelers, the Pirates, the Penguins. There's an exhibit on the "Steel Curtain" defense. There's Mario Lemieux on a wall, hoisting the Stanley Cup. There's a recording of the first Major League Baseball game broadcast on radio, on KDKA. There's a film, narrated by Joe Morgan, about the Negro Leagues' Homestead Grays. There are Super Bowl rings and hockey sweaters and game-used baseball bats and gloves and other memorabilia. There are exhibits devoted to high school football and boxing.

Amid these eye-catching displays, the case was easy to miss. It was four feet high, five feet long, and tucked away in a corner. Hanging from the ceiling a few feet away, thirteen lantern-like lights threw beams away from it and toward ten life-size photos of Pittsburgh sports heroes: Tony Dorsett, Franco Harris, Roberto Clemente, Bill Mazeroski, Lemieux, more. The room's alignment meant that the case and its contents were kept, quite literally, in shadow.

The items under glass were all connected to the first team to win a championship in the famous, and long defunct, American Basketball Association—the ABA. Every basketball fan knows about the ABA, even if he or she has never seen a live ABA game: red-white-and-blue ball, games in front of sparse crowds in armories and small-college fieldhouses, Afros and slam dunks everywhere. What every basketball fan likely doesn't know is that the first team to win the ABA championship remains the only Pittsburgh team to win a professional basketball championship: the 1967–68 Pittsburgh Pipers. The items under glass didn't reveal much about that achievement or the man most responsible for it. In fact, they barely acknowledged them at all.

On the far left side of the case rested a dull silver bowl: the 1967–68 ABA championship trophy. Mounted next to it were seven Topps basketball cards, the kind from a bubble-gum pack, featuring seven members not of the '67–'68 Pipers but of another ABA club: the 1971–72 Pittsburgh Condors. Mounted behind the cards were a Pipers game program, its cover bright orange, and a set of game notes, its cover black and dark green. But the only mention of Connie Hawkins was in black type on a small white placard near the trophy.

In 1968, NBA Hall of Famer Connie Hawkins . . . was a star player for the Pipers squad.

He was a bit more than that.

Shawn Hawkins wore a gleaming gold necklace with a giant H at its center, and he had the long body and long, goateed face of the grandfather he knew only so well, of the man whose legacy he had been fighting to fortify. Shawn was no Connie, but there was no shame in that, and he wasn't a hoops slouch himself—a six-foot-six forward who averaged more than 12 points over 60 games for Long Beach State in the mid-2000s, then played professionally overseas. Having just turned forty when we met for lunch in Pittsburgh in April 2023, he recalled a day when he was ten. It was 1992, the year that Connie was inducted into the Naismith Memorial Basketball Hall of Fame. For a time, Connie's house was a block from Willie Stargell's, and the summer basketball league that bore his name had blossomed into one of the best in the country. But his NBA career, just seven years, had not earned him the measure of wealth that many of his contemporaries enjoyed. The money hadn't lasted, but his friendship with Jerry Colangelo—a titan in the sport, the owner and president of the Phoenix Suns, the franchise that had brought Hawkins to the NBA—had. The Suns hired Hawkins to work in their community-relations department, as a team ambassador. He was moving to Phoenix.

"He was trying to sit me down and tell me, 'Things are going to change. I'm going to move to Phoenix,'" Shawn told me. "He was able to get on his feet again."

What do people think of when they think of basketball in Pittsburgh? Do people even think of basketball in Pittsburgh? Some people surely do, and when they do, they probably think of something tied directly to the slam dunk. No straw man here. They probably do. They might think of *The Fish That Saved Pittsburgh*, the 1979 cult-classic film about the fictitious (yet strangely realistic) Pittsburgh Pythons—starring Julius Erving, Kareem Abdul-Jabbar, Meadowlark Lemon, and, of course, Hawkins. They might think of Jerome Lane, the stout standout forward for the University of Pittsburgh in the late 1980s, who was responsible for one of the most famous dunks in basketball history: his shattering of the backboard at Fitzgerald Field House on January 25, 1988, against Providence. Actually, they might think first of Bill Raftery's famous call of that dunk for ESPN: "SEND IT HOME, JEROME!" Maybe they remember that John Calipari, before he coached Marcus Camby at UMass and Derrick Rose at Memphis and a couple of dozen NBA-bound skywalkers at Kentucky, was born in the 'Burgh's 'burbs.

Do they think of Connie Hawkins? Or, to put it better, do people think of Pittsburgh when they think of him? Slight chance it's the first thing. Hawkins represents any number of thoughts and memories and identities to those who knew him or watched him or have heard of him. He was a hero of New York prep and playground basketball mythology, a god of the game from Bedford-Stuyvesant and Boys High School, a predecessor of and influence on Erving and Jabbar. He was the face of perhaps the most egregious breach of justice in basketball history. He was forced to leave the University of Iowa, was banned by the NBA, was cost hundreds of thousands of dollars in income and endorsements, was tarred with the slimiest stigma in sports—*point-shaver*—even though there was never any evidence, any reasonable or logical reason to believe, that he had shaved any points. He won a lawsuit against the NBA—the league settled it with him for $1.3 million, but no one would deny that its acquiescence was a victory for him—that allowed him, finally, to play in the league. He was the first great player the Phoenix Suns had. And Connie Hawkins remains a redemption story still unfinished, because before Erving and Thompson showed up, The Hawk tore up the ABA while he was in Pittsburgh, the first pilot in a league-wide flight show, and there's barely a remembrance of him there. Shawn Hawkins is committed to finishing it. Shawn wants formal apologies from the NBA and the Manhattan District Attorney's Office, which investigated and coaxed a false confession out of a callow, teenaged Connie. He wants more recognition and some acclaim for the first true superstar in the first professional league that put the dunk at the center of its branding and identity. He's chasing the justice his grandfather didn't receive.

"I have pictures where he's going around Kareem and those types of guys," Shawn told me. "He did it in the summer leagues all the time, in the years where it wasn't done in the NBA because of his years of exile. People didn't get to see his best years. The years when people would have got to know those dunks were the years he was playing in the parks and in the ABA. He should have been playing at the highest level at that time."

This has been a quest for him, and joining him in that quest, and joining us at our restaurant table, were two people close to him. The first was his girlfriend, Renee Robinson, a former Division I basketball player at Morgan State, who had played in the Connie Hawkins League herself as a kid. The second was Vince Lackner, a Harvard alumnus who played for the Crimson men's basketball team, now a Pittsburgh tax attorney who had befriended Connie and played pickup ball with and against him for years.

"Here in Pittsburgh," Shawn was saying, "he wasn't getting his due—i.e., how we're talking about him now. The museum, they have the one thing about the Pipers and about him. They don't highlight it. The things he's done for this city and was able to accomplish, despite all the obstacles in front of him, should be celebrated at the highest level here."

In the minds of those who knew or knew of him, Connie Hawkins is all those labels and figures and more. "He was Julius before Julius. . . . He was Michael before Michael," Larry Brown once said. "He was simply the greatest individual player I have ever seen." He is certainly all those lofty comparisons and designations before anyone thinks of him as *the star of the first ABA championship team*. But the truth is that, when it comes down to what he could do on a basketball court, when it comes down to what he did on a basketball court, that season in the shadows was his finest hour. That season was Connie Hawkins at his best.

By age eleven, Hawkins was six foot two and could dunk. At Boys High, he was a Parade All-American, and he idolized Elgin Baylor, sometimes sneaking into the old Madison Square Garden, on Eighth Avenue between 49th and 50th Streets, with his friends to watch Baylor whenever the Lakers came to town to play the Knicks. Baylor had entered the NBA at a time when circumstances were favorable to him; the league had adopted the twenty-four-second shot clock and widened the lane from six feet to twelve just a few years before his debut. At six foot five, he was three inches shorter than Hawkins would grow to be, but he could leap so high and hang in the air for so long that he created the template for the guards and forwards who would give the sport so much of its glamor and grace. "The pro game suits my freelance style of play," Baylor wrote in his autobiography, *Hang Time*. "I like a fast pace. I thrive in an offense that runs."

Hawkins, from his youngest days in the game, could thrive in either a fast or slow tempo, could get out on a fastbreak and swoop in for a dunk or post up, waving the basketball above his head with one hand as if he were playing keep-away with a child. At our restaurant table, Shawn shook his head in admiring disbelief at that image. His grandfather's hands were ten and a half inches long and eleven inches wide.

"Fifth-largest in NBA history," Lackner said. "His hands were so big they could palm Sunday."

"He was able to dunk three balls," Shawn said. "My granddad had huge hands. He would throw one up, then would have two in his hands, dunk those, then dunk the last one on the way down."

"You know how many likes that would get on Instagram?" Renee said.

Too many to count. Hawkins was such a prodigy that, in the summer of 1958 or 1959—no one could quite pin down the year, not even the *New York Times*, which left the detail murky in a February 2002 article—he played in a legendary pickup game at St. Andrew's Playground in Bedford-Stuyvesant. Among the game's competitors were Brown, Oscar Robertson, Lenny Wilkens, Jim Brown—perhaps the greatest football player of all time—and Bob Gibson—one of the greatest right-handed pitchers of all time. At the time of the game, Hawkins would have been sixteen or so. Robert Cornegy Jr., a former Bed-Stuy councilman, was a terrific basketball player himself, nearly seven feet tall. He would go to St. Andrew's often to watch Hawkins. "Between his leaping ability and his ability to control the ball in his hand," Cornegy once said, "it seemed like he would stay in the air forever."

Boys High won the city championship in Hawkins's junior and senior seasons, and Hawkins's duels against Wilt Chamberlain and his role as Jumpin' Jackie Jackson's wingman—and Jackie's role as his—lifted him to must-see status at Rucker. "I'd go watch him," Kareem Abdul-Jabbar wrote in his memoir *Giant Steps*, "and not only learn new moves, I'd get taught a whole new concept of the game. These were my Sunday revelations. The Hawk would snare a rebound and swoop downcourt as each of his teammates circled in their own improvised patterns. He would fake his man a couple of times, as if testing his engines, and then gun it. Palming the ball, waving it around in one of his huge hands, he'd take off some 20 feet out and glide to the basket like a Black Phantom, then hang, hesitate while two or three defenders each took their separate shots at him, somehow circle underneath the basket, let go of the ball, and put it in off the backboard—with English. All he needed to top it off would've been a victory roll. No one had ever done that before. No one had thought about doing it."

Every college in America wanted him. Every college in America couldn't have him, because every school in America wasn't willing to do what it took to get him. That is, every school wasn't willing to bend its academic admission benchmarks for a student who grew up poor, even by the standards of Bed-Stuy, and who needed so many years of tutoring that he didn't reach an eleventh-grade reading level at Boys until he was about to graduate. The University of Iowa was willing. The Hawkeyes had a not-so-secret weapon: Arlo Wilson, the Iowa alumnus of all Iowa alumni, the Iowa booster of all Iowa boosters, the president of the Iowa Touchdown Club . . . and a New York–based businessman with enough dollar bills to lay a footpath for Hawkins from Bed-Stuy to Iowa City in the fall of 1961. Grades? Just put Connie on academic probation. Give him time to adjust and figure out those college classes. A fake job at a gas station? Done. Tuition money and pocket cash under the table? Connie got $150 a month, which was beyond anything he knew or dreamed. But those ploys weren't as seedy or as damaging to his reputation, to his future, as another association he had already made would be, this one right in the neighborhood.

Jack Molinas was a Brooklyn guy, too, book-smart and street-smart and a damn good small forward—Stuyvesant High, Columbia University, less than a season with the Fort Wayne Pistons before the NBA banned him for betting on games, then Brooklyn Law School. He had shaved points at Columbia, part of the New York–based scandals of 1950 and 1951 that rocked the sport. He could sweet-talk anyone, and at six foot six and two hundred pounds, connected to bosses within the Genovese crime family, he could use other methods of persuasion if he had to. Connie Hawkins was poor, so poor that his mother's apartment had no hot water, so poor that his shoelaces were rope and wire. Connie Hawkins was naive and ignorant, so ignorant that he didn't know that Jack Molinas had been barred from pro basketball, so naive and trusting that he never questioned why a street-smart Brooklyn guy would sidle up to him in the first place. When Jack Molinas wanted to find another player to loop into his gambling network and point-shaving scheme, Connie Hawkins was an easy mark.

Hawkins wasn't yet a senior at Boys High when, at the Manhattan Beach courts in Brooklyn, Molinas sidled up to him. This was how Molinas and Joe Hacken, his partner in fixing, worked—get to a needy kid early, lure him into the operation, groom him, ask him to play in a few charity games for a few bucks, then, once the kid was playing college ball and Molinas and Hacken had established a relationship with him, push him to fiddle with the point spread. From 1957 to 1961: four years, 27 schools, 36 players paid $70,000 to influence 43 games—the scheme stretched like poisoned taffy across the country.

In December 1960, while Hawkins was back in New York between semesters, Molinas gave him a sum of money. Some published reports have said it was $200; some have said it was $250. Hawkins considered it a loan, insisting thereafter that there was never any mention or expectation that, by accepting the money, he had agreed to throw games. But after detectives from New York County District Attorney Frank Hogan's office arrested Dave Budin, a schoolteacher and former Brooklyn College player who was working for Molinas, Budin named names, implicating several players who supposedly were involved in the point-shaving scams. He included Hawkins, even though he had never met him. Hogan's prosecutors brought

Hawkins and another city high school standout, Roger Brown, in for questioning.

"The police put me and Roger in a hotel for two weeks," Hawkins once said, "and every day for eight hours, we had to go to the district attorney's office. They asked me so many confusing questions that my head began to spin. They didn't believe that it was a loan. They didn't believe that I knew nothing about crooked ball games. They didn't believe me when I didn't even know what a point spread was. Those people wouldn't believe me if I told them my own name. They said I was trying to protect Molinas. I was frightened. I thought they were going to put me in jail if I didn't say what they wanted."

On its face, the accusation that Hawkins had thrown games made no sense. He was an eighteen-year-old freshman at Iowa, and even if he hadn't been on academic probation, he wouldn't have been allowed to play for the Hawkeyes—because *no* freshmen were allowed to play varsity college basketball then, per NCAA rules. (The exception to those rules was the 1951–52 season, when the association gave freshmen an extra year of eligibility to make up for the shortage of players because of the Korean War.) Even if he had wanted to shave points, he never would have gotten on the court to carry out the sleazy act. But his fourteen days in front of the prosecutors were such a stew of contradictions and denials and confessions made out of terror and without a lawyer that, although Hawkins was neither charged with a crime nor even mentioned in the indictment against Molinas, the stigma of being a cheat, the perception and presumption of guilt, stuck to him anyway. Iowa coach Sharm Scheuerman told Hawkins it would be best for everyone if Connie left school voluntarily; his departure was, in effect, an expulsion. No other college would touch him. The NBA had rules against gambling or associating with gamblers. Its franchises blackballed him. He was eligible for the draft each year after his exit from Iowa, and no team picked him, until finally NBA commissioner Walter Kennedy and the league's board of governors officially banned him in 1966.

Where did he go? Where could he go? He had to go to a place

where he could get a fresh, clean start, or something close to it. He had to go to a place that wasn't a basketball place, not really. He went to Pittsburgh.

The name of the housing project where Shawn Hawkins lived his earliest and roughest years was Robinson Court, in the Hill District of Pittsburgh. The grandson of a Hall of Famer, growing up in a housing project? Yes. What did Connie Hawkins have to hand down? "He was always fighting for crumbs when he deserved a bigger portion," Shawn said. You couldn't get a taxi to drop you off in Robinson Court or pick you up in Robinson Court. You couldn't even order pizza in Robinson Court, Shawn told me. No delivery guy would venture there. The kids who got out were the ones who could play ball. "Any good basketball player you can name in the city of Pittsburgh is normally from the Hill District," Shawn said. "My grandfather had a house in Point Breeze, the east end, by Homewood."

John Edgar Wideman, who was from Homewood, wrote extensively about the neighborhood, and he probably spoke for many of its natives when, in *Hoop Roots*, he wrote this:

Growing up, I needed basketball because my family was poor and colored, hemmed in by material circumstances none of us knew how to control, and if I wanted more, a larger, different portion than other poor colored folks in Homewood, I had to single myself out. . . . Fear and love, love and fear raised the stakes of the game. Engendered the beginnings of a hunger, the hunger driving the serious players I admire most, who never seem satisfied no matter how well they perform.

It was one neighborhood in Pittsburgh. It could have been any similar neighborhood in America. It was John Edgar Wideman: point guard for the University of Pennsylvania, decorated novelist. It could have been Oscar Robertson in Indianapolis, Bill Russell in Oakland, Wilt Chamberlain in West Philadelphia. It could have been Connie Hawkins in the very neighborhoods that Wideman knew so well. "Even though Pittsburgh has a rich basketball history, it's not a basketball city," Shawn told me. No, it isn't. Not compared to cities that are basketball cities. Pittsburgh has no NBA franchise and nothing comparable to it. "The thing we did have," Shawn said, "was Connie Hawkins."

He arrived in September 1961, the major acquisition of the Pittsburgh Rens, one of the eight franchises that composed Abe Saperstein's attempt to take on the NBA: the American Basketball League. A nightclub owner named Lenny Litman ran the team. Hawkins hadn't been arrested, hadn't been charged. Why not sign him? So Litman did. Hawkins was nineteen, in the prime of his life, though when he suited up for the Rens, he wrapped himself in enough athletic tape that Herschell Turner, who played in the ABL and was later one of Hawkins's teammates with the Pipers, once said, "Johnson & Johnson should have sponsored him." In that '61–'62 season, Hawkins was the ABL's most valuable player, which would have been wonderful and remembered around Pittsburgh forever . . . except the league lasted only until December 1962, when it folded. That year-plus was enough time, though, for Hawkins to grow close to Litman's brother David and David's wife Roslyn, both of whom were attorneys.

To Saperstein, an opportunity that closed somewhere opened another opportunity somewhere else. He signed Hawkins to play for the Globetrotters, and Connie toured with the team for four years, a time in exile that would later leave him bitter for reasons beyond his standing outside a locked window, peering in at life in the NBA. He hated having to kowtow to Saperstein's preferences and prejudices, having to play what he called "the role of the grateful boy," knowing that Abe wouldn't approve if Hawk started driving a fancy car or—God forbid—dating a white woman. The typical Globetrotters show didn't sit well with him, either. "What we were doing out there," he once said, "was acting like Uncle Toms, grinning and smiling and dancing around. That's the way they told us to act, and that's the way a lot of white people like to think we really are."

After Kennedy formalized Hawkins's ban from the NBA in '66, Connie's connection to the Litman family, a bond that had grown tighter even while he was touring with the Globetrotters, changed the course of his career and his life. The parks and playgrounds and summer leagues remained his domain, the place where he could prove he belonged with, and often above, the best players in the world. But pickup games in parks and playgrounds didn't pay the bills. David and Roslyn Litman, in November 1966, filed an antitrust lawsuit on Hawkins's behalf against the NBA. And after entrepreneurs and promoters Constantine Seredin and Dennis Murphy, among others, gathered enough investors to put the ABA together—"There's only one basketball league," Murphy once said, "so why not have another?"—and persuaded George Mikan to serve as its commissioner, Hawkins finally got a genuine second chance. Mikan cleared Hawkins and Roger Brown to play, and David Litman persuaded Gabe Rubin, the Pipers' owner and president, to sign Hawkins to a two-year contract worth $40,000—a pittance for the quality of player the Pipers were getting. The brief length of the deal mattered greatly to Litman, though, because he wanted to make sure Hawkins could jump immediately to the NBA, with no contractual restrictions or obligations, if they won their lawsuit.

Come the fall of 1967, Pittsburgh's experiment with elite professional basketball could commence. It was a dicey arrangement from the start. The Pipers were, according to one writer, "perpetually broke." Rubin reached a three-year agreement with Charles Strong, the executive director of Civic Arena, for 29 home games in the team's first season. The Pipers had to share the Arena with the Penguins, and it was always unavailable on the last Saturday of March, when it hosted a dog show. Accused of stealing the franchise's name from the Cleveland Pipers, who had played in the American Basketball League earlier in the decade, Rubin gave two reasons for selecting the moniker: One, Pittsburgh was "the home of pipe mills," he said, "before there was a Cleveland." Two, he was fond of Carnegie Mellon University's bagpipe band. (The school, as of October 2023, offered a major in bagpiping.) The squad's uniforms were orange and turquoise—the same color scheme as that of the Flint Tropics, Will Ferrell's fictitious team in the 2008 ABA spoof *Semi-Pro*. Hawkins wasn't the only Pipers player barred from the NBA. Charlie Williams, the team's best guard, had failed to report a bribe that had been offered to one of his teammates at Seattle University. When Pipers coach Vince Cazzetta called him and asked if he wanted to come to Pittsburgh to play, Williams volleyed the question back: "What kind of players do you have?"

"Well," Cazzetta said, "I have Connie Hawkins."

"I'm coming," Williams said.

The Hawk was a magnet to draw players to Pittsburgh and a curiosity to them once they arrived. He claimed that, during his travels with the Globetrotters, he had become fluent in fifty to sixty languages. "He learned one word in every country," Barry Leibowitz, another Pipers guard, said, "so he thought he was fluent in fifty or sixty languages. And nobody was going to argue with him." The beauty and substance of Hawkins's game, though, was the more powerful tractor beam, the aspect of him that the Pipers would remember for years thereafter. Steve Vacendak had led Duke to two Final Fours, in 1964 and '66, as a combo guard, and he met Hawkins for the first time at the Pipers' training at the University of Pittsburgh. "He was just astounding," Vacendak told me. "I had never been around someone who was so capable of not only dunking the ball but doing it in spectacular fashion. First of all, he was long. He had huge hands, long arms, long legs, and he was built more along the lines of a grasshopper, I think. I don't even know what creature he would be comparable to. His body wasn't his dominant feature. His arms and his legs were. They happened to be attached to his body, but he was notably slender."

Vacendak thought Hawkins a nice guy, someone who rarely got angry, even on the court. "But when Connie wanted to get back at someone who was being super-aggressive," he said, "he would dunk on them or reach around them or make them look funny. He'd do something like he was saying, 'OK, you tried that stuff. Now take some of this.' It wasn't a physical move. It wasn't him colliding with the guy's body or pushing him back. He didn't do that much at all because he could reach around him, and he knew how to use his arms and legs. He knew how to leverage his body, and he knew how to leverage someone else's body."

And he had advantages, by playing in the ABA that season, that he wouldn't have had playing in the NBA. No Wilt. No Russell. No Nate Thurmond. Fewer taller, bruising centers planting themselves under the basket. The league had a three-point shot, which drew players away from the lane and the rim, which in turn opened up driving lanes.

"It was beautiful," Vacendak said. "There were so many dunks and long shots and people going up and down the court. It was amazing. That first year, the ABA was more like the Rucker League than the NBA was. They weren't going to come out there and bounce the ball and bounce the ball and score 82 points. The fans wanted offense, and they got it. Look at the players who came through after that first year."

He named them: Erving, George Gervin, Charlie "The Helicopter" Hentz, who in November 1970, while playing with the Carolina Cougars, delivered two backboard-shattering dunks at Dorton Arena in Raleigh.

"These guys were just wonderful, and a very important part of the dunking aspect is that the ABA forced the NBA to become more colorful, to be more open. We took them and turned them on their ear.

"There was a distinct thirst, if not hunger, for the dunk, and the ABA filled that."

There was little thirst, however, for pro basketball in Pittsburgh. No one could blame Hawkins. He was scoring more than 24 points and grabbing more than 13 rebounds a game when, in early February 1968, he suffered a hematoma of the gastrocnemius—a swollen left calf. The injury kept him out of one game, but he returned to play through it and through two bad knees and was even better in the second half of the season. He finished as the league's most valuable player and leading scorer, putting up 26.8 points a night, but few people showed up on those nights to see him. The Pipers averaged 3,200 spectators for their games at Civic Arena, which wasn't bad by the standards of that first ABA season. But in a town with a long-established love affair with prep sports and a blue-collar sensibility that made it fertile ground for hockey to flourish, the Pipers struggled to cultivate a loyal fan base. It didn't help that they scheduled most of their home games for Tuesday and Friday nights, forcing them to compete for interest with the area's high school basketball teams. That they won the Eastern Division with a 54–24 record, the best among the ABA's eleven franchises that season, registered with the Western Pennsylvania public only so much. Sometimes, Bill Neal, a longtime columnist and reporter for the *Pittsburgh Courier*—for a spell the most widely circulated Black newspaper in the United States—would walk from the local YMCA to Hawkins's favorite restaurant with him, cars zipping past them. "You wouldn't hear a horn blow," Neal told me. "In comparison, he took me to Harlem for the Rucker years later, and it was like walking with Jesus. Horn. 'Hawk!' Horn. 'Hawk! Put your money away. It's no good here.' People didn't appreciate him as much in Pittsburgh. The Hill District, they went to the games. But Connie was very much taken for granted. He wasn't 'The Great Connie Hawkins' because people didn't know."

The Pipers breezed through the first two rounds of the ABA's postseason tournament. The region reacted with a yawn. One of the first-round games at Civic Arena, against the Pacers, drew just 2,189 spectators. The parking lot was full, but only because the Western Pennsylvania Restaurant Association was holding a food fair in the downstairs exhibition hall. Cazzetta had been lamenting the dormant atmosphere at his team's home games for months, and now the play-offs were no better. "I know the town went crazy when the Pirates won the World Series," he had said during the season. "Well, I don't expect the town to go crazy if we win the [championship], but I do wish I could notice a little feeling, a little enthusiasm. The only team in pro ball that has won more games is the Philadelphia 76ers. We have the highest [winning] percentage in the American Basketball Association—the most valuable player, Connie Hawkins. Yet it doesn't feel electric in the city. It's almost a feeling like, 'Who cares?' And I can't get used to this."

In the finals, the Pipers' opponents were the New Orleans Buccaneers. It took Hawkins's scoring 47 points in Game 4, a 106–105

Pittsburgh victory at Loyola University Field House, to tie the series at two, but his brilliance came with a cost. While making a cut late in the game, he tore the medial collateral ligament in his right knee. Hawkins sat out Game 5, which the Buccaneers won in Pittsburgh, 111–108, putting them within one win of the championship and putting the Pipers on the edge of elimination.

By skipping Game 5, Hawkins had six days to rest before Game 6 back in New Orleans. "If Connie can continue his recovery," Rubin said, "he will play, and with Hawkins in there, I feel we can win." What was developing was the kind of story that makes sports compelling: the wounded superstar, playing through pain when his team needed him most. The narrative's drama only intensified when the Buccaneers carried a 13-point lead into halftime. But the Pipers outscored them 59–40 in the second half, and Hawkins performed as if he were in perfect health. He finished with 41 points and 12 rebounds. The Pipers won, 118–112, to force Game 7 at home. By then, the people of Pittsburgh had caught on that they had a chance to celebrate a championship, something the city hadn't done since Mazeroski's ninth-inning home run beat the Yankees in the 1960 World Series . . . nine years earlier.

A crowd of 11,457 filled Civic Arena on the night of Saturday, May 4. His right leg still wrapped in a fraying white bandage from the top of his thigh to just below his knee, Hawkins managed 20 points and 13 rebounds, acting as much as a threatening defensive presence as he did the locus of the Pipers' offense. In one Associated Press photo from the game, Hawkins leaps in the lane—his legs straight down below him, his arms splayed to the sides as if he were hanging from a crucifix, each of those limbs so taut with muscle that they look like hawsers—to block a shot. The ball was in Hawkins's hands for the final seconds of the Pipers' 122–113 victory; he dribbled out the clock, moving with a slight limp, as fans streamed down from the stands onto the court. In the champagne-soaked locker room, he hugged a few of his teammates, shook hands with all of them, and wept.

Two years later, Willis Reed, the New York Knicks' center and captain, established himself as the everlasting embodiment of the Wounded

Superstar Narrative, and for good reason. Hobbled by a torn muscle in his right thigh, he emerged from a tunnel onto the court at Madison Square Garden before tip-off of Game 7 of the NBA Finals, throwing thousands of Knicks fans into ecstasy, inspiring his team to wipe out Chamberlain, Jerry West, and the Los Angeles Lakers by 14 points. Connie Hawkins was Willis Reed before Willis Reed. The difference was that his stage wasn't the biggest and brightest in the world of basketball. His stage was a town that barely cared. He simply didn't have nearly as many eyes on him, and those eyes wouldn't stay on him. That June, Bill Erickson, a Minnesota attorney, bought a majority share of the Pipers from Gabe Rubin and moved them to Minneapolis.

"Taking the ball and swinging it," Shawn Hawkins was saying, his voice rising, "he was the first to do that, and he doesn't get any credit for it. They give Dr. J the credit for it."

Credit was hard to come by for Connie Hawkins. He had earned a fair amount in the aftermath of the Pipers' championship. Bill Sharman, who had been coaching the NBA's San Francisco Warriors and left to take a job with the ABA's Los Angeles Stars, had attended Game 7 of Pipers-Buccaneers. "Hawkins is as good as anyone in the NBA," Sharman said. "I don't say he's as valuable as Bill Russell is to the Celtics, but he can do more things than Russell. He's amazing." Yes, he was the most amazing basketball player in the world who couldn't play in the NBA . . . until David Wolf joined the Litmans in making it a life's mission to clear Hawkins's name.

Wolf had gone to Columbia University's journalism school, wore a black toupee, and possessed a sharp intellect and a gruff personality. Before becoming a well-respected boxing manager—Ray "Boom Boom" Mancini was one of his fighters—Wolf embarked on an investigation into Hawkins's ostracism and the dubious reasons for it. It led to one of the most important pieces of sports journalism ever published: his comprehensive treatise, in the May 16, 1969, issue of *Life* magazine, detailing why Hawkins's banishment from the NBA was unjust.

"Evidence recently uncovered," he wrote, "indicated that Connie Hawkins never knowingly associated with gamblers, that he never introduced a player to a fixer, and that the only damaging statements about his involvement were made by Hawkins himself—as a terrified, semiliterate teenager who thought he'd go to jail unless he said what the D.A.'s detectives pressed him to say."

In the court of public opinion, Wolf's piece—the foundation of *Foul!*, his seminal 1972 biography of Hawkins—was the finest amicus brief anyone could have filed on Hawkins's behalf. A month after the article's publication, Kennedy settled Hawkins's lawsuit and lifted the NBA's ban against him. He entered the league at last at twenty-seven; the Suns had won a coin toss with the Seattle SuperSonics and won his rights.

He never left Pittsburgh, though, neither in spirit nor body. "People would drop everything to watch The Hawk play," Father Jack O'Malley, a priest and a friend of Hawkins's, once said. "Then you would talk to him like he was your next-door neighbor." Hawkins and Bill Neal founded the Connie Hawkins League in 1975, a year before he retired, and at a banquet one year honoring Hawkins, the guest speaker told the guests: *If there had not been a Connie Hawkins, there would not have been a Dr. J.* The next morning, when Neal accompanied him to the airport, the speaker handed him a card and said, *Bill, here's my number. If Connie Hawkins ever needs anything, you call me.* Then Julius Erving flew home.

Hawkins himself played in the league for three years. He stuck to pickup from then on, usually at Mellon Park in Point Breeze. "Mellon remains a magnet on summer weekends for Pittsburgh's high school, college, pro, and playground royalty," Wideman, who played frequently at the park, wrote in 1984 in *Brothers and Keepers.* "The court's run down now. Scarred backboards, rims bent and loose, two cracks in the asphalt steps. Neglected, going to seed, the buckling, gray rectangle is a microcosm of the potholed city. Tradition and location conspire to preserve Mellon's uniqueness. Over the years, Pittsburgh's best have always played at Mellon. And since the park's not really in anybody's neighborhood, it's a no-man's land, the perfect place for a battlefield, one of the only inner-city basketball courts where white and Black players confront one another." Vince Lackner, the attorney and former Harvard guard, was one of those white players who confronted The Hawk. He got to face him for the first time in 1981.

"I was seeing the legend with the grapefruit-like handle of the ball," Lackner told me. "You're awestruck the first couple of times when you realize who he is."

"Think about this," Shawn said. "You think about the origin of the dunk and how basketball evolved. Wilt, Bill Russell—those are strictly inside guys. Those guys played nowhere but inside. But my grandfather is the first hybrid. He's the first guy to go inside/outside. He's the first LeBron. He's the first Magic, the first Julius Erving, the first guy to be six-eight, six-nine, to play multiple positions and bring the ball up."

How much earlier might the dunk have become an essential aspect of basketball had Hawkins not remained shrouded in such obscurity for so long? How much sooner would the sport have advanced in its popular appeal if The Hawk had been a household name even in the town that was his home for the prime of his career? Brady Smith, the Western Pennsylvania Sports Museum's director of marketing and communications, told me in May 2023 that while there was no definitive timetable for a new, more comprehensive basketball exhibition, "it will likely happen in the next two to four years." As of this writing, Shawn Hawkins is still waiting on behalf of his grandfather, who died in October 2017, for a formal apology from the NBA and from the Manhattan District Attorney's Office. The work that David Wolf began with his marvelous journalism has never ended. The search for the justice that Connie Hawkins is owed and the respect that he deserves—in the sport of basketball, in the city that ought to have embraced him fully long ago—continues. The push to find him a place in the light goes on.

II

THE BAN

Basketball was changing, improving. The players were getting taller, stronger, nimbler. The game was reaching more people, creating more fans. This progression was picking up speed and seemed unstoppable. Damn if some of the sport's power people didn't try anyway. They had their reasons. Those who stand in the way of something better always do.

Nothing could seem stranger in retrospect. Imagine removing the home run from baseball or the forward pass from football. Imagine being in charge of a sport, and imagine that a particular play had emerged organically from athletes themselves at all strata of that sport. Those athletes had taken it upon themselves to test the boundaries of the rules and, in doing so, had made the sport better, more enjoyable to take part in, more enjoyable to watch. Imagine that this play unleashed an inherent freedom and euphoria that had been dormant within the sport for too long. Imagine that this play allowed athletes to explore the sport's physical and emotional possibilities and was emblematic of the sport's expansion and accessibility, of its breach of the country's race- and class-based barriers. Then, imagine that this play was deemed impermissible, that the people in charge of the sport had determined that the play wasn't actually part of the sport at all.

On March 28, 1967, the National Basketball Committee—the organization that enacted the rules for US college and high school basketball at the time—did that. *All* of it. It banned the slam dunk.

In a halting voice over the phone, the old man asked if I would call him back in ten minutes. He needed a moment to ruminate on the topic we would be discussing. David Lattin had turned seventy-nine less than two weeks before, and there is no telling how many times someone has asked him to travel, in his mind, back to March 19, 1966. To the championship of the NCAA men's basketball tournament. To Texas Western, the first team with an all-Black starting lineup to reach a championship game, with Lattin as one of those starters and one of the team's stars. To Kentucky and head coach Adolph Rupp, the archetypes of blue-blooded and white-skinned basketball. To the Miners' 72–65 victory and its ripples and implications and its status as a racial and cultural touchstone—the film *Glory Road* and the books and Don Haskins and all the tremors from that game that shook the sport thereafter.

"We were just youngsters trying to win," Lattin told me, "and we had no idea how big it was going to be later or what it meant. Coach Haskins knew, but we didn't."

Coach Haskins was smart. Against Kentucky, he understood the weapon he had in Lattin and how to best wield him. Six foot seven and 225 pounds in his playing days, a Houston native, Lattin had taken a detour before landing with Haskins in El Paso. He had first enrolled, in 1963, at Tennessee A&I (now Tennessee State University), a historically Black college that had won three straight NAIA championships from 1957 through 1959. He left A&I after just a year; having been suspended for a minor disciplinary infraction and seeking a higher quality of basketball, he later accepted Haskins's scholarship offer to play at Texas Western. But he made at least one lasting impression in

Nashville. When Perry Wallace debuted for Vanderbilt in 1967, he became the first Black varsity basketball player in the history of the Southeastern Conference. In junior high and high school, Wallace played so much pickup ball at A&I that he came to know and admire Lattin for his combination of flair and power on the court.

"He would get the ball, and he would go down the floor," Wallace once said, "and he would do the Michael Jordan dunk. His legs were spread apart the same way, and he'd be flying through the air. And everybody under the basket went, 'Oooooh, shit! Time to leave. Time to go. Don't even mess with this. Get out of the way.'"

During practices at Texas Western, Lattin would dunk the ball one hundred times, and before each game, in the layup line, he would jam it six times, seven times, eight. "Just to make a point," he wrote in his autobiography, *Slam Dunk to Glory*. "I brought cockiness, coolness, a certain 'take you down' attitude to the team."

Kentucky was a terrific squad, entering the game with a 27–1 record, its leading scorer—at more than 22 points a game—a lean six-foot-four guard named Pat Riley. But the Wildcats, dubbed "Rupp's Runts," didn't have a starter who was taller than six-five—or who was Black—and Haskins banked that Lattin could take them down mentally. "I knew a lot was being made of the white-Black thing," Haskins once wrote, "and although I didn't care about it, I wasn't going to ignore it." So he told Lattin: *David, on our first possession, I want you to take it to the rim and dunk on someone. Just knock them over. Just dunk it like they ain't never seen it dunked.* Haskins didn't care if Lattin was called for traveling, an offensive foul, or a felony. The instructions were to run someone's ass over. The crude stereotype of Black players as nothing more than brutes and thugs had been prevalent throughout college basketball ever since their presence in the sport had started to increase. "At first," DePaul coach Ray Meyer once said, "the whites seemed afraid to play against the Blacks." Haskins didn't subscribe to such bigotry, but with a national championship at stake, he was damn well going to use it to his and the Miners' advantage.

After Riley sank a free throw for the game's first point and for the only lead that Kentucky would hold in the game, Bobby Joe Hill,

Texas Western's point guard, brought the ball up court on the Miners' second possession. The Wildcats aligned themselves in a one-three-one zone in which only one player would be guarding Lattin down low.

"Every team we played knew better than to do that," Lattin told me with a laugh.

Every team except Kentucky, apparently.

"Yeah," he said. "One-on-one under the basket. Don't do that."

Hill zipped a pass from the top of the key to Lattin. Riley, at the bottom of the zone, was the only Kentucky player to make even a passable attempt at fending Lattin away from the rim. He slid over in front of Lattin and jumped with him. He might as well have been leaping to stop a thundercloud. Lattin rose over him and, with two hands, slammed the ball through the hoop.

The reverberations, tangible and intangible, of that dunk would fan out for years in the minds of those who were involved in it and who witnessed it. Lattin's jam was as early and as decisive a turning point as the Miners could have hoped for. In the locker room afterward, Lattin grinned and, in a soft voice, said, "I did it for psychological reasons. Did you hear that crowd? The Kentucky players heard those cheers and roars. I know they did."

Texas Western's victory was the first in a series of dominoes to go down around college basketball. "The reason the game was so significant wasn't just that we beat them," Lattin told me. "The significance was that it opened the doors for universities, especially in the deep South, for African Americans to go to school. Once they opened the doors for the athletes, it opened them for other kids, as well. I'm proud of that." As he should have been. But there was an opposite reaction—if not an equal one, not in the long term—to Lattin's dunk. Yes, more Black students and more Black athletes were entering colleges and college sports, and for much of white America, that was a terrifying trend, one that had to be stemmed or, if possible, stopped altogether. "For Blacks, it was a triumphant statement of why segregation was wrong," Perry Wallace said in 1996, after he'd gone on to become a trial attorney in the US Justice Department and a law professor. For whites, "the specter of David Lattin, big, strong, dark, fantastically physical—and the 'in-yo-face, yo-mama' dunk was his favorite—was a scary thing."

Not to Haskins, obviously. And not to Riley, who, while at Linton High School in Schenectady, had played against and beaten Power Memorial High and Lew Alcindor on a snowy December night in upstate New York less than five years earlier. He wasn't wired to view the Miners as anything other than his opponents, and the broader, deeper ramifications of the game revealed themselves to him only after time had softened the pain of the national championship loss. "They were playing for something a lot more [important] than I think people realized at the time," he once said. "I mean, it wasn't written about much back then, but it was basically five Black players—or so the perception was—against five Southern white guys. Now, I'm from New York. So I kind of resented that."

His head coach resented something else.

There was a time, oddly enough, when Adolph Rupp didn't think the dunk was so bad. Through his first seven years as Kentucky's basketball patriarch, he didn't have a player come through his program who could or would dunk. In 1937, one did. Robert Marion "Clug" Cluggish, from Corbin, Kentucky, was six foot ten, with a narrow head and wide ears, and once he entered the Wildcats' starting lineup as a sophomore, he became the central attraction of their pregame warm-ups, putting on a show by dunking repeatedly. When the players would charge onto the court just before game time, guard J. Rice Walker would dribble the ball the length of the floor, Cluggish going with him stride for stride. As Walker approached the basket, he would jump, as if he were shooting a layup, and loft the ball toward the rim, and Cluggish would throw it down, an early iteration of an alley-oop.

Walker and Cluggish attempted the same routine at Madison Square Garden on December 31, 1938—New Year's Eve in New York— before a big game against Long Island University. In the half-lit arena, a spotlight tracked their movements. LIU fans packed the Garden that

night, and when Cluggish this time missed his dunk attempt, clanging
the ball off the back of the rim and launching it thirty feet into the
air, those fans "went wild," Fred "Cab" Curtis, a Kentucky player,
later said. "They laughed and stomped their feet and jeered for what
seemed like an hour. Even in the semi-darkness, I could see Adolph's
face was fiery red. He was furious."

Kentucky lost the game, 52–34, and in the team's Pullman car on
the train ride back to Philadelphia, Rupp stood up. *All the starters take
lower berths*, he said. *Any subs who played get into the uppers.* He then
pointed at Cluggish. *And Clug, you sleep in the aisle.*

"That's the night," Curtis said, "Adolph turned against the dunk."

Even if the story happened exactly as Curtis told it, it's awfully
convenient to suggest that one player's miscue was enough for Rupp
to start seeing the dunk as a blight on the sport. As more Black players streamed into college basketball's talent pool, it became clear that
whatever appreciation Rupp retained or lost for the dunk was less
about the act itself and more about who was performing it. That quick
trip from Lexington to Louisville in 1964 to recruit Wes Unseld—the
trip on which he had crossed paths with John McLendon at Unseld's
house, the only trip that Rupp ever made to Unseld's house—had not
materialized of his own choosing. John Oswald, UK's president, had
been pressuring Rupp to bring in more Black players, an agenda that
angered the coach. "Harry," Rupp once said to his top assistant, Harry
Lancaster, "that son of a bitch is ordering me to get some n——s in
here. What am I going to do?" He wouldn't do much of anything for
another three years; he didn't sign a Black player until Tom Payne in
1969.

Those changes apparently changed Rupp's view of the dunk from
the days when Clug Cluggish was firing up the Wildcats and their
fans in the layup line. By the time officials were pursuing a ban in
earnest, Rupp was calling the dunk "show-off tactics." Lattin has
long believed that Rupp was directly responsible for the ban, that
the first basket of that '66 national title game was such an affront to
him, and a symbol of the changes ahead for college basketball, that
Rupp couldn't abide it and leveraged his status in the sport to rid it of

the dunk. Haskins received forty thousand pieces of hate mail in the aftermath of the Miners' victory, but poor, poor Adolph's grasp on the levers of the game was weakening, and he knew it. It wasn't just that players were dunking. It was that Black players were dunking. And they were dunking while they were beating his team. "He was definitely embarrassed about that," Lattin told me. To Lattin, Rupp—his forty-two years coaching Kentucky, his 876 victories, his four national championships—was so towering a figure that he could have the dunk outlawed single-handedly. But with or without his assent, the gears were already in motion. Some coaches, of course, had been lobbying for years to have the dunk removed, and even Bob Kurland's presence and greatness at Oklahoma A&M didn't persuade his coach that the dunk was a worthy asset and deserved a place in the sport. At a Big Eight Conference luncheon in December 1966, Hank Iba delivered a speech in which he predicted that the height of the rim would eventually be raised from ten feet to eleven, and he called for the dunk to be eliminated. (Remember: As much as he and his team benefited from Kurland's size, Iba had believed that the NCAA's ban on goaltending would make Kurland a better player. There's no reason to think he wouldn't have felt the same way about a ban on the dunk.)

There were two people in the luncheon audience whose attention Iba wanted to catch with his speech. One was Norvall Neve, the commissioner of the Missouri Valley Conference and, more importantly, one of the twenty members of the National Basketball Committee. The other was more influential. The other was John Bunn, the committee's executive director and rules editor and interpreter.

Few people in basketball had stronger connections to its origins than Bunn. A former player and assistant coach under Phog Allen at Kansas, he spent ten years as both the athletic director and head coach at Springfield College—the site of James Naismith's fateful brainstorm that birthed the game. "What Knute Rockne was to football and John McGraw to baseball," one Springfield newspaperman wrote in August 1979, after Bunn's death, "John Bunn was to basketball. The importance of his presence in the game is incalculable, his contributions immeasurable. . . . As possessor of one of basketball's keen minds, Bunn rose to the position of absolute authority for the sport."

There were two other figures of comparable power, official or otherwise, to greenlight so significant a change. Ed Steitz, who was the committee's assistant rules editor in 1967 and who would become its editor in 1968, had such an encyclopedic command and recall of college basketball's regulations that questioning him and his reams of research and data was a futile exercise. Walter Byers, meanwhile, was in his seventeenth year as the executive director of the NCAA, having assumed that position at age twenty-nine in 1951, the same year the position was created, after working in the bureaucracy of the Big Ten Conference. A quirky loner from Kansas City, Byers as an older man wore a toupee and cowboy boots, and he enforced an often-peculiar set of policies within the offices of the association's headquarters. Employees worked half days on Saturdays, and they could neither drink anything at their desks nor take any breaks. Sally Jenkins of the *Washington Post* once referred to his tenure atop the NCAA as "a tyrannical monopoly under a dictator-president." So banning the dunk, or anything else, wasn't exactly a concept he was likely to find repellent.

And if there were ever a moment in time when an institution such as the NCAA would be inclined to crack down on anything that had even a whiff of personality, anything that gave off the scent of the counterculture, 1967 would have been it. Four years after the March on Washington. Three years after the Civil Rights Act of 1964. One year before the assassinations of Martin Luther King Jr. and Bobby Kennedy. All amid the Vietnam War and the Merry Pranksters and Berkeley and Wisconsin and Kent State and the Black Panthers and the Beatles and the Stones and Marvin Gaye and Norman Mailer, all as college sports and their popularity and their revenues were growing at a rate so fast that only someone blindfolded to the world could manage to see the whole enterprise as "amateurism." In Byers's last year as NCAA president, 1987, the men's basketball tournament would rake in $43 million in revenue, and he'd come around to the reality that college sports was big business, that the athletes who played football

and basketball at its highest levels were *de facto* professionals, and that
the system was inherently corrupt for cutting them out of their right-
ful share of the profits. "Protecting young people from commercial
evils is a transparent excuse for monopoly operations that benefit others," he wrote in his 1995 memoir, *Unsportsmanlike Conduct*, referring
to the NCAA as "the collegiate cartel." But in 1967, when the debate
about the dunk was raging, he was nowhere close to that epiphany.
Hardly anyone was. When a recruiting scandal was revealed or the
sport seemed to be breaking away from its foundations in *any* regard,
the impulse and instinct were to regulate college basketball back to
the way it used to be. "I still see the 1950s and 1960s as a romantic
era—at least in the minds of a public that was deeply shocked when
coaches and young heroes it admired went wrong," Byers wrote in
Unsportsmanlike Conduct. "These ideals lived also in the minds of faculty and athletics officials who wanted to keep college sports the kind
of campus and student activity they nostalgically remembered from
their own younger days."

Byers died in 2015, and some of that inherently stifling and oppres-
sive view of college sports died with him. "My father was in many
ways the face of college athletics as the place where the truest ideal of
amateurism got played out," his son Fritz told me one day over the
phone. "That very much changed, and this is something that he and
I talked about as it changed and then talked at length about when he
was writing his book. That's all true. Whether his view of banning
the dunk was somehow to preserve a distinction between college basketball and pro basketball, I don't know. That would be a fair infer-
ence." Considering Byers's intellectual journey, from the guardian of
college sports' image of lily-white amateurism to a pragmatic capital-
ist, it's a bit surprising that he couldn't foresee the manner in which
college hoops was already evolving—and that he was so naive as to
believe he or anyone else could stop it. But only a little surprising. The
shock that Black players' presence and performance delivered to the
system was apparently so profound, especially once a young man from
Harlem decided to go west, to Southern California, to pursue both his

education and a national championship, that all other considerations fell away.

Lew Alcindor spent the summer before his eighth-grade year practic-ing dunking. He had never done it before, but he was familiar enough with it and the accepted norms of organized basketball then to know that it was rare. Teams did not like opposing players throwing it down against them, and it was common, once a prospective dunker was air-borne, for defenders to cut his legs out from under him to send him crashing to the court. Many players didn't bother risking such injury. Alcindor didn't care. "I was six foot eight," he once wrote, "and I was determined to leave my mark on the game." In one game, with sixty people looking on, he "slammed the ball through the hoop as if I'd been doing it all my life. The spectators jumped to their feet, screaming and clapping. When that ball went through the hoop, it was as if I'd followed it, like Alice in Wonderland falling down the rabbit hole into a strange new world. I felt unstoppable."

In March 1965, Alcindor took a recruiting trip to UCLA, walk-ing across campus and noticing the kind of foliage—weeping wattle, bristly oxtongue, brilliant greens and yellows—that he had never seen in his New York neighborhood. In an office set inside a corrugated-steel Quonset hut, he met John Wooden, who greeted him by saying, "Welcome, Lewis," and asking Alcindor about his high school grades and potential fields of study at the university. Alcindor's career at Power Memorial had been so astounding—a 79–2 record, a 71-game winning streak, three city championships, a city record 2,067 points—that no college coach had bothered to talk to him about academics. For a kid who already had met King and read Malcolm X, who was already on an intellectual trajectory that would stretch well beyond sports, who would refuse to play for the 1968 US Olympic men's basketball team to protest the racial injustice and inequality in America, Wooden's question was all he needed to hear. He decided then and there that UCLA was for him.

That was off the court. On it, Wooden thought that Alcindor could be lethargic at times, especially on defense—a byproduct, the coach believed, of Alcindor's size. He was so much bigger than everyone he played with or against that it was easy for him to dominate a game, at least one at the high school level. During Alcindor's first year at UCLA, he worked daily with one of the freshman team's assistant coaches, Jay Carty. Six foot eight, 220 pounds, and a former NBA player, Carty could bump, push, and knock Alcindor around in a way that would prepare him for varsity competition. He also marked a point on the backboard a foot and a half above the rim and had Alcindor jump to touch it over and over again. Alcindor's vertical leap improved substantially because of the drill. Having already learned and mastered his skyhook—perhaps the greatest offensive weapon in basketball history—thanks to his coaches and mentors in Harlem, he was now every bit as unstoppable as he once felt.

"People don't realize how strong Lewis is," Wooden once said. "His muscles are long and supple, but there's a lot of strength in them. His height and maneuverability make him physical, but it isn't a question of overpowering anyone. His basketball is his maneuverability rather than his power."

If anything, dunking stripped Alcindor's play of some of its grace. Seven feet, one and a half inches, languid, with a ballet dancer's footwork, he was the rare big man whose game was less aesthetically pleasing when he slammed the ball home. That blemish was a small price to pay to increase the potency of a player who was the most imposing force in college basketball even when he was ineligible to play varsity college basketball. Alcindor had 31 points and 21 rebounds as the UCLA freshmen beat the Bruins' varsity team, 75–60, in November 1965, and his sophomore season—the only one in which he was permitted to dunk the basketball—was statistically the best of his collegiate career. He averaged more points (29.0), shot a higher percentage from the field (.667), and grabbed more total rebounds (466) than he did as either a junior or a senior. The Bruins went 30–0, winning 27 of those games by at least 10 points and 17 by at least 20. They rolled through the NCAA Tournament, beating Wyoming by 49, Pacific by 16, Houston and Elvin Hayes in the national semifinals by 15, and Dayton by 15 in the final.

That championship game, at Freedom Hall in Louisville, was telling. Alcindor dunked three times in the Bruins' 79–64 win, but what's striking about watching the game is how dominant he *wasn't*. He finished with 20 points and 18 rebounds. He showed off his sky-hook. He made some terrific, smart passes out of the post to get open perimeter shots for his teammates. But he didn't assert himself in any overt fashion; he didn't try to take over the game. For his first field goal, Alcindor moseyed downcourt, set up in the lane, caught a pass from forward Lucius Allen, and stuffed the ball in. UCLA 15, Dayton 4. Early in the second half, with the Bruins up 16, he caught the ball on the left block, faked to his left, spun back right to the baseline and dunked over the Flyers' Don May, who was six-four and helpless to do anything against Alcindor except foul him, which he did. Minutes later, cradling the ball as if his right arm were a lacrosse stick, Alcindor hooked a pass from the low right block to the opposite side of the court to guard Lynn Shackelford. Shackelford missed a fifteen-foot jump shot, but Alcindor gathered the rebound, jumped, and slammed the ball through the hoop to give UCLA a 52–31 lead. It was his last dunk of the game. It would be the last dunk in an official NCAA game for another nine years. Lew Alcindor was too tall, too good, too emblematic of this new reality in college basketball. Something had to be done. Just two days after UCLA's victory, something finally was.

The National Basketball Committee did what committees do. Its members met. They reached a decision and implemented a policy. Then they were shady about how they had reached that decision. Newspaper headlines on Wednesday, March 29, 1967, told basketball fans from coast to coast that from now on, if a player on their favorite college or high school team dunked during a game, the basket would not count, and his team would lose possession of the ball. The fans weren't told much more. Who on the committee supported the ban? Who opposed it? Who had lobbied the committee in favor or against the ban? Those questions went unanswered. And the undercurrent of the decision—its racial component—went unmentioned.

Bunn and Steitz were out front as the committee's spokespeople and chief elucidators for the reasons behind the ban. The vote, Bunn said, had been overwhelming in favor of ditching the dunk. "There were very few negative votes," he said, and the committee's hope was that the ban would "equalize the defense and offense in play around the basket . . . because the dunking maneuver does not give the defense an opportunity to block the shot."

Plenty of coaches were incredulous. College basketball was thriving, expanding its reach around the country. Why stymie the game's evolution? Why stymie the players'? "I am completely shocked and surprised that the rules committee would even propose such a change," said Houston's Guy Lewis, who, years before his Phi Slama Jama teams, was already invested in recruiting highflyers. "It will change my theory of coaching, because it has taken a long time to find players capable of dunking the ball." Referees worried that the ban would make their jobs more difficult. The dunk had always been the unwritten exception to the rule that a player's hand couldn't touch the ball once it was inside the imaginary cylinder above the rim. Now, refs would have to look more closely and more frequently to determine whether a player's hand was in the cylinder and exactly when he had taken his hand off the ball. Most maddening was the seemingly arbitrary, reactionary nature of the ban. "I'm really mad," Michigan coach Dave Strack said. "I think they should listen to the coaches more. They change the rule with no consideration for the coaches or the players."

Based on Bunn's quotes, though, it didn't take a hoops savant to understand that the committee had spent some time considering at least one player and his effect on the sport. Bill Becker of the *New York Times* wrote that Alcindor was "the obvious object of the rule"—the Anti-Alcindor Rule, as it became known—and Wooden acknowledged years later that a committee member had revealed to him that Alcindor's name had indeed come up during the discussion of the ban. Walter Byers, too, had Alcindor's dominance on his mind as he presided over the change.

"He was aware that Alcindor was dunking with ease over everyone," Fritz Byers told me. "I know my father took note of that. I have no memory of him saying, 'We have to put an end to that.' But I really know my father's view was, 'That's not basketball. Dunking is not real basketball.'"

Alcindor's coach agreed. Even a faint show of support from Wooden for Alcindor might have at least given the committee members pause, but Wooden never provided it. "I've never liked the dunk," he said in 2000, when he was ninety. "I thought it was the best thing for basketball when they outlawed it, and I didn't like when they put it back in. I think it brings on selfishness, showmanship, too much individual play." Wilt Chamberlain, meanwhile, was in his eighth NBA season—a league that Walter Byers apparently would not have considered "real basketball"— when he was asked for his opinion on the ban. "It's like penalizing Bob Hayes five yards because he can run a 9.1 hundred and nobody else in pro football can," Chamberlain said. "Dunking takes a lot of moves, agility, subtlety, timing, coordination. It's not just a big man's tool."

No, but it wasn't going to be tolerated, and Alcindor believed he understood why. "Clearly, they did it to undermine my dominance in the game," he wrote in *Giant Steps*, his 1983 autobiography. "Equally clearly, if I'd been white, they never would have done it. The dunk is one of basketball's great crowd pleasers, and there is no good reason to give it up except that this and other n———s were running away with the sport." Robert Bowness, an assistant coach at Hunter College in the Bronx, took the pulse of the playgrounds and parks after the ban, and like Alcindor, players there saw it as something sinister, something laced with racism. "If a guy is seven feet tall, he's going to score from in close whether he stuffs or just lays it in," Bownes told Pete Axthelm in *The City Game*. "That rule wasn't put in to stop seven-footers. It was put in to stop the six-foot-two brothers who could dazzle the crowd and embarrass much bigger white kids by dunking. The white establishment has an uncomfortable feeling that Blacks are dominating too many areas of sports. So they're setting up all kinds of restrictions and barriers. Everyone knows that dunking is a trademark of great playground Black athletes, and so they took it away. It's as simple as that."

The ban makes even more sense, if such a thing could make sense, in that broader context. Rick Telander likened it to a measure out of Victorian England, when "amateur" was a synonym for "gentleman" among the upper class, when any encroachment from the working class in, say, a local soccer club caused the snobby and wealthy to retreat into their own select way of playing the game—to keep the lowbrow out. "The dunk followed that same arc—'It's not right. It's not proper,'" Telander told me. "It's absolutely an act of rebellion. It's more than just two points. It's not just 'Duck your head and run back up court.' Fashion always comes from two places: the top and the bottom, the very, very rich or the outcast. It goes back in American history, too. The boast was always considered very lowbrow. That's what the 'scum of the earth' did, the trash and the pioneers. That's also where the dunk came from. It was a barbaric yawp." It was a statement, an assertion, and the members of the polite and powerful portion of society didn't like it. The point of the ban, then, wasn't to hamstring one player. It was to hamstring any player who was predisposed to throw one down, and Rupp, Iba, Wooden, and other coaches who supported the ban had plenty of candidates for neutering. As author Andrew Maraniss has noted, Rupp and Kentucky didn't have UCLA on their regular-season schedule, but they did have Vanderbilt and Perry Wallace on it—twice, since both schools were in the Southeastern Conference (SEC). Before Wallace's death in 2017, people speculated to him that his presence might have had something to do with the ban. He himself did not draw that direct connection. "At the time," Wallace told Maraniss, "I didn't have that level of paranoia or self-importance. I just found out that somebody changed the rules. I'm more comfortable that the major person was Kareem, and in general Black players were doing most of the dunking. I was just part of the equation, part of the formula. When you look back, you see it was a silly, suspicious rule, and I think it said a whole lot about the times. I'm like a lot of people; without any evidence, I strongly suspect that it was racially motivated, and like many things that you look back on, it really stands out like your proverbial sore thumb."

Ed Steitz scoffed at the notion that Alcindor or any other specific player was the target of the ban. The suggestion, he once said, was "a lot of baloney"; the dunk had to go because it was costing schools money and jeopardizing players' safety. The breakaway rim hadn't been invented yet. There was no hinge, no spring, no give in the stiff, standard hoop to absorb the force that an elite athlete applied when he brought his hands and arms down with all his might and weight. So every dunk threatened to destroy the entire hoop-backboard–stanchion apparatus. There had been "1,500 injuries and nearly a quarter of a million dollars in damaged equipment," Steitz said in 1977. "They were tearing down rims and backboards. Games and tournaments could not be completed. Television commitments could not be fulfilled."

Still, even if one gives Byers, Bunn, and Steitz the benefit of the doubt that they weren't making a concerted effort to neutralize Black players' impact on college basketball, one has to acknowledge that the three of them were so officious that the chances are good none of them ever stopped to consider the disproportionate effect that banning the dunk would have. Steitz, in particular, was concerned at all times whether the rules maintained a sense of balance in the flow of action. Basketball, he believed, shouldn't tip toward one style of play or another. He was the driving force, for instance, behind the NCAA's full-time implementation of the three-point shot in 1986, and the timing of that innovation and its promise of increased offense coincided with the rise of the bare-knuckled Big East—exemplified by John Thompson, Patrick Ewing, and the smothering defense of their smart, ferocious Georgetown teams—into the best conference in the country. Similarly, in the late 1960s, Steitz worried that the sport would devolve into nothing more than giants stuffing the ball home, that the dunk would either rob basketball of its motion and beauty or never allow those qualities to flourish.

"The athleticism that is in today's game wasn't in the game back in those years," Steitz's son Bob told me as a way of describing the thinking that his father and others like him used to justify the ban. "It just wasn't. You didn't have six-four guys playing above the rim. It just wasn't happening. You did have guys like Lew Alcindor and some bigger players catch the ball, turn, dunk it. And was that really a shot? The thinking was, 'That's not a shot. It's called a dunk shot, but you're just throwing the ball through the basket. You have to be able to shoot the ball. That's how James Naismith did it with the peach basket.'"

As it turned out, Ed Steitz and everyone else who wanted to eliminate the dunk had it exactly backward. The dunk didn't limit the possibilities within basketball. It expanded them. It didn't turn the sport into a battle of size and brute strength. It lifted it into the ether, and the ban deprived those who loved basketball of witnessing some of its best at their best. Julius Erving, David Thompson, Pete Maravich, Artis Gilmore, Bob Lanier, Sidney Wicks—the rule hamstrung all these wondrous athletes and more, and for what?

The ban was bookended by unbeaten seasons—UCLA in 1967, and Bob Knight's Indiana Hoosiers in 1976, the last Division I team to complete a season without a loss. To coincide with the nation's celebration of its bicentennial, the '76 Final Four was in Philadelphia, where the National Basketball Committee this time voted to bring back the dunk. "In less than a minute," Big Ten commissioner Wayne Duke said. Three years later, the committee dissolved for good; the NCAA and the National Federation of High School Associations took on rule-setting for themselves.

"Revocation of the dunk was the worst thing that happened in this country since Prohibition," St. John's Lou Carneseca said. "Let's see, the Volstead Act was passed in 1920 and repealed in 1933. That's thirteen years, and we repealed the dunk in eight. That's progress." But the more delicious reaction was from a retired coach who said he was "violently opposed" to the dunk "for years. But after thinking it over, I believe the dunk shot has a place in basketball." What lovely timing by Adolph Rupp, to see the light so late.

In July 2022, I contacted Paige Kadish, the NCAA's associate director of library and research, to ask for access to the association's library, specifically its "Presidential Collection," to search for anything from

WILTON N. CHAMBERLAIN
401 N. Salford Street   Ac.
S.A., A.A., Basketball Captain, Track, A.A. Representative, School Improvement, Locker Aide, Teacher's Aide.
Our favorite basketball player kept the competitive teams buoyed up for three years . . . good food and music are "George" with "The Dipper" . . . hasn't time for talkative and inquisitive people . . . dreams of becoming an educated hobo.

In his senior yearbook entry at Overbrook High School in West Philadelphia, Wilt Chamberlain said he aspired to be an "educated hobo." *(Photo by Barry Galman)*

Chamberlain towered over his teammates at Overbrook High School. *(Photo by Barry Galman)*

Even on one knee, Chamberlin was a giant for a high schooler. *(Photo by Barry Galman)*

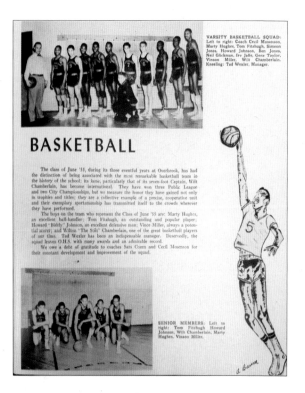

This page from Chamberlain's senior yearbook provides an indication of his lofty status at Overbrook High School.
(Photo by Barry Galman)

It was hardly surprising that Chamberlain was the tallest member of his class at Overbrook High School.
(Photo by Barry Galman)

David Thompson wasn't permitted to dunk legally throughout his college career at North Carolina State. *(North Carolina State University)*

Joe Fortenberry was a terrific semipro player before and after his stint on the US Olympic Team.
(Oliver Fortenberry)

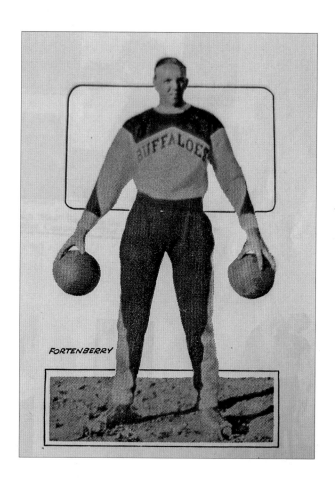

FORTENBERRY

(Above) Joe Fortenberry had gigantic hands, and his fingers were so big that he wore a size-15 ring. *(Oliver Fortenberry)*

Joe Fortenberry was the subject of a *New York Times* article that helped introduce the slam dunk to a national audience. *(Oliver Fortenberry)*

(Above) A placard at North Carolina State details the achievements of Lorenzo Charles the 1982–83 Wolfpack. *(Photo by Mike Sielski)*

The 1982–83 national champions. *(Photo by Mike Sielski)*

(Above and below) Lorenzo Charles's dunk helped the 1982–83 North Carolina State Wolfpack become a national sensation. *(Photos by Mike Sielski)*

Lorenzo Charles (center) and teammate Sidney Lowe celebrate the 1983 national championship with Jim Valvano, who wears the net like a necklace. *(Photo by Mike Sielski)*

At Jimmy V's Osteria & Bar in downtown Raleigh, it's always April 4, 1983.
(Photo by Mike Sielski)

Jim Valvano's mantra is ever-present at the Raleigh restaurant that bears his name.
(Photo by Mike Sielski)

Lorenzo Charles's grave is just a short walk from Jim Valvano's at Oakwood Cemetery in Raleigh. *(Photo by Mike Sielski)*

Mac McClung won the 2023 and 2024 NBA Slam Dunk Contests.
(Photo by Mike Sielski)

Ja Morant, shown here taking a jump shot during a morning shootaround, is the most thrilling dunker in the modern NBA.
(Photo by Mike Sielski)

Walter Byers's archives that might be relevant or helpful to my research. If I could spend a couple of days at the association's headquarters in Indianapolis and page through Byers's papers Robert Caro–style, maybe I could uncover a document that provided a clear-cut, no-doubt explanation for why the dunk had been banned. I suggested as much to Fritz Byers when I interviewed him, and he agreed.

Kadish responded promptly to my inquiry, telling me that the library was "closed to outside researchers due to COVID." She could, however, send me what they had.

Within the week, Massillon Myers, one of the NCAA's assistant directors of communication—i.e., a spokesperson—emailed me links to a few old association manuals, convention proceedings, and basketball guides and several newspaper and magazine articles about the dunk ban. The material wasn't all that revealing, and much of it wasn't relevant. Next time, I contacted Myers. Could I see Walter Byers's papers? No, he said. They weren't open to the public.

With Fritz, though, I figured I had an ace in the hole: the president's son on my side. I had told him about the NCAA's obstinance, and he seemed puzzled and disappointed. On October 27, 2022, I wrote back to Kadish and Myers, asking again for access to the Walter Byers papers. This time, I copied Fritz on the email. I wrote in part:

Mr. Byers told me during our conversation that he would have no issue with my seeing the papers and using them to help write my book. I would think that such formal acknowledgement and permission from the Byers family would be enough for me to gain access to these archives.

Please understand: I'm trying to tell this story as thoroughly and accurately as possible. Access to Walter Byers' archives— his letters, memos, notes, etc. during his time in charge of the association—will allow me to get this story right. That's my only goal. I hope you're willing to help me.

Later that day, I received a response from Myers.

Hi Mike,

Thanks for reaching out. We looked into it again and due

to the Record Retention Policy that is created by the NCAA, the Presidential Collection is for internal use only. Unfortunately, we cannot give you access to the materials.

Thanks again and good luck with your research.

Massillon

Myers sent his email at 2:58 p.m. I sent my response at 3:30.

Hi Massillon,

I'm disappointed in the association's response to my request. Let's be clear and honest here: It's not that the NCAA can't give me access to the Walter Byers archives. It's that the NCAA *won't* give me access and, presumably, would deny Walter Byers' son access to them, too. As I mentioned in a previous email, I'm not on some kind of investigative witch hunt here. I'm trying to write a book and, in doing so, give a complete and accurate accounting of an important period in college sports history. I don't see what the NCAA's objection here could be.

I'll be sure to research and report about the '67 dunk ban, the reasons for it, and the implications of it as thoroughly and tenaciously as possible. When the time comes for me to write this section of the book, I'll also be sure to explain within the text that the NCAA refused to allow me access to the Presidential Collection and did not provide any explanation or reason for rejecting my request beyond, *We didn't want to let him see this stuff.* My readers will then be free to speculate to themselves and draw their own conclusions about why the association chose to be so secretive.

No one from the NCAA ever responded, as if the association preferred to keep the past as vague as possible. No further context or explanation could be fully satisfying anyway. A decade's worth of dunks had vanished. Countless opportunities to add more thrilling moments and memories, during an era when college basketball was already gaining a stronger foothold in American culture, had been missed. Consider what was to come. Imagine what might have been.

12

THE SUMMIT OF SLAM

The meeting, on a stretch of East Coast sand, did not come about through happenstance or serendipity. It was not random. There was a purpose behind it, for the aspirant at least. To him, it was a rite of passage. For basketball, it was a sign of the future.

The older, taller, and more famous of the two men had settled himself in a prime spot on the sand of Riis Park in Queens. It was a gorgeous Saturday afternoon in the summer of 1969. Lew Alcindor was still Lew Alcindor then. He would not convert from Christianity to Islam and change his name to Kareem Abdul-Jabbar until 1971, though he had embraced the faith a few years earlier, as a freshman at UCLA. On March 22, 1969, he had completed his college basketball career with a magnificent performance in the Bruins' 92–72 victory over Purdue in the national championship game: 37 points, 20 rebounds, his control of the game's direction and outcome total . . . even though he was forbidden from dunking the ball. On April 7, 1969, the Milwaukee Bucks had selected him with the first pick in the NBA draft, and the presumption around the sport was that a team that had won just 27 games the season before, as a first-year expansion franchise, would instantly become one of the league's best merely for Alcindor's presence.

(The presumption was correct. The Bucks went 56–26 and reached the Eastern Division Finals in '69–70, and Alcindor was voted Rookie of the Year.) But this day at the beach was not about basketball for him. The outdoor courts close to the shore, strips of black against the beige sand, held no interest to him. He wore sandals, sunglasses, and a yellow dashiki, and he relaxed by paging through a copy of *Soul on Ice*, the collection of essays by Eldridge Cleaver that charted Cleaver's journey from prison inmate to Marxist activist.

The younger man, who had not yet had the opportunity to reveal his nascent greatness to most of the basketball world, had come to Riis looking for Alcindor. "I was fully equipped," Julius Erving told me years later. "He was committed to chilling at the beach and watching girls or whatever his MO was. I was going there to play basketball." Erving was nineteen, having finished his freshman year at the University of Massachusetts, having not played a second of varsity college basketball yet. He and five of his teammates from Roosevelt High School on Long Island—Leon Saunders, Lennie Carter, Ralph Burgess, Robert Mayrant, Tommy Taylor—would pile into Mayrant's Rambler and drive anywhere in New York for a game. "Ralph always knew how to fix the car if it broke down," Erving said. The National Basketball Committee's edict banning the dunk also applied to the nation's high school programs, of course, so Erving and his buddies were itching to show their stuff whenever and wherever polite society permitted, and they barnstormed from Harlem to Brooklyn to Queens to Hempstead to do it.

"It was, 'Hey, let's go find some guys to beat up on,'" Saunders told me. "This was not unusual for us to do. We always felt pretty confident because we had Julius. We had twelve players on the team at Roosevelt, and eleven of them could dunk. You couldn't dunk during the game, but you could dunk during warm-ups. That was a part of what we did to intimidate teams at the other end. We would be as creative as possible with various types of slam dunks, and we used to play a game in terms of how we lined up, where the best dunker—which was always Julius—would be first."

They pulled up at Riis and headed straight to the courts. Games were already going, but from what the Roosevelt crew could tell, there was no one close to Alcindor's height anywhere. A few guys stood around. They had the next game, were waiting to play. Erving asked them where "the seven-footer" was. They pointed to the beach. Erving meandered over to Alcindor. It was as if, he would write later, he was allowed an audience with a world leader . . . except Alcindor was just twenty-two, just three years older, full of fierce anger at the station of Black people in 1960s America, anger that Erving did not share. Alcindor, remember, was a Malcolm X votary—shake up the system and threaten the establishment by any means necessary. Erving was a Martin Luther King Jr. adherent. Shake up the system? Not Erving. He considered himself a product of it, and he valued order too much to put the system at peril through strident protest. The older man saw the dunk as the ultimate act of defiance—why, after all, had White America banned it?—saw it on the same continuum as his revolutionary politics. He was among those who thrust it to the forefront and forced a reckoning with the sport's inevitable advancement. The younger man would take that rebellious act and make it mainstream, be happy to talk about it and stylize it and popularize it, to show those who didn't look like him that there was nothing to fear from men who could fly.

"Hey, man," Erving said, "I'm Julius."

He knew Alcindor was The Man, and Erving wanted to be The Man by beating The Man. But even though Erving's reputation preceded him to the beach at Riis Park, The Man was too busy reading to be bothered.

"So . . . Julius has come," Alcindor said.

"You're not playing ball today?" Erving asked.

No, he was not. No man atop a throne ever deigns to prove himself to a challenger. The next moment indicated why. Alcindor held up his hands. Erving held up his. They pressed their palms together. Each man, Erving recalled later, had to measure himself against the other in whatever way possible. It turned out that Erving's hands were longer and wider. All the better to grab a basketball, to grab *basketball*, and hurl it into the future.

From the instant that Erving began his career in professional basket-ball in 1971, through what he called "the side-door entrance of the ABA," he would think of himself as hidden in Abdul-Jabbar's shadow. Abdul-Jabbar had been a champion in college, would be a champion in the NBA, was a leader, a presence that loomed over all of basket-ball. He was the star by which Erving steered, and their meeting that Saturday in Queens has stayed with him, fresh in his memory, for the rest of his life for that reason. For their rivalry. For the similarities and differences between them. "It was something that gets talked about," he told me. "I talked about it. Now you're talking about it. It was the creation of a lifetime conversation for multiple generations."

That conversation continues still. Julius Erving would like to have the last word.

13

GOD ON HIGH

He was a rival to Erving and an exemplar to a generation of dunkers. He was the best player in the history of the best conference in college basketball. He could have been so much more.

What it must have been like to see David Thompson in the flesh and in the air . . . hanging up there near the rim . . . at once in motion and somehow perfectly still . . . his violent takeoff framed in complete contrast to the peaceful sight of him in silent flight . . . arms outstretched and legs spread and his whole body, all six feet and four inches and 180 pounds of him, high above everyone else on the court. *Violent* is the right word. David Thompson leaped violently, leaving the ground even from a standstill as if he were a gymnast who had sprinted onto a springboard to launch himself into a vault. He leaped violently whether the basketball was in his hands or not. In fact, the entire sequence was a better representation of his effect on a game and his influence on the sport if the ball was not.

For if the ball was not in David Thompson's hands, then it was possible, even likely, that he would cut toward the basket. And one of his North Carolina State teammates—the teammate who did, at that instant, happen to have the ball in *his* hands—would loft it toward the rim. And Thompson would initiate one of his violent leaps . . . neurons firing, knees bending, planar muscles flexing . . . until he and the ball occupied the same air space. And the ball would be, for a moment and at last, in his hands. It could not be the briefest of moments. No, it could not. There would have to be a lapse of time—a half second, a quarter second—and during that time Thompson would have to make a decision, maybe more than one. Was he high enough to drop the ball through the hoop? Did he have to bank in a shot softly off the backboard? Did he have a clear angle to use the glass? Could he shoot a finger roll? Should he shoot a finger roll?

There was one option, of course—the option that would be most likely to succeed, that would most likely result in two points for him and for the Wolfpack, that would demoralize any opponent and exhilarate everyone on his team and any spectator inside Reynolds Coliseum in Raleigh—that was unavailable to him. This was what the National Basketball Committee and the NCAA and those who had acquiesced to them had done to college basketball: from the fall of 1972 through the winter of 1975, they had stripped the most exciting player in the sport of his ability to carry out the most exciting play in the sport. The truest testament to David Thompson's greatness over his three seasons at NC State wasn't the 2,309 points he scored or the Wolfpack's unbeaten 1972–73 season or its two Atlantic Coast Conference Tournament championships or its 1974 national championship or the fact that he was the ACC Player of the Year three times or the National Player of the Year twice. It was that he popularized the alley-oop to the point that it became a staple of basketball, and he did it without ever hammering down an alley-oop dunk.

Mo Howard was a Philadelphia guard with everything that label connotes, with the toughness and the quickness and the upbringing to have seen some stuff. Philly in the 1960s was nothing but tight neighborhoods and little streets in those neighborhoods and row houses on those little streets and often gangs on the corners outside those row houses. That kind of environment, Howard figured, was bound to breed and shape a better ballplayer than just about anywhere else in America. So . . . when Howard decided to play college ball in College Park, to play for Lefty Driesell at Maryland, what was he going to see there out of a teammate or an opponent that he hadn't seen already? That was the way he looked at it, and that was why he was incredulous in the fall of 1972, when he got on campus and his new buddy and backcourt mate, John Lucas from Durham, North Carolina, kept talking about someone he'd played pickup against back home. The NCAA had just lifted the prohibition on freshmen playing varsity ball that year, so Howard and Lucas could suit up right away for the Terps. *Trust me*, Lucas kept saying. *Just wait.* The dude had a nickname—DT—and he was a sophomore at NC State, set to play varsity for the first time, finally, and he was spectacular.

"Now, I'm from Philadelphia," Howard told me. "I'm thinking to myself, 'There's no way they're playing pickup basketball like this guy's describing in North Carolina, OK? They can't be that frickin' good.'"

Thompson may not have the street cred that Howard prized so much, but he'd hardly had it easy as a kid in Shelby, a town of fifteen thousand less than fifty miles west of Charlotte. He was the youngest of Vellie and Ida Thompson's eleven children—Vellie worked picking up supplies for an Army surplus store—and was stuck in a segregated school until eighth grade. That same eighth-grade year, young David dunked a basketball for the first time, when he was just five foot eight. By his tenth-grade year at Crest Senior High School, he could jump from a standstill ten times and touch the rim with his elbow each time, and he started playing pickup at Gardner-Webb College, which was within walking distance of his house. There was a weight room in the gym; he used it, did toe raises and leg extensions, and on the court went up against Artis Gilmore, George Adams, and Ernie Fleming—all of whom went on to play Division I ball, all of whom went on to either play in or be drafted into the NBA, all of whom were at least an inch taller than Thompson would ever be.

"Artis and Ernie," Thompson once said, "would just drive me through the floor."

See, Mo? The kid was tough. He just didn't show it like some others did.

"He was really the most humble player I ever played against," Bobby Jones, who was at North Carolina while Thompson was at NC State, told me. "He would never do anything or say anything to motivate you or make you think, 'This guy's lording it over you.' He was really focused on his job on the court."

It was a surprising thing to hear, if only because most players who define themselves through dunking the basketball often aren't so humble.

"David's background probably contributed to that," Jones said. "He came from humble beginnings, and he remembered where he came from and was very appreciative of that, obviously, and had parents who really raised him in a way to say, 'You don't brag about what you've done. You let other people talk about you.'"

Soon those people wouldn't be able to stop.

Two hundred schools recruited Thompson. Two ended up on NCAA probation. A Duke alumnus bought him a suit coat, pants, and tickets to the 1971 ACC Tournament. Later, Thompson scrimmaged with NC State assistant coach/recruiter Ed Biedenbach—an improper interaction between college coach and potential player, per the NCAA—and spent the night on NC State's campus during a basketball camp before he had registered there as a student. The association ruled that the university should have charged Thompson eight dollars for sleeping in the dorm room, as if it were a motel. As their punishment for plying Thompson with such lavish gifts, both the Wolfpack and the Blue Devils would be ineligible for postseason play during the 1972–73 season.

Thompson picked NC State after Biedenbach issued him a challenge, daring him to forge his own identity there, arguing that he would be considered just the latest in a long line of fine players at North Carolina or another blue-blooded program. Early in his freshman year, Thompson demonstrated how special he would be. He and the other freshmen in the program scrimmaged in Carmichael Gymnasium, the campus physical education building, across the street from Reynolds Coliseum, until mid-October, when they could practice with the varsity players on opposite ends of the Reynolds courts. Time and again in those workouts, Thompson would catch the ball in the high post and have the man guarding him at his mercy. If he wanted to drive to the hoop, he could; none of his teammates was quick enough to stay with him. But he was also a terrific jump-shooter, and because his vertical leap was so high—forty-four inches—no defender could block his shot or even obstruct his view of the basket. When it came to stopping Thompson, the best of all the bad options was to deny him the ball by overplaying him on the perimeter, so he and fellow frosh Monte Towe, a five-foot-seven point guard, developed a countermove to that strategy. Thompson would fake toward the high post, then go backdoor on his defender, and Towe would loft the ball toward the rim for him. The first time they tried it, Towe threw a terrible pass, "one," he said, "that was about to go out of the gym." It didn't matter that Towe's alley-oop attempt was so far off the mark, and it didn't matter that Thompson couldn't palm a basketball—that throughout his college and pro careers, he generally either had to lay the ball in with two hands or cup it against his right wrist for a tomahawk dunk. He turned Towe's mistake into something marvelous; he went up, caught the ball, and stuffed it.

As far as NC State's coaches and players were concerned, Thompson and Towe might as well have discovered fire. Art Musselman, the program's freshman coach, started calling the alley-oop as a set play, and head coach Norm Sloan, with Biedenbach's help, installed it into the Wolfpack's offense early in the 1972–73 season, once Thompson and Towe were sophomores and the team's starting backcourt. The more they ran it, the better they got at it. Biedenbach would sit at practice or on the bench during games, shake his head at Thompson, and think, *How did that happen?* Once, Towe floated an alley-oop pass toward Thompson that looked certain to sail out of bounds, but Thompson caught the ball behind the backboard, pulled it in front of the rim, and laid it in— all in midair. "He jumped as high as was necessary," Biedenbach once said. "It was remarkable how high he would get up and control the ball. His equilibrium was even more fantastic." Landing was hell on Thompson's knees, but he and Towe were so in sync, their connection so strong and reliable and almost telepathic, that they set a goal of getting the Wolfpack at least three alley-oop scores a game—a goal they usually reached or even surpassed.

"If they didn't invent it," former NC State athletic director and coach Les Robinson once said, "they definitely perfected it."

And no, they did not invent it, though many who covered them like to say that they had. Don Patterson, who wrote for the Greensboro *News & Record* for forty-three years, looked into the history of the alley-oop in 1998, and he possessed enough historical integrity to acknowledge that Bill Russell and K. C. Jones had pioneered it at San Francisco, even if few gave them public credit at the time. "For all the hoopla surrounding the play," Patterson wrote, "no one knows for certain when or where the alley-oop originated. But it's been around since at least the mid-1950s, when players such as K. C. Jones and Bill Russell at San Francisco and Vic Molodet and Ronnie Shavlik at NC State started passing and catching the ball above the rim for slam dunk finishes." Once Thompson and Towe started deploying the play routinely, though, the press took notice, describing it with a variation of *allez hop*, a French exclamation often used when a circus acrobat was about to leap. The term had been Americanized in the 1930s as the title of a popular syndicated comic strip, and now Thompson had come along and compelled the country to expand the vocabulary of basketball.

"We brought it out to light," he once said.

It took time for the alley-oop to catch on. After NC State implemented it, a couple of years went by, Towe once said, before he and Thompson noticed other teams using it regularly. An alley-oop was risky; the pass might be bad, and its recipient might fumble the ball, might miss the layup, or might end up crashing to the floor. Plus, not every team had someone like Thompson. Maryland, for instance, would have seemed to have an ideal collection and alignment of talent to make the alley-oop a staple of its fastbreak offense. The Terrapins had a six-nine center in Len Elmore, a six-eleven forward in Tom McMillen, and a couple of quicksilver six-three guards in Howard and Lucas. But the alley-oop wasn't part of their arsenal. "The big guys got the ball out, and we'd just take off," Howard told me. "The game had become a little faster. Before, you'd walk the ball down the court and run the plays. Now you had backcourt guys who were becoming more athletic, guys who could run and jump. But nobody did it like Thompson—nobody. In that era, it was him, and then about ten rungs below was everybody else."

There was a reason I spoke to Mo Howard, specifically Mo Howard, about David Thompson. I wanted the perspective of one of Thompson's college opponents, preferably one who had to guard him a few times, and Howard was and did. It is one thing to hear the stories of an athlete's greatness from his family members or teammates, from those predisposed to think of him favorably or even see him as flawless. It is another to hear them from his foes, from those who had a stake in his defeat or failure. The rivalry between NC State and Maryland in the early to mid-1970s was among the best in all of college basketball, maybe the best, even if it was relatively one-sided. The Wolfpack won seven of its nine games against the Terrapins during Thompson's three seasons in Raleigh, including two ACC Tournament championship games and one semifinal, and seven times the final margin of victory was six points or fewer.

The first of those losses, the first game that Thompson played against Maryland and that Howard played against Thompson, came on Sunday, January 14, 1973, at Cole Field House. Each team was 11–0. The Terps were ranked second in the nation, behind UCLA, in the Associated Press Top 25, and the Wolfpack was third. For each fan base, each local and state media contingent, the game's significance was enormous. Mark Whicker, later a longtime columnist for the *Philadelphia Daily News* and the *Orange County Register*, was still a student at the University of North Carolina when he traveled 285 miles, from Chapel Hill to College Park, to cover the game. One of Howard's closest friends, a fellow Philadelphia high school phenom, drove down to sit in the bleachers. There was no way Joe Bryant—future NBA veteran and father of Kobe—was going to miss this game. But there was another unbeaten team that promised to command more of the country's attention and interest that day.

Russ Potts, Maryland's sports-marketing director, had urged Lefty Driesell and athletic director Jim Kehoe to schedule the NC State game on Super Bowl Sunday. Driesell and Kehoe thought no one would be bothered to watch college basketball on the day of America's biggest football bacchanalia, but Potts believed that the captive audience of folks staying home, waiting for the 16–0 Miami Dolphins to face the Washington Redskins, would lead to a gigantic rating for Terps-Wolfpack. It did. When the game tipped off that afternoon, twenty-five million people tuned in without it being televised on a national network. C. D. Chesley, who owned a company that produced ACC games, finagled and coaxed 145 TV stations across the country to carry the game. By comparison, the famed 1968 prime-time matchup between UCLA and Houston at the Astrodome had been broadcast on just 120 stations. And that game's stars—the Bruins' Lew Alcindor and the Cougars' Elvin Hayes—were already household names. NC State–Maryland would be Thompson's unveiling to the nation.

"It was like a can't-miss," longtime college basketball analyst Billy Packer said in 2018. "Nobody even realized at that time how great David Thompson was."

Thompson entered the game as the ACC's leading scorer, at 25.5 points a game, but because he hadn't fared as well against the tougher teams on the Wolfpack's schedule, plenty of people were still skeptical that he was as good as his reputation suggested. A fan at the game called Thompson "the flop of the year," and a sportswriter said flatly, "Thompson is a myth."

Mythical that day, certainly. But no myth. By the game's final half minute, Thompson had scored 38 points. Driesell had half the Maryland roster try to stop him at one time or another. No one could. "We had six different guys guard him," Howard told me, "and I know that, on one of those alley-oop plays, he was up so high that, if I'm not mistaken, he may have hit his shoulder on the backboard." With twelve seconds left in regulation and the game tied at 85, Sloan took a time-out but did not call a play in the huddle, leaving it up to his players to freelance their way to a good look at the basket. Near the top of the key, NC State center Tom Burleson dribbled the ball three times. "Ponderously," Whicker said. Thompson tried to cut toward Burleson to get the ball, but Maryland's Bob Bodell stepped into the passing lane. Elmore, the Terps' center, not only gave Burleson ample room to shoot but shouted at him to do so. Burleson took him up on his goading, firing an eighteen-foot jump shot with six seconds left. The ball caromed off the rim once and then again before Thompson glided over to lay it in with three seconds to go. That final basket, he said later, was the easiest one he made all day. NC State 87, Maryland 85.

"DT was God," Whicker told me.

The NC State locker room throbbed with sound and celebration for several minutes after the game, the starkest of contrasts with the rest of Cole Field House and those morose Maryland coaches, players, and fans. "It was so silent," Howard said, "you could hear the roaches crawling on the floor." Thompson was the last Wolfpack player to exit the locker room after describing, re-describing, and analyzing his putback, noting that he had indeed paid mind to his critics' baseless belief that he was overrated, that against a more formidable opponent like Maryland, he wouldn't and couldn't live up to the hype around him. "That just goes to show what people know," he said. The notion that he had shown the country what college basketball was and could yet be, that he could send both hard-core fans and ho-hum observers into states of rapture and keep them buying tickets and tuning in and coming back for more if only he and players like him were allowed to dunk, never occurred to him. He carried himself, one writer observed, with an impassive enthusiasm, his face a blank slate, admitting that he had no appreciation or sense of the quality of his play while the game was taking place, that he concentrated so intensely that any possible distractions fell away from his frame of perception. When the Wolfpack's coaches and players arrived back on campus at 8 p.m., two thousand fans and students were waiting at Reynolds Coliseum to greet the team, chanting, "WE'RE NUMBER ONE!" In fourteen months' time, they would be.

Seventeen days later, NC State beat Maryland again, this time at Reynolds, this time 89–78, this time with Thompson scoring just 24 points but enhancing his legend nonetheless. Clad in a red NC State blazer, Jim Holshouser, the governor of North Carolina, attended the game, and afterward, John T. Caldwell, the university's chancellor, stopped a Wolfpack player on the way into the locker room to tell him, "You're all beautiful." But no one compared to Thompson. When Wolfpack forward Joe Cafferky back-rimmed a jumper during the game, Thompson ran in from the right side, jumped to catch the ball, and laid it in as he glided past the basket. On the Maryland bench, Howard and his teammates peeked at Driesell to make sure their coach wasn't looking at them. Then they leaned back to hide from him as they high-fived each other.

That moment stayed on Howard's mind through Maryland's two-point loss to NC State in that year's ACC title game, a victory that completed the Wolfpack's 1972–73 perfect season—27 games, 27 victories, no participation in the NCAA Tournament because of the probation penalty from Thompson's recruitment. And it was still on his mind come March 9, 1974: the teams' conference-championship rematch at Greensboro Coliseum. The arena's capacity: 15,262. The price of a ticket: seven dollars. At stake between the 25–1 Wolfpack and the 23–4 Terrapins: a berth in the NCAA Tournament. It would be the last year that the bracket did not include at-large teams, just conference champs and independents. Acknowledged as one of the greatest games in college basketball history, NC State's 103–100 over-time win was not Thompson's greatest game. He scored 29 points, yes, but he needed 24 shots to do it. He exited late in regulation for a spell, with the score tied at 97, with a severe leg cramp. And though Thompson got to the rim for a couple of alley-oops against Mary-land's taller players, Howard guarded him more in that game than he had or would in any of their other encounters, prevented him from scoring on an alley-oop, and held him without a point for eighteen minutes. "I did everything I could to not let him get the basketball," Howard told me. "The bigger guys didn't have the intensity to not let him get the ball. I was thinking, 'Shit, this guy ain't gonna alley-oop me.'" Thompson, after all, was the only NC State player on the floor with the potential to embarrass him in that manner.

"There were so many unbelievable plays from this guy," Howard said. "I had seen the alley-oop dunk before, but I'd never seen anybody do it with the verticality, the height. You couldn't throw the ball over his head going to the basket. He would catch everything, and it would always end up with him dropping the ball into the basket— literally dropping the ball into the basket. We'd never seen anything like him. *We'd never seen anything like him.*"

They weren't the only ones. The 1974 NCAA Tournament was practically teed up for Thompson and the Wolfpack; NC State would host the East Regional at Reynolds, and the Final Four would be in Greensboro. In his first game, Thompson had 40 points and 10 rebounds as the Wolfpack eased past Providence, 92–78, and afterward, Friars coach Dave Gavitt dared to question whether college basketball was better off for banning the dunk and, in turn, dulling Thompson's game. "Can you imagine what a show that would have been if the dunk shot was legal?" said Gavitt, who in five years would be among the founders, the principal one, of the Big East. "Just think about it for a minute. I've always been an advocate of the return of the dunk, and last night made me that much more conscious of it. Think what Thompson would be with it." Two days later, midway through the first half in the regional final, Pittsburgh's Lou Hill was about to take a jump shot when Thompson leaped to try to block it, his fingertip grazing the ball—he was actually called for goaltending—his feet bumping into the shoulder of his teammate Phil Spence. Legs bicycling as he fell, Thompson landed headfirst. The impact of his skull striking the floor sounded, a witness said, like a bowling ball dropped from atop the backboard. Blood puddled on the court from a gaping gash in his head, and his eyes rolled back as he lost consciousness. Urine flooded his shorts, an indication that his nervous system wasn't functioning.

"My teammates," Thompson later wrote in his autobiography, *Skywalker*, "feared I was dead."

Wheeled out of the arena on a stretcher, Thompson woke up in the back of an ambulance on the way to Rex Hospital in Raleigh. The scene was so terrifying, and Thompson's status a subject of such curiosity, that CBS's Walter Cronkite called the hospital, eventually getting Jim Manley, NC State's team doctor, on the phone. Manley told him that Thompson had suffered a concussion and needed fifteen stitches to patch up his head. Forty-eight minutes after he had left, Thompson strode back into Reynolds and sat on the NC State bench next to Sloan, a huge white bandage wrapped around his head, the crowd giving him a rousing ovation. It was the most dramatic aspect of the Wolfpack's 100–78 victory.

"The day he hit his head in Reynolds, then came back to the arena in the second half," Whicker told me, "was probably the most hysterical day I've experienced in sports."

Whicker did not use *hysterical* to mean *excessively humorous*. He used it to describe the hysteria, the chaos and commotion. Thompson had acquired the most valuable quality a famous athlete can own: sports heroism. He wore it like a magic cloak. He had come back from an injury that at first seemed to have put his career at risk. He had rallied, shown a measure of courage, and against UCLA in the national semifinals, he only reaffirmed that he possessed those traits. In the second half, he dropped in an alley-oop over Bill Walton as he was fouled by Dave Meyers, converting a three-point play and giving the Wolfpack its first lead. He then scored four straight points in the final minute of the second overtime, assuring an 80–77 upset of the Bruins, who had won the previous seven national championships. NC State's 76–64 victory over Marquette, to win its first NCAA title and complete a two-season stretch in which it won 57 of its 58 games, was practically a coronation.

It was also the high point of Thompson's life in basketball. NC State went 22–6 in 1974–75, his senior year, and didn't qualify for the NCAA Tournament. "That gave Thompson only one season in the national spotlight," Jack McCallum wrote in *Sports Illustrated* in 1999.

"Had he been able to use his vertical leap for show-stopping jams . . . the Thompson legend would have grown a hundredfold." Those who followed the Wolfpack closely knew how right McCallum was. In an early-season game against Buffalo State, a 144–88 rout, Thompson set an ACC record with 57 points, and 22 of those points—39 percent of Thompson's offensive output—came when he and Towe collaborated on 11 alley-oops. Buffalo State played zone all night, never attempting to guard him one-on-one. "I would repeatedly sneak in through the back door, catch Monte's high arching passes, and score, score, score," he once wrote. "I thought they'd catch on after a while, but much to my surprise and delight, they did not." The next morning's edition of the *Durham Sun* featured a headline that hinted that its author, confronted with Thompson's magnificence, had simply thrown his hands in the air: *Thompson—Impossible to Describe.*

His final basket at Reynolds Coliseum, on March 1, 1975, against UNC-Charlotte, didn't count. Less than five minutes remained in the game, the Wolfpack up by double-digits. Thompson took off on a breakaway, and for once, he did not lay the ball in with any finesse. He hammered down a tomahawk windmill dunk, as if he were showing the world what might have been, what everyone might have beheld, over his three seasons at NC State. The crowd roared like a jet engine. Norm Sloan described it later as a "touch of class." The referees, per the dunk ban, assessed Thompson a technical foul. He did not care. "That was my statement on the subject for all to see in plain view," he wrote. "It was the *dunk*, and what it meant metaphorically, that was principal to me." There could have been no better way for him to exit—by demonstrating what he could have done and had not been permitted to do. "Fame," he once said, "is fleeting." But his feats, to those who had been alongside him for the ride, were anything but. Tim Stoddard, a teammate of Thompson's at NC State and, later, a major-league pitcher for fourteen years, believed that there was nothing on a basketball court beyond Thompson's grasp, that he could jump higher than anyone, could deke and drive past any opposing team's best defender. A sea of hands would grasp at a rebound, and Thompson's, Stoddard once said, were always above everyone else's, always came away with the basketball. It didn't matter that he could, and did, drink too deeply of the waters of that fleeting fame and sports heroism. It didn't matter that he sipped Boone's Farm wine on a recruiting trip while he was still in high school. It didn't matter that he started going to campus parties at NC State and pounding beers regularly as a freshman. It didn't matter that he was drinking daily as a senior and one night slammed his Pontiac Grand Prix into a tree, his ears filled with the Stevie Wonder and Isley Brothers tunes that had been blasting from his radio, his brain blurred by alcohol. None of it mattered. DT was indefatigable. DT was everlasting. DT was God.

And the pros believed it, too. The Atlanta Hawks took him first overall in the 1975 NBA draft, and the Denver Nuggets took him first overall in the 1975 ABA draft, the picks just two and a half weeks apart, the contract offers to him identical: $2.5 million over six years. Thompson chose Denver; the ABA's faster, freer style of play and the Nuggets' roster, coached by Larry Brown and full of exciting, young players, appealed to him more. Julius Erving already had established himself as the king of the league. Yet there appeared universal agreement, from the instant he entered the ABA, that Thompson was a worthy challenger to the throne. "Everybody knows about Dr. J," the Nuggets' Willie Wise said, "but I don't think you can say 'Dr. J' and not mention David Thompson in the same breath."

Bobby Jones was in his second season with the Nuggets, his second professional season, when Thompson joined them. He noticed how Denver's opponents would react to Thompson's dunks, especially those that humiliated a player who had tried to stop him: hands up, maybe the defender lamely tried to jump with Thompson, maybe he just remained flat-footed and let Thompson sky over him, whatever. The player would act, in the moment, like nothing had happened. Just another basket. Don't worry about the arena humming or shaking. No biggie. But then, Jones would keep an eye on the man as he trotted to the other end of the court: the opponent's eyes would bug out, as if he were in shock.

Sometimes, Jones's would, too. One night during Thompson's rookie season, in a game against the San Antonio Spurs at McNichols Arena in Denver, Jones fought for position near the free-throw line, Thompson lingering behind him, as a Nuggets player took a shot. Jones pushed his man into the middle of the lane as they vied for position, but the opponent boxed him out and pinned him down. The shot hit the back of the rim solidly, and as the ball arced toward him and over his head, Jones felt two knees pressing against his back and shoulder blades. Thompson's knees.

"David jumped over me and the other guy and caught the ball and threw it back down," Jones told me. "As he did that, he toppled over both of us. We caught him so he wouldn't break his neck. That was one of the most amazing dunks I've ever seen."

The amazement built to a crescendo as the games and days passed. Against the Nets later that season, Nuggets swingman Ralph Simpson heaved an alley-oop pass that looked too far for Thompson to reach. But reach it Thompson did, catching the ball behind his head—and behind the backboard—with his right hand and jamming it. He competed in the ABA's Slam Dunk Contest at halftime of the All-Star Game and led the Nuggets into the finals against Erving's New York Nets, and once the NBA absorbed the Nuggets and three other ABA teams after the league folded that year, he at first missed neither a beat nor a dunk. He went *mano a mano* with Walton again, driving baseline during a 1977 preseason game against the Portland Trail Blazers— the defending champion Portland Trail Blazers—Walton half-sliding, half-running over to impede Thompson's path to the basket, the two of them going up at the same time. "And Bill came down a lot sooner than David did," said Jones, who was there. "David threw the ball down so hard it shattered the backboard, and the rim was somehow still attached by two little metal strips. It sort of dangled down, but it was like an explosion. It was spectacular. Maybe Vince Carter might be an exception, but I've never seen anyone jump with the explosiveness that David had." He dropped 40 points in Denver's regular-season finale, a loss to the New Orleans Jazz in April 1977 that also happened to be the last professional game in the career of his friendly foe Mo

Howard. "There wasn't anybody in the whole league," Howard, who appeared in 23 games that season for the Jazz, said, "who could guard that guy." At Cobo Hall in Detroit on April 9, 1978, he capped the subsequent regular season by torching the Pistons for 73 points—still the fourth-highest single-game total in NBA history—in a last-ditch attempt to beat out the Spurs' George Gervin for the scoring title. (Gervin scored 63 himself that night against the Jazz to edge Thompson, 27.22 to 27.15.) He signed a contract with the Nuggets for five years and $4 million. No NBA players had ever been paid more.

DT had everything. DT was already letting everything slip away.

He first smoked marijuana as a rookie, then tasted cocaine during the '76 ABA Finals, in a hotel room in New York. It was available at any and all parties he attended—pro sports and disco and the social scene in America's cities in the late '70s and early '80s, was there ever a faster lane?—and he used it more extensively during the 1979–80 season, when a foot injury limited him to 39 games and he had more free time. The rumors and leaks increased until the circumstantial evidence became too obvious and powerful to ignore. He resigned his captaincy. He missed team flights. The drugs and drinking transformed his personality, he acknowledged later, making him edgier and quicker to anger. In 1982, Doug Moe, the Nuggets' head coach, suspended him two games for showing up late to practice, arguing that the organization had coddled Thompson for too long, and a *Los Angeles Times* story laid bare the player-coach conflict and referenced the "innuendo that Thompson has dabbled with drugs." Thompson denied it on the record: "If you're hurt and you're Black and you make a lot of money, the first thing anybody says is that you're into drugs." When the *Denver Post* published a seven-story exposé of his addictions in June '82—and when, in the report's aftermath, the Nuggets traded him to the Seattle SuperSonics—it might have seemed ridiculous for Thompson to try to keep up his one-man charade. Not to him. He met with media members at the Sonics' training facility and was close to crying as he denied everything. The *Post* had lied about him. Moe had lied about him. No, he didn't have a cocaine problem. No, he hadn't skipped or shown up late to practice. "It has to hurt you when something negative like that is said," he told reporters that day. "But I'm planning on disproving all the negative things that have been said."

He lasted less than two full seasons in Seattle. After a loss in Philadelphia to Erving and the 76ers in March 1984, with the Sonics' next game in East Rutherford against the Nets, Thompson and four teammates rented a limousine and zoomed up the Jersey Turnpike into Midtown Manhattan . . . to Studio 54. There, during a fight with a club employee, Thompson tumbled down a staircase and tore the medial collateral and posterior cruciate ligaments in his left knee. He never played in the NBA again after that night. Instead, he entered a twenty-eight-day program in Denver. He was charged with assaulting his wife and spent time in jail. He declared bankruptcy, selling his 1974 NCAA Championship ring for $44,427.

"The lift you get from cocaine, high as it is," he once wrote, "is nothing next to the slam dunk that comes afterwards."

It took Thompson years to get and stay sober, to come to terms with and learn from his past. "You can't do anything about it," he once said. "I'm happy with my career. I did something that very few people ever did." Like Earl Manigault before him, his life has been laced with nostalgia for who he was and poignancy for who and what he might have been. In 1997, a reporter asked him the sharp, direct, natural question: What would your career have been like without the drugs? "Hard to say," Thompson told him in something close to a whisper.

At the 2009 Naismith Memorial Basketball Hall of Fame inductions, a fellow North Carolinian picked Thompson, an inductee himself in 1996, to accompany him to the stage as his presenter. "I was eleven years old in 1974," Michael Jordan said that night. "I was in love with David Thompson." The NCAA, in 2013, held a celebration for the seventy-fifth anniversary of the men's basketball tournament. Seated next to Kareem Abdul-Jabbar for the festivities, Thompson joked to him, "You killed all my college highlights." He could still dunk in 2016, when he was sixty-two, as if he were making up for lost time, which he was.

"I've always thought that one of the biggest tragedies of college basketball," Monte Towe once said, "is there was no dunking when David Thompson played."

It was a tragedy of Thompson's life, too. Just not the only one. Just not the biggest. Over the months I spent researching and writing this book, I emailed Thompson several times requesting an interview—something, anything, even just a brief phone conversation—and I reached out to friends and acquaintances of his to lobby on my behalf. "He doesn't answer emails," Mo Howard said after I told him of my frustration, and another source said, "I feel like he's just not interested, but I understand that you would like him to tell you that." He never did. He never responded. In December 2023, North Carolina State honored him by unveiling a statue of him in the courtyard outside Reynolds Coliseum. Life-sized, set on a pedestal, the structure depicts Thompson in midair, in mid-leap, his arms taut, his hands clutching a basketball above his head. When the sculptor consulted him about the statue's design, Thompson advised him, *Just make it look like I'm alley-ooping, and it'll be great.* It does. It is. But it only leads to a question bittersweet and perhaps impossible to answer. The dunk ban had deprived him, and everyone who loved basketball, of so much. His addictions had deprived him of even more. How much greater could David Thompson have been? It's hard to say. It's so hard to say.

14

JULIUS

More than anyone, he brought the dunk down from the clouds and into people's living rooms. First, though, he had to introduce himself, as only he could.

Inside the **Ernest N. Morial** Convention Center, hard on the shore of the Mississippi River, a man who once could soar at last took a seat. It was a Sunday in early April, a gorgeous afternoon in New Orleans, the off-day between the semifinal games and the championship game of the 2022 NCAA Men's Final Four. Canceled in 2020, all 67 of its games played in Indianapolis and closed to the public in 2021, the NCAA Tournament had returned to normal for the first time since the COVID-19 pandemic began, and the presence of four traditional powers of college basketball—Duke, North Carolina, Kansas, and Villanova—in a city renowned for its nightlife had made the weekend of this Final Four an especially lively scene. The NCAA's "Fan Fest," a carnival of basketball parlor games and celebrity appearances, of pop-a-shot competitions and autograph-seeker lines that inched along like conveyor belts, siphoned some of the crowds from the French Quarter into the convention center. There, one attraction drew more interest and attention than any other. More than 160 people—fathers, sons, mothers, daughters, middle-aged men in Philadelphia 76ers jerseys, younger men wearing various other NBA jerseys, the curious, the devoted, the longtime appreciators of aerial artistry, the kinds of dudes who just want someone of prominence to acknowledge them and maybe, just maybe, sign their shirts—snaked around the carpeted floor in a roped-off area fit for a Disney World ride. They gripped basketballs and glossy magazines, high-top sneakers and brand-new pens, and kept their eyes turned to an empty table. The line for a seventy-two-year-old man, for Julius Erving, was so long that the festival's officials stopped allowing people to wait in it.

AT&T had sponsored this appearance by Erving, the sort of quick fly-in, fly-out trip that famous retired athletes make often, in which they are compensated handsomely for minimal effort and bask in the reassurance that they, though retired, are still famous. An emcee from the company—early forties, his hair combed in a perfect black pompadour, his mouth filled with flawless teeth—introduced Erving with a lengthy soliloquy in which he used the word *innovator* several times. As in, *He was a true innovator, an influence on everything that came after him*. Then, through a doorway in a portable room divider, fifteen minutes after his scheduled arrival time, Erving materialized: sleek gray suit, black sneakers, a shock of white hair capping his head as if he were a six-foot-seven-inch alp.

When the applause subsided, the emcee wouldn't let Erving get to the autographs just yet. He handed him a microphone. Had to give the folks a taste. Had to let everyone see some of Erving's personality. Without hesitating, the emcee mentioned the reason that Erving had captivated so many basketball fans during his sixteen-year professional career, the reason that so many of those fans had been willing to stand in line, thirty-five years after he had played his final game, just for the briefest of encounters with him.

"The slam dunk," the emcee said. "You gave it grace, suave. You gave it flair, style."

Erving grinned a sheepish grin. What memories flashed through his brain just then? The takeoff-from-the-foul-line flight he embarked on to win the 1976 ABA Slam Dunk Contest? The rock-the-cradle classic from January 1983, when he scooped up a loose ball in his right hand and wrist like a jai alai ball in a chistera, swooped down on the Lakers' Michael Cooper, and sent the Spectrum into a frenzy? That had to be top of mind always for him, didn't it? A big game between the league's two best teams, Erving soaring over one of the NBA's best defensive players for the greatest in-game dunk of all—maybe the greatest dunk of all, given the setting and circumstances and context—the sequence foreshadowing the championship to which he would lead the Sixers later that season, when they'd wipe out the Lakers in four games in the finals . . . had to be, right? No. The aftermath of that transcendent moment and others came to mind first. "You're making my knees hurt, talking about all that slam dunking," he said, and he laughed, but he went from sheepish to serious in a heartbeat.

"There's a price you pay, the physical taxation on your body," he said. "Bill Walton is walking around here. He used to dunk the ball a lot, close to the basket. He's walking now, and his knees are hurting. His feet are hurting. I'm not hurting as much as he is. But believe me, I hurt. That's part of the sacrifice because of the glory that you get when you are able to do something like a Vince Carter or a Clyde Drexler or a Michael Jordan or a Julius Erving or a Kobe Bryant."

This is not how sports heroes are supposed to speak during public appearances. They are supposed to play to the crowd and hand out one harmless hello after another. They are not supposed to say to the gathered masses something that the gathered masses either did not want to hear or weren't at all interested in hearing. Sports heroes are not supposed to be poignant and wistful. They are not supposed to lament, to a convention center full of strangers, the cost of the talents and trademarks that made them great. Here was Julius Erving, though, the immortal Dr. J., throwing into stark relief the lasting significance of an act that, to someone unfamiliar with the history of basketball, to someone who fails to recognize or acknowledge the degree to which sports can shape and have shaped the mores and norms of American society, might seem nothing more than the most direct way to send a leather ball through an iron hoop. The dunk had catapulted him and those players who followed and modeled themselves after him—those players he himself had just named: Jordan and Bryant and Drexler and Carter—into varying spheres of stardom. The dunk—and, more specifically, Erving's iterations of the dunk—had elevated basketball from a minor pastime in this country into a multibillion-dollar global industry. The dunk had made The Doctor a king. Just ask the people who were standing there in line.

"If they're at that game and you make a play and you posterize somebody, they remember that, and they like to talk about it," Erving said. "They talk about it like they did it. And that's what it is. It is a shared experience."

Ready, at last, to share it again, he sat down and began to sign.

On Wednesday, October 20, 1976, a telephone rang inside the Spectrum, the brown-walled, oblong arena in south Philadelphia that was, at the time, the Sixers' headquarters and home court. Seated in his office, at once excited and nervous in anticipation of the call, Pat Williams, the team's general manager, answered. On the line was Roy Boe, the owner of the New York Nets of the American Basketball Association. It was 1:40 p.m. The course of the Sixers franchise, along with that of professional basketball in the United States, was about to change forever.

"He starts with small talk," Williams told me, "and my heart is beating like a trip-hammer."

Julius Erving had been holding out of the Nets' training camp for two weeks. The team's player-personnel people had concluded that they had to trade him, but Boe didn't want players in return for Erving. He wanted cash. The ABA was dissolving, Boe was moving the Nets to the NBA, and he needed money to pay a territorial fee to the New York Knicks. Erving was his meal ticket: three ABA championships, three scoring titles, four MVP awards with the Virginia Squires and the Nets, the Afro, the nickname. To Boe, it was more important to be in the NBA than it was to retain the best player in a league that would soon be defunct.

Irwin Weiner, Erving's agent, already had told Williams that, for the then-princely sum of $6 million—half to Erving at $450,000 annually over a six-year contract, half to the Nets—Dr. J would be happy to play in Philadelphia . . . as long as Boe signed off on the deal. First, though, Williams had to get Fitz Dixon, the Sixers' owner, to understand that Erving was worth such a deal; for Williams, no easy task. When the two met to discuss the matter, Dixon asked, "Who is Julius Erving?" Only after Williams assured him that Erving was "the Babe Ruth of basketball" did Dixon give the move his blessing.

Now, on the phone, Boe finally stopped stalling and delivered the news that Williams was eager, even desperate, to hear: the Nets would accept the Sixers' offer. Adrenaline surged through Williams. He flashed a thumbs-up sign to the other man in the room, Jack Mc-Mahon, the Sixers' top scout, who reacted with such exuberance that he nearly fell out of his chair.

The reasons for Williams and McMahon's joy went beyond wins and losses, though, beyond the fact that the Sixers, by acquiring Erving, had instantaneously elevated themselves into championship contenders. Erving was not merely a marvelous scorer. His fluid grace on the court, his leaping ability, and his eleven-inch hands combined to make him a player unlike any in basketball, his game defined by dunks that had to be seen to be believed . . . except no one in Philadelphia, or most of the United States, had seen them. Yes, the Nets were based in the nation's largest media market, and that market had more than its share of basketball junkies. But the ABA had no franchise in the City of Brotherly Love and no national-television contract.

"It was word of mouth, just little trickles," Williams told me. "Unless you were an ABA fan—and there weren't many of them—and walked into a building, the greater world had no idea who this guy was. The ABA purists will tell you that the greater stage never saw him at his best. His best was from twenty-one to twenty-six. The wear and tear were just beginning. The first five years, he was invisible, but the word was 'You haven't seen anything like this guy.'"

Even at the University of Massachusetts, Erving had been anonymous relative to the nation's other college basketball stars: LSU's "Pistol" Pete Maravich, Jacksonville's Artis Gilmore, North Carolina's Charlie

Scott, St. Bonaventure's Bob Lanier. Previewing UMass's first-round matchup against Marquette in the 1970 National Invitational Tournament, Owen Davis of the *Chapel Hill Press* wrote: "Massachusetts qualified for the NIT by winning the Yankee Conference. To do that, it had to beat Vermont, Connecticut, New Hampshire, Maine, and Rhode Island. In that conference, basketball isn't even a major winter sport. Hockey is." Seventeen minutes into that game, though, Marquette—the only nationally ranked team in the tournament—couldn't shake the Minutemen. A sophomore at the time, Erving was dominating play, wowing the Madison Square Garden crowd and infuriating Warriors coach Al McGuire, who while sitting on the bench turned to one of his assistants, Hank Raymonds.

"Who the fuck is that?"

"Coach, that's Julius."

"Who the fuck is Julius?"

To answer McGuire's question, you have to travel back in time to 1956 and head to Roosevelt, New York, a hamlet in the southern center of Long Island. At Parkside Gardens, a public-housing project there, Julius Erving—"June" to his mother, his elder sister, and his younger brother—was at age six so desperate to peek out the window of his family's third-floor apartment that he would don his blue Keds, sprint across the room, and jump once he reached the sill, hoping to glimpse the sky. His parents were divorced, and on days when his father visited him, June plopped himself onto the seat of a swing set outside the Gardens, pumped his legs until, as the swing rocked him higher and higher, he leaped out of it as if he were a pebble in a slingshot. And his father marveled at how high and how far the child could jump.

Julius was a rule follower, throughout his childhood and for most, though not all, of his adult life. His mother, when he was young, told him that he must respect his elders, must stay quiet in class and listen to his teachers, must complete his schoolwork before he could go outside to play basketball or anything else. He listened to her, always. "I stand by the rules, move with care and respect and wariness," he wrote in his autobiography, *Dr. J.* "I enjoy rules, and games have rules. A basketball court has rules and order and laws and requirements; it is regulated. I like that aspect of it: the predictability of a universe, the basketball court, the football field, where we are all set in motion by the same strictures and standards." It was an interesting and perhaps unexpected perspective from someone who set himself apart from his teammates and competitors through the spectacular fashion in which he defied basketball's, and human physiology's, limits and expectations. While interviewing Erving for a 1985 *Esquire* profile, seated across a table from him in the offices of Erving's eponymous capital holding company, writer Mark Jacobson told him, "What you do affirms the supremacy of all beings. Seeing you play basketball has enriched my life." The man, the name, and the money behind the Erving Group offered a polite thank-you.

"Every serious hoop fan remembers the first time he saw Julius Erving play basketball," Jacobson wrote. "My grandfather . . . probably had the same feeling the first time he saw Willie Mays go back on a fly ball."

Erving's first dunk came on an eight-foot playground basket, and neither he nor any of his peers paid it much mind when, as a five-eleven sophomore at Roosevelt High School, he dunked on a ten-foot hoop. "Everyone else," he once said, "could do it." As a junior, six foot four now, he was a tight end on Roosevelt's football team, and after practice one day, he walked into the gymnasium, still clad in his shoulder and thigh pads and, having taken off his cleats on the way to the locker room, in stockinged feet. His best friend, Leon Saunders, followed him.

"Somebody threw him a ball, and he picked up the ball and dunked it in his full football pads," Saunders told me. The act sparked a discussion among the athletes in the gym: How big was a basketball rim? Could you dunk two balls at once? The teens didn't know the specific dimensions, that the diameter of a hoop is eighteen inches but the diameter of a men's basketball is just less than nine and a half inches, that in theory no, one could not dunk two basketballs at once, but that in practice an athlete whose hands were big enough and strong enough to squeeze each ball just enough to test the thresholds of the ball—its elasticity outside and its air pressure inside—could do it.

"Then he picks up another ball," Saunders said, "and dunks them both at the same time. It wasn't like he took a running start or there was anybody in front of him. He just bounced the ball, grabbed it—he could grab a ball in each hand easily—just walked up to the rim and dunked two balls. This was more than a demonstration. This was: 'This is what I can do.'"

Erving played high school football for just that one season. Ray Wilson, Roosevelt's basketball coach, pressed him to focus on one sport, though Wilson wasn't so enamored with Erving's skills and potential that he would turn the team over to him: Erving came off the bench his junior season . . . and still scored 18 points a game. "We use Erving whenever we need him the most," Wilson said at the time. He wore ankle weights for a while—so that he would feel lighter on the court, like a hitter putting a doughnut on his bat to swing in the on-deck circle—but eventually disposed of them. "My spring is natural," he once said. "I felt grounded" with the weights. His individual statistics as a senior were outstanding—23 points and 13 rebounds a game, as Roosevelt reached the second round of its league playoffs—but there was a growing gap between the conventional numbers he put up and the gobsmacking manner in which he compiled them. During a week-long stay in Schroon Lake, New York, at the Shamrock Basketball Camp, run by NBA veteran Wayne Embry, Erving raised his hand when the Knicks' Harthorne Wingo, one of the camp's counselors, wanted someone to "give him a run." Erving did . . . and jammed over him. But that dunk was pie for Erving compared to one that he delivered weeks after he graduated from Roosevelt. He and Saunders sauntered into the gymnasium at Kennedy Rec Center in Hempstead, where a pickup game was raging and where one player, whose first name was Bob, was dominating. *Julius, Julius, glad you're here*, Saunders remembered a couple of players saying. *You gotta put this dude Bob in his place. He's just dunking on everybody.* Early in the next game, Saunders took a jump shot. It was long. The ball hit the back of the rim and careened straight up into the air. Bob jumped to pull down the rebound, but Erving jumped with him, rose over him, and dunked it on his way down. "The whole gym," Saunders told me, "fell on the floor."

That October, the 1968 Summer Olympics were held in Mexico City—the Olympics of John Carlos and Tommie Smith, of George Foreman pounding and thumping the heavyweight field, of Czechoslovakian gymnast Vera Caslavska quietly shunning the Soviet national anthem to protest the invasion of her homeland. And they were, too, the Olympics at which Bob Beamon, a native of Queens and an alumnus of Jamaica High School, long-jumped twenty-nine feet, two and a quarter inches, winning the gold medal and establishing a world record that lasted twenty-three years . . . all just a couple of months after Julius Erving threw one down on him at Kennedy Rec. (Beamon confirmed the account for me through a public-relations representative.)

"He probably would have dusted Julius in the long jump," Saunders said. "But going straight up? That was a different story."

Ray Wilson had been a teammate, at Boston University, of Jack Leamon, the head coach at the University of Massachusetts. And Erving found both UMass's pastoral Amherst campus and the free-flowing system that Leamon ran so appealing that his college choice was relatively easy. A state school such as UMass, he told me, would give him a more "regional perspective, not just local but regional," exposing him to a broader swath of people than even the integrated communities of Long Island had, to what he once called "the white world. I feel prepared, but I am also, for the first time, intimidated."

He had no need to be. Pickup games at UMass's Boyden Gymnasium soon became must-see events. Like all freshmen throughout college basketball, Erving couldn't play for his university's varsity team, and like all players throughout college basketball, he wasn't allowed to dunk in a game. So five or six dozen people crammed into the gym to watch him show off and slam, reverse and rock the cradle, during workouts and warm-ups. The UMass freshmen went unbeaten, 17–0, and over Erving's sophomore and junior seasons with the Minutemen, the most difficult aspect of the game for him was quelling his instinct to jam the ball on a fastbreak. Put simply, he did everything better than everyone else. Pat Williams once heard of a conversation between two sportswriters, one of whom had covered Erving at UMass.

"Tell me about this young Jewish kid, this Julius Erving."

"Well, for starters, I don't think he's Jewish."

"How come?"

"He's Black, for one thing. And for another, I'm not sure he's not from another planet. I saw him make some moves that aren't supposed to be humanly possible."

"So why don't you write about them?"

"I'm not sure anybody would believe me."

Every aspect of his greatness was a whisper on the wind. In fact, Erving was so under the radar at UMass that he wasn't initially invited to the Olympic development program in 1970. He ended up being a late arrival to the camp but didn't remain on the roster for the 1972 Games; he lost his amateur status in 1971, turning pro after his junior season. There was a benefit to his early departure from Amherst, though: because he was no longer eligible for college basketball, there was nothing stopping him from playing in the Rucker Pro League.

Their feet would dangle in the air just a little longer than the man they came to see, white sneakers swinging off the roofs and ledges of the brick apartment buildings that towered over Rucker Park and provided a helicopter-high view of the court . . . of the goings-on in the Pro League . . . of the genius creation of Holcombe Rucker . . . of the professional hoopers who would flock to Harlem in the summer to compete against the guys who had made their bones on the playground, the guys who had the benefit of mystery . . . *How good were they really? What if they got their shot?* . . . a helicopter-high view of the one who best straddled both of those worlds . . . a prime place to watch Julius Erving. Teenagers and young men and women from Harlem, from throughout the five boroughs, dozens of them, even hundreds, swarming around and above the court—all of them drawn by Erving's reputation, by the nickname that Leon Saunders had given him in high school and that Rucker would make immortal.

The Doctor? Dr. J? Saunders gets the credit for those everlasting sobriquets. He and Erving were playing at Roosevelt Park one day, and Saunders was so pedantic about the rules, knew them so well and stuck to them so rigidly and insisted that his friend do the same, that Julius muttered to him, *Man, you're like you're some kind of professor.* Saunders fired back a retort: *Who are you to argue? Who are you, a doctor?* Passing in the halls of Roosevelt High, they'd acknowledge each other with their new pet names. "He'd say, 'Professor.' And I'd say, 'Doctor,'" Saunders told me. "Nobody else called me 'Professor' but him, and nobody else called him 'Doctor' but me."

Not until Rucker. In his first game, the Westsiders, his team in the Pro League, took on the Cincinnati Kings, with Nate "Tiny" Archibald and a couple of Notre Dame standouts: guard Austin Carr and forward Sid Catlett, who'd starred at DeMatha High School and had a cup of coffee in the NBA. Rain forced the game indoors, and on the Westsiders' first possession, Erving lifted off from the right side of the foul line—"I can picture it forever," said Peter Vecsey, who coached the team—and dunked over Catlett, who was six foot eight. "We've seen scenes with people at Rucker coming out of the stands and doing dances," Vecsey told me, "and there's me and my assistant coach, Butch Bissell, doing the same thing. It was, 'What the fuck was that?'"

The more Erving came around, the more his rep spread, and the courtside ringmasters had to start paying him his proper respect in the proper Rucker way. "Everybody in the league had a nickname: Sky King, Helicopter, this and that," Saunders told me. "We go there, one of the first times he played there, and the guy on the mic says, 'Julius, I've heard of you, man. What's your nickname, man?' Julius said, 'I don't know if I have a nickname, man.'"

The mic man suggested "The Claw," a reference to the size of

Erving's hands. Erving didn't like it. He looked over at Saunders. *If you're going to call me anything,* he told the guy, *call me "The Doctor."*

"That's the first time it became public," Saunders said. "That's when it stuck. The guy was salivating. 'The Doctor—I can work with that. Here comes The Doctor. He's ready to operate.'"

He could not be so free, so imaginative, in college. After one Rucker game, fifty kids took the court, all of them mimicking him, dunking imaginary basketballs behind their backs. He felt, he once wrote, an "intense emotional connection" with those who attended his games there, for they seemed to understand that they were watching him blossom into the player he was always supposed to be, that they were discovering him at the very same time that he was discovering himself—"this Black community [who] don't have very much. This is their park—their outlet and their experience." Now they had him. Now he was part of them. In one game, he drove on six-foot-nine center Tom Hoover, who had played in the NBA and ABA for five seasons, and Hoover knocked him to the deck with a warning: "Don't be coming in here with that weak stuff." The next time Erving got the ball and took it to the rim, Hoover jumped to try to prevent him from dunking, and Erving jammed the ball with such force that it broke Hoover's right hand.

"I'll tell you something else, man," Saunders said. "I really look at Julius, and it would be hard to say I have no bias, but I thought he was a better dunker than Michael Jordan in this sense: If you really look at Michael, Michael had a much better handle than Julius. He would basically use his handle, get a step on somebody, and once he got a step on you, he rose and would finish in great fashion. Julius would just jump in your face, just jump over you, and dunk on you. 'I don't have to fake you out. I don't have to get a step or a lane. I'm just going to jump over you and dunk in your face.'"

On Sunday, September 9, 1973, the Westsiders beat the Courtsmen at Mahoney Gym, on the campus of City College of New York, 135–124, to win their second straight pro league title. For the three thousand people on hand, Erving scored 27 points and, according to one witness, unleashed "a magical assortment of smashing dunks." But the true treat for those New Yorkers, in a way, was yet ahead. A month earlier, on August 1, after Erving had spent his first two ABA seasons with them, the Virginia Squires had sent him back to Long Island by trading him to the New York Nets.

Against Al McGuire and Marquette, in that who-the-fuck-is-he game, Erving finished with 18 points, taking just 13 shots—"I don't think we gave him the ball enough," Jack Leamon said after his team's 62–55 loss—and impressing McGuire from beginning to end. "Erving will be a pro," he said. A year later, Erving took advantage of a measure the ABA had implemented, and that the NBA didn't have, to try to entice young, rising talent: an economic hardship rule that allowed players to leave college early. Believing that he had accomplished everything he could at UMass, he turned pro, and Earl Foreman, the owner of the Squires, bought his rights for $10,000. The only franchise Erving negotiated with, they signed him to a four-year, $500,000 contract that included a "sheepskin clause," a $10,000 bonus once he completed his degree. The rule was a necessity. The ABA was regarded as a ragtag collection of small-time teams that needed gimmicks to draw attention to itself. So everyone in the league, including its player-personnel directors and coaches, was willing to take chances, including and especially when it came to scouting and acquiring talent. Al Bianchi, the Squires' coach, and Johnny Kerr, their general manager, struggled even to get their hands on game film of Erving from his years at UMass, and once they did, they could barely make him out amid the grainy gray, black, and white of the moving images. It wasn't until Erving took part in a Squires tryout camp in Richmond that Bianchi and Kerr understood who and what they had in him. Just shaking his hand was incredible; Kerr never forgot it. "I never saw such long fingers," he once said. "They were the fingers of a pianist or a surgeon." At camp, Erving dashed up and down the court, dunking over fellow first-timers and Squires veterans alike. *Look what we found*, Bianchi thought. During a pickup game, one player's shot caromed off the back of the rim, high into the air, and every player on the floor, it seemed to Kerr, jumped to try to grab it.

"Out of the middle of the pack came Julius . . . up . . . up . . . up," Kerr once said. "He cupped the rebound with one hand and then slammed it through the rim, all in one motion. The gym went silent. All the players just stopped for a few seconds. This was a tryout camp, and I had just watched one of the best plays I had ever seen in my life. I didn't know he'd become a living legend, but he had greatness about him that you could just sense. A young Julius Erving was like Thomas Edison. He was inventing something new every night."

After Erving's second year with the Squires, it became obvious to him and anyone else who understood his value to the ABA that his contract had left him terribly underpaid. He led the league in scoring (31.9 points a game) and in minutes played per game (42.2) during the 1972–73 season and spent his nights literally dreaming of dunking. He demanded a new deal, precipitating a snarl in which two NBA teams, the Atlanta Hawks and Milwaukee Bucks, battled for his rights, only to have Foreman deal him to the Nets. The trade was wild. Foreman was so revenue-strapped and so desperate to be out from under Erving's contract, even if The Doctor was the bargain of all bargains, that all the Squires got in return was forward George Carter and, in Foreman's words, "a lot of cash."

The Nets got the figure who—over more than a half century since the trade, through the franchise's persistent relocating, from the ABA to the NBA, from Uniondale to East Rutherford to Brooklyn—still embodies their brightest days. Jason Kidd, Kenyon Martin, Kevin Durant, Kyrie Irving: none of them springs to mind first when someone thinks of the mostly woebegone Nets. Erving, with that sphere of an Afro, with his red-white-and-blue jersey dotted with stars, does. And should. "He has all the moves ever invented," Phil Pepe wrote in the *Daily News* on August 1, the day after the trade, "and a lot that never were invented." His return required his reintroduction to hoops fans in the New York area and an introduction to those who had never heard of him and who otherwise might never know who he was. Such was the lot of those who played in the ABA. The nostalgia for it that exists today, the warm memories, didn't exist, couldn't exist, then. It was just an upstart struggling to stay alive.

"Julius Erving symbolizes the ABA," Bob Costas, who began his professional broadcasting career as the play-by-play voice of the league's Spirits of St. Louis, once said, "and the mystique that exists about Julius to this day is there because he began his career in 'the other league.' How many people really saw Julius with the Virginia Squires? . . . The ABA was like basketball's Wild West, and Julius Erving, George Gervin, James Silas, and the other ABA stars were the gunfighters."

And as everyone knows, every great gunfighter needs to win a duel.

The people in charge of the ABA were under no illusions about the condition of their league as it entered its ninth season. Despite its star power—Connie Hawkins, George McGinnis, Erving, more— franchises were folding, or relocating and then folding, every year. Two, the San Diego Sails and Utah Stars, went under during that 1975–76 season. Rather than committing to keep the league afloat, its top-drawing teams—the Nets, with Erving, and the Denver Nuggets, with their sky-walking star, David Thompson—were eyeballing the NBA, looking to bolt to a stabler, more lucrative situation. To juice interest, and with less to lose with each passing day, the league's decision-makers tried a new format for its midseason All-Star Game at McNichols Arena: the Nuggets, as the defending champions and the game's hosts, would take on a squad of players picked from the ABA's other six teams. That wasn't all. The country-western singers Glen Campbell and Charlie Rich would perform before the game, and, at the suggestion of Jim Bukata, the league's public-relations director, there would be a slam dunk contest at halftime.

Five players, all of whom would already be in Denver for the game, would take part: Erving, Thompson, George Gervin, Artis Gilmore, and Larry Kenon. Including a non–All-Star in the contest would have required flying in a non–All-Star for the contest, and no one in the league was about to spend that extra money. Erving asked Kevin Loughery, the Nets' head coach, if the contest ought to have a white participant, and in fact, the league invited the Nuggets' Bobby Jones to compete. Jones declined. "I wanted to win the All-Star Game," he told me. "I didn't have the energy to do what those guys did."

On January 27, 1976, with 17,798—the largest crowd in ABA history—on hand, with $1,200 in prize money at stake, the five competitors were briefed on the rules before commencing with the contest. Each of them could attempt up to five dunks in a two-minute span. One of the dunks had to be from a stationary position; one had to have the player start his move from the foul line, ten feet away, or beyond. Two contestants would dunk on one basket and three would dunk on the other, the public-address announcer told everyone, "to take pressure off the rims and backboards." Based on "artistic ability, imagination, body flow, and fan response," four judges would determine the winner. The panel: former Knicks star and Nuggets general manager Vince Boryla; Nuggets super-fan Alberta Worthington; high school standout LaVon Williams, who was "Mr. Basketball" in Colorado before heading off to the University of Kentucky; and Barry Fey, a former guard at Penn who, as a concert promoter, had set up the pregame festivities with Campbell and Rich.

Gilmore, the tallest competitor at seven foot two, appeared unsure of what to do, as if he hadn't practiced or planned his dunks or was, for whatever reason, holding back. Gervin and Kenon were a little looser, but there was a mood of tentativeness in the arena until Thompson got the ball. Fresh from a remarkable career at North Carolina State and in his rookie season with the Nuggets, he had been nervous throughout the days leading into the contest, so eager was he to live up to the home crowd's expectations and hopes. His teammates had been pumping him up, encouraging him, letting him know which of his dunks they thought were his best. From the right side, he charged toward the hoop and hammered down a powerful right-handed slam. Working quickly, he ripped off a double-pump two-handed reverse and, from the left baseline, a 360-degree spin and jam, establishing himself as the man to beat.

But now, it was Erving's turn. Standing directly under the basket, he dunked two balls at once—a nod, perhaps unconsciously, to his Roosevelt days. Then he walked out to halfcourt, then back to the free-throw line, then back to the opposite free-throw line, counting and measuring his steps as he went. Before the contest, he had made a $1,500 bet with Doug Moe, then an assistant coach with the Nuggets, that he could take off from the foul line and dunk during his descent. He paused, bent at the waist, then started, a slight stutter step, then a sprint into four floor-eating strides from the midcourt stripe to just inside the foul line, then . . . whoosh. Up.

"I've described Julius as more of a glider than a jumper," Jones told me. "He was more of a long jumper."

The crowd let out a communal *Whoa*. Erving lost the bet to Moe, but he didn't need another dunk to win the contest. After a reverse from the right side, he swooped in from the left side, grabbing the rim with his left hand and windmilling the ball through the hoop with his right, then finishing with an "Iron Cross" dunk from the right base-line, spreading his arms and dunking the ball without looking at the basket. All the game's players greeted him at halfcourt to congratulate him. The judges' decision was a formality.

"It was something else," Erving told me. "It's still talked about today. I didn't know it would have such a lasting effect on basketball history, and neither did any of the other players. I don't think any of us really knew. We were the ABA, and we were crowd-pleasers. Yes, we made history, but the intention wasn't making history."

The All-Star Game—and, in turn, the dunk contest—was sup-posed to have been broadcast nationally but ended up being televised in just five markets: Denver, Indianapolis, Louisville, San Antonio, and St. Louis. Since the game didn't end until after 2 a.m. Eastern time, the ripples from the contest didn't start spreading immediately. Only after *Good Morning America* and the *Today* show featured Erving and Thompson did the magnitude of the event begin to reveal itself. "Merger plans had long been in the works between the ABA and the NBA," ESPN's Eric Neel once wrote, "but the contest no doubt has-tened them." Afterward, Erving said that he was unlikely to compete in another dunk contest ever again, that his knees were "75 percent of what they used to be." (He did, in fact, compete in another: the NBA's 1984 contest, where he finished second to the Phoenix Suns' Larry

Nance.) But he and the ABA had already ignited, or at least accelerated, an insurrection within pro basketball. The slam dunk was cool,
and the ABA had embraced it, which made the ABA cool, which
made the NBA seem stuffy and stiff in comparison, mostly because
it didn't have the athlete who, more than anyone, had made the slam
dunk cool.

In Philadelphia, Pat Williams had watched those TV highlights of
the contest.

"That," he told me, "is what really put Julius on the stage."

Erving never missed a game during his three-year career with the
Nets, leading them to the league championship in 1974 and 1976, and
was at times seemingly too good to be true. Long before San Antonio
Spurs coach Gregg Popovich figured out that he could scream at his
franchise centerpiece, Tim Duncan, and that Duncan would take the
criticism without complaint, and that the other, lesser players would
understand Popovich gave the team's superstar no special dispensation,
Kevin Loughery used the same psychological tactic with Erving. Doc
messed up, even when he didn't. Doc was no different, even if he was.

One night, Erving dunked over three defenders, and Loughery
called a time-out for no reason other than to pull Erving aside and tell
him, *You just played the greatest three-minute stretch of basketball I've ever
watched.* Rod Thorn, an assistant under Loughery, had never seen a
player catch and dunk an alley-oop pass with one hand until he saw
Erving do it. The shame was that his exploits took place so often under
the blanket of the ABA's obscurity. In Game 6 of the '76 ABA Finals,
Erving scored 31 points, pulled down 19 rebounds, and blocked four
shots as the Nets rallied from a 22-point deficit in the third quarter to
beat the Denver Nuggets, 112–106, and win the series in six games. As
they stormed the Nassau Coliseum court, Nets fans nearly trampled
Nuggets play-by-play voice Al Albert, who climbed atop a table to
escape. Albert lost his microphone and headset. The phone and cable
lines he needed for his broadcast were cut. His television monitor
crashed to the floor. The chaotic scene was a bittersweet valedictory

for The Doctor's tenure: the passion and adoration that he would earn over his career in the NBA, with the Sixers, would manifest itself in that final game . . . and never again with the Nets. Attendance was low throughout the ABA. So was revenue. The franchises were too regional. The league was falling apart.

"Everybody thought we were in the hinterlands," Bill Melchionni told me. "We were minor-league."

Four ABA teams merged with the NBA in June 1976. "I can say without a doubt," broadcaster John Sterling, who was the Nets' radio play-by-play voice at the time, once said, "that what finally convinced the NBA to merge was a chance to get Julius in the league." Melchionni, who had become the Nets' general manager immediately after that championship series, began fielding phone calls from civic leaders and chambers of commerce around the country, begging to have Erving and the Nets come to their cities to play exhibition games, offering as much as $50,000 as enticement. "We were scheduled to play two games in Vegas," Melchionni told me. "Guys would ask, 'How many minutes is he going to play?' And I'd say, 'It's an exhibition game. He's not going to play forty-eight minutes.'"

The calls stopped, of course, after Wednesday, October 20, 1976. The last day that Julius Erving belonged to the ABA. The first day that the NBA belonged to Julius Erving.

There's a narrative about the NBA, and if you're at all familiar with the history of pro basketball, you're familiar with the narrative.

The narrative goes like this: In the late 1970s, the league was in a bad way. Drug use and abuse, of cocaine in particular, was rampant. The lack of a dynastic team and a run of small-market franchises winning championships—Portland in 1977, Washington in 1978, Seattle in 1979—caused fan interest to fall. TV ratings plummeted to the point that CBS, the league's primary rights holder, had to tape-delay games in the NBA Finals. Then . . . along came Magic Johnson and Larry Bird in the fall of '79, bringing with them the thirty-five million people who had tuned in to their battle in that year's NCAA Championship

Game, joining the league's marquee teams—Bird, the Celtics; Magic, the Lakers—and returning them to glory and breathing life back into one of sports' best rivalries. From a four-year deal with CBS for $74 million when Bird and Magic debuted, the NBA by 2002 had contracts with ABC, ESPN, and TNT, each of which was six years, the sum of which was worth more than $4.6 billion, and you can trace that ascension by drawing a line from Bird and Magic—not *Bird and Johnson*, always *Bird and Magic*—to Michael to Shaq and Kobe. That's the narrative, boiled down: Bird and Magic saved the NBA. It's difficult to dispute it.

"I think," Julius Erving told me one day over the phone, "that's bullshit."

There are only so many occasions when an athlete of Erving's stature and accomplishments reveals the full depth and dimension of his ego, of the indignation that even the slightest of slights causes him. Here was one of those occasions. Bird and Magic saved the NBA? *Hell, no*, Julius Erving said. *Hell, no.*

"Obviously it was a great rivalry between the two individuals and the two franchises because they played for the NCAA championship, then moved on and it was pretty much Magic playing for the NBA championship, Bird eventually," he told me. "It's a good story. It was a good story. But truth be told, I think in terms of the popularity of the league, the league was never more popular than it was after the ABA joined the league. Eleven All-Stars in that first All-Star game were from the ABA. That's what saved the league."

He actually understated the number of ABA players. There were twelve players in that 1977 NBA All-Star Game who had been in the ABA the season before. He was one of them, and he regarded the inconspicuousness of that fact as another piece of proof that he doesn't get the credit he's due for the sport's success. When those TV talking heads compiled their rankings of the best players of all time—Wilt or Russell? Michael or LeBron? Does Kobe or Oscar make your top ten?—how often do they leave The Doctor off their lists? Too frequently for his taste. Do they know that, if you combine his ABA and NBA careers, he scored 30,026 points—and that just seven players scored more? That he made sixteen All-Star Games? That he won four Most Valuable Player awards—as many as LeBron and more than Bird or Magic or Steph Curry? That he won three championships, too? "When the naysayers take the ABA piece out," he said, "it dilutes my career."

It also strips away the context, timing, and effect of Erving's entrance into the NBA. The Sixers acquired him just two days before their first game of the 1976–77 regular season, and his arrival coincided with what might have been Philadelphia's high-water mark in twentieth-century American social culture. The nation had celebrated its Bicentennial in the city that summer. Philadelphia International Records, led by the production team of Kenneth Gamble and Leon A. Huff, had supplanted Motown as the source of the country's best and most popular soul music. The O'Jays, Billy Paul, Harold Melvin & the Blue Notes, Teddy Prendergast: These and other artists had been and would continue carrying the sweet and funk-filled sound of "Philly Soul" to the top of the R&B charts week after week. The Phillies— the city's major-league baseball team, loaded with talented players, Mike Schmidt and Steve Carlton among them—had just qualified for the playoffs for the first time in more than a quarter century. The Flyers—the infamous and innovative "Broad Street Bullies"—had won the Stanley Cup in 1974 and '75 and, in January '76, had defended the honor and superiority of North American hockey (literally) and Western civilization (metaphorically) by routing the Soviet Red Army team.

Now the Sixers, coming off their first winning season in five years, had added basketball's greatest attraction. On October 26, 1976, they beat the New Orleans Jazz, 111–101, for their first victory of Erving's first season with them. Still getting acclimated to his new team and working himself into game shape, he came off the bench, missed seven of his ten shots, and scored just ten points. Still, the crowd at the Superdome, 27,383, was the largest ever to have seen a professional basketball game.

"The Doctor arrived in town just when the NBA needed a big image lift," *Philadelphia* magazine's Robert Huber wrote in April 2008, "mid-'70s, a shining light in the coke-addled, pampered, arrogant, sex-crazed brotherhood of pro ball—the best brother, pure playground but responsible and winning, and better in this way, too: dignified, a family man, smart, a stand-up guy in his careful baritone, a dream for white suburbia. For God's sake, he lived in white suburbia. Not all gated-up but comfortably, and he used to joke that he was white—off the court."

On the court, he was melding those two worlds, making the playground palatable to wider, whiter audiences. "The 76ers are undoubtedly the dunk champions of the NBA," the *Philadelphia Inquirer*'s Bill Livingston wrote in November '76. "It is that accolade that sets them apart, that has been partially responsible for a long line of sellouts on the road." Fred Carter, a guard on the team, was more succinct about the phenomenon: "The dunk has come back. It's more than just a basket." Which made Erving, the shot's primary purveyor, more than just another superstar. The Sixers won a league championship, reached the finals four times, and won at least 50 games nine times during Erving's eleven seasons with them. His favorite dunk of all time? Over Elvin Hayes and Wes Unseld in the late 1970s at the Capital Centre, when Hayes and Unseld were with the Washington Bullets, when the Bullets and the Sixers were fighting for supremacy in the Eastern Conference. "With Hayes and Unseld, when you went in there, you put your life on the line, mostly from Unseld," Erving told me. "I don't think Hayes was going to hurt you. So I turn the corner and go in and I'm airborne, and suddenly we end up chest to chest, and he's got both arms up like it's a field goal, like the goalpost in football, and I move the ball over to the middle and throw it down really hard." And the building, he remembered, got quiet . . . so quiet. "Really, for his teammates, it showed the power he had to control a game," Bobby Jones, Erving's teammate with the Sixers for eight years, told me. "It's kind of a motivation for everybody else: 'Look what this guy just did to them. What can I do?'" His career was a testament to the truth that, contrary to those who had dismissed the dunk as too showy and self-centered, individual excellence and panache didn't have to come at the expense of team success.

"When you say 'the best player,' I didn't think of myself that way, either," Erving told me. "My whole approach to basketball was a team approach as opposed to an individual approach. So the idea of individual glory and honor, at the start of the game I wasn't looking to do that. I was looking to win and enjoy my teammates and also treat the fans to my game. George Gervin and I talked about how we often played to please the crowd or tried to steal the other person's crowd. It starts with the dunk line in warm-ups. Part of the preparation was, 'All right, let's go out here and steal this crowd so that, at the end of the game, they'll be cheering for us, even against their home team.'"

That universal worship for Erving has lasted throughout his life. People are different around him, he told me. They become childlike, wide-eyed, even now that he is in his seventies and they might be in their forties. "They're like a son," he said, despite the revelation that his image as a faithful family man was just that: an image. "I've had two children out of wedlock," he told Huber, "but I can walk down the street holding my head up high. There are ten thousand children who I've been the catalyst for in all that I've done." Maintaining that measure of idolatry around Erving requires separating his personal flaws and foibles from his athletic exploits . . . and remembering not to separate him and his impact from his era. If the dunk is a symbol of basketball's progress and Black athletes' role in that progress—that they could own the game and take it to places it had never been before—then Erving's importance can't be overstated. He was a transformative figure, a conduit, maybe the conduit, for the sport's acceptance and growth in the mainstream.

"He was—clearly," Leon Saunders, who has worked in the music industry for more than forty years, mostly as a talent agent, told me. "There are a couple of players who changed the game, and Julius is clearly one of them. Wilt and Russell brought that game into the paint. Julius brought the ball above the rim from outside, from the wing. I referred to it as 'an Afro-American aerial ballet.' That's how I saw what Julius was doing. That was the best description I could come up with. That's what he created in professional basketball. You had to do more, and Julius was the single personage that made it clear this game had to change."

At his springtime appearance in New Orleans during the 2022 Final Four, Erving noted how closely the ABA foreran the NBA's evolution, particularly in its accent on its players' individuality and creative freedom and the appeal that those qualities would have to fans. "Hopefully it won't be forgotten because it was an important time in my life—probably the most fun that I had playing basketball," he said. "I probably had more fun playing in the ABA than I did in college or even the NBA. The NBA was the most significant platform because that's the one that exists today and that's how most of you know me. But the ABA, the five years over there were extremely, extremely important." He should have been the greatest attraction in the sport, and with the Sixers, he would be. But when he entered the NBA, he was as much myth and mystery as he was man. "Everybody has seen LeBron James," Melchionni told me. "Three-quarters of the country probably never saw Doc. I've always made the statement: the Red Sox never should have traded Babe Ruth, and the Nets never should have sold Dr. J."

The ABA retains a cultlike following today, a zealotry among hoops history buffs and that ever-shrinking club of people who have some connection, tangible or emotional, to the league. Even at the time, those lucky enough to have seen Erving play regarded it as an experience so vital to their devotion to the Nets that, once he left, they had no desire to continue following them at all. In declaring that he was returning his season tickets, Mike Duarte wrote a letter to franchise vice president Barry Elson that read in part: "With Julius Erving being sold to another team, I have absolutely no interest in attending Nets games. . . . Erving is the only basketball player in the world who could provide incentive for me to travel out to Long Island to see a basketball game." Another ticket holder, Fred Schruers, asked, "Am I going to watch Roy Boe run up and down the court with three million dollars and slam dunk? Am I crazy? I'd rather hole up in my apartment with two frozen pizzas and try to pick up the Doctor on my short-wave." But they were the exceptions, the ones already in the know. The general public—the fans who come and go, who flipped through TV channels and stopped on a game because they had noticed someone doing something different and interesting, who learned of basketball superstars through chats at the office watercooler—knew little about Dr. J before he entered the NBA, before he penetrated the national consciousness to a depth and degree he hadn't even while in New York, before he revealed the magic intrinsic not only in the game's blazing future but in its shadowed present. And those kinds of fans, the most casual of fans, the fans who would be drawn to pro basketball by the millions throughout the subsequent two decades, could only take the word of the fortunate few who had ventured to Nassau Coliseum for a respite from Vietnam and Watergate and the trammels of that time . . . those who sought and found a night of entertainment that felt more like something sacred and supernatural . . . those who would swear, hands to their hearts, may God strike them dead, that Julius Erving could fly.

15

DR. DUNK

He had neither the flashy personality nor the gaze-at-me game that some of his contemporaries did. But on an afternoon in the Pacific Northwest, he gave everyone a glimpse of what was ahead for the NBA: the dunk as standalone entertainment, as an act of value and pleasure in and of itself.

Darnell Hillman's face was a blank slate, not a smile or a grimace or any other indication of emotion to be found, as if he were a tradesman with a task to complete, a carpenter with a bench to build, indifferent to all the people in the stands who were eyeballing him. White tank top. Blue shorts. Black dome of hair. Shoulders slightly sloped as he moved around the Memorial Coliseum court in Portland. No prancing. No strutting. No Broadway-style bow. No exultant scream. No biceps flex. No sign of bravado at all from the eventual champion of the NBA's first slam dunk contest, from the league's first official lord of flight.

Hillman was two and a half months shy of his twenty-eighth birthday, so he wasn't a kid anymore, not by any definition, and maybe that was why he seemed so low-key out there on the court. Basketball was never much of a show performance to him; it had always been, to a great degree, work. He had served in the US Army. He had competed abroad, in Europe and the Middle East, and even in college he had met men who had talked to him about the need to make America a place where justice was more than merely a great notion, who had used the spectacle of sport to show him and the rest of the world what they had meant. He had lived some, seen some things. When Hillman was in high school in northern California, spending all his free time in the playgrounds and gyms of San Francisco, his teachers would give him a quarter for every time he jammed a ball home during a game, so he could buy a cinnamon roll and a carton of milk in the morning. Dunking was a revenue stream for him even then. It was a job. This one, on June 5, 1977, would take him less than two minutes to finish.

In the mid-1970s, a battle over basketball waged between two of the three major television networks in the United States. NBC had NCAA hoops. CBS had the rights to the NBA. And NBC was kicking CBS's tail. To that time, seven of the ten most-watched televised basketball games ever were college games, including the top four. (The 1975 national championship game, between UCLA and Kentucky, was number one on the list.) NBC was filling its national schedule on Sundays with attractive college matchups, and the strategy was working. On March 7, 1976, for example, its telecast of Marquette's 72–66 victory over South Carolina drew a 24 share; the Knicks' 92–81 loss to the Bullets in Washington, on CBS, drew an 18 share. CBS and the NBA needed something—more star power, great teams in bigger TV markets, gimmicks, something—to goose viewership. The network started televising four regional games each Sunday to draw more localized audiences and introduced a recurring feature called "Red on Roundball," in which Red Auerbach—while still the general manager of the Celtics—would offer a brief tutorial on basketball's finer points.

"And," the Associated Press reported before the 1976–77 NBA campaign began, "the package will be further enhanced by a slam dunk contest to run throughout the season."

The idea for the contest was CBS's. Keith Overpeck of the Louisville *Courier-Journal* reported in January '77 that "there must have been a CBS official staring bleary-eyed at his television" a year earlier, watching the ABA dunk contest, the showdown between Julius Erving and David Thompson in Denver. Now Erving and Thompson were both in the NBA—Erving with the Sixers, Thompson still with the Nuggets. So CBS would stage a dunk contest of its own, Overpeck wrote, "to brighten the halftimes of its National Basketball Association telecasts." Each of the league's twenty-two teams would select what Colleen Kolibas, a CBS production secretary, described as its "best, most well-known competitor," and a single-elimination tournament of one-on-one dunk-offs would whittle down the field to its winner, who would receive $15,000 in prize money. An interesting and diverse trio comprised the judges' panel. There was former Celtics guard Sam Jones. There was ex-referee Mendy Rudolph. And there was Larry Bortstein, a freelance sportswriter. Portly, bespectacled, and not tall, Bortstein would have seemed at first an odd choice to judge any sort of athletic competition, but he didn't take himself or the event too seriously—and neither did CBS or the NBA. "It was fun," he said after the contest had ended. "But they didn't have a sponsor and spent a lot of money."

What they wanted, of course, was an Erving-Thompson rematch and the ratings that presumably would come with it. Thompson was in, but what about Erving? "Some problems with him and his law-yer," Kolibas said, which was true. Through his agent, Erving de-manded a $10,000 appearance fee for the contest. He declined to enter when he didn't get it.

Now, even in a best-case scenario, the contest's championship round would feature Thompson and . . . who? Kareem Abdul-Jabbar? His name and his status would generate some interest. What about his serious-if-dour demeanor, though? Would he bring the energy and panache that Erving would? Unlikely. No one compared to Dr. J. One way or another, CBS and the NBA would have to settle for someone else.

Hillman learned to earn his school-day-snack money by apprenticing under Willie Wise, who was a senior at Balboa High School when

Hillman entered as a freshman and, at six foot five, was four inches shorter. Wise would be one of the best and most well-rounded players of the ABA's early years, winning a league championship with the Utah Stars in 1971, and he taught Hillman during their year together the importance of practicing his dunks: how to hold the basketball, how to time his leap, how to seize the right opportunity to rock the rim. Hillman also took up high-jumping, but at six-nine, he was so tall for a high jumper and his limbs were so long that he struggled to refine his technique and maximize the spring in his legs as he approached the bar. "I didn't have a particular style," he told me. "I only cleared six-six in high school, but I was probably jumping five or six inches over that. My trailing legs were always the problem."

After transferring from Balboa to Hiram W. Johnson High in Sacramento when his family relocated, Hillman visited college after college among the twenty that offered him basketball scholarships. He came away from most of his recruiting visits feeling vaguely dirty about the process, about all the meetings with alumni and boosters who kept offering to slip money to him on the sly. The one place where that didn't happen, he told me, was San Jose State, coached by Dan Clines. "I got none of that," he told me. "They were very honest with me. They told me I was going to have to earn my position."

The Spartans went 16–8 in 1968–69, Clines's only winning season among the five years he was their head coach, and Hillman was terrific as a sophomore, averaging more than 15 points and 14 rebounds. But the moment from Hillman's two years at San Jose State that lasted, that shaped the rest of his athletic career and in particular his ability to dunk, happened not on a basketball court but in the university's high-jump pit.

Though NCAA regulations prevented him from playing varsity basketball his freshman year or, of course, dunking at all once he was eligible to play, Hillman could compete in the high jump. In the spring of 1968, he was in the pit one day, honing his technique, the bar set at just six feet. Nearby, running quarters on the track, just a few months before he and Tommie Smith medaled in the 200-meter dash at the Mexico City Olympics and raised their black-gloved fists in the air to protest the treatment of Black Americans, was John Carlos. Once he noticed Hillman practicing, Carlos veered off the track, strode over to the pit, knocked the bar off its supports, and grabbed Hillman by the lapels of his shirt.

If I ever see this bar set at this height again, he told Hillman, *I'll come down here and kick your ass all over this field.*

Carlos was six foot four and powerful, already a gold medalist at the 1967 Pan-American Games, and it took Hillman—maybe 210 pounds clinging to his six-nine frame—a minute or two before he could wrestle out of the Olympian's grip. He looked Carlos up and down and thought, *Here's a world-record holder, and he's taking the time to come off his practice and give you something.*

"Mr. Carlos," he asked, "what would you like me to do?"

Carlos reset the high-jump bar to seven feet.

This, he told Hillman, *is where you practice every day.*

San Jose State had a meet scheduled the following Saturday in Modesto. "So all of that week, I was not getting over the bar," Hillman told me. "But every time I looked around the field, thinking I might get away with lowering this bar, just to gain some confidence, he had his eyes on me."

At that Saturday meet, Hillman cleared six feet, eleven and a half inches—still the tenth-best mark in school history. "When I landed in the pits," he said, "I jumped up and ran all over the field looking for John, and I found him and told him, 'Thank you. I did it. I get it. I understand what you were doing.' You set your goals high, not so high that you can't reach them but high enough that you have to work for them."

Carlos's counsel helped Hillman become a better dunker—once he was allowed to dunk, that is. He could tap into his adrenaline and aggressiveness and still control his body well enough to do whatever he wished once he was in the air. In college, for instance, he grew adept at leaping high enough and far enough away from the rim that he could throw the ball through the hoop while still keeping his hand outside the cylinder—a more difficult maneuver than anything he'd have to try once he turned pro, once he didn't have to worry about such restrictions. "I was able to take my high-jumping skills and talent and convert them," he told me. Carlos's influence on Hillman was as profound in another arena, as well. In the fall of 1968, seven San Jose State football players vowed to boycott a game against Brigham Young University over the Mormon Church's then-racist beliefs and policies toward Blacks. The San Jose State administration responded not by backing the players but by threatening to revoke their scholarships. Hillman joined Carlos and several other athletes in a counter-threat: if the football players' scholarships were taken away, all the Black athletes at SJS would refuse to compete in their respective sports. The university backed down.

That single basketball season at San Jose State was all Hillman had there to show what he could do. He planned to go to summer school in 1969, ahead of his junior year, to make up a couple of credits, but when his mother went into the hospital, he withdrew from the university to get a job. Within that sliver of time, he was drafted into the army. "I asked for a deferment and then a hardship exemption," he once said, "and they declined. I said, 'The hell with it. I might as well go in and get it over with.'" For his two years of service, he mostly traveled the world, playing more than three hundred games for the All-Army team. While dunking during pregame warm-ups in Yugoslavia as part of the CISM World Military Games—he was named the most valuable player of the event in 1970—Hillman broke a rim, delaying the opening tip-off by forty-five minutes. The crowd jeered him by whistling at him. "In Europe, they don't boo," he told me. "They whistle. It was like thirty thousand people, and you get thirty thousand people whistling at you, and it's piercing." The incident only intensified the respect and awe in which Hillman's teammates held him; though Hillman was an enlisted man, an officer/point guard named Mike Krzyzewski carried his bags for him. "It was a pleasure to do that," Krzyzewski once said. It wasn't as if Hillman couldn't manage on his own. Each of his hands, spread to its widest, could touch twelve piano keys, and when Hillman cradled Krzyzewski's first daughter, Debbie, a few months after she was born, she disappeared into his palms. "I couldn't see her," Coach K said years later. "I could not see her."

Once his tour ended, in 1971, Hillman had a choice. As a first-round pick of the NBA's San Francisco Warriors and a second-round pick of the ABA's Indiana Pacers, he was at the center of a bidding war, one that the Warriors weren't keen to wage. "He wanted us to give him a contract that would give him more than Nate Thurmond, Jerry Lucas, and Jeff Mullins," San Francisco general manager Bob Feerick said, citing three of the team's best and best-known veterans. (Thurmond was earning the highest annual salary of the trio: $150,000.) So Hillman rejected the chance to play for his hometown team and picked the Pacers instead.

Immediately, on a team that had won the ABA championship in 1970, that had won 58 games the following season, and whose stars were forward George McGinnis, center Mel Daniels, and Connie Hawkins's old friend and rival Roger Brown, Hillman became one of the primary attractions. He was credited with having a forty-inch vertical leap, but it was likely much higher; standing flat-footed, he could jump four to six inches over the backboard square. With a running start, with the chance to use his high-jumping skills, he could put the rim against his sternum, or he could dunk a basketball, lower his arm through the hoop all the way to his armpit, and pull his arm out again. His pregame routine, one dunk after another in and out of the layup line, drew fans to Fairgrounds Coliseum, the Pacers' home arena, hours before tip-off. As his first act to hook and hold the attention of the children who attended his basketball camps, he would sprint toward a basket, jump, and kick the rim. "Every day," he told me, "I expected to kick the backboard."

A guy like that needed a nickname, and the newspaper story that bestowed upon Hillman the nickname of all nicknames, the moniker of all monikers, the autograph in permanent marker, ran in the *Indianapolis Star* on Sunday, February 13, 1972. The headline was something out of a Ken Kesey novel; it was so '70s, it should have been printed in Day-Glo-pink Bocklin: *Dr. Dunk Turns on The Hep Pacer Crowds.* The subhead was kitschy: *DARNELL, THE STUFFIN' MAN.* And the writer, Robin Miller, began the piece like this:

"Dr. Dunk's the name, and stuffing's his game."

Hillman was not some cult hero or sideshow; he was a quality player, a terrific wing and post defender. "Just because you can jump doesn't mean much," he said in 1972. "It's how you use and learn to use your jumping ability. . . . Some players get psyched shooting, but I get psyched up jumping." As just one example, in February 1973 the Pacers beat Erving and the Virginia Squires in overtime, 127–119. Erving scored 35 points in regulation but, with Hillman guarding him, none in overtime. Meanwhile, Hillman finished the game with just 16 points, but he had eight during the extra session, accounting for the margin of victory by himself.

That night marked a rare occasion that any of Erving's opponents could say they got the better of him. But Dr. J deferred to Dr. Dunk on a more personal, and maybe a more culturally significant, matter. In the army, Hillman had been forced to shave his head. He hated it, and when he got out, he told himself, *I'm never getting another haircut.* He happened to see a photograph of the communist revolutionary Angela Davis. "She had a beautiful Afro," he told me. "There were a lot of student movements of all kinds, activists pushing things. When I saw her Afro, I said, 'This is where I'm going to make my statement.'" He grew his hair out until it was a small planet, thirteen and a half inches in diameter. "He had a big two-bedroom, two-bathroom condo for an Afro back in the day," said longtime college basketball coach Fran Dunphy, who, after finishing his college playing career at La Salle, had been one of Hillman's teammates on the All-Army squad. "It was his trademark." Hillman would even invite Erving to his home whenever the Squires, the Nets, or the 76ers flew into Indianapolis to play the Pacers, and he would help him tend to his 'Fro. They used a hair dryer and an angel food cake cutter; its thin prongs made it ideal for plucking and shaping thick, curly hair. "I told Julius, 'All you need to do is go to your barber and have him trim the ends, clip all of the broken ends off, get it evened up, and you're good to go,'" Hillman told me. "We had quite a few guys in that league who had pretty sick Afros."

There were guys like that everywhere in America. Hillman himself was an emblem of the nation in the early to mid-1970s, of all its extremes—his appearance and the presumptions about him that it surely inspired (*Is Doctor Dunk really a member of the Black Panthers?*), his connection to the Civil Rights and Black Power Movements through his time at San Jose State and his friendship with Carlos, a young man compelled by his government to serve his country during an unpopular war, the self-discipline that such a man reveals and acquires for that experience, the circumstances that led him to make his home and ply his distinctive skills in the Midwest, in the heartland, at a time and a place where anyone walking down the street might view him as exotic and even dangerous. Hillman did his best to keep those forces from interfering with or jeopardizing his career. He didn't see himself as a symbol. He didn't care to be a symbol. "I was here to play basketball," he told me. "All that other stuff, I didn't want it to affect my being on the court." He was plenty exotic there as it was. A display advertisement splashed on multiple pages within the Friday, December 19, 1975, edition of the Louisville *Courier-Journal* promoted a game at eight o'clock that night between the Pacers and the Kentucky Colonels "featuring 'Doctor Dunk' Darnell Hillman" and, beforehand, a high school girls' basketball game. ("Good Seats Available At Freedom Hall Box Office Open 10 a.m. 'til Gametime.") An ABA team that played winning basketball was one thing. An ABA team that had a player such as Hillman—the kind of player who separated the league from the staid NBA—was another. One never knew what such a player might do.

"If I got an opening in the ball game, and knowing how to explode off the floor, that's what I wanted to do," he told me. "Get me a couple of dunks, and I was happy after that. I tried to bring your house down. Most of those who could dunk wanted to be the one who busted a ball game wide open, and I certainly could do that. Four or five feet from the rim, I could probably still glide over you. You were still in danger."

The Pacers' transition from the ABA to the NBA was not as smooth as they would have liked. Under Bobby "Slick" Leonard, their head coach and general manager, they finished the 1976–77 season, their first in the NBA, with a 36–46 record, but the dunk contest and Hillman's participation in it offered a glint of light in a mostly dark year. The league had sent out a memo to its teams telling them to hold intra-squad "dunk-offs" to determine who would be the representatives in the contest. Leonard's wife, Nancy—the Pacers' assistant GM—walked into practice one day to inform the coaches and players about the contest's details. Without taking any questions, she said, *And Darnell's going to represent the team.*

"We had Danny Rounfield, who was a great leaper; Mel Bennett, who could jump very well; and Jerome Green," Hillman told me. "We had some leapers on the team who would have loved to have been in it. But nobody challenged her. She was the coach's wife."

Even without Erving's participation in the contest—Darryl Dawkins stepped in as the Sixers' entrant—CBS and the NBA held out hope that a couple of the league's established and emerging standouts would end up squaring off. Abdul-Jabbar, in his second season with the Los Angeles Lakers; Moses Malone, in his first season with the Houston Rockets; and Thompson were all part of the field. As that field winnowed, though, those matchups didn't materialize. Thompson injured himself during one of the TV-taping sessions and had to be replaced by Gus Gerard—floppy-haired, thin, without DT's magnetism. CBS's executives were so desperate to have Thompson in the contest that, once he was healthy again, they allowed him to reenter, only to have him lose to Ron Lee, a rookie with the Phoenix Suns.

Hillman, meanwhile, was emerging as a contender. In early January, he beat Malone in the contest's first round and the Bulls' Mickey Johnson in the second. On Sunday, February 13, Erving wowed a sellout crowd of 19,938 at Milwaukee Arena, scoring 30 points and dunking four times—one of them a windmill slam over Jabbar—in the NBA All-Star Game. The day would prove a rough one for Jabbar, because after the game, he and Hillman met in the contest's semifinals. Not quite as fresh as Hillman, given that he had just played a full game, Jabbar still warmed up for the contest by dribbling along the baseline, pumping the ball in front of the rim, bringing the ball down to his knees, and lifting it back over his head to throw it down. "At seven-two and certainly for his length, that was a pretty remarkable dunk, to hang that long and pull that off," Hillman told me. "Nobody really understands how high a guy of that height could jump."

After winning a coin toss, Hillman decided to have Jabbar, who had spent the first six years of his NBA career with the Bucks, go first. "This was his home," he told me, "and it was a full house." Maybe Jabbar would try to feed off the energy and emotion of the fans who once loved him. Hillman would go the other way. He had a set routine of dunks that he planned to perform methodically: three reverses, one 180-degree two-handed circle, and a rock-the-cradle move that he called "The Hammer," in which he would cup the ball with one hand, clench his other hand into a fist, and "bang that ball through your arm down into the hoop. You've got to have some pretty good hops to do those dunks."

It turned out that Jabbar had no home-court advantage at all. The fans were so docile that the public-address announcer had to exhort them: "We're going to be asking for some crowd noise. We're going to be zeroing in with the cameras for some crowd close-ups. So let's make some noise. C'mon, let's have a big Milwaukee cheer." Attending the All-Star Game as a spectator, just a year removed from his retirement after eleven NBA seasons, former Bucks guard Jon McGlocklin watched the contest with his son Shannon and realized quickly that his friend and teammate was going to lose. "Kareem is the most dominant player in the game today," McGlocklin said during a chat with a local reporter, "but he's not as spectacular as Julius Erving or even Hillman." No, he was not. Dr. Dunk won and advanced to the championship round, which would be held in June at halftime of an NBA Finals game. Any resemblance to what the Slam Dunk Contest would eventually grow to be in its heyday, in the era of Jordan and Dominique Wilkins and Spud Webb, would be purely coincidental.

It was the sort of sports transaction that might—might—warrant a paragraph or two in the local sports section or a mention on the six o'clock news, a deal between two teams that had gone nowhere. On April 14, 1977, with both of their regular seasons already finished, with no postseason berth ahead for either of them, the Pacers and the New York Nets consummated a trade that had been in the works for a couple of months. Indiana got guard John Williamson. New York got a first-round draft pick . . . and the rights to Darnell Hillman. Until Hillman signed a new contract with the Nets, however, he was not considered to be on their roster. So one of the finalists in the NBA's first slam dunk contest was, technically, not an NBA player. Unfamiliar with the New York region, Hillman came back to Indianapolis and, for the two months between the trade and the contest's championship round, worked out at tiny Marian College. The conditions were spartan. The college's old, abandoned gymnasium had holes in its ceiling. Pigeons nested and flew through it like it was an oversized birdhouse. "There was no air in there," Hillman told me. "All I could do was open the doors, and each day, I would have to damp-mop the floor because of all the pigeon droppings on it." To pass his free time, he started playing in a parks-department softball league. A liquor store, The Bottle Shoppe, sponsored the team.

The contest's other finalist had a similar story to tell. A six-foot-nine power forward and Brooklyn native, Larry McNeill had played for the Kansas City Kings from the moment he entered the NBA in 1973 until September '76, when the Kings traded him to the Nets. And he was the Nets' representative in the dunk contest . . . until they waived him in December. Like Hillman, just because McNeill wasn't in the NBA didn't mean he couldn't be in the NBA's dunk contest. And like Hillman, he kept out-slamming all his opponents. Never missing a cheeky opportunity to promote itself, the *New York Post* sponsored McNeill to keep him in the contest. In each round, he wore a red jersey with the tabloid's name across the front and his nickname, "The Hawk," across the back. He stayed in shape by working out at a public-school gymnasium on 123rd Street in Manhattan and playing for a semi-pro team on weekends. "Hopefully I'll be back before the season is over," he told the *Kansas City Star* on February 18, 1977.

"Bills are starting to pile up." Less than a week later, his hopes were fulfilled. The Golden State Warriors signed him on February 24.

This was, of course, not the clash-of-the-dunking-titans matchup that CBS and the league had aspired to create at the season's start. Mingling with other NBA officials in the league's hospitality room at the Spectrum in Philadelphia before Game 5 of the finals—the series between the Sixers and Portland Trail Blazers was tied at two— Blazers vice president and general manager Harry Glickman learned that the contest's championship round would take place at halftime of Game 6. Then he learned that the finalists were Hillman and McNeill. "Do they have tickets?" Glickman said. His incredulity turned to anger after the Blazers' 110–104 victory in Game 5 when CBS pushed to have Game 6 begin at 10:30 a.m. West Coast time so that the network could carry, in its entirety, a non-major golf tournament: the Kemper Open in Charlotte. Glickman and NBA commissioner Larry O'Brien vetoed the request, and CBS settled instead for a noon tip-off.

The gulf between who the league and its fans had wanted to be in the contest and who ended up being in the contest was never wider or more apparent than at Game 6. His team facing elimination, Erving threw down dunk after dunk in the pregame layup line, and with each one, the Memorial Coliseum crowd cheered. When Hillman and McNeill took the court at halftime, boos greeted them. Adding to the contest's honky-tonk feel was the short-sleeved warm-up pullover that Hillman wore. Royal blue trimmed with bright yellow, the shirt had the words BOTTLE SHOPPE stripped across the front in white. John McNelis, the store's manager, had asked him to wear it.

Finishing the contest in a timely manner was a high priority—no need to delay the start of Game 6's second half—so the rules were rigid: Each contestant would attempt five dunks and only five dunks, earning two points for each one he made. Each judge would then as- sign an overall grade to the five dunks on a 1-to-10 scale. In loosening up, McNeill repeated the same sequence: he'd dunk the ball with two hands, hold on to the rim, and pull himself into a chin-up. *If that's all he's going to do*, Hillman thought, *man, I've got a great chance of taking this.*

Sure enough, McNeill relied on that one style of dunk, and the judges scored him accordingly: 8.5s across the board. Hillman's variety gave him an inherent advantage. He went through his routine of five: 8.5, 9.0, 9.5. Since neither he nor McNeill missed a dunk, the final score seemed closer than it was: Hillman 37, McNeill 35.5.

When it was time for his post-contest interview with CBS's Don Criqui, Hillman rose from the bench and pulled on the BOTTLE SHOPPE warm-up again. It had cost McNelis $250 to sponsor the softball team. For days after the contest, he had customers streaming in, asking if his store was the same Bottle Shoppe that Hillman had advertised. "I just say, 'Yes, he's one of our many stars,'" McNelis said later. "I never expected to get that much return for my money."

McNelis was a lot happier with CBS than the Blazers or basketball fans around the country were. At least the network had televised the full dunk contest live. Once the buzzer sounded on the Blazers' 109–107 championship-clinching victory, CBS didn't bother showing the postgame celebration in the team's locker room. The network's operations people in New York calculated that CBS would pull in more viewers on the East Coast—and more revenue—by showing the Kemper Open. So they cut immediately from the game to the tournament, where Chi Chi Rodriguez was on the fairway.

Was the NBA's first dunk contest a success, either at the time or in retrospect? It's hard to call it one. Criqui toed the party line as much as he could afterward. "The kids loved it," he told one reporter. "The reaction was favorable across the nation, but I don't know if they'll do it again next year." They didn't, and it was Brent Musberger, CBS's play-by-play voice for the Finals, who crystallized the small-time nature of the contest when he joked with Criqui during the telecast: "Don, tell Darnell to hold up. I've got Julius Erving. He's saying, 'I want the winner.'"

Hillman got his $15,000 but little else. The NBA never officially acknowledged him as the first dunk-contest winner, and he told me that when he contacted the league to find out why, "the story they gave me was that because the dunk contest the first year didn't have a major sponsor, they never recognized me. But anybody who was there saw it." He never even got a trophy, not until the Pacers splurged for one for him in 2017, after Indiana's Glenn Robinson III won that year's contest. What he got was the self-respect and pride that accompanied vanquishing so many big names and overcoming the odds and his relative anonymity.

"I wasn't the one they wanted to win," he told me. "Julius, David Thompson, Dawkins, and George Gervin—they wanted one of those four to take it. I'm quite aware of it.

"I had never been to the All-Star Game. In the ABA, in order to dunk in the contest, you had to be an All-Star. So I never got to be there. When the leagues got together, I took a shot at it. Seeing how they were talking about those guys and wanted them to win, I had to do everything and anything to earn that title."

He still views his championship as a validation of the ABA's legacy. "The NBA's thing was, if you were shorter, you were a point guard," he told me. "Any taller than that, you'd be a two-guard. Taller, you'd be a small forward, big forward, and center. The ABA's concept was, it's not about your height, but it's about your skill set. We had big men who could go out to the three-point line, put the ball on the floor, or shoot. Our game meant that, if a big guy was out there shooting it, somebody had to guard him. That opened up the middle and allowed everyone else to drive in the paint and get your stuff off. The country was now adjusting to the skill set of the player, not the size."

That's the truest, most lasting legacy of the '77 contest: it opened the door to the flamboyance that followed, to the generation of players who took the NBA where the ABA had already been inclined to go. The next step beyond Hillman's relative modesty was Darryl Dawkins's Look Out Below Dunk, his Yo Mama Dunk, his dozens of other dunks with star-spangled names, his two shattered backboards—when he broke one of them over the Kings' Bill Robinzine in 1979, he called it his Rump-Roastin'-Bun-Toastin'-Glass-Flyin'-Robinzine-Cryin' Dunk—and the total acceptance of the dunk throughout the college and pro games: Darrell "Dr. Dunkenstein" Griffith, Kenny

"Sky" Walker, Jerome Lane sending it home, the understanding that the dunk wasn't a gimmick or a parlor trick, that it enhanced the quality of and appreciation for basketball itself. There would have been no life on Planet Lovetron without Darnell Hillman first leaving the earth.

Not that the process happened overnight. It didn't. It would be six years before there was a Final Four defined by the dunk—defined so fully that it culminated with what remains college basketball's most consequential slam. It would be seven years before the NBA—with Denver and McNichols Arena hosting the 1984 All-Star Game, with the memories of who David Thompson had been still fresh—brought the contest back. And it would be eleven years before the NBA Slam Dunk Contest would reach its apogee in popularity, in the rivalries within the competition, and in the figures who made themselves immortal by filing flight plans for journeys that began within the bounds of a basketball court and ended beyond anyone's imagination.

16

WRONG PLACE, RIGHT TIME

The Final Four that was supposed to be all about the dunk, that capped the slammin', jammin' takeover of college basketball, lived up to that expectation . . . with the most unexpected of endings, authored by a sweet soul reluctant to step into the spotlight.

On Fayetteville Street in downtown Raleigh, inside the main dining room at Jimmy V's Osteria and Bar, it's always coming up on midnight Eastern time on Monday, April 4, 1983, and Lorenzo Charles is not yet fully cognizant of what his good fortune and marvelous instincts have wrought. Connected to a rust-brick Sheraton, the restaurant is a popular gathering place in town, patrons wielding forks to twirl linguini and crack into arancini at lunchtime, then grabbing drinks in the early evening before a big North Carolina State basketball game. Above those customers and fans, an everlasting reminder of the program's greatest moment of glory is just a glance away. Affixed to a beige wall near the ceiling is a rectangular scoreboard, crimson in color, and on that scoreboard, the details never change: the 00:00 on the clock, the teams, the final score. WOLFPACK 54, COUGARS 52. Here, the scoreboard, like a da Vinci or Delacroix, represents the highest form of art, and Lorenzo Charles had both of his hands on the brush for the final, finishing stroke.

For anyone with a passing interest in and familiarity with college basketball's past, the name *Lorenzo Charles* conjures one memory: the closing seconds of the 1983 national championship game. NC State versus Houston. Jim Valvano's walking-the-wire underdogs against Hakeem Olajuwon and Clyde Drexler and the rest of Phi Slama Jama. Tie game. Forty-four seconds to go. And there was Charles, a sophomore power forward, standing under the basket as his teammates, with a growing sense of panic, passed the ball around the perimeter; as guard Dereck Whittenburg heaved a last-ditch shot from thirty feet out; as nine players on the court at University Arena—"The Pit"—in Albuquerque, New Mexico, stiffened into total motionlessness, Charles the only one moving, jumping, catching the ball a foot in front of the rim and dunking it a half second before the buzzer; two NC State players hugging Charles but the others swept up into the pandemonium at halfcourt; Valvano running around like a madman; Charles vanishing from view into the joyous chaos as if he were stepping into W. P. Kinsella's cornfield. Glance at the scoreboard again: WOLFPACK 54, COUGARS 52.

On an afternoon in January 2023, that scoreboard loomed behind me as Cozell McQueen and Ernie Myers—two of Charles's teammates on the '83 NC State team, two of his closest friends—shared story after story about him. Charles died in June 2011 when a bus he was driving for Elite Tours, the company for which he worked for the last ten years of his life, swerved off Interstate 40 near Raleigh and crashed. He was forty-seven, a middle-aged man who had done something unforgettable and extraordinary when he was nineteen and who, over the next twenty-eight years, never ceased to be surprised that people remembered he had done something unforgettable and extraordinary. In 2008, he shepherded then-candidate Barack Obama's entourage throughout a campaign stop in the Raleigh-Durham-Cary region of North Carolina, and before boarding a plane to depart, Obama had the Secret Service page Charles so that he could meet him. Sometimes Charles drove the Duke men's basketball team to games and events, and Mike Krzyzewski would talk to his players about Charles's career, and Charles could barely contain his glee when he called McQueen to fill him in. *Yo, Co, Coach K remembered me. Nobody forgets the dunk, Co.*

When McQueen entered the restaurant, he greeted me with a warm hug, even though we had never met before. An important reserve on that Wolfpack team, six-foot-eleven and still as lanky as he was when he played college ball, he was Charles's roommate at NC State. At the time of Charles's death, both of them lived in Cary, not even a mile and a half from each other. McQueen was both happy and hesitant to speak in any depth about his friend.

"He should know," he said, nodding his head to the right like he was shaking water out of his ear, toward Myers. "When you start asking me stuff . . ."

"He gets kind of emotional," Myers said.

"Got to be careful," McQueen said. "We'll talk if we have to."

His voice was weak and halting.

"I'm going to try to get through it."

Still sitting, he turned his head and torso to the left. Away from me. Away from Myers. Away from the table.

"So ask away."

Lorenzo Charles did not come from a basketball family. His father, Herman, had been a marvelous baseball player in Panama before immigrating to the United States, where he and his wife, Silvia, lived in Brooklyn's Starrett City housing project, near Jamaica Bay. Herman was a small, thin man who rose each morning at three and began his workday, as a butcher and meat-packer, at five. Silvia earned extra money as a typist. Lorenzo, when he was a boy, loved electric toy trains and did not pick up a basketball until two years before he graduated from Brooklyn Technical High School. He eventually would top out at six-foot-seven, and "he was always a big muscular guy," said Myers, who grew up in the Bronx and had seen Charles play in high school. Gil Reynolds, Charles's AAU coach with the Vanguard Oilers, was an influential figure in the borough—the *New York Post*

called him "the godfather of basketball in Brooklyn"—and a notori-
ous taskmaster. "He was a loud coach," Myers told me. "He would
embarrass his players on the bench, screaming and hollering. I would
feel sorry for those guys."

Compared to Reynolds's histrionics, the prospect of playing for Valvano must have seemed a breeze to Charles. NC State had hired Valvano—
Queens-born and street-smart, charismatic and hilarious—in 1980,
and he immediately began building a recruiting pipeline between the
Northeast and Raleigh. Five key members of that 1982–83 championship team—Charles, Myers, Dereck Whittenburg, Sidney Lowe, and
Thurl Bailey—were from either New York or the Washington, DC,
area, and Charles was maybe the longest shot of them all. Though
he had averaged more than 20 points and 14 rebounds as a senior at
Brooklyn Tech, though the New York *Daily News* had selected him to
its high school all-star team, he was so raw that he didn't catch the eye
of many Division I coaches. "He wasn't heavily recruited," Valvano
once said. "I liked his size and strength." Typing up a report on New
York–area players for *High School Basketball Illustrated*, Tom Konchalski,
the renowned and respected amateur scout, was honest, unsparing,
and deliciously colorful in his evaluation of Charles: "pro upper body
coupled with velvety touch so why isn't he better?—answer: little to no
intensity. roams court with panther potential yet executes like Bambi
in shorts and may lack stamina and agility . . . terrific 15' turnaround
jumper (no slouch from stripe, either) but ordinary post moves debit
present performance—good bounce off stride, fair off two feet—if he
learns to play harder perhaps high majors who are ogling, not buying,
should have made purchase [*sic*]."

It took him a year to learn. He dunked during a pickup game at
Carmichael Gymnasium; grabbing the rim with both hands, he broke
it—and the backboard with it. He didn't move as the glass shards
showered him; it was as if he were standing in his own individual ice
storm. He felt guilty for ending the game. But he contributed little his
freshman season, just two points and six minutes a game, and when
Myers traveled to campus for his recruiting visit, he let him have it,
even though Charles was a year older. *Lo, man, what's up?* Myers asked

him. *Vee's telling me you don't play hard. You don't work hard. You've got to get in shape to get up and down the court.* Charles's first season with the Wolfpack was so disappointing that Valvano, not ready to trust that he would develop into a contributing player, brought in another power forward, Alvin Battle—a move that motivated Charles to practice and play harder the following season.

He needed, because of his laconic personality, such motivation. Charles didn't talk much. His friends thought him funny, with a dry sense of humor, but strangers didn't warm up to him right away. "If he wasn't smiling, you were like, 'OK, I'm walking on the other side of the street,'" Myers told me. "He was one of those guys where if you didn't know him and he walked into a party or something, even football players were like, 'I ain't messin' with that dude.'" He and McQueen, classmates and teammates, became close quickly—Charles quiet and often glowering and from the big city, McQueen affable and boisterous and hailing from Marlboro County in South Carolina, each one's disposition filling the gaps in the other's. "A great guy, gentle guy," McQueen told me. "Had the power to be a mean guy. Wasn't in his DNA. If he wasn't smiling, you'd think he was a thug. You'd think he was a bodyguard. Massive arms, massive shoulders, big strong butt. Lo was a powerful man. Sometimes I didn't think he knew how strong he was. To give you an idea, one day, we were in a hurry, and his car was in a shop."

Charles needed a ride to see his girlfriend, so he begged one from McQueen, who owned an old burgundy Monte Carlo. As McQueen dropped him off at a stop sign, Charles casually slammed the door. "Man," McQueen told him, "you're going to break my window." McQueen hopped out to check for any damage, and sure enough, he couldn't roll the window down. Just by closing the door, Charles had knocked the window off its track.

"Oh," Charles said in his long, slow baritone. "Sorry. My fault."

The two of them were inseparable, and they were together in their campus apartment on May 30, 1982, when a few members of the NC State football team knocked on their door and asked to use their phone to order a pizza from Domino's. As the group waited outside and the delivery man pulled up, the football players told Charles and McQueen, *We're getting ready to take this pizza.*

"Me and Lo look at each other," McQueen told me. "We walk around the corner. But Lo is standing on the curb." He was still in sight of the delivery man. *I'm not doing nothing wrong,* he said to McQueen. *I'm just watching.*

Two months later, in July, Charles was arrested and charged with larceny from a person, a felony under North Carolina law that carried a prison sentence of as long as ten years. He was alleged to have stolen two pizzas and an asbestos bag from the delivery man; the total value of the items was fifty dollars. To this day, McQueen and Myers insist that the only reason that Charles was charged was that he had a relatively famous face.

"The football players weren't as visible on campus as we were," Myers said. "They wore helmets. If you're a Domino's pizza guy, you know who Lorenzo Charles is. He was the only one the guy could identify."

Charles, smartly, agreed to a plea bargain. He served a thirty-four-hour term in the jail in the nearby town of Apex, completed three hundred hours of community service—tutoring kids in rec centers, washing state-owned cars—paid a twenty-dollar restitution fee to Domino's, and underwent thirty hours of group counseling. He never admitted any guilt in court, and he never implicated any football players. "That's the thing New Yorkers do: They're not Judas. They ain't gonna rat," said McQueen, who reiterated that he and Charles never suspected that anyone was going to rob anyone that night. "I was right there. The guy had nothing to do with it at all. He didn't even get a slice."

The incident and arrest hung over him like an anvil until February 23, 1983. In Durham. At Cameron Indoor Stadium. On the campus of Duke University. In *Survive and Advance,* ESPN's 2013 documentary about Valvano and the 1982–83 Wolfpack, the filmmakers lead the viewer to believe that Whittenburg's return from a badly sprained ankle rescued NC State's season. No doubt it helped, but there was another occurrence that benefited the team, and another player, that goes unmentioned in the film. During pregame introductions, Cameron's public-address announcer called out Charles's name, and dozens of Duke fans held up pizza boxes. Some even threw them toward the court; the boxes pinwheeled down from the stands and landed near Charles's feet. Then Charles's best buddy added to the indignity; McQueen was so pumped up that when he tried to give Charles a high-five, he missed Charles's hand and smacked him in the face.

"So Lorenzo's already pissed," Myers said. "And then the game starts, and he took it out on Duke."

The Wolfpack crushed the Blue Devils, 96–79, and Charles had what was then the best game of his career: He scored 13 points, six more than his season's average; missed just two shots from the field; pulled down five rebounds; and outplayed Duke center Jay Bilas. Over NC State's last 13 games that season, he averaged 11.5 points and 8.5 rebounds. He was a different player from the Duke game on. "He was *dunking*," Myers told me. "His game developed. It was out of anger. That was the turning point for Lorenzo Charles."

The day after I met McQueen and Myers at Jimmy V's, I met the only North Carolina State player who has an entree named after him on the menu there. The "Whitten-burger" is a chuck/short rib patty with lettuce, tomato, and onion. Dereck Whittenburg ordered it—no bun. Before we talked about Charles, Whittenburg brought up a dunk contest that he won at the Baltimore Civic Center in 1976, when he was a sophomore at DeMatha Catholic High School in Hyattsville, Maryland. He beat a couple of scholastic phenoms, Gene Banks and Albert King. The outcome of the contest isn't surprising if you know a piece of trivia about Whittenburg: he and David Thompson are cousins. "Dunking," he told me, "is in my family."

Having been a college coach for a quarter century, Whittenburg was an executive producer on *Survive and Advance*, and the documentary thrust the story of the 1982–83 Wolfpack back to the forefront of basketball fans' minds around the country. Even thirty years after his death from testicular cancer in 1993, Valvano had never really left the public conversation, thanks to the prominence of the V Foundation for Cancer Research and the resonance of his acceptance speech at the

1993 ESPYs, when he won the Arthur Ashe Courage Award. But *Survive and Advance* reminded everyone of just how improbable NC State's wire-walk to the national championship was: the Wolfpack's 17–10 regular-season record and the understanding that the team needed to win the ACC Tournament just to qualify for the NCAA Tournament; the late-game comebacks; the succession of redoubtable opponents— Virginia with Ralph Sampson, North Carolina with Michael Jordan and Sam Perkins, University of Nevada, Las Vegas (UNLV) with Sidney Green, Houston with Olajuwon and Drexler.

Sixty-eight million people watched the film, according to Whittenburg, and they traveled back to a transitional time in college basketball: the ACC was the first of thirteen conferences during the '82–83 season to implement a three-point shot and a thirty-second shot clock. Those new rules wouldn't apply to the NCAA Tournament, but the future was clear. The sport was speeding up and spreading out.

"The college game had become ultimately boring," Valvano wrote in his eponymous autobiography. "The games were slow and low-scoring. . . . Ours had become a game of coaches, not players. We had taken a beautiful, action-packed thing and made it into a chess match. It took about as long as a game of chess, and about as many points were scored. It was ridiculous and horrible. The players all wanted to play, not hang back."

Charles was an exception. He didn't mind hanging back. He would grow to six-seven and add several pounds of muscle over his four years at NC State, getting up to 240, his body tapering into a V from his shoulders to his feet. He could squat 500 pounds, bench-press 250, and curl a 165-pound dumbbell with each arm. "He was put together like a Greek god," Myers said, the classic post player who was at his best in a slower, halfcourt-oriented style of game. He was athletic but not fluid, and he was a poor free-throw shooter through his freshman and sophomore seasons, making just 66 percent of his attempts. It was less surprising, then, that he had 12 rebounds—the same number as Sampson—to help the Wolfpack beat UVA in the ACC Championship Game than it was that he twice sank a winning free throw to save NC State's season. He hit one with three seconds to beat Wake

Forest, 71–70, in the ACC Tournament quarterfinals, then went to the line with 23 seconds left and the Wolfpack down one to Virginia in the West Regional Final. In the huddle, Valvano spoke to his players as if he presumed that Charles would make both shots. The truth was that Valvano felt like there was a fired-up ferret inside his stomach, but he never betrayed his anxiety to Charles or the rest of the team. He tried to reassure Charles with a Dick Vitale–style monologue: *Lo, baby, this is it. We've come this far—team of destiny, the Cardiac Pack. It's on you. Knock them both down. When you do, we're calling time-out again. Then we'll talk about defense. But there's no defense now, baby, because you are the man. Brooklyn, New York's own, Lorenzo Charles, the guy from the Big Apple, my guy Lo—do it, baby.* Lo did it. He made both. "I know now that 'Zo won't ever get rattled," Valvano said later. "All season, I've been waiting for him to get as tough as he looks. Now, the waiting's over." NC State won, 81–78, and moved on to the Final Four.

CBS had acquired the telecasting rights to the NCAA Tournament in 1981, paying $48 million for a three-year contract to wrest the month of March away from NBC. The power of TV as a popular cultural force was perhaps at its zenith; wide-scale access to a television did not fragment viewing habits and content consumption in the way the Internet has. Quite the opposite: A major sporting event, a long-running sitcom or drama, or even a made-for-TV movie was a shared experience for much of America, sometimes commanding an audience that these days only a Super Bowl can. On February 28, 1983, less than three weeks before the first game of the NCAA Tournament, CBS aired the final episode of M*A*S*H*, and nearly 106 million people tuned in. Later that year, in November, *The Day After*—an "ABC Sunday Night Movie" about the fallout of a nuclear war—drew 100 million viewers. The teams that reached the 1983 Final Four would compete on a grand and vast stage, and the public was finding the productions and performances more thrilling with each passing year. Michigan State's victory over Indiana State in the 1979 championship game—Magic Johnson versus Larry Bird—remains the most watched Final Four game of all time, pulling more than 35 million viewers, and the sport was starting to reap the rewards of reinstituting the dunk in 1976. "We put it back in because it's an appealing way to score," NCAA rules guru Ed Steitz once said. "The fans liked it, and the players liked it."

As if to prove Steitz's point, the teams that rose to the top of the tournament in the early 1980s were often fastbreaking and highflying, with stars who were or would be famous for dunking. Louisville won the 1980 national title behind Darrell Griffith, a six-four guard who scored 23 points a game that season, touted the "over twenty ways" that he could dunk the ball, and was nicknamed "Dr. Dunkenstein." Marty Blake, the director of the NBA's scouting service, went so far as to say of Griffith: "He is the one player coming out this year who is sure to be a superstar. He's like Larry Bird and Magic Johnson, as close to an immediate star as you can find." (Griffith was a fine player for the Utah Jazz, averaging 21 points and shooting 48 percent from the field over his first five seasons with them. But it was a stretch even then to suggest he'd be on Bird's or Johnson's level. If anything, a player's ability to dunk had started to warp evaluations of him; it was easy to think a player was better than he actually was or would be just because he was a tremendous dunker.) The '82 Final Four could have played entirely above the clouds: Louisville again; Houston; Georgetown with Patrick Ewing as a freshman, before his knees began to betray him; North Carolina with Jordan, Perkins, and James Worthy. But '83 marked the pinnacle of the dunk's influence on college basketball—not in NC State's 67–60 semifinal victory over Georgia, maybe the most uneventful game the Wolfpack played in the Tournament, but in that Final Four's next two games.

For the third time in four years, Louisville had reached the national semifinals; coach Denny Crum had no one on his roster taller than six-nine, but the Cardinals were willing to play run-and-gun ball with anyone, even their opponents in Albuquerque: the Houston Cougars. Olajuwon and Drexler would be Hall of Fame NBA players, but coach Guy Lewis had long been an advocate for incorporating the dunk into the college game, and he built a team that did more than incorporate the dunk into its strategy. Benny Anders, Michael Young,

Larry Micheaux—dunking *was* Houston's strategy. In the game that inspired sportswriter Thomas Bonk, in January '83, to coin the nickname "Phi Slama Jama," the Cougars dunked 29 times in a 112–58 win over Pacific. They had 161 through their first 32 games of the '82–'83 season; one out of every seven baskets they scored was on a dunk. They were 30–2 heading into the Final Four. Louisville was 32–3. These two prevailing narratives of the weekend—NC State's march through the tournament and the titillating matchup in Saturday's second game—were so attractive that Albuquerque couldn't handle the flood of fans from the four schools, some fifteen thousand people in all, into the city for the weekend. The NCAA and the Albuquerque conventions and visitors bureau had set aside eight thousand first-class hotel rooms, and those rooms filled so quickly that about seven hundred fans—and the NC State team and traveling party—had to stay in Grants, a town eighty miles west of the University of New Mexico campus. Still, the expectation, at least throughout the country, was that the NC State–Georgia game was all but irrelevant. The winner would be nothing more than a lamb to be sacrificed. Houston-Louisville was the real championship game, and the Cougars carried themselves like they couldn't conceive of losing. Late in the Wolfpack's win, Houston's players, Walkman earphones wrapped around their heads, sat directly behind the NC State bench.

"Walked in with an arrogant air," McQueen said at Jimmy V's.

"We were taken aback by that," Myers added. "They assumed they were going to win."

Based on what they were about to do to Louisville, they would have been fools to assume otherwise. Down eight midway through the second half, Houston ripped off 12 straight points, eight of them on dunks. Anders cut Louisville's lead to two when he stole a pass in Houston's defensive end, dribbled downcourt, and swerved to the right and slowed down to allow the Cardinals' Charles Jones to catch up to him. Anders was six-five. Jones was six-nine. And Anders, the ball in his right hand, his right arm extended like a crane, tomahawked down a dunk over Jones, who fouled him. Drexler gave Houston a three-point lead when Anders, after another steal, fed him an in-stride pass on a fastbreak and Drexler leaped with the ball in his right hand, changed his mind in midair, and jammed it with two hands instead.

"When you were under the basket and they came down with all those thunderous dunks," Hank Nichols, one of the game's referees, once said, "you looked around for a bomb shelter."

The Cougars threw down 19 dunks in their 94–81 win. It was, Ed Steitz said, "the most electrifying game I've ever seen. If we banned the dunk now, fans would hang all the members of the rules committee." Roger Valdiserri, Notre Dame's longtime sports-information director and spokesperson, held up a handwritten sign along press row. WELCOME TO THE 21ST CENTURY, it read.

"It built on the shards of possibility explored by prior innovators like Julius Erving and David Thompson," Robert Weintraub wrote in an oral history of the game for ESPN.com, "and then extrapolated, creating an entirely new paradigm. Now the dunk could be the objective of an offense, not just an occasional happenstance. Now teams could attack the rim at every opportunity, and there would be no purist backlash. . . . Houston and Louisville brought Rucker Park to the Final Four."

Over the forty-eight hours before the national title game, Charles and McQueen joked with each other about which one of them would have to guard, or attempt to guard, Drexler. *You gotta guard him. . . . I ain't gonna guard him. . . . Who's gonna guard him? . . . Thurl's gonna guard him.* Valvano's defensive philosophy was simple: *Don't let the opponent's best player beat you.* But Houston had so much talent that his best recourse was to draw on a strategy he had used throughout the postseason: he would throw multiple defenses at the Cougars—box-and-one, triangle-and-two, diamond-and-one, one-three-chaser—to try to confuse them. There was, however, one ironclad rule that his players had to follow. Dunks, Valvano later wrote, were "the *raison d'être* of the Phi Slama Jamas." Dunks energized them. Dunks got them playing faster and freer and with more confidence. Dunks demoralized their opponents. *Do whatever you have to do,* Valvano told the Wolfpack. *Foul them. Grab them. Root yourself in the lane and steel yourself against the collision and take the charge.* But under no circumstances could any Houston player dunk the basketball in the 1983 national championship game.

Olajuwon was the only one who did. Once.

Charles was a nonfactor for most of the game. He scored NC State's third and fourth points, on a rebound putback, but was mostly invisible from that basket until the last minute. "Hakeem was blocking everything," Myers told me. "Lo couldn't adjust to that." Despite the low score, the teams played at a remarkably fast pace, given that the altitude in Albuquerque, roughly five thousand feet, deprived the athletes of oxygen, and the score swung at times based on which team and players happened to be tiring and which happened to get their second wind. NC State was up by eight at halftime, but late in the second half, Houston seemed to seize control, leading 52–46 with less than four minutes left in regulation. Then Lowe swished a long jump shot from the top of the key, and Whittenburg hit even deeper jumpers on back-to-back possessions to tie the game. After Houston freshman Alvin Franklin missed the first free throw in a one-and-one situation and McQueen corralled the rebound, Valvano called a time-out with 44 seconds to go.

Since the tournament was not using a shot clock, the Wolfpack could hold the ball as long as necessary to take the last shot and give the Cougars no chance to score in regulation. Valvano instructed his players to melt as much clock as possible before running one of the team's time-honored offensive sets. Lowe would drive into the middle of the Houston defense and, depending on which side the help defender came from, kick the ball to either of NC State's best outside shooters: Whittenburg or sophomore guard Terry Gannon. If no help came, if Houston guarded Lowe one-on-one, he would continue driving to the basket in the hope that he would score or get fouled. There are varying versions of what Valvano said to Charles in that moment. In one—from Tim Peeler's book *Legends of N.C. State Basketball*—he was deadly serious. "Lo," he told Charles, "you haven't done anything all night. I wish you would wake up." But in a 1987 speech to a group of financial professionals, Valvano's description of the situation had much more levity. "He's from Brooklyn. I'm from Queens. Two city kids," he said during the speech. "Right after I diagrammed the play, I thought, 'What if it didn't work?' I called Lorenzo over. I said, 'Lo, c'mere.' He said, 'What's up, Coach?' I said, 'Look, pay attention. It's very important. If this play doesn't work, anything that's up near the basket, make believe it's a hubcap.'"

All of Valvano's words in that huddle, all of his best-laid plans, went to pieces once Lowe inbounded the ball to Gannon and Gannon tossed it back to Lowe just across the midcourt stripe. Houston surprised and discombobulated the Wolfpack by coming out in a one-three-one halfcourt trap. NC State's players threw 12 passes—several of which were weak and dangerously close to being stolen—and took 29 seconds off the clock before any of them dribbled even once, so fearful did they appear of the Cougars' tenacity and speed. Charles lingered on the right side of the court, near the lane. For the first 43 seconds of that final possession, he was the only NC State player who didn't touch the ball. With nine seconds left, just as Lowe snapped a bounce pass to Bailey in the left corner and Bailey, like a harried quarterback, chucked the ball to Whittenburg beyond the top of the key, Charles shuffled closer to the basket, positioning himself under the cylinder. It was a terrible place for a potential offensive rebounder to be. NC State's last shot was likely to come from one of their guards—Whittenburg, Lowe, Gannon—which meant that shot was likely to come from at least fifteen feet out, which meant, if that player missed, the ball was likely to hit the rim and carom several feet away from the basket . . . and away from Charles.

"Most people say I was the guy who was in the right place at the right time," Charles admitted later. "Actually, I was in the wrong place at the right time."

With Anders bearing down on him, Whittenburg reached for Thurl Bailey's pass with both of his hands. Anders knocked the ball out of Whittenburg's grasp for a half second, but Whittenburg grabbed it again and lofted it toward the rim. He thought his shot was going in.

"Little short," he told me. "Lo and I will be linked together for the rest of my life."

Had Charles been anywhere else on the floor, he wouldn't have had the necessary view of Whittenburg's shot to know—unlike Bailey and Olajuwon—that it would be an airball, so short of the rim that he could jump to catch it and dunk it without risking an offensive-goaltending call.

On the CBS telecast, play-by-play announcer Gary Bender went silent, seemingly out of shock, when Charles dropped the ball through the hoop. Color analyst Billy Packer delivered the perfect punctuation mark.

"They won it," Packer said, "on the dunk."

Charles looked around, puzzled, uncertain, as if he were poised to fall back on defense. He wasn't sure how much time, if any, was left in the game. He hadn't heard the buzzer. He couldn't hear his teammates. The noise at the bottom of The Pit was deafening. "The loudest Final Four game I've ever been to," longtime basketball writer Dick "Hoops" Weiss told me. From the bench, Myers and backups Walt Densmore and Mike Warren dashed to Charles, group-hugged him, and assured him that the game was, in fact, over. In the stands, Herman Charles watched with a father's fierce pride as his son won North Carolina State its second national championship. "That's my boy," he said.

It was fitting that the '83 Final Four had been won with a dunk. It was ironic that an NC State player had been the one to do it. "For him to dunk the ball at that moment to win the game," Houston's Michael Young said in 2011, after Charles's death, "it was one of the most heartbreaking moments I have ever felt in my whole career." The kid responsible for it, a fishing hat now mashed on his head, climbed on top of the backboard with his friend McQueen and smiled while everyone else whooped and hollered around him. Back at the team hotel in Grants that night, the players and coaches celebrated with fans and boosters, and when the party finally broke up, Charles and McQueen—sharing a suite, roommates again—lay on their beds in silence until Charles bolted up, laughing, still in giddy disbelief. *Yo, Co, I just made the final shot for the N-C-Double-A Championship.*

"He didn't process it at the time, but it was the biggest dunk in the history of college basketball," Myers told me. "And he never felt that throughout his life."

When the Wolfpack returned to the Final Four in 2024, for the first time since 1983, it gave people around the country cause to recall Charles or, perhaps, learn about him for the first time. He had capped an era of college basketball in which the slam dunk had reigned supreme, and he and his teammates had helped propel the sport into the modern media age, and the afterglow warmed them for weeks, for months, for years.

More than thirty-two million people had seen Charles's dunk on CBS. The '83 national title game is the third most-watched Final Four game of all time. A North Carolina newspaper transformed a photograph of Charles's dunk into a life-sized poster; he hung one in the bedroom of his campus apartment. People recognized him on the street, stopped him, asked him for autographs. He had never imagined himself becoming a basketball star, had thought he would be an average player at NC State, but now he had become more than that. The dunk accelerated his improvement. It made him more assertive. "The joke around Reynolds Coliseum," Don Markus wrote in the Bergen *Record* in December 1984, "is that Charles will dunk anything that moves." Valvano once joked that "a little boy walked by in practice, and Lorenzo tried to dunk him. . . . He gathers himself better than most players I've ever had. And then, when he goes [up], he's just too strong to stop."

He liked the reaction of the fans in Reynolds Coliseum, he once said, whenever he slammed one home. It made them go wild. It made the building shake. It shook up the other team. Maryland coach Lefty Driesell liked to say that he would promise recruits' and players' mothers that their sons wouldn't have to guard Charles, who over his junior and senior seasons encountered nightly double- and triple-teams in the post and fought through them to score more than 18 points a game and shoot 56 percent from the field. He had made himself more than a one-dunk wonder, but ahead of the 1985 NBA draft, as much as teams admired his work ethic, he had added another twenty-five pounds to gird

himself for an 82-game season against professionals, and his game had
suffered for it. The Atlanta Hawks took him with the 41st overall pick,
but he appeared in just 36 games for them that season, his only one in
the NBA. He earned $70,000, enough to buy his father a Rolex, then
accepted a six-figure salary to play in Cantu, Italy, for a team sponsored
by Squib, a soft-drink company. "The Italian Mello Yellow," Charles
once said. Spain, Turkey, Argentina, the Continental Basketball Association, the Global Basketball Association—he played in all of them,
played professionally for another fifteen years, held on as long as he
could. His basketball career never made him financially comfortable
later in his life, and he never finished his degree at NC State. He married, stayed local, drove for UPS, made less than fifteen dollars an hour
for Elite Tours, allowed his body to get billowy, listened to family and
friends who urged him to exercise and eat better, and laughed them
off. The interactions with his passengers pleased him. He chauffeured
the Duke men's lacrosse team to two Final Fours. He had Coach K in
his bus . . . and Coach K had remembered him . . .

"He didn't feel like he had failed," one of his friends said. "He
didn't hang his head."

On June 26, 2011, Charles visited an NC State basketball camp to
meet Mark Gottfried, who had become the Wolfpack's head coach
just two months earlier, and Gottfried's staff. The next day, McQueen
was in his car when Myers called him. *Something happened to Lo*, Myers
told him. *I've been trying to call him. He won't answer his phone.*

"When they told me . . . where he had the accident," McQueen
said in Jimmy V's, "man, it was around the corner from where I live,
man, off of 40 on the backside. It's just mind-boggling."

Less than two miles north of the restaurant is Oakwood Cemetery, seventy-two acres, chartered in 1869. There, an eight-step stone
staircase and a dozen strides separate Valvano's and Charles's graves.
They receive so many visitors that when I met Robin Simonton, the
cemetery's executive director, she never bothered to open a map to
find their plots. "I don't even have to look," she said. One dunk in one
game . . . one instant . . . one play that never fades . . . it was enough
to make sure that no one would forget Lorenzo Charles.

17

FLYING BLIND

Dunking was once thought to be the final frontier for women's basketball, the gap that had to be closed before the women's game would receive a similar measure of respect to the men's. Now that today's female stars enjoy and have earned so much of that respect, it's easy to overlook the women who first showed that the full breadth of the sport, everything that it offered, was within reach.

Where do you start with the story of the trailblazers who raised the dunk to the highest reaches of women's basketball? Here are three of them, each with her own story within that broader story, each of those stories full of delicious details, each of those stories intersecting at so many points and at so many angles that if you tried to connect the dots among them, you'd end up scribbling a spiderweb across your sheet of looseleaf. Do you begin with the one who thought she had been the first woman to dunk in a college basketball game, only to learn that, oh no, sorry, there actually had been someone who beat her to the punch a decade earlier? Do you begin with that true pioneer and the long-missing videotape of her dunk—the confirmation of her achievement, a lost ark of slam and jam—that a diligent reporter dug up a quarter century later? Do you begin with the woman who was tethered to both, who was a teammate to one and family to the other, who had the privilege of having the greatest basketball player of all posterize her during a pickup game, who became a national sensation for a fleeting moment after she threw down a dunk that she herself barely even saw?

Confused? Understandable. Curious? Good. Let's start at the end. That will clear everything up.

In March 2009, Reed Albergotti found what every good journalist who wants to write a good feature needs: a good news peg. Bound for Baylor University and the WNBA, years before she was imprisoned for ten months in Russia for carrying a scant amount of hash oil, Brittney Griner was finishing up her senior season at Nimitz High School in Houston, where she had dunked 52 times in 32 games. She was six foot nine; it was only a matter of time, once her college career got underway, before she threw one down for Baylor. A sports reporter for the *Wall Street Journal* at the time—we were coworkers for three years there—Albergotti decided to track down and write about the first woman to dunk: Georgeann Wells of the University of West Virginia. It all lined up, too. Wells reportedly had dunked in a game against the University of Charleston on December 21, 1984. It was coming up on the twenty-fifth anniversary of her slam. "Total coincidence," Albergotti told me.

Better yet, the circumstances would make for an entertaining read. President Richard Nixon had signed Title IX—the seminal law that outlawed federal discrimination by sex and gender and paved the way for the expansion of women's collegiate sports—in June 1972, which placed Wells's dunk near the top of that wave of change as it was just beginning to crest. Three months before Title IX's passage, tiny Immaculata College—an all-women's institution just outside Philadelphia, run by the Sisters, Servants of the Immaculate Heart of Mary, with an undergraduate enrollment of just eight hundred—won the first of its three consecutive national championships. Theresa Grentz, the Mighty

Macs' best player, was six feet tall and a multiskilled force in the post, but dunking was hardly a consideration for her or any of her contemporaries. "I could get my wrist above the rim, but I couldn't get high enough to force the ball down through," Gretz, who was inducted into the Naismith Hall of Fame in 2022, told me. "Dunking was not something we practiced or worked toward. It just wasn't a thing."

The influx of talent to the sport post–Title IX would inevitably make it one. At Northland High School in Columbus, Ohio, the six-foot-seven Wells had tried to dunk in games but couldn't quite get there. Once Wells got to West Virginia, though, her coaches, seeing the public-relations potential in her leaping ability, made her dunk up to twenty times after each practice. They would even bring a reel-to-reel video camera to games throughout the 1983–84 season, Wells's sophomore year, hoping they might capture proof of Wells dunking. It was as if they were searching for Sasquatch or the Loch Ness Monster, except their odds of success were much better.

The Mountaineers' game against Charleston—four days before Christmas, early in Wells's junior season—was at a neutral site: Elkins, West Virginia, at a gym inside the Randolph County Armory. West Virginia was cruising to an easy victory, up 23 points at halftime, when guard Lisa Ribble pointed out that Charleston's players weren't hustling back on defense. There were opportunities to get Wells a breakaway, to give her time and space to build up speed, gather herself, and dunk. "Let's go for it," Ribble said to her. A few minutes into the second half, Charleston scored, and on the ensuing inbounds pass, Ribble lofted the ball down the court for Wells, who dribbled a few times and one-handed the ball down through the basket. "There was no question about it," Bill Fiske, West Virginia's associate head coach, told the Associated Press immediately after the game. "The place went crazy. There must have been five hundred people hanging around outside the dressing room afterward wanting her autograph. Everyone wanted to prove they were there."

Two factors that went unmentioned in any contemporaneous reports about Wells's dunk or the Mountaineers' 110–82 win made her feat even more distinctive. In the late 1970s, the invention and widespread implementation of the breakaway rim—the spring-and-hinge mechanism that allowed players to stuff the ball through the hoop or grab the rim with little concern that they would break either the backboard or the bones in their hands and wrists—made dunking easier for everyone. It seems unlikely, however, that in 1984 the armory would have been outfitted with the latest in basketball technology. Additionally, a standard men's basketball has a circumference of 29.5 inches and weighs between 20 and 22 ounces, and just that season, the NCAA had introduced a smaller ball for women's games, one that had a 28.5-inch circumference and weighed 18 to 20 ounces and that remains the standard size in the sport to this day. But there's no indication that West Virginia and Charleston used that smaller ball; "Wells," Greg Garber wrote for ESPN.com in July 2009, "apparently dunked with an old-school men's ball."

Then, eight days later, in the closing moments of a 109–76 victory over Xavier at the University of Cincinnati, Wells dunked again.

"This one was awesome," she said. "It was much better than the first one. I had confidence all the way that I could do it. On the first one, I was kind of scared, but now I know I can do it."

The first one was the historic one, though. The first one was the one that interested Albergotti. During an online search, he dug up an old photograph of Wells dunking. He started to write a caption for it when a fairly unsettling thought occurred to him: *Wait a minute. How do I know that the dunk in this photo is the first one? How do I know this dunk even happened during a game? What if it happened during a practice? I don't know what's true in this photo and what isn't.* So he called Kittie Blakemore, who was West Virginia's head coach from 1973 through 1992, to confirm the origin of the photo.

Blakemore told Albergotti that the picture was indeed from a practice. *There is no photo from the game,* she told him. *There's video of the game and the dunk, but no one has it.*

Funny enough, it was Charleston coach Bud Francis who had made sure to videotape the game, positioning someone on the east side of the armory to capture the action. The Mountaineers hadn't toted their cumbersome video equipment to Elkins. Fiske presumably had called the Associated Press himself to relay the news of Wells's dunk; why would any newspaper or television station be covering a West Virginia–Charleston women's basketball game in 1984? But Francis, thinking that it would be humiliating for the Charleston players and program to be known around the country as the victims of the first dunk in women's college basketball, refused either to release the tape or to give it to West Virginia, and he kept on refusing until the day he died, in 1999. Without a photo or the video, there was no public visual evidence that Wells had dunked, and she had heard for years from people whose skepticism was laced with sexism: *There's no proof that you dunked, and I don't believe that you did.* The doubts had to be especially galling for Wells considering that she had a fantastic career at West Virginia, scoring 1,484 points, grabbing 1,075 rebounds, and blocking 436 shots—the last mark still a school record. She wasn't an uncoordinated scrub. It wasn't a stretch to think a player of her size and skill could dunk.

"It blew my mind," Albergotti told me. "I couldn't believe that somebody would be that petty. You have to think back to that era— West Virginia in 1984, women's sports, and the racial undertone, a Black woman embarrassing the other team. It was not, 'This is an amazing achievement,' which is how most people would look at it to-day. It made sense at the time that he would have this reaction. Imagine you had this really important moment in women's sports today. You'd be shamed on Twitter into turning over the tape."

Albergotti thought he could help. He suggested to Blakemore that he could contact Francis's family. *Don't stick your nose in this mess,* Blakemore, who died in 2020, told him. The situation was so sensitive that she feared that, if Albergotti tried to find the tape, the person who had it might destroy it. Undeterred, Albergotti called Ford Francis, Bud's son, who said that he did have some old tapes of his father's games. Ford kept them in a basket next to his television, but he had no idea, he said, whether any of them contained the footage of Wells's dunk. None of them was labeled WELLS or WVU or DUNK. One of them, however, was labeled ELKINS. Bingo. Albergotti flew to Ford's house to get the tape and made a digital copy of the video . . .

and of Wells's dunk. His next step was to show it to her—a challenge, given that she had not responded to his emails and phone calls. Eventually, he tracked her down.

"I think I surprised her," he told me. "She doesn't like to be in the spotlight. I played the video for her on my laptop, and she was just totally blown away. She cried. It was just such a cool experience to see her reaction to it. I think she felt like something had been taken away from her."

The *Journal* published Albergotti's story on March 20, 2009. You can still watch the video of Wells's dunk on the paper's website. Any doubts about what Georgeann Wells had done were dead. There were two women—teammates, friends, national champions—who had believed all along.

Both of them had their idols. In Shelby, North Carolina, Charlotte Smith would watch NBA games on the floor-model television in her grandmother's house with her cousin Dereck Whittenburg. The games always featured the same player: her uncle David Thompson. Each summer during his professional career, Thompson would return to his home state to visit his family. In 1982, all the parents and grandparents and aunts and uncles and cousins piled into a recreational vehicle and drove to Knoxville to attend the World's Fair. That was a onetime treat, though. Mostly, Thompson played basketball with his younger relatives on a driveway hoop. "He was very influential in my life," Smith told me. "It was really cool to have him home those summers. I remember thinking, 'Wow, look at his lifestyle. I want to be just like my uncle and play pro basketball when I grow up.'"

Throughout elementary, middle, and high school, Smith was taller than all the boys in her grades, growing to be six feet. "There were very slim pickings when it came to dating options," she said. One day, she watched the Shelby High boys basketball players go through their pregame layup line, and a couple of them dunked. *Shoot*, she thought, *I wonder if I could do that*. She jumped into the line with them, grabbed a ball—men's sized—and dunked it on her first try. "They went crazy:

'Oh, my God! Oh, my God!'" she told me. "It was like they didn't believe it. So I did it probably three times. All the doubting Thomases saw it with their own eyes." But she never had the opportunity in an official high school game to do it.

Sylvia Crawley never did, either, though she knew, well before she entered Steubenville High School in eastern Ohio, that it was possible for a woman to dunk. Crawley had a particular poster of a particular athlete on her bedroom wall when she was a kid. "Very few little girls had this," she told me. In the poster, the athlete, a basketball player wearing Converse sneakers, was dunking. The athlete had even autographed it for Crawley: *Keep it in the family, Cuz. Love, Georgeann.* Yes, Wells and Crawley were cousins.

For all their admiration for their highflying family members, Crawley and Smith ended up signing to play at the University of North Carolina—Crawley entering school in the late summer/fall of 1990, Smith a year later—for the same reason: head coach Sylvia Hatchell and her staff had tempted them with the prospect of meeting Tar Heels alum Michael Jordan. Finally, in the summer of 1991, while working at Jordan's basketball camp, Crawley stood next to him for the annual counselors' photograph—Jordan six-six but Crawley six-five herself. "And he's leaning on me, talking trash, in the picture," Crawley said. "I'm like, 'Get off me, Mike.'" That night, Jordan joined the male counselors and Crawley for a pickup game. Whenever she was the only woman playing pickup with guys, Crawley would usually just tell them, *Guard who you want to guard, and I'll take who's left* . . . and she'd end up guarding the worst male player on the court. This time, she said nothing, and her four teammates picked up the four worst male players on the other team, leaving her with . . . Jordan. *Oh, y'all scared of Mike? I ain't scared of Mike. I'm not afraid.*

As expected, Crawley had no more success stopping Jordan than the men on the court would have, and in one sequence, she found herself alone under the basket, the only player between Jordan and the rim as he blasted off the floor for a dunk. "I literally watched him jump over my head," she told me. "I'm watching to see, first of all, what his tongue and legs were doing and where his hand is going, how he's grabbing the rim, how he pulled back on the rim. I just sat there and took in the whole thing. Everybody gets out of the way. No one wants to be dunked on. But it was my honor to be dunked on because I got to see the whole mechanics of a dunk."

The tutorial promised to have practical benefits for her and the rest of the Tar Heels. In the wake of four consecutive losing seasons, Hatchell had sought to build a more athletic team at Carolina, and she managed to recruit four players who could dunk: Crawley; Smith; Gwendolyn Gillingham, who was six-seven; and future Olympian Marion Jones, who would win five medals, including three golds, in track and field at the 2000 Olympics in Sydney—only to have them stripped after she admitted to using performance-enhancing drugs. (At five-ten, Jones was also the shortest of the quartet.) "Why not dunk?" Hatchell once said. "It adds something to the women's game that nobody else has." George "Bulldog" Smith, the athletic department's strength and conditioning coach, designed a training program to increase the explosiveness of each player's jumping ability: fewer bench presses and forearm curls, more power cleans and snatches and plyometrics. Smith said that she added seven inches to her vertical leap in one summer. In another pickup game, this one inside Woollen Gym—a fieldhouse on UNC's campus with multiple courts, one of which had a rim that was slightly less than ten feet high— Crawley caught an alley-oop pass from a teammate and, on that lower rim, dunked the ball. That Crawley didn't drop the ball was itself an achievement for her, an indication of how far she had come. As a freshman, she'd had so much trouble adjusting to the velocity with which Division I players snapped the ball to each other that the Tar Heels' guards would scream at her for fumbling their passes. Sometimes the ball would smack her in the face. "I was literally tortured with every pass as a center," she said. "It got to the point where nobody would pass to me." To strengthen the ligaments and muscles in Crawley's long, delicate fingers, Smith had her dig her hands into buckets of sand fifty to a hundred times before practice, then fired basketballs at her—high passes, bounce passes—until, eventually, "my whole game opened up," she told me. "I could catch the ball. I could palm the ball. Now I was ready to dunk the ball."

The Tar Heels' layup lines became jam sessions during the 1993–94 season, as Crawley, Smith, Gillingham, and Jones would dunk back to back to back to back. One group of opposing players took photos of them. "The other teams would watch us in awe," Smith told me. No North Carolina player ever dunked in a game in '93–'94, but then, no North Carolina player had to. The team won 32 of its first 34 games entering the NCAA Tournament championship game against Louisiana Tech, then won the program's first and so far only national title when Smith, who had 20 points and 23 rebounds in the game, drilled a three-pointer at the buzzer for a dramatic 60–59 victory. When she realized that Hatchell was calling an inbounds play to set her up for the Tar Heels' final shot, "it felt like the weight of the world was on my shoulders," Smith once said. And that feeling lingered some even after the championship, as she entered her senior season, because of the pressure people, especially UNC's male athletes, were placing on her to dunk during a game. "It was an open discussion mostly among the football players," she told me. "We all shared the same dining space. 'When are you going to dunk? When are you going to dunk?' Here it is, my senior year, and I'm thinking, 'Man, it's my goal to dunk in college, and this is it.' The clock was winding down."

On December 2, 1994, in an interview with the Raleigh News & Observer, Smith reaffirmed how much the expectations were weighing on her: "This is my last shot, and I think there'll be more pressure on me than ever before." Two days later, on Sunday, December 4, the Tar Heels hosted North Carolina A&T, and less than twenty seconds after the opening tip, A&T's Samara Dobbins threw an ill-advised pass. Smith stole the ball and, with no other players near her, lifted off and dunked it. Relief washed over her, though there was little celebration of the moment, either during the game or afterward. Play continued. Smith had to backpedal to join her teammates on defense, and once Carolina finished toying with A&T, winning 113–58, the public reaction to her achievement, to the first dunk in a women's basketball game in ten years, was underwhelming to say the least. Perhaps bitter over the game's outcome, Tim Abney, A&T's coach, said Smith's basket was "a semi- or a fraction" of a dunk. A reporter got Thompson on the phone for comment, and he expressed surprise that his niece hadn't dunked sooner. "It was just a matter of time," he said. That was pretty much how Hatchell and Smith felt, too. "It wasn't as good as I have seen her dunk before," Hatchell said, and Smith was disappointed in herself. "It wasn't the dunk I expected," she said.

It was the only time that Smith ever dunked during an official game, either in her four years at Carolina or her six in the WNBA. She suffered a torn hamstring in the pros, "so it was difficult for me to do anything other than stay grounded," she told me. Smith also has undergone four knee surgeries, all of them, she said, to clean up the damage that the impact of landing after leaping and dunking had done to her. The head coach at Elon University since 2011, she does not often mention her career—the national championship and her role in it, her 1994–95 national player of the year award, the dunk—to her players.

"I don't really talk about myself a lot," she said. "They know my history."

Then she paused, just to laugh and move her tongue into her cheek.

"They know they play for one of the GOATs."

The winner of the only slam dunk contest in American professional women's basketball never dunked in a professional game. Or a collegiate game. Not once. Sylvia Crawley kept waiting for an opportunity that never came, and people kept wondering and asking her about it, and maybe that's why, when she was one of six players chosen to compete in the 1998 American Basketball League dunk contest, she was so enthusiastic about it.

Don't remember the American Basketball League? Don't blame you. It was around for just two years, starting in 1996 and folding in December 1998, the primary competitor to the WNBA but without the financial and promotional backing of the NBA. Like the ABA in 1976, the ABL needed some novelty to have any hope of surviving. Hence, a dunk contest at the All-Star Game, held at Disney's Wide World of Sports Complex near Orlando. Hence, the invitation to Crawley, who was playing for the league's franchise in Denver, the Colorado Explosion. She happened to live in a townhouse complex with several members of the Denver Broncos. They had questions and suggestions: reverses and rocked cradles and everything else they'd seen Dr. J and MJ and 'Nique do.

Guys, Crawley told them, *I can't do all that stuff. I've got one right-handed, jump-off-the-left-leg dunk.*

They asked what kinds of dunks the other women in the contest would do.

The same exact dunk, y'all, she said.

Boooorrrrrring.

They gave her an idea that might work: Dunk blindfolded. Crawley liked it. It had some flair, and if there were any tilt in the rim, its lowest part would be at the front. All Crawley had to do was pace off the correct number of strides to make sure her timing was right and that she would reach the rim: eight big steps out from the basket when she walked, four strides back in when she ran in to dunk. "I have long legs," she said. She practiced at practice with the Explosion. She practiced in her free time with her friends on the Broncos. Still, she didn't want to take any chance that she would miss the dunk or, even worse, lose her sense of direction. So her mother made her a special blindfold, cutting a piece out of the cloth and sewing a strip of sheer black hosiery over the hole—a special eye-patch that would allow Crawley to see the basket. She practiced with the jury-rigged blindfold and dunked every time. The plan seemed foolproof.

At the contest, Crawley took her eight steps to lay out off her path to the rim and marked the spot where she would jump to dunk. Then she had her sister, Helen, put the blindfold on her . . . except Helen tied the blindfold so tightly around Crawley's head that Crawley couldn't open her eyes. All she could see was her nose and her feet.

"We're talking through our teeth so nobody knows we're fighting," Crawley told me. "I'm saying a prayer, 'Dear Lord Jesus, if you never do another thing for me, please allow me to dunk on national TV. Please.'"

She never let on how panicked she was. She did a Mile High Salute—in honor of the Broncos—dribbled twice, saw her mark on the floor, and took off, legs in a Jordanesque splay. "And my hand connected," she said, "and I was cheering harder than everybody in the stadium. My sister almost had a heart attack. She had one job, and she almost blew it. I could have passed out in that moment."

Crawley got $5,000 for winning the contest. She got to be interviewed on *Good Morning America* and on talk shows hosted by Keenan Ivory Wayans and Sinbad. She got to be part of a photo shoot for *Rolling Stone*, with Kobe Bryant and the skier Picabo Street. ("It was very abstract," she told me.) She got to play professionally in sixteen countries, got to learn how to speak French and Spanish and Italian and Korean. And she, like Smith, like Wells, got to be a footnote.

"We have not done a good enough job of cataloging women's basketball history," Smith told me. "When I was in high school, I was thinking that I would be the first woman to dunk in college. I knew nothing about Georgeann Wells. Never heard of her. Even when I was in college, even when I dunked in the game, I did not know much about Georgeann Wells. So here I am thinking I'm the first woman in history to dunk, but I'm not. Her story needs to be told.

"Now that I'm however many years removed from dunking in a game, it's almost like I'm invisible to history, because nobody really talks about that dunk. I've seen documentaries. I've seen videos. I've seen social-media posts. It's like, 'OK, but what about me?'"

As of March 2024, the brightest light in college basketball—men's or women's—was Iowa's Caitlin Clark, whose long-distance marksmanship and dazzling passing are reminiscent of Pete Maravich and within the women's game have elevated her, in her similar style of play and popularity, to a plane approaching Stephen Curry's. Clark was her own traveling road show; her presence in the 2023 national championship game, LSU's 102–85 victory over the Hawkeyes, was a primary reason that viewership of the game more than doubled that of 2022. But the sport has grown, through Clark and her peers and predecessors, without the dunk becoming a major factor within it. Just nine female players had dunked during an NCAA game through January 2024, and there had been 37 dunks in WNBA history through July 2023—with Griner responsible for 26 of them. "People are putting more baskets in from 25 feet than they are dunking," Smith told me. "Point blank. Period." In this way, those trailblazers who shattered this particular glass ceiling by jumping through it—Wells, Smith, Crawley—stand out all the more. Smith is right. They should not be forgotten. So few have been like them since. How many more will there be?

18

THE HIGHEST HEIGHT

The slam dunk—its history and its evolution, its story and its impact—at its climax.

On the West Side of Chicago, the 1800 block of West Madison Street specifically, it was freezing to the point of danger, the air's slightest stirring an invisible knife. There was no snow, no precipitation of any kind in the city on Saturday, February 6, 1988, just the kind of weather that is peaceful and beautiful through a closed window and will remain peaceful and beautiful as long as you remain on the safe side of that window. The temperature never broke 9.1 degrees Fahrenheit and dived to a low of 1.2, and wind gusts that topped out at nearly 29 miles per hour sent the windchill factor plummeting to anywhere between minus 19 and minus 26 degrees. In a parking lot outside Chicago Stadium, kerosene tanks warmed a large tent full of reporters and columnists, whose gloved hands and fingers pounded away on typewriters and TRS-80 laptops. There wasn't enough room in the aging and outdated arena to accommodate them.

They were there to cover the NBA All-Star Game, which would be played the next day. But the weekend's individual competitions would be staged that afternoon, and they had their own purchase.

The undercard was the Three-Point Contest; Larry Bird had won the first two, in 1986 and '87, so his attempt—his successful attempt, as it turned out—to defend his crown would be its primary source of suspense. Still, there was no disputing that the main event would be the Slam Dunk Contest. The field was seven dunkers deep, among them Greg "Cadillac" Anderson, the San Antonio Spurs' exciting rookie forward; the Golden State Warriors' Otis Smith; and two members of the Portland Trail Blazers with the respect and reputations to make them contenders for the title: Jerome Kersey, who had been the contest's runner-up the year before, and Clyde Drexler. (The field might have been stronger and deeper had another standout dunker chosen to compete. But as he had every year since entering the NBA in 1984, the Sixers' Charles Barkley turned down his invitation. "There's no dunk I can't do," he said, "but I don't want any part of it.") The remaining three entrants, though, promised to deliver the loudest thunderclaps and draw the most attention. All of them had previously been champions: the Atlanta Hawks' Dominique Wilkins, in 1985; his diminutive teammate Spud Webb, in 1986; and the contestant who had beaten Kersey in 1987, at Seattle Center Coliseum, and this time would enjoy a home-court and home-crowd advantage: Michael Jordan.

Jordan loved what he called "this raggedy old place," loved everything about it: the tradition and the history and the mystique and the wooden seats and the labyrinth of staircases and the tiny locker rooms that had just three or four shower stalls that spat out hot water some of the time. He loved the psychological edge that the spartan conditions gave the Bulls, similar to the one that the Celtics enjoyed at Boston Garden—the only arena in the NBA that was older. Chicago Stadium's walls were brick and limestone. Presumably, they would retain ample heat even during the worst of a Windy City winter. But the building was also nearly sixty years old and not quite what it used to be, having opened on St. Patrick's Day 1929; it would close in 1994 and be razed in 1995. It wasn't much warmer inside than it was outside, so chilly that Jordan mentioned it when, three hours before the dunk contest, he encountered Walter Iooss on the court.

"Hey, Michael, how are you doing?" Iooss asked him.

"Eh, cold."

Before Jordan commenced with his shunning of *Sports Illustrated*—
the cover of a March 1994 issue, showing him swinging and missing
during his attempt to play Major League Baseball, with the headline
"Bag it, Michael!," had offended him—his relationship with Iooss,
SI's preeminent photographer, was perhaps his closest with anyone
at the magazine. A trim man with a hawkish, goateed face and pur-
poseful look, Iooss at the 1987 dunk contest had meticulously set up
his photography equipment in the hopes of capturing a perfect shot of
Jordan (or whoever else happened to win the contest), only to fail to
get a photo that showed Jordan's face clearly. "If you couldn't see the
player's face," Iooss told me, "the shot and the dunk were worthless."
He carried that lesson with him that July, when he covered a kids' basketball camp in Lisle, Illinois, that Jordan was overseeing—his "Flight
School." The two of them got to know each other better, and after
having his assistants paint a wide strip of asphalt blue to complement
Jordan's red uniform and climbing into the basket of a cherry picker so
he could shoot from a downward angle, Iooss took what he considered
his finest photo of Jordan: a portrait—one of the fifty times Jordan
was on *SI*'s cover, the most of any athlete—in which he hovered in
the air at the right side of the basket, the basketball in his right hand
and pulled behind his head, his left hand extended in front of him and
so close to the rim that he might clutch it, his concentration fully engaged on the act of dunking, the pure and brilliant color of the court
making it seem as if he were set against a springtime sky. *My muse . . .*
that's what Iooss called him.

Glancing around Chicago Stadium, toting his strobe light kit,
Iooss surveyed the scene to figure out where to position himself. He
explained to Jordan the problem that he feared he would encounter
again: He would take a series of photos that didn't reveal the dunkers'
faces. It would be beneficial if he knew ahead of time what route each
contestant would take to the basket.

"Maybe," he suggested to Jordan, "you could let me know which
way you're going to go."

It was, Iooss told me later, either the dumbest question he ever asked or the smartest. To Jordan, everything was a challenge. Everything was a game. He was pleased to play this one.

"Sure," he said.

"How are you going to do that?" Iooss asked.

"You watch," Jordan told him. "I'll put my finger on my knee." He would subtly point to the direction that Iooss should move.

"You're going to remember that?"

"You watch."

On paper, the player who had won the 1986 Slam Dunk Contest probably shouldn't have still been an underdog in the 1988 Slam Dunk Contest. But Anthony Jerome Webb was just five feet, seven inches tall . . . on paper . . . still too much of a long shot for anyone to see him any other way. He was bestowed his nickname not long after his birth, when someone in Parkland Hospital in Dallas thought aloud that the baby's head was so big that it resembled the Soviet satellite Sputnik. "Sput" became "Spud," and Spud became . . . an employee at the Woolworth's-style store that his family owned, Webb's Soul Mart, which sold boots and shirts and beer, tennis shoes and black-eyed peas and potatoes. A teenaged Spud would stock shelves and weigh beef and pork with the butcher and practically had to stand on a milk crate to make sure he could see over the counter and operate the cash register. Then he'd hit the local Boys & Girls Club and the parks near his home in the projects to play ball.

Nobody recruited him out of Wilmer-Hutchins High School. Nobody offered him a Division I scholarship. He was five-four and had played just one year of varsity. All-district—26, 27 points a game. Big deal. Nobody recruits a five-four kid with one year of varsity ball under his belt, no matter how many points he scores or how high he can jump. It was a sin, too, a stupid one, because Spud could *jump*. "We'd walk to the gym and play a bunch of games," he told me, "and as soon as the game was over, everybody dunked. I did it for about two years, throwing it up there, missing, missing, missing, all those years. Finally I get one, and everybody was like, 'About time 'cause we're tired of seeing you chip away at the goal.' That's how I learned to dunk: throwing it up in the air, throwing it off a wall, throwing it off a backboard." So he went to Midland Junior College, grew a couple of inches, led the Chaparrals to the 1982 National Junior College Athletic Association national championship, scored 36 points in the title game, and was named the tournament's most valuable player. Division I schools noticed him then. He arrived at North Carolina State in the fall of '83, the Wolfpack on top of college basketball, Spud amazed at the lines for tickets that wound around campus like giant sidewinders. The Pack came within a game of another Final Four berth in 1985, losing to Chris Mullin and St. John's in the regional finals, and Spud put up the sorts of numbers over his two seasons that often lead to an ACC point guard getting picked in the first round of the NBA draft . . . more than 10 points a game . . . nearly six assists a game . . . nearly two steals a game . . . except no team drafted him until the fourth round—back when the draft had seven rounds—and after the Detroit Pistons picked him, they waived him . . . because no one would believe that a five-seven guard could survive or even thrive in the NBA, even if he had a forty-two-inch vertical leap.

The Atlanta Hawks signed him. After Doc Rivers suffered a fractured wrist, Spud started the 1985–86 season opener at The Omni, and Spud—who had never *seen* an NBA game before in person, let alone played in one—had 12 points and 10 assists. Back then, that performance and another few like it were all it took to puncture the cling-wrap-thin wall separating just another backup point guard from a pop-culture curiosity. Hair high and tight . . . eyes like saucers . . . soft features that made him look twelve when he was really twenty-two . . . Spud wasn't a man in the public's eyes. Spud was a kid, and how was this kid competing with supermen? A week before the 1986 Slam Dunk Contest—in Spud's hometown, Dallas—Hawks general manager Stan Kasten told him, *We want you in it.* So now Spud had to fly from Indianapolis, where the Hawks beat the Pacers in the teams' last game before the All-Star break, to Los Angeles, because before he even stepped on the floor at Reunion Arena for the contest, he was going to be on *The Tonight Show Starring Johnny Carson*. Indiana to

Hollywood, Hollywood to North Texas. "I don't know how I had the energy," he told me. "I was lucky I was twenty-two." No Jordan to contend with—he had a broken foot. Dominique was there, trying to go back-to-back, but once Spud did a couple of double-pump dunks and a 360 slam and a two-hand reverse after he bounced the ball off the backboard—all those, even though he couldn't palm the ball—the story was just too good.

"I'm pretty sure everybody in America said, 'OK, maybe this guy can squeeze one in,'" he told me. "I know that's what they were thinking, but I knew the repertoire of dunks I could do because I'd been doing them since eleventh grade."

The '87 contest in Seattle was a washout for Spud—torn meniscus, just 33 games that season. But '88 was his chance to shock everyone a second time and build on the best night of his basketball life. Without '86, he wouldn't have been driving a Corvette, wouldn't have had a shoe deal with Pony and an endorsement deal with Coca-Cola, wouldn't have savored the sheepish pleasure he felt when, the first time he and Wilkins climbed on the Hawks' team bus after Spud had out-dunked him, head coach Mike Fratello and the players started riding Dominique and didn't stop. *We're gonna run the first play for Spud. He's the man now.*

"It was funny," Webb told me, "because Fratello and Doc were like, 'Don't mess with Dominique. He's pissed.'"

Of course he was pissed. Why wouldn't he have been pissed? Dominique Wilkins discovered dunking in the way a prospective addict would discover a potent performance-enhancing drug with no negative side effects. Nothing else in his life had been so wonderful. Nothing else had made him such a better version of himself. He was thirteen, at Patterson Park, playing in the Baltimore Basketball League, and he was dribbling the ball on a fastbreak, and all he did was rise up and all he heard was people cheering and there was no movement or sound in between. He didn't realize what he had done because he had never done it before. He backpedaled downcourt on defense before the

referee called out to him, *Come back! Come back! You got fouled.* Little
Dominique had shocked himself. "I knew I was a gifted athlete, even
at that age," he told me. "I knew I had leaping ability. But I didn't realize
that, in a game situation, I was able to do that."

He was sixteen when he hopped a bus to Washington, North Carolina.
"Baltimore," he told me, "had a high crime rate, and I told my mom,
'I'm leaving.'" He had family from his mother's and father's sides down
there, but he wasn't sure where he would live until the morning after
he got to Washington, when Dave Smith, the basketball coach at the
town's public high school, spotted him on a playground and took him
back to Smith's home. Smith showed him a bathroom, a bedroom, and
the kitchen. *You can have all this,* he told Wilkins. *The only tradeoff is that
you have to play for my high school team.* Cool by 'Nique. That was 1976.
The same year that the dunk ban, in college and high school basketball,
disappeared. "When I went to college, dunking was back in," he said.
"For me, man, it was a breath of fresh air."

As a high schooler, Wilkins had a 47-inch vertical leap—he would
reach 48 inches in the pros—and could clear six-six in the high jump.
The coaches at the University of Georgia sold him on his opportunity
to shine there, not to blend in the background at NC State or UNC or
another ACC school but to star in Athens. He declared for the NBA
draft in 1982, after his junior season—UGA lost to Lorenzo Charles
and the Wolfpack in the following year's Final Four—and the Hawks
were so hot to keep the local hero in-state that, after the Utah Jazz
selected Wilkins with the third pick, Atlanta traded John Drew, Freeman Williams, and $1 million for him. The Hawks sold 900 tickets at
$400 apiece within five days of the trade's consummation. They had
their meal ticket, their crowd-pleaser, and with Ted Turner's Supersta-
tion TBS beaming Hawks games to cable-TV customers nationwide,
Wilkins flew into the homes of hundreds of thousands of hoops fans
outside Atlanta.

His teammates were as gobsmacked as the fans and viewers. "He
jumps so high," longtime Hawks center Tree Rollins once said,
"he's always open." Six feet, seven inches and two hundred pounds of

liquid stone, Wilkins was perhaps, pound for pound, the most ferocious dunker ever, double-pumping with such force and speed that he
seemed a piston still operating at full capacity while airborne. A big
man who tried to block one of Wilkins's dunks might as well stuff
his fingers in a thresher's maw. Wilkins considered his finest dunk
to be a baseline shimmy-and-drive, with 40 seconds left in regulation, to beat the Milwaukee Bucks in January 1984. Bob Lanier, the
Bucks' center then, who was six-eleven and wore a size 22 sneaker,
was covering the rim, "and I remember turning in the air," Wilkins
told me, "and when I turned back around, he was going down and
I was still going up, and I dunked on him, and that was the end of
the game." The entire sequence appeared completely spontaneous, as
if Wilkins were making up his moves in real time. He was. Because
of his track-and-field background, he didn't have to choreograph any
of his dunks. Knowing that his footwork and sense of timing, honed
from his years as a high jumper and runner, wouldn't waver, he could
allow the combination of anger and instinct within him to take over.
"I played angry because of the way I grew up in Baltimore," he told
me. "It was a natural thing, but it was always under control. I used
the dunk as a tool to keep guys from wanting to challenge my shot. It
was a tool for intimidation, but it was also a crowd motivator. It was a
momentum-changer. It really was. It got everybody around me fired
up when I dunked. So that was a big part of it, but it was just to strike
fear into people."

He had been nervous, not himself, in 1984, in his and the NBA's
first contest, too rattled by the presence of his idol, Erving, who didn't
even win. Doc finished second to the Phoenix Suns' Larry Nance,
who toted two basketballs in his hands and dunked them one after
the other to take the title. "But that second contest" in '85, he said, "I
said, 'I'm not coming to compete. I'm coming to win.'" And he did,
beating Jordan. It mattered that much to him. It mattered that much
to all the competitors—to their marketing potential and their possible
shoe deals and their standing and esteem around the league and in the
culture.

"Whoo, man," Wilkins told me, laughing. "Dunk contest was everything, bro. It was Ev. Ree. Thing."

Walter Iooss's career as a professional photographer got off to a better start than Michael Jordan's career as a professional basketball player did. When Iooss was fifteen, his father had given him a gift, a camera, and in July 1961, two weeks after graduating from East Orange High School in northern New Jersey, he got his first assignment from *Sports Illustrated*: to take pictures of an eighty-plus-year-old Connecticut man named Archie Chester who had built a sailboat without a blueprint so he could sail down to Florida and back. The job paid Iooss $100, and his father, Walter Sr., had to drive him to Connecticut, and the photo ran on the last page of the issue. A humble beginning? To be sure. But no more humiliating or painful than the first time Jordan tried to dunk in an NBA regular-season game: October 26, 1984, against the Washington Bullets. Jordan caught a pass on the left wing, faked, drove into the lane, and jumped, only to have Jeff Ruland—the Bullets' six-ten, 240-pound metal filing cabinet of a center—jump with him. Ruland extended his left leg—maybe accidentally, maybe on purpose, who knows such things in the heat of a game?—and Jordan bumped it as he came down, crashed to the floor, and stayed there, prone on the Chicago Stadium court, for twenty seconds before pushing himself up. *Welcome to the league, rook. Don't give a shit if you have an Olympic gold medal and a colossal shoe deal on the horizon. Don't give a shit who you think you are. Don't try to embarrass me by jamming over me.* How far Iooss and his muse had come . . .

Though he would soon stand as a symbol of the best of basketball, though he would become as mainstream and establishment as an athlete gets ("Republicans buy sneakers, too"), Jordan still retained at least the patina of insurgency in the winter of '88. There was a hint of upstart to him then, and he was only starting to shed it. Remember: here was a kid who apparently had been cut from the varsity basketball team at Emsley A. Laney High School in Wilmington, North Carolina, only to start for Dean Smith and UNC as a freshman. (That tale, of course, turned out to be tall. Despite his repeated assertions through-out his life that he was cut, Jordan was not. His coach, Pop Herring, merely assigned him to the jayvee team his sophomore year.) Here was a kid who had been introduced to the country as "Mike Jordan" in newspaper articles and TV chyrons. Here was a kid who, left open with the Tar Heels down one to Georgetown in the final 15 seconds of the 1982 NCAA Championship Game, had dared to take and make the winning jump shot. Then, after he had been named the national player of the year in 1983–84, once the Bulls selected him with the third pick in the '84 NBA draft, he entered the league as a challenger to its two kings: Bird and Magic Johnson. If he wanted the title of *Best Player in the World*, he would have to take it from one or both of them.

He knew how he would do it. Bird and Magic were inherently team players first: both brilliant passers, both with limitless court vision and telepathic anticipation, both six-foot-nine, neither known primarily for playing above the rim. There, Jordan believed, was his advantage, his place to gain traction. He could distinguish himself from them through his athleticism, particularly his 48-inch vertical leap. He was already Bird's and Magic's superior as a scorer. His game wasn't about setting up his teammates. Put Jordan and four five-nine guys named Bob on the floor together, and he could take on any NBA starting five by himself while the Bobs stood around and stared. The manner in which he could and did score was what made him so captivating, but his leaping ability and lateral quickness could allow him to be a better defender than Bird and Magic were, too, and he committed himself to that aim. "To some extent," he wrote in one of his autobiographies, "I think it was hard for people to believe anyone who jumped and dunked could also be a complete player. But that's what I did at North Carolina, and that's what I was trying to do in the NBA." Besides, as much as he respected the pair, they were not his models. "When I came into the league," Jordan wrote, "I wasn't nearly as enamored with Magic Johnson and Larry Bird as I was with Julius Erving. As a kid . . . the only player I really knew about was Dr. J."

Any comparison between Erving and Jordan was appropriate, even at that early stage of Jordan's career. Throughout that summer and fall of 1984, he was demonstrating the same crossover appeal—both in how he performed on the court and how he carried himself off it—that Erving had. In leading the '84 US Olympic team to a gold medal at the Summer Games in Los Angeles, he won over America and, in a greater feat, America's orneriest coach: Bob Knight. It was during the Olympic team's training, too, that Jordan met for the first time with Sonny Vaccaro, then an executive with Nike, who had targeted him to be the company's new spokesperson. The contradictions and complements within Jordan, Vaccaro believed, would vault the upstart shoe company past Adidas and Converse. "Jordan was the complete package," authors Dan Wetzel and Don Yaeger wrote in their chronicle of the sneaker wars, *Sole Influence*. "His game was street enough to be legit on city playgrounds, yet [he was] polished enough to work in suburban living rooms. In a league that is predominantly Black but plays to a majority white fan base, he was perfect." Maybe the riskiest part of Vaccaro's gamble was that he had decided Jordan would be his quarry after watching just one of his games: the NCAA championship against Georgetown. "How was I so confident in Michael Jordan when I only saw him play one game and make one shot that I remembered?" Vaccaro told me. "I don't know. I've been good at that. There's no question about it. When I made a bet on a kid, history proves it out." He wasn't wrong. In 1996, he pulled off a similar coup for Adidas, signing Kobe Bryant after seeing him at the summertime ABCD Camp and rekindling a friendship with Kobe's father, Joe.

By all rights, Adidas or Converse should have been the front-runner to sign Jordan; he loved the former's sneakers, and he wore the latter's throughout his three years at UNC. But Adidas showed little interest, and Converse, which already had Erving, Bird, and Magic, made an offer that didn't come close to the five-year, $2.5-million deal—plus an annuity, plus the "Air Jordan" brand—that Nike gave to Jordan. "Nike would have been OK," Vaccaro told me. "They just wouldn't have been the Nike of today without Jordan. We know that. If another company would have done it with Michael, they could have. But no one wanted to offer him five cents, and no one offered him a signature shoe. What Jordan did for himself and Nike was put them on Mount Rushmore. He changed marketing."

Jordan's aerial skills and charisma gave Nike so much to work with and were so astonishing that, even with four decades' hindsight, the coverage of and reaction to his arrival in the NBA was accurate, almost prescient, in its anticipation of his greatness. "Michael Jordan," one journalist wrote while the Bulls were still finishing up training camp, "makes Michael Jackson's Moonwalk look like a lead-shoe imitation." Quinn Buckner, who would become one of Jordan's closest friends, was a backup guard for the Celtics. "Oooh, Michael Jordan, I don't know if you can even put it into words," Buckner said in October 1984, and Jordan hadn't played a game in the league yet. Once he shook off Ruland's ill-humored introduction to the league, his signature dunk, in which he cuffed the ball with his right wrist, rocked it in front of his chest, and slammed it down, quickly emerged as the vogue move throughout the sport. Roy Marble, a prep phenom from Flint, Michigan, and, later, the University of Iowa's all-time leading scorer, copied the dunk, adding a little flair of his own by flipping the ball behind his back, and he wasn't the only one to try. "Jumping," he said, "has become the thing in Flint." Jordan's influence on younger players was so profound, in fact, that it worried one of the sport's most respected, and loudest, voices. "So many kids are relying on their great legs, and that's all," Dick Vitale said in November 1984. "It seems like these kids get reputations, and they feel like they have to show their peers how they can fly up to the sky and dunk all the time. Hey, you've got to be able to stop on a dime and shoot the J, or you become very ordinary."

When Nike released its first Air Jordan sneaker, black and red, during Jordan's rookie season, the NBA fined him $5,000 a game for wearing shoes that didn't conform to its rules about uniforms' color schemes. Nike paid the fine, then cut a commercial that showed a glimpse of Jordan in the sneakers before the screen splashed a giant X and the word BANNED over his feet. "It would have cost millions of dollars," he once wrote, "to come up with a promotion that produced as much publicity as the league's ban did." The company's image of rebelliousness was crystallized. So, over time, was Jordan's image as the sport's ideal manifestation of fitness and agility, of elegance and accessibility, and of the single-minded chase for excellence. He was both introspective and ruthless and knew that he was, and he could express that self-awareness more intelligently than most athletes could. "There are plays that stand out in your mind, things you did that, when you see the replay, it almost seems like you're watching someone else in your body," he once wrote. "I remember one dunk early in my career. . . . I don't remember what year it was, but the replay was in slow motion. It looked like one of those Apollo blast-offs in slow motion. I just kept going up. I knew I was watching myself, but I couldn't believe how it looked. I remember thinking, When does jumping become flying? That's how it looked to me. When people would ask whether I could fly, especially when I was younger, I always said, 'Yes, for a little while.'" When Wilkins beat him in the 1985 contest, it was less a blow to Jordan's reputation than an indication of where the NBA was headed. Wilkins was in his third season. Jordan was in just his first. They would be going at each other like that for a while, but Jordan's persona and the feline-like way he moved on the court would prove more enchanting to more casual basketball fans. The difference was small but significant. Jordan was more charming, and his playing style was more beautiful. Billboards—Nike advertisements that showed Jordan stretching out his arm until it was taut, a basketball in his hand as if he were poised to dunk—sprang up along highways and in city centers around the country. "People not only want to watch him play," his Bulls teammate Orlando Woolridge said in October 1985, "but they identify with him."

Then, for a while, they couldn't watch him. On October 29, 1985, at Oakland Coliseum Arena, Jordan took off toward the rim against the Golden State Warriors, in the third game of the Bulls' season, and upon landing broke the navicular bone in his left foot. The injury so depressed him that he spent several days at home, crying, and his parents flew to Chicago from North Carolina to console him. He decided against surgery and didn't play for four and a half months, and when he did return to the Bulls' lineup in mid-March, Stan James, one of the three ortho-pedists who examined him during his convalescence, believed Jordan shouldn't play because his foot hadn't fully healed. Shaped like a side-ways apostrophe and located in the middle of the foot, the navicular is essential to walking and running, and James estimated that Jordan had at least a 10 percent chance of reinjuring himself. "It's a very difficult and unpredictable fracture," he once told me. Bulls owner Jerry Reins-dorf and general manager Jerry Krause didn't want Jordan to risk it; Jordan was disgusted and accused them of wanting to lose games for the sake of getting a higher draft pick. He was going to play, and Reinsdorf and Krause, whom he regarded as his nemeses from then on, would have to deal with it. The Bulls won six of their final ten regular-season games to sneak into the playoffs as the eighth and last seed in the Eastern Conference, drawing the Celtics in the best-of-five first round.

That '85–86 Celtics club—with Bird, Kevin McHale, and Robert Parish in the frontcourt; with Dennis Johnson and Danny Ainge in the backcourt; with a rejuvenated Bill Walton coming off the bench—went 67–15, lost just three postseason games in winning the NBA cham-pionship, and is generally regarded as the best team in the history of an already storied franchise. That context is vital to appreciating what Jordan did during that three-game Celtics sweep and how much his performance mattered to his stardom and legacy. The series' first two games were at Boston Garden, and in just the first half of Game 1, Jordan drove past Celtics guard Rick Carlisle for a baseline slam, cut backdoor on Bird and took a pass from John Paxson for another dunk, and stole the ball and cruised the length of the court for a one-handed jam.

"That's just an ordinary stuff by Michael Jordan," analyst Tommy Heinsohn said on the Celtics' telecast.

"That's a 3 or a 4," play-by-play voice Mike Gorman deadpanned.

Jordan finished with 49 points in a 19-point Bulls loss. Somehow, he was even better three nights later in Game 2. In a brief pregame in-terview with CBS's Pat O'Brien, he said, "I don't think one man can beat the Boston Celtics," but damn if he didn't come as close as anyone could. He dunked just once in Game 2, zooming around McHale and over Bird in the fourth quarter, scoring mostly on an array of pullup jump shots and trapeze-artist layups, hitting two free throws with no time left in regulation to tie the game only to have the Celtics pull away to win in double overtime, 135–131. His 63 points that night remain the most that any player has scored in an NBA playoff game.

"I would never have called him the greatest player I'd ever seen if I didn't mean it," Bird said after Game 2. "It's just God disguised as Michael Jordan."

Jordan read Bird's comments in the next day's newspapers. The praise astounded him. It gave him a fresh, stronger credibility. The public's perception of him and even Jordan's own perception of himself—from a player who probably would be an immortal to one who, according to Bird, already was one—changed and remained fixed from that point on. His 37.1 points per game in 1986–87, the following season, was the NBA's highest single-season average in nearly a quarter century, but he was aware throughout the year how frequently he scored on drives to the basket and dunks. The following offseason, knowing that teams would try to force him to shoot from the perimeter more, he began working on his outside shot. Simultaneously, the Detroit Pistons—the "Bad Boys" who would reach the NBA Finals in three consecutive years and win back-to-back championships—began crafting their "Jordan Rules," the grueling defensive approach that they employed against him: double-teaming him on the perimeter, bumping and hammering him whenever he darted into the lane or lifted off the floor. It would take Jordan a couple of years of training and weight lifting to gird his body against that punishment, to withstand it and thrive in spite of it, but the result, a better and stronger Jordan, was inevitable. "He hadn't won a championship yet," the author and sportswriter Rick Telander told me, "but after the broken foot, he was a man on fire, a man obsessed."

Jordan's comeback and the symbiotic relationship between him and those who covered him—they needed him, and he understood he needed them—gave bone and muscle to his mythology. Interacting with the media and playing to a crowd, as he would at the '88 contest, came easily to him, and as he separated himself from his peers, every anecdote about him was suffused with a greater significance. Telander,

writing for *Sports Illustrated* then, once descended into Jordan's basement to play eight ball against him. "He's no good," Telander told me,
"and I'm no good. All of a sudden, this light went off in my head: 'No,
no, you're not going to win.' This is a nothing game, but he did not
want to lose. If I'd have beaten him, God knows he might have hated
me forever." For Jordan, there was never any such thing as a nothing
game, not in a casual night of billiards with a sportswriter, not in
the entertaining pageantry of a slam dunk contest—*the* slam dunk
contest—held in the arena and among the fans he knew so well.

The evidence of Jordan's impact was all around as the contest neared
its beginning, and Iooss looked around to take it all in: the benches,
the press table, the eighteen-thousand-plus people in the stands, people
everywhere, the whole place packed and intense. Brian McIntyre, the
NBA's public-relations director, had made certain to give Iooss a prime
spot to shoot, along the baseline. Wielding a Hasselblad with a super-
wide lens, Iooss kept his back to the basket's stanchion as, throughout
the contest, Jordan signaled to him which way to angle himself and his
camera. On the TBS telecast, Bob Neal, Steve "Snapper" Jones, and
Rick Barry offered their appraisals of the dunks, each of which culminated in a satisfying clank of Chicago Stadium's loose rims. There were
five judges for the event: four former NBA players—Gail Goodrich,
"Jumping" Johnny Green, Randy Smith, and Tommy Hawkins—and
former Bears star Gale Sayers. Later, Goodrich would insist that at no
time did the judges ever confer with one another about their marks, that
they showed no favoritism to any of the contestants, and in the first two
rounds, no one gave that possibility much thought. The overriding
question was which two of the three favorites—Jordan, Wilkins, and
Webb—would advance to the finals.

Spud made the question easier to answer. Spud wasn't quite himself,
was still hampered by his recent knee surgery, didn't have his usual
spring. Spud missed two of his three attempts in the first round and
was eliminated. He settled in on the sideline to watch the rest, mar-
veling as Jordan and Wilkins cruised into the championship round,

delivering the matchup everyone wanted. Each man would get three tries. Jordan won a coin toss and deferred. Wilkins would dunk first. The odds were not in his favor. The sound inside Chicago Stadium for a Bulls game routinely reached 130 decibels, louder than the average rock concert, as loud as a military jet's takeoff from an aircraft carrier. "There's no question," said Doug Collins, who was coaching the Bulls then, "it's the loudest place in sport." The judges could fight their subconscious biases as best they could, but they weren't robots. 'Nique understood the forces he was up against. "Of course," he told me. "Look, you're in Chicago. But at the same time, he knew as well as I knew it was going to be a competition. I knew that we were going to bring the best out of each other. And we did."

Dominique: bounce the ball off the backboard, jam with two hands—*50 out of 50.*

Michael: reverse—*50 out of 50.*

Dominique: a baseline power dunk. He nearly hurled himself into the first row of seats—*50 out of 50.*

Man, Spud Webb said to someone, *can you believe these guys going at it like this?*

Michael: rock the cradle—*47 out of 50.* There was nothing but boos at 130 decibels.

Dominique: a two-handed windmill off two feet. "I don't think the judges appreciated that dunk," he said immediately after the contest. "When you come all the way around with two hands like that . . . it's something that no one else can do." He was right in two ways. One, it is usually more difficult to jump with both hands above your head than it is with one. John Fontanella, a longtime professor of physics at the US Naval Academy, once explained why: *By raising just one hand, you have lowered your center of gravity. You're now pushing your hips to the height that your belly button previously reached.* Two, the judges did not appreciate the dunk—*45 out of 50.* Wilkins led by 48 points.

At midcourt, Jordan bounced the ball and caught it with one hand. It was, he said later, "the only time in the contest I was nervous. I knew I needed something spectacular to win." He then looked up, happened to catch the eye of someone courtside, and smiled.

Julius Erving pointed toward the backcourt. *Go back. Go back.* His signal was obvious, and Jordan picked up on it. "The man who started it all," Jordan said later, "told me to take off from the free-throw line." Just like Doc had done in 1976. The old king was asking the new king to complete the circle.

Jordan, his head down, moseyed to the far baseline, and looked back at Iooss. Jordan moved his hand slightly, telling Iooss to shift to the right. He began dribbling up the court, picking up steam. This impressed Erving. When he had beaten David Thompson with that foul-line flush twelve years earlier, Doc had sprinted in from halfcourt. He had neither counted off his steps nor tried to dribble the ball. Michael was doing it the way he'd do it in a game: bounce, bounce, bounce, step and a half, *go*. "I put a little extra pump in there," Jordan said later. Doc thought that was cool. It's safe to assume that the acquaintance sitting next to him—Mike Tyson, in the middle of his three-year reign as the heavyweight champion of the world—did, too. And it's safe to assume that everyone else in Chicago Stadium thought it was cool, as well, right up to the moment that Jordan back-rimmed the dunk.

The crowd gasped, then fell silent, then whistled and whooped again. Jordan had one more chance. "Mythology is so important," Telander told me. "Everyone needs that moment of crisis." The expression on Dominique Wilkins's face remained flat until he started shaking his head skeptically. He knew the deal before Jordan ever took off the second time. Everyone did.

On TBS, Neal said, "The only way he's going to lose this competition is if he misses this dunk."

He did not miss. "His dunk," Erving told me, "was better than mine." Under the basket, Iooss snapped a photo that will last forever: Jordan's full face visible, his mouth twisted in a grimace of concentration, the basketball in his right hand and near his ear, his right arm cocked, his shoulders wide and legs parallel so that he resembles the Greek letter Pi, the giant red scoreboard looming behind him and showing the tally that is about to change—WILKINS 145, JORDAN 97—the background a panorama of the arena, the five judges seated behind a table draped in a white cloth that had GATORADE written across it, every person's head turned toward Jordan and the basket, their desire and expectation that he would win the contest written in their wide eyes and half-open mouths.

"The passage of time makes things more important," Iooss told me. "As Michael's star kept exploding into the stratosphere, it mimicked what he did best: just flying through the air. Once the picture started appearing in *Sports Illustrated*, it started to take on a life of its own." He and Jordan, in 1991, collaborated on a book, *Rare Air*, that Iooss once bragged sold eight hundred thousand copies. Click on the Michael Jordan gallery on walteriooss.com, and the first photograph displayed is that one. In August 2020, an archival print of the photo—"Michael Jordan, 'Slam Dunk,' Chicago, IL, 1988"—was bought through Christie's auction house for $35,000.

50 out of 50.

His work completed, perfection achieved, Walter Iooss kissed his camera.

The passage of time can also make things seem absurd in retrospect, as some of the details of the '88 contest and its aftermath do. Jordan received $12,500 in prize money for winning. Second prize? Not a set of steak knives, but close. Wilkins walked away with just $7,500 . . . and the belief that he had helped lift the dunk contest, and maybe the dunk itself, to its apex.

"The fact that people are talking about that contest thirty-four years later lets you know it's the greatest of all time, no matter what anybody says," Wilkins told me. "I don't know if you'll ever see a dunk contest again where you had two great players going head-to-head—Hall of Fame players who wanted to know who the best was. That's the difference. The level of competition was off. The. Charts. It was off the charts. I don't know if you'll ever see that again."

Why not?

"They make so much money they probably don't care," Webb told me. "Then they worry about their reputation, their brand. I don't get it. If you say you're a competitor, compete."

Different era. Different players. Different priorities. The author Rich Cohen published, in late 2023, a book called *When the Game Was War*, in which he argued that '87–88 was the greatest season in NBA history, an inflection point for the league: Bird and the Celtics formidable but in decline, Magic and the Lakers clinging to their dynasty, Isiah Thomas and the Pistons poised to usurp Showtime with Bad Boy basketball, Jordan and the Bulls taking the first steps of their climb toward their six championships. It is difficult to dispute Cohen's thesis or Jordan's importance within it. Nike's Air Jordan campaign reached its acme in 1988 and 1989, around and after the '88 dunk contest, when Spike Lee, playing the character "Mars Blackmon," joined Jordan for a series of comedic TV spots. In one, Jordan dunked as Lee clung to the rim as if it were a life raft, the ball slamming into Lee's chest and belly: "Mike, that's cold, man." In another, Lee/Mars asked Jordan, "What makes you the greatest player in the world? . . . Is it the vicious dunks?" Eventually, the two concluded: "It's gotta be the shoes." From the '87–88 season to the '88–'89 season, NBA attendance increased by close to 1,700 people per game, the highest jump from one year to another in league history, according to historian Robert Bradley. In February '88, Jordan was in the last season of his rookie contract, which paid him less than $900,000 that year in salary and bonuses. By the first day of the 1993 postseason, Jordan was in the fifth year of an eight-year, $25.7-million extension, and the NBA and NBC had reached an agreement on a four-year, $750-million extension of their television deal—a 25 percent increase from what the network had paid to acquire the league's TV rights just four years earlier. After grossing $986 million in revenue in 1984, the year it signed Jordan, Nike grossed $9.2 *billion* in 1998, the year Jordan retired from the Bulls for the second time. He was the ultimate rising tide. Everyone and everything connected to pro basketball was a boat.

"I don't think anybody could have predicted it," Telander told me. "Nike couldn't have. Nobody could. There can't be another Michael. You can't have that era. When you take people out of their moment, you lose all perspective.

"With Michael, it was as if everything that was barbaric had been sanitized and beautified. He was a gorgeous, photogenic man, magnificently white teeth. His face is purely symmetrical."

Remember, too, the era: the late 1980s, men who were Masters of the Universe and three-piece peacocks, go-getting young financiers and corporate climbers who were making millions and hanging out in cigar parlors, going to tailors to make sure their Armani and Versace were looking clean and sharp. The 17,000-square-foot flagship location of Bigsby & Kruthers, Chicago's renowned high-end menswear retailer, was right there on Michigan Avenue along the Magnificent Mile. Suddenly Jordan was wearing those suits, with the diamond earring, with the silk tie just so, all other adornments stripped away, ultra-macho and still . . . dignified.

"Very tolerable to White America, tolerable particularly to women, and tolerable to the Black community, too," Telander told me. "Video, slow-motion, the dunk contest, everything coming to the forefront—what an athlete looks like is important. And his physique—if you had to draw the perfect physique for what any man would want to look like, it would be Michael Jordan. Not too muscular. Every striation of muscle is defined: his deltoids, the ball out in front, his hands cradling that thing, looking straight ahead with this earnest look of defiance and acceptance of fate. 'You and I and the ball are going to meet.' That photo is on more kids' bedroom walls . . ."

No one inside Chicago Stadium that day, other than Walter Iooss, knew that he had snagged the shot that would help shape a legend. In all likelihood, no one would have cared. The people in the building wanted to talk to Michael Jordan, to touch him, to *be like Mike*, to jump and glide and dunk like Mike, to share a precious second with him, and after the contest ended, they tried to surround him, disciples of a man who now seemed to them more than just a man. Hundreds of them filled the corridors throughout the arena. There seemed nowhere for Jordan to go, no way for him to leave. Communicating by walkie-talkie, two security guards, Gus Lett and Joe Rokas, scouted out an escape route for him. A car idled outside. The guards shepherded Jordan through the basement, through a door, and into the car, and it drove away into the arctic night.

19

SKIN DEEP

The dunk becomes so routine, so universal, that it becomes a joke, in the best and worst of ways . . .

All of them had come to see him. All of them. The baby boomer woman who was sitting right behind the Delaware Blue Coats' bench on this Wednesday night in February 2023, whose husband was a basketball referee, and who knew, from the first time she saw the little guard with the floppy hair, that he'd be a hell of a player. The five sophomores and juniors from Sterling High School in southern New Jersey who were holding handmade signs that read "MCCLUNG FOR PRESIDENT" and "THE DUNK CONTEST HAPPENS IN DELAWARE." The children who poured into Chase Fieldhouse—hand in hand with their parents or in giggling, chattering clusters—for a chance to catch the reigning NBA Slam Dunk champion doing his thing . . . or maybe just to catch a free T-shirt once the dance team started chucking them into the stands. Sure, maybe some of the attendees were more jazzed about the free apparel. But a G League franchise's ticket sales don't increase by a factor of five, as the Blue Coats said theirs had, on merchandise giveaways alone. This was as special as a night in the NBA G League gets. All because of Mac McClung.

Since winning the dunk contest in Salt Lake City four nights earlier, McClung had been swept up in a media hurricane, and he himself was the source of the publicity storm. Basketball's glitterati had credited him with pulling the contest back from the brink of obsolescence. For a brief period, the public had stopped being bored with it. "Mac Mc-Clung has personally saved the slam dunk contest with his performance tonight!!" Magic Johnson posted on X/Twitter. How could anyone not be a sucker for the story? McClung had signed a two-way contract with the 76ers on February 14, though he insisted that the Sixers didn't sign him just so he would technically be on an NBA roster in time for the contest . . . which was on February 18. His final attempt in the competition was a 540-degree spin-o-rama that was a reasonable facsimile of the trademark move of his favorite dunker: Vince Carter. Then, after McClung's victory, the Sixers immediately assigned him back to the Blue Coats, their affiliate in the G League. He was the Shane of slam, the hero who had ridden into town, stared down the villain—the villain in this case being indifference to what had once been a favorite tradition of the NBA season—saved the day, and moseyed out again.

A thousand unread text messages waited for him on his smartphone. He had received so many interview requests that the Blue Coats' staff couldn't handle them all; the Sixers' public-relations department needed three people to sort through the requests. CNN, *SportsCenter*, *Good Morning America*: Either he had appeared on each already, or he soon would. There had been 520 million online views of the NBA's Skills Competition, Three-Point Contest, and Slam Dunk Contest in the first twelve hours that the videos of those events were available. Three hundred million of those views were of McClung and his dunks. He had added 250,000 followers to his Instagram account in less than forty-eight hours and scored a one-year endorsement deal with Puma, becoming the rare kind of insta-celebrity who cuts across any number of demographics and causes people to break out of their respective pop-culture silos. Now here he was in Wilmington, and the gym was going gaga for him.

A six-foot-two, twenty-four-year-old white man who had been

an official NBA player for all of four days, and who was no longer an NBA player, had resurrected the Slam Dunk Contest. The notion sounded like a joke. There was a time when that's exactly what it would have been.

Ron Shelton was writing a brilliant sports movie when he provided himself the setting and inspiration to write another brilliant sports movie. It was the mid-1980s, and Shelton was in Hollywood, toiling away on a script for a comedy about the magic of baseball and life in the Carolina League: *Bull Durham*. A former minor-league infielder in the Baltimore Orioles' organization, Shelton had also played basketball at a big Southern California high school (Santa Barbara High) and a small Southern California college (Westmont). He wasn't old enough yet where he had to stop playing completely. "I was just a guy," he told me, "but I was a guy who had a lot of game for a white guy in his mid-thirties." So on Monday, Wednesday, and Friday afternoons, when he needed to step away from his typewriter, he'd head to an outdoor court near Hollywood, at Cahuenga and Santa Monica Boulevards, to play pickup. One day, he showed up at the court to find it locked with chains. An old dude was sitting nearby. Shelton asked him what had happened.

Oh, the dude said, *the city and the police closed the court up while they're doing an investigation.*

What investigation?

Well, you know, Charlie got shot by Willie.

He got shot?

Yeah, Charlie's dead. Willie's in jail.

What happened?

Well, they got in an argument on the court.

It must have been a block-charge thing, Shelton said, *because that's all we ever argued about.*

It was, the old-timer said, *and Willie said, "I'm going to the glove box."*

Shelton didn't know what the old dude meant.

Everyone around here knows what "going to the glove box" means. He went to the glove box in his car, got his gun, and shot him.

"So," Shelton told me, "I moved my game indoors."

He relocated to what he called the "old, cramped, wonderful gyms" around Los Angeles—five-on-five, three-on-three, college guys, former NBA guys, "really good players." The games were so spirited, the arguments and smack-talk so colorful and creative, and the stakes for some of the players so high that Shelton started thinking, *This is a movie.*

"Because this is a culture," he told me. "It's a democratic place where you're judged only by the quality of your game—which is to say, your character—and disputes are resolved after the argument is honored. You can insult my girlfriend, my momma, and I can insult yours—your manhood, my manhood. People are laughing. It gets a little testy sometimes. Then, somebody goes to the top of the key and shoots a shot, and if he makes it, there is no question that he won the argument. And if he misses it, there's no question that you won the argument. There are no lawyers. There are no appellate judges. I thought, 'How civil is this?'"

So once he finished *Bull Durham*, he got to writing again. In Shelton's telling, the playground court would be a bastion of democracy, of honest and fair and ferocious competition, of rules unspoken yet universally accepted, and the ability to dunk would be the ultimate arbiter, the place where the winners, truly, were separated from the losers.

And when it came to dunking, white guys were . . . generally speaking . . . well, if not losers, then at least second bananas. How else to view the manner in which the inflow of Black players had changed basketball? They had set themselves apart, reconstituted the entire game, in ways overt and subtle. Anyone could watch five minutes of an NBA game, posit the demographic breakdown of the league's talent, then scan the rosters of the thirty franchises to confirm that guess: that, as of 2023, more than 70 percent of NBA players were Black and fewer than 18 percent were white. Or anyone could take, say, Bobby

Jones. Hall of Fame forward for the Denver Nuggets and the Sixers for twelve seasons, from the mid-1970s to the mid-1980s. One of the best defensive wing players ever. Six-foot-nine leaper. Pale as paper. Grew up in Charlotte. His dad and his brother played at Oklahoma. Structure was all Jones knew in the sport. "I've never seen a guy take a charge in a street game," he told me. "Guys were more creative in that environment, and I certainly missed a lot growing up in the suburbs."

Having played college ball at North Carolina during the era of the ban, Jones had never attempted a dunk until he entered the ABA in 1974. In one of his first games with the Nuggets, he stole the ball, steamed toward the hoop on a breakaway, and lifted off to dunk . . . except he planted his foot so far from the rim that his knee gave out and he tumbled into the stanchion. He pretended that he'd injured his knee, that it had buckled without warning and he had perhaps strained a ligament. The truth was that he was embarrassed. But as a teammate of both Julius Erving and David Thompson, Jones had two up-close and first-class examples in the art of taking off and finishing at the rim, so he got the hang of it soon enough. He read a magazine article early in his career that listed five NBA players who "didn't play their color," and he was among those five. "So I was a white guy," he told me, "but I 'played Black' because I could jump. It never impacted me as a player in the league because I fit in with the guys who could elevate—not to the level of David or Julius, but I could block a shot or put it in the hole on a fastbreak."

Jones was regarded as such an outlier that, in March 1976, *Sports Illustrated*'s Curry Kirkpatrick wrote: "He goes up where no Caucasian has ever trod before." Another eleven years passed before a white player trod in the NBA Slam Dunk Contest—the Seattle SuperSonics' Tom Chambers, in 1987—and another nine years passed after that before a white player trod high and well enough to win it. Brent Barry was a rookie with the Los Angeles Clippers in 1996 when one of the team's public-relations representatives, having seen Barry dunk during practices, lobbied to get him into the contest. At the Alamodome in San Antonio, Barry twice took off from the free-throw line and dunked, mimicking Erving's winning move at the 1976 ABA event, but even in that nod to the past, Barry couldn't help but come off as square. There was such a chill in the Alamodome that he kept his red and blue Clippers warm-up on and zipped up to his neck, a less-than-chic look that only reaffirmed the perception that the contest was no longer as hip or prestigious as it had been.

A victory by another Los Angeles rookie in 1997—Kobe Bryant—wasn't enough to dissuade the league from doing away with the contest in 1998 and replacing it with "2Ball," in which NBA and WNBA players teamed up in a shooting competition. And when the contest returned in 2000, even Vince Carter's repertoire of powerful and graceful slams—he windmilled one home after first tucking the ball between his legs while in midair—had the effect of eating a candy bar: the sugar rush lasted only so long. Jordan was gone for good after his two-year dabble with the Washington Wizards, and for the better part of a decade, a pair of post players whose games were based on a mixture on physical strength and sound fundamentals were atop the league's food chain: Shaquille O'Neal and Tim Duncan. The dunk contest devolved into a caricature of itself, getting lamer and lamer. Blake Griffin jumped over a Kia Optima. Dwight Howard dressed like Superman. More and more average and quasi-anonymous players entered the contest . . . and won it: Jeremy Evans, Terrence Rosse, Hamidou Diallo, Derrick Jones. The *Washington Post*'s Jerry Brewer, in a column that ran on February 18, 2023, noted that the contest had lost its magic and would likely never recover it. It was harder for players to impress fans and viewers with their preplanned and staged dunks; any spectacular, spontaneous slam during a game could be watched millions of times online. The factors that had made the contest a must-see event—the scarcity of opportunities to see the league's best dunkers, the star power of the participants—were gone. Once, players needed to compete in it to enhance the league's profile and their own marketability. No more.

"It's a shame that time and consumption habits have conspired with the players' changing attitudes to dull the experience," Brewer concluded. "Without an inspired concept to refresh the legacy, it won't last much longer."

That night, the NBA unveiled what it apparently considered an inspired concept, in the short, white form of Mac McClung.

Good luck finding a basketball fan of a certain age who can't quote at least one line from *White Men Can't Jump*, Shelton's movie—and it is *his* movie; he wrote and directed it—about the uneasy and hilarious partnership between two streetball hustlers, one Black, one white. Before he had written a word of the script, he came up with its title, and he ran it past a few people he trusted. One was Victoria Thomas, who turned out to be the film's casting director. One was his daughter, who was seventeen and thought it was "the coolest, sexiest title ever," he said. One was the woman he was dating, the woman who eventually became his wife: the actress Lolita Davidovich. "That was my demographic, algorithmic test—women of different universes," he told me. "They thought it was great. That was good enough for me."

As the title makes clear, Shelton presumes that the average viewer will have already accepted, or at least be familiar with, two common stereotypes: that Black people are better at basketball than white people and that one of the reasons they're better is that, in a sport in which leaping is essential, white people have a harder time getting off the ground. Those low-level premises, in and of themselves, wouldn't make for much of a movie, and any engagement with them, in the hands of a lesser artist, would be akin to juggling torches. But the film works because Shelton spends much of his time upending those and other racially based presumptions. Plus, he can write like a sonofabitch. In a phrase the critic Roger Ebert used to describe another screenplay, Shelton "has an ear for dialogue not as it is spoken but as it is dreamed," and the first twenty minutes of *White Men Can't Jump* crackle as few films do as the characters engage in verbal swordplay.

After Woody Harrelson's Billy Hoyle gets the better of Wesley Snipes's Sidney Dean in a shooting contest, Sidney tells a scrawny, mouthy friend to "shut your anorexic, malnutrition, tapeworm-having, overdosed Dick Gregory, Bahamian-diet-drinking ass up." When Sidney and Billy hustle a temperamental player named Raymond,

Raymond vows, "I'm gonna go to my car, get my other gun, shoot everybody's ass." *The glove-box scene.* When Sidney compliments Billy for being tougher than the average white player ("You're a real cool customer on the court. Real chill out there. Can't be rattled in your game. You don't even fall for that 'n——' shit out there"), Shelton is referencing the same racial dynamics that have been at play in the sport for years—at least as far back as 1966, when they gave Dave Lattin and Texas Western such a psychological advantage over their opponents. Sidney is fly. Sidney talks fierce trash. Sidney twirls in reverse no-look layups and screams as he slams down two-handed dunks. Billy shoots jump shots. Billy throws bounce passes. Billy wears dorky outfits: long-sleeved shirts under short-sleeved tees, socks whose elastic has gone limp. It's the tough, flamboyant Black guy versus the soft, unathletic white guy ("a slow, white, geeky chump," as Billy calls himself), and we all know who has the edge there, right?

Stereotypes all around, it seems: Black men are thugs. White men will outsmart them. Not so fast. Go a layer deeper, and you pick up on how subversive Shelton's plot and his drawing of the characters really are. Sidney is the relatively stable head of a nuclear family; he plays street ball so he can earn enough money to buy a house and move himself, his wife, and their newborn to a better neighborhood. Billy is the ne'er-do-well who won't settle down with the girlfriend who loves him, who is drowning in gambling debt and nevertheless squanders his money, and who hints that he's from a broken home. (Sidney: "Fuck you. Your mother's an astronaut." Billy: "My mother was too drunk to be an astronaut.") In a film in which a Black male character quotes poet John Keats and a female Hispanic character—Rosie Perez's unforgettable Gloria Clemente—becomes a runaway champion on *Jeopardy!*, Billy, the white jock, is the least intelligent figure by far. "At the end, he loses the girl, and he's sort of oblivious to it," Shelton said. "He hasn't learned anything. Rosie's the one with the future, not Woody."

In one scene, Billy tells Sidney, "You're like every other brother I met on the playground. . . . You'd rather look good and lose than look bad and win." But that's not true. Sidney will do anything to come out on top, even hustle his own partner, which he does the first time he and Billy team up. Meanwhile, winning matters less and less to Billy as the story progresses, and proving that he can dunk matters more and more. It's his number-one insecurity. He and Sidney stop at a decrepit basketball goal in a seedy part of LA, and when Sidney bets their winnings that Billy can't dunk—and gives him three chances to try—Billy immediately makes a preemptive excuse, wondering if the rim is too high: "Is this shit regulation?" The climax of the film, the great triumph and celebration, isn't over Sidney and Billy teaming up to win the big game, though they do. It's that Billy has finally jumped high enough to throw down an alley-oop jam.

"You have to accept the tropes, then try to turn them upside down," Shelton told me. "It's like making a Western. There are certain things that the audience needs, and there are certain archetypal truths. I try to humanize everybody. We get to literally go home with Wesley. We see his family. We see his wife. She's got a life. He keeps telling Woody: 'You've got to listen to the woman. You've got to listen to the woman.' The main thing about clichés is what Sam Peckinpah said, 'Embrace the cliché. Then light it from a different angle. Then it's not a cliché anymore.'"

In *Elevating the Game*, his 1992 rumination on the connection between basketball and Black culture, the critic Nelson George noted that the sport's two styles—the creative, highflying "schoolyard" manner of play associated with Black players and the disciplined, indoor-oriented "classroom" approach associated with white athletes—had melded into something more beautiful and complex. "The schoolyard style has now enriched classroom philosophies so thoroughly that the differences aren't so easy to discern," George wrote. "Put simply—because of schoolyard experimentation, all players now do things once thought impossible."

McClung was the embodiment of that socio-racial-athletic blending, even as a native of Gate City, a southern Virginia town that, according to census data, has just two thousand residents and is in a county whose population is more than 97 percent white and less than 1 percent Black. His father, Marcus, who was a tight end and linebacker at Virginia Tech in the early 1990s, started having Mac do plyometric exercises—pop squats and burpees and box jumps—when the kid was in seventh grade. His legs strengthened by those workouts, Mac dunked for the first time when he was fifteen. "One foot, one hand, pretty boring," he said.

At Gate City High, he broke the state's single-season record for points—a record that had been held by Allen Iverson. Two years at Georgetown, one at Texas Tech, ricocheting from the Bulls to the Lakers to the Warriors, from the NBA to the G League and back again, all since going undrafted in 2021—when it comes to reaching basketball's peak, McClung would seem the ultimate example of someone whose fingernails and palms were bloody from the climb. But a point guard who had dunked just twelve times in college and who had just two games of NBA experience wouldn't have gotten a shot in the dunk contest unless he already had built-in buzz, and McClung had that since high school, when his buddies started posting videos of his dunks on social media and his acrobatics went viral. Two videos of his dunks had generated more than 2.4 million aggregate views on YouTube, and what stood out to Trey Mines, McClung's AAU coach, when he first saw those videos was McClung's confidence. "He was this white kid doing crazy things with the basketball," Mines once said. "Then you watch him jump, and it's like, 'Whoa, wait a minute. This isn't real. No, this kid isn't doing that.' I used to tell Mac all the time: he's the swaggiest white kid I knew." His vertical leap at the 2021 NBA Draft Combine, 43½ inches, was the seventh highest in combine history. Coby Carl, McClung's coach with the Blue Coats, described him to me as "freak, effortless athlete. His athleticism shows up with his speed, with his first burst. Even starting out at practices, he's able to get up and go." He was a natural dunker, even if he didn't appear to be one.

That was the problem. Whether one wanted to acknowledge it or not, McClung's appearance—his height, his story, his skin tone— surely had played into the image of him as an underdog, into the reaction to his victory, and into the decision to include him in the contest in the first place. In early October 2023, McClung had been in Japan with the Golden State Warriors, who opened their preseason with two games in Tokyo against the Washington Wizards. There, he said, he got a phone call from Michael Levine, the NBA's senior vice president of entertainment and marketing, who told him that the league wanted him in the dunk contest. Four months later, after averaging more than 19 points and shooting better than 57 percent from the field in 18 games with the Blue Coats, McClung signed with the Sixers, bristling at the idea that anything other than merit factored into the decision. "I've done everything they've asked," he told me. "That's the reason they wanted to give me a chance."

His involvement in the contest was greeted with skepticism, if not outright resentment, for its novelty and its possible implications. During a podcast interview, Kevin Durant had asked, "What are we doing?" when he learned that McClung would be included, and Jesse Washington of the ESPN-owned website Andscape.com had said that McClung was chosen to compete solely because he was white. Washington later apologized, and the questions and assertions seemed silly when in February 2024, McClung—still in the G League, now with the Osceola Magic—returned to the contest to defend his title. And did.

"There was a lot of backlash. So many people didn't want it to happen," McClung told me. "I'm not going to judge anyone for their opinions. I guess that does matter 'cause it's not usual to see white guys dunk like that. So I get it. But that's not even a thought in my head. That's never really been important to me. I was from a town where there were a lot of white people, but I was always playing basketball in northern Virginia or Florida. I just see energy instead of color. My parents were so good. They really just taught me to judge energy and judge kindness, not the color of your skin."

White Men Can't Jump debuted in theaters in late March 1992, and Shelton couldn't have timed the film's release better to fall into the flow of the zeitgeist. *Elevating the Game* had been published that January. Less than a year earlier, Jordan and the Bulls had won their first NBA championship, and in four months, the Dream Team's domination of the Barcelona Summer Olympics would reaffirm Jordan's status as the globe's king of sports. (In the opening sequence of *White Men*, Kadeem Hardison's character, Junior, isn't wearing a Lakers jersey; he's wearing a Bulls jersey with JORDAN 23 on the back.) The NBA's Slam Dunk Contest was the domain of Black dunkers and Black dunkers alone—Barry hadn't won it yet—and had become a touchstone of American entertainment, so much so that, in the early '90s, Foot Locker began holding its own annual "Dunk Fest," which featured star athletes from the NFL and Major League Baseball, Deion Sanders and Ken Griffey Jr. among them. The movie's costumes—bright pinks and oranges and sea blues, tank tops—became fashion staples of the decade. "It traveled," Shelton told me. "I got all these notifications that kids dressed differently after that movie. It changed the playground look. Guys were dressing like Woody and Wesley and those guys."

There was a major news event that was on Shelton's mind as he made the film: the beating of Rodney King, on March 3, 1991, by four Los Angeles police officers and their subsequent trial for assault charges. The verdict—and the officers' acquittals—came down on April 29, 1992, one month after *White Men* had opened, and the riots in the verdict's aftermath raged while the movie was still in theaters. Shelton solicited advice from the cast members, most of whom were Black, on how to preserve the film's energy and themes without his having to soften the language too much. "I just wrote it as I saw it," he told me. "When the actors came in to rehearse, I just said, 'Anything you're not comfortable with in the script, tell me.' They embraced the script. They loved the script. The N-word was in there about six times, because it's very common on the court, and they said, 'We don't really want to say that.' I said, 'Then don't.' I don't come in there as a dictator. I say, 'This is the story as I see it. Now I want you to interact with it and make it your story.'"

What could have been a powder keg turned out to be a hit. The film had just a $16 million budget. Shelton told me that Joe Roth, the chairman of 20th Century Fox, "had that number as a carrot for production: 'If you can make it for no more than $16 million, it's a go.'" It grossed $91 million. The basketball sequences had enough

20

MORT DE LA DUNK . . . ?

No sport can ever stay the same. No sport should. And yet . . .
if the dunk is no longer at the core of the thrill of playing and
watching hoops, if it's taken for granted as just another part
of the game, what then? What has basketball gained, and what
has it lost?

In November 2017, *The Atlantic,* whose pages and website are usually reserved for think pieces about domestic politics, global conflicts, and
technological and scientific trends and breakthroughs, published an
essay by Sam Riches lamenting the "slam dunk's day of reckoning."
The news hook for Riches's piece was that Vince Carter—the most
direct successor to Erving, Thompson, Jordan, and Wilkins—would
be turning forty-one in two months and was nearing the end of his
NBA career. Carter wasn't quite as close to retirement as Riches believed; having just begun his twentieth season, he would play two
more, for the Atlanta Hawks, before walking away satisfied he had
accomplished what he had set out to do when he entered the league.
Though he had been obsessed with the Slam Dunk Contest when
he was a kid, videotaping and studying each one, and though he approached his debut in the contest as if it were a meaningful game—"I

authenticity—you could see Snipes and Harrelson as guys who could really play—and though Shelton, who had earned an Academy Award nomination for his *Bull Durham* screenplay, didn't get one for *White Men Can't Jump*, he accomplished something maybe more difficult. He took the chance that people could stand to laugh at themselves more, and the film's staying power is a testament to his success in revealing the individuality and shared humanity of his characters . . . and of us. That's a hell of a high-wire act; a 2023 remake couldn't pull it off and flopped. When Sidney Dean hammers down a rim-rocking slam, snatches a wad of bills out of a competitor's hand, and screams, "AAAAHHH, give me my money!" he is doing what any great dunker or filmmaker has to do: he is going all in, no regret, no hesitation, accepting the risk that he might fail or be made a fool. *Bull Durham* might be the better film, but *White Men Can't Jump* is the braver one.

Outside Chase Fieldhouse, more than an hour after the game had ended, ten to fifteen people bundled against a cold, breezy night and gathered to wait for McClung to emerge. Exhausted after winning the dunk contest the first time, after the weekend of his life, he had dragged himself through a rough night: shooting 2-for-9 from the field in 24 minutes, clanking one jump shot after another off the front of the rim, scoring just seven points in the Blue Coats' 116–111 loss to the Motor City Cruise, trying to feel normal again and failing to come close.

When he finally did exit the arena, wearing just a white T-shirt and black pants against the chill, he stopped to scribble autographs and pose for photographs, flashing a peace sign in every picture. One woman told him, "It was so fun watching you." A Black teenaged kid in a black hoodie said, "I'm going to get him to sign my forehead, bro." It didn't matter that Mac McClung hadn't dunked once in the game. For the people crowding around him in the middle of the night, a moment with a man who already had done the impossible, and in a year's time would do it again, was enough.

was there for business," he once said—he had wanted to be seen as more than a dunker. That was why, after winning the contest in 2000, Carter never competed in it again. Dunking had done more for him than just make him a showman. Dunking had helped him become an All-Star eight times. Dunking had helped him win the NBA Rookie of the Year Award and an Olympic gold medal. But Riches hinted that dunking—as a gravitational force for the NBA, as a primary reason for players' fame and respect and the public's fascination with pro basketball—would probably retire with Carter.

"Compared to forty years ago," Riches wrote, "the dunk is not what it once was. . . . Today's dunks are mostly utilitarian, about function rather than form; they are cold and clinical in contrast to what they once were. There are exceptions, of course, but the overall impression is one of sanitized creativity. The artfulness of the dunk has largely been lost—if not forgotten, then ignored."

The dunk's potency—its use as an instrument to shift a game's momentum, as a measure of toughness and bravado and, for lack of a better word, *manhood*—had been draining away. Carter . . . the AND1 Tour, with its fusion of streetball and hip-hop and Globetrotter sensibility . . . Shaquille O'Neal blasting a backboard into shards and bits or causing the stanchion to rock and creak as if an earthquake had hit . . . all of these once-novel displays grew relatively stale. People had seen them before or felt like they had. *Sports Illustrated*'s Jack Mc-Callum, in November 1981, had asserted that "the dunk has become basketball's highest art form." But fewer players and fans now viewed it with the same awe and reverence, and the mindsets of the people building and coaching NBA teams and the people suiting up for those teams had dulled the act of dunking into exactly what Riches described. With certain exceptions, it was, as offensive efficiency became more paramount, little more than a prosaic tool for putting the ball through the basket. The number of dunks each season, for example, had increased by 35 percent from 2001–02 to 2018–19, but that jump was mostly a function of a simultaneous increase in scoring: an NBA team averaged fewer than 95 points in '01–'02 and more than 111 in '18–'19. Even a popular innovation such as the "self-oop"—players tossing the

ball off the backboard, catching it, and throwing it down—developed
not out of the quest for artistry but the desire to solve a practical problem: What happens when a player has picked up his dribble, is stuck
or trapped, and doesn't have anyone to pass to but himself? "What has
brought the self-oop to the forefront," the *Wall Street Journal*'s Robert
O'Connell wrote in February 2024, "isn't style but strategy."

The shift toward efficiency was about maximizing offensive production while, over the long term, minimizing risk. At its core, the
philosophy was simple: A made three-pointer was 50 percent more
valuable than a made two-pointer, and players were more likely to
make shots—dunks and layups—near the rim. So a smart general
manager should stock his or her roster with players who could more
easily score from those areas of the court, and sheer math would carry
the team to victory. In certain contexts, though, a dunk can be the
riskiest play in basketball—not just for the player carrying it out but
also for the player trying to prevent it—and that risk has been height-
ened in the age of social media, where a single seven-second snippet
of action—one rim-rocking dunk, one player getting posterized—can
live forever. Carter once called this dynamic "the fear of," meaning
that players were hesitant to compete in the Slam Dunk Contest because of the negative feedback they might receive if they failed to
perform well or suffered a humiliating experience. "I wasn't afraid,"
he said. "I wasn't scared of the result." But he believed other players
were, and he wasn't the only one. "They don't want to look bad,"
longtime NBA guard Nate Robinson, the only three-time winner of
the contest, once said. "They don't want to mess up their—I hate to
say it: they don't want to look silly, man. It's about the reputation more
than going out and just showing people that you're human."

The flip side to that fear has been an increased reluctance to challenge and defend against dunks—to shy away from jumping with a
prospective dunker in an attempt to snuff the slam. Even as field-goal
attempts and scoring skyrocketed throughout the first twenty-four years
of the twenty-first century, the rate of blocked shots per game has held
relatively steady since the league started tracking the statistic in 1973.
On March 18, 2024, the Utah Jazz's John Collins, who is six-nine, tried

to block a dunk attempt by the Minnesota Timberwolves' Anthony Edwards, who is six-four, as Edwards surged through the lane. Edwards went up so high and threw the ball down so hard over Collins that NBA media and fans reacted with an explosion of online content: posts loaded with capital letters and exclamation points, multi-angled replays of the sequence, and declarations that Edwards had just delivered the best in-game dunk of all time. For the 3.86 million subscribers to its YouTube page, the website Bleacher Report posted a link to the dunk with the headline: *Anthony Edwards DISRESPECTFUL Poster Dunk on John Collins.* To its 1.3 million followers on Twitter/X, Hoop Central, an NBA analysis and aggregation site, sent out a candid clip of Edwards signing autographs after the game. In it a young fan asks him for his jersey. "I gotta give it to Collins," Edwards replies with a smirk. That Collins had suffered a head contusion when Edwards landed on him only added to the dunk's instantaneous mythology and, one would assume, Collins's embarrassment. In light of the play and its viral fallout, one can understand why it's the rare modern player who doesn't mind being dunked on, who recognizes that there is a time to get and a time to be gotten. Better to avoid the mocking, or the possibility of it, altogether. "They just don't want to be on a video where their friends are giving them crap about it, whereas I really don't care," Andrew Bogut, a seven-foot center who spent fourteen years in the NBA, said in 2016. "My job is to protect the basket. . . . Nine times out of ten I'm going to block it. One time out of ten I'm going to be on *SportsCenter.* I don't care."

Carter, of course, was responsible for an all-time posterization—maybe *the* all-time posterization—during the 2000 Summer Olympics in Sydney. Six-foot-six, he flew so far over French center Frederic Weis, who at seven-two had him by eight inches, that he was practically sitting on Weis's right shoulder when he hammered down an explosive jam. Ricky Cobb, who operates the nostalgic Twitter/X account @Super70sSports, will occasionally post a photograph of the dunk—Carter soaring, Weis cowering underneath him, Weis's face turned to the left and pressed against the insides of Carter's thighs—with this laugh-out-loud line: "Vince Carter always carried an EpiPen in case any opponent was allergic to nuts." The French press and public were, for a while, merciless toward Weis, giving the play a name: *Dunk de la Mort*. The Dunk of Death. There was more to him and his story than that moment, though, so much more. Weis had played in four straight French league All-Star games ahead of those Olympics. The New York Knicks had made him their first-round draft pick in 1999. He was proud to contribute to the silver medal that France won at Sydney. His son had been born with a severe form of autism, and the diagnosis threw Weis into such a deep depression that, in January 2008, he swallowed a box of sleeping pills in an attempt to kill himself. He subsequently recovered to forge a career in broadcasting. Carter's dunk did not destroy Weis, but one could be forgiven for thinking that it might have.

"Did having his legacy permanently marked by that experience help?" Sam Borden, who profiled Weis for both the *New York Times* and ESPN, said. "It definitely didn't help."

Borden has a Master of Fine Arts from Fairfield University in Connecticut, and the subject of his thesis was masculinity in sports. His primary conclusion, he told me, was that "feelings in masculinity— particularly in positions in sports, like 'I am an NBA player,' or accomplishments in sports, like 'I dunked on this guy'—are fleeting." And athletes should recognize that most of their successes and blunders are evanescent; one will likely follow the other, so they shouldn't turn haughty over their triumphs or judge themselves so harshly for their failures. Did you crack a long home run and feel like Roy Hobbs as you watched the ball sail into the second deck? Savor that trot around the bases, son. You'll probably strike out later in the game. Did you feel indestructible after slamming over Frederic Weis? Well, enjoy it while it lasts, because you might airball your next shot. "The realization the vast majority of those athletes come to," Borden said, "is that whatever your feelings are about yourself as a man, it has to come from something deeper than what you're doing on a court or a field." The thesis's title was *Male Fraud*. Maybe some of the players whom Carter, Bogut, and Robinson were talking about should read it.

"There's a certain element of permanence that makes that more significant than it maybe would have been in another time," Borden told me. "The simple act of getting dunked on isn't necessarily the emasculating thing that those guys are thinking of. It's the idea that it will become—and this is where Frederic has some significance—part of your legacy. If you and I are playing and there's no camera, sure, I'll take a swing at it. Nobody will know except for you and me. The notion that it could become identifiably part of who you are, like it did for Fred, is a real deterrent for a lot of guys. That's probably a shame, especially if you're a defensive purist."

As a varsity player at Highland High School in Medina, Ohio, Daryl Morey could dunk a tennis ball, maybe a volleyball, but never a basketball. "I blame my small hands," he told me. Medina is about thirty miles south of Cleveland, so the man who spearheaded the analytics revolution in the NBA grew up a fan of the terrific Cavaliers teams of the late 1980s and early 1990s: Brad Daugherty, Mark Price, Larry Nance, clubs that were never quite good enough to get past Jordan's Bulls in the Eastern Conference playoffs. In his nightmares, Morey can still see Jordan hovering over Craig Ehlo in the final second of Game 5 of the teams' 1989 first-round series, Ehlo on his way down, Jordan hovering still and drilling that jump shot from the foul line to break the heart of everyone in northeast Ohio.

"I refused to watch the fucking Bulls for the longest time," Morey told me, "because I knew I'd have to fucking watch the fucking shot that fucking Michael made against fucking Ehlo."

It's reasonable to credit Morey, for his thirteen years as the general manager of the Houston Rockets, for being one of the two figures most responsible for shaping the NBA into a league that prized the three-point shot over just about anything else. The other figure couldn't appear more dissimilar from him. In the trite, reductive way these discussions have been framed, Morey is the nerd, and Steph Curry is the jock. Morey is numbers and trends and spreadsheets; he graduated from Northwestern, and his first full-time job in sports was with the firm STATS Inc. Curry is creativity and jazziness and *Holy crap, can you believe he did that?* Morey was the league's Billy Beane. Curry was the league's most captivating player since Jordan. Morey is work. Curry is fun. Take this scene: In January 2016, the Warriors—on their way to a 73–9 regular season, the best record in league history—visited Philadelphia to face the Sixers, who were on their way to a 10–72 regular season, one of the worst in league history. Nevertheless, a quick glance around the Wells Fargo Center made it clear that Curry's presence alone made the game an event. Toddlers wore the Warriors' colors, blue and gold. A teenaged girl held up a sign that read: *Hey 76ers, Can The Process Bring Us Steph?* Before Curry began his warm-up routine, lingering around the three-point arc, taking ordinary jumpers and trying trick shots, the Sixers took a telling precaution to protect him. To prevent spectators from getting too close to the court and, in turn, too close to Curry, they had members of the Center's security detail hold a yellow rope around three-quarters of the court—both baselines and the sideline opposite the scorer's table.

"That's not normal?" Curry joked after the game. "I've never seen that before. I mean, I've seen people show up to watch us warm up, but that was a little different."

He had emerged as maybe the most marketable man in the sport. Over the previous year, sales of his jersey had increased 581 percent, and his merchandise sales had increased 453 percent. Three digits, no typos. "Steph is getting to that point where he's transcending the game in a lot of ways," Warriors coach Steve Kerr, who had been a teammate of Jordan's for more than three seasons with the Bulls, said that night. "People who wouldn't otherwise be interested in basketball are interested in Steph, and that's how it was with Michael. . . . He does amazing things, and the crowd, even though they're cheering for the home team, is legitimately thrilled to watch him do his thing."

Curry in his prime stood alone: not merely the world's best long-range shooter but perhaps its best ball-handler, too, able to create his shot anytime from anywhere. Morey wasn't getting Curry, so in Houston, he did what he thought was the next best thing: he traded for James Harden, made him the nucleus of the Rockets' offense, and surrounded him with spot-up shooters. Harden might launch a stepback three. He might shake a defender with his killer crossover dribble and drive all the way to the rim. Once there, he might drop in a layup, dunk, draw a foul, or kick the ball out to an open teammate for what Morey regarded as the most important shot in basketball: the corner three. The corner three is the shot with the highest return on the shortest distance. It's just 22 feet, one and three-quarters feet closer to the basket than any other shot from behind the arc, so Morey and other managers like him sought out players who could shoot it well, and coaching staffs designed their game plans and schemes to create more opportunities to take it. A player who could "catch-and-shoot"—who could quite literally stand still in the corner and hit a three once someone passed him the ball—took on exponentially more value.

The prevalence of such a player also has had its costs, however, more than a lot of analytically inclined minds might have first wanted to acknowledge. Kirk Goldsberry noted in *Sprawlball*, his spatial and statistical breakdown of the changes in offense since the NBA's implementation of the three-point shot, that the league's accent on efficiency had led to more catch-and-shoot threes and fewer "acrobatic tries in the two-point area." As efficient of a shot as the dunk is, the maddening sight of a smaller NBA player knifing to the basket, a clear layup or jam awaiting him, before kicking the ball out for a shot from 24 feet had become common. And it was driving a lot of fans insane, "those of us," Goldsberry wrote, "who go to arenas to watch some of the best athletes in the world performing basketball actions we can achieve ourselves only in our dreams or via our game consoles."

The average nationally televised NBA game in 1995–96, Jordan's first full season after his first retirement, pulled in nearly three million viewers. Viewership has hovered at roughly half that ever since, though in fairness fewer people watch sports—or anything else—on linear television. Still, LeBron, Steph, more three-pointers, more scoring, the influx of international talent—none of those factors has caused or contributed to a similar spike in interest or popularity. A similar spike hasn't happened. Widespread national interest in professional basketball, over the last three decades, peaked with the player who had tormented young Daryl Morey. It peaked with Fucking Michael Jordan. It peaked, one might argue, just when the dunk peaked.

Morey, whom the Sixers hired as their team president in 2020, told me that he has spoken frequently with one of his mentors, the renowned baseball writer and statistician Bill James, about the question of whether a heavy emphasis on data necessarily strips the artistry away from a sport, basketball specifically. They agree, Morey said, that "the league office has to take an active role, and this is where the NBA really beats all the other sports that I've seen. You have to take an active role in making sure, with the rules you set, that when teams optimize—and teams are going to optimize, whether you have data or not; they're just better at it now—you are creating a more interesting product. The data doesn't make it more interesting or less interesting. It just says, 'Here's the gravity of the rules, and we're going to push you there.' If that pushes you to a less interesting sport, then the league needs to get involved."

In other words: the rules can push back. The NBA doesn't have to return to the kill-or-be-killed style of the mid-1990s and early 2000s—each game a slow-motion stock-car race, players trading paint, bumping and bodying and hacking each other, often crashing spectacularly—and it doesn't have to resign itself to players and teams scoring so easily, with such high efficiency and such little resistance, that the sport might as well be a glorified shootaround. It can encourage its officials to, as the cliché goes, *let 'em play* a little more, give defenders a fighting chance by no longer blowing their whistles over the slightest hand check, provide the freedom and incentive for a shot-blocker to . . . block more shots. It would make dunking the ball more challenging, more impressive, and more exciting.

Those tweaks, though, can do only so much to restore the exhilaration that characterized basketball's advancements in the 1970s, '80s, and early '90s—the sensation that everything about it was fresh and spontaneous, like a man suddenly deciding, out of a desire to create something beautiful and everlasting, to string a high wire between two skyscrapers and walk across it. There's no going back to the era when a dunk inspired Gatsby-like wonder in those who witnessed it, not unless the sport's leaders bring Phog Allen's dreams to fruition and adopt the radical measure of raising the rim a foot or two. Radical, yes, but it might be worth contemplating someday. The typical NBA player grew by more than three inches, from six feet, four inches to six feet, seven inches, between 1952 and 1987, then has decreased slightly ever since, to six-six. That recent trend makes sense. Taller, stouter post players were deemed less important as the three-pointer's effect and influence increased and the sport became perimeter-based. But the rise of several players who are six-eleven or taller, who years ago would have been consigned to staying near the basket, and who now—because of their nimbleness, ball-handling and passing skills, and shooting ability—function as giant point forwards could eventually compel a reformulation of a basketball court's balance of size and space. Magic, LeBron, and Kevin Durant have begotten Victor Wembanyama, Giannis Antetokoumpo, and Nikola Jokic. And if, over another thirty-five years, the average height of an NBA player increases another three inches, to six foot nine, raising the rim won't sound so radical. It will be a necessary measure to maintain the spiritual quality that makes the sport so special . . . and that always has. Look up. The soul of the game lives on in the sky.

ACKNOWLEDGMENTS

If I named and thanked everyone who helped me write this book, the hardback would be too heavy to pick up.

The people I met in and around Murray State University could not have been kinder or more generous with their time and insights into Ja Morant and his effect on the school and the town. I spent a terrific afternoon in Pittsburgh with Shawn Hawkins, Renee Robinson, and Vince Lackner as they described their relationships with Connie Hawkins—Hawk the man, Hawk the grandfather, Hawk the icon. Oliver Fortenberry did more than tell me his father's story; he basically gave me a grand tour of Joe Fortenberry's life and of West Texas. I'm grateful for his and Ed Wright's hospitality.

Kathy Lafferty mined the archives at the University of Kansas for reams of John McLendon material. Jeffrey Monseau of Springfield College pointed me in some good directions for primary sourcing on James Naismith and basketball's origins. Barry Bookhard, Andrew Maraniss, Dave Winder, Annabelle Myers, and Dave Sholler lent the kind of behind-the-scenes assistance that often goes unrecognized but enables someone like me to write something like this.

Mike Jensen, my former colleague at the *Philadelphia Inquirer*, smoothed over sections of this book and gave me liberal access to his dual expertise in hoops and words. Tyler Kepner read an early draft of the manuscript and tidied up some of its sloppiness. Susan Canavan, of Waxman Literary, and Pete Wolverton, of St. Martin's Press, were ideal companions on the journey to publication. My father-in-law, Bob Zilahy, was a wizard in preparing the photographs inside this book for publication. My wife, Kate, and my parents, Ann and Chuck Sielski, doubled as eagle-eyed copy editors for the manuscript. And my family members and friends provided support and encouragement throughout the long process of researching and writing *Magic in the Air*. I love and owe all of them more than I can say.

My sons, Evan and Gabe, inherited my modest athletic ability, so they'll likely never dunk a basketball in their lives. I hope that, with their sharp minds, good humor, and kind hearts, they'll settle for making their dad feel like he can touch the stratosphere himself.

SOURCES AND BIBLIOGRAPHY

Every chapter of this book was its own tiny book, and that structure required a method of research and reporting that was deeper and more diverse than any writing project I'd taken on before.

I conducted as many interviews—in person, over the phone, via email and text message—as possible. Some of my subjects, including Kareem Abdul-Jabbar and David Thompson, declined to speak with me, turned down interview requests through their representatives, or simply did not respond to my requests or questions. I did my best to compensate for their absence. I took advantage of geographic proximity where I could: I attended a 76ers–Memphis Grizzlies game and shootaround to speak to Ja and Tee Morant, for instance, and because Bob Kurland's daughter Barbara Rintala and I live less than thirty minutes from each other, we were able to meet for coffee to talk about her father. I traveled to various cities and towns around the country to meet with and observe subjects and to get a feel for certain environments and settings: Amarillo, Texas; Murray, Kentucky; New Orleans, Louisiana; Pittsburgh, Pennsylvania; Raleigh, North Carolina; Wilmington, Delaware. YouTube is a truly magical place; there, I watched full games, clips of games, interviews, documentaries, podcasts, talk shows, and more. It's almost as magical as Newspapers.com, where I unearthed information, context, confirmation, and details that sometimes made my head spin. Carl Agard provided me with a digital copy of Jackie Jackson's unpublished and unfinished memoir. Oliver Fortenberry opened up his father's archive of articles and memorabilia to me; I felt the weight of Joe's 1936 Olympic gold medal in my hands.

With permission, I have reused or replicated a small amount of my work for the *Philadelphia Inquirer*. I cited many sources within the book in spots where I believed attribution was natural and necessary and didn't disrupt the flow of the narrative. The major sources that I relied on are listed below.

ARCHIVES, DATABASES, AND PERSONAL COLLECTIONS

Carl Agard

Almanac.com

Ancestry.com

The Association for Professional Basketball Research

Basketball-Reference.com

Black Fives Foundation

Central Intercollegiate Athletic Association

Christie's Auction House

City of Philadelphia

City-Data.com

DraftExpress.com

Federal Bureau of Investigation

Foot Locker

Oliver Fortenberry

The Harlem Globetrotters

Walter Iooss

John McLendon Foundation

LA84 Foundation

Murray State University

Rachael Naismith

NBA

NCAA

National Weather Service

North Carolina State University

Oklahoma State University

Overbrook High School

Pacific Marine Review

Panhandle Sports Hall of Fame

Pro Basketball Encyclopedia

Purdue University

RemembertheABA.com

Rensselaer Polytechnic Institute

RunRepeat.com

Sacramento Sports Hall of Fame

Sears

Society of American Baseball Research

Spotrac.com

Springfield College

SportsMediaWatch.com

SS *Manhattan*

TedSilary.com

TheHoopsGeek.com

Tom Konchalski

US Census

United States Holocaust Memorial Museum

University of Kansas

University of North Carolina at Chapel Hill

Virginia Union University

West Virginia University

Western Pennsylvania Sports Museum

BOOKS

Abdul-Jabbar, Kareem. *Coach Wooden and Me: Our 50-Year Friendship On and Off the Court.* New York: Grand Central Publishing, 2017.

———, and Peter Knobler. *Giant Steps: The Autobiography of Kareem Abdul-Jabbar.* New York: Bantam Books, 1983.

———, and Raymond Obstfeld. *Becoming Kareem: Growing Up On and Off the Court*. New York: Little, Brown and Company, 2017.

Abrams, Jonathan. *Boys Among Men: How the Prep-to-Pro Generation Redefined the NBA and Sparked a Basketball Revolution*. New York: Crown Archetype, 2016.

Allen, Forrest C. *Better Basketball: Technique, Tactics, Talent*. New York: McGraw-Hill, 1937.

The Association of Gentleman Pittsburgh Journalists. *Integrating Pittsburgh Sports*. Charleston, SC: History Press, 2006.

Axthelm, Pete. *The City Game: Basketball from the Garden to the Playgrounds*. New York: Harper's Magazine Press, 1970.

Baylor, Elgin, with Alan Eisenstock. *Hang Time: My Life in Basketball*. New York: Houghton Mifflin Harcourt, 2018.

Beckham, Barry. *Double Dunk: The Story of Earl "The Goat" Manigault*. Los Angeles: Holloway House, 1980.

Berkow, Ira. *Red: A Biography of Red Smith*. Lincoln: University of Nebraska Press, 1986.

Brewer, John M., Jr. *Black America Series: African Americans in Pittsburgh*. Charleston, SC: Arcadia Publishing, 2006.

Byers, Walter, with Charles Hammer. *Unsportsmanlike Conduct: Exploiting College Athletes*. Ann Arbor: The University of Michigan Press, 1995.

Caponi-Tabery, Gena. *Jump for Joy: Jazz, Basketball, and Black Culture in 1930s America*. Amherst: The University of Massachusetts Press, 2008.

———, ed. *Signifyin(g), Sanctifyin', & Slam Dunking: A Reader in African American Expressive Culture*. Amherst: The University of Massachusetts Press, 1999.

Chamberlain, Wilt, and David Shaw. *Wilt: Just Like Any Other Black Millionaire Who Lives Next Door*. New York: Macmillan, 1973.

Cherry, Robert. *Wilt: Larger than Life*. Chicago: Triumph Books, 2004.

Cohen, Joel. *Big A: The Story of Lew Alcindor*. New York: Scholastic Magazines Inc., 1971.

Cohen, Rich. *When the Game Was War: The NBA's Greatest Season*. New York: Random House, 2023.

Cohen, Stan. *The Games of '36: A Pictorial History of the 1936 Olympics in Germany*. Missoula, MT: Pictorial Histories Publishing, 1996.

Cohen, Stanley. *The Game They Played*. New York: Carroll & Graf Publishers, 1977.

Croatto, Pete. *From Hang Time to Prime Time: Business, Entertainment, and the Birth of the Modern-Day NBA*. New York: Atria Books, 2020.

Cunningham, Carson. *American Hoops: U.S. Men's Olympic Basketball from Berlin to Beijing*. Lincoln: University of Nebraska Press, 2009.

Dawkins, Darryl, and Charley Rosen. *Chocolate Thunder: The Uncensored Life and Times of the NBA's Original Showman*. Toronto: Sport Media Publishing, 2003.

———, with George Wirt. *Chocolate Thunder: The In-Your-Face, All-Over-the-Place, Death-Defyin', Mesmerizin', Slam-Jam Adventures of Double-D*. Chicago: Contemporary Books, 1986.

Diem, Carl, ed. *The XIth Olympic Games, Berlin 1936: Official Report*. Berlin: Wilhelm Limpert, 1936.

Ellsworth, Scott. *The Secret Game: A Wartime Story of Courage, Change, and Basketball's Lost Triumph*. New York: Little, Brown and Company, 2015.

Erving, Julius, with Karl Taro Greenfield. *Dr. J: The Autobiography*. New York: Harper-Collins, 2013.

Fitzpatrick, Frank. *And the Walls Came Tumbling Down: Kentucky, Texas Western, and the Game That Changed American Sports*. New York: Simon & Schuster, 1999.

Fortenberry, Beth. *Slam Dunk: The True Story of Basketball's First Olympic Gold Medal Team*. New York: Hybrid Global Publishing, 2019.

Francois, Francis B. *Two Guys from Barnum, Iowa, and How They Helped Save Basketball*. Costa Mesa, CA: Francois Press, 2008.

Frey, Darcy. *The Last Shot: City Streets, Basketball Dreams*. New York: Houghton Mifflin, 1994.

George, Nelson. *Elevating the Game: Black Men and Basketball*. New York: HarperCollins, 1992.

Goldsberry, Kirk. *Sprawlball: A Visual Tour of the New Era of the NBA*. New York: Houghton Mifflin Harcourt, 2019.

Goudsouzian, Aram. *King of the Court: Bill Russell and the Basketball Revolution*. Berkeley: University of California Press, 2010.

Green, Ben. *Spinning the Globe: The Rise, Fall, and Return to Greatness of the Harlem Globetrotters*. New York: HarperCollins, 2005.

Grundy, Pamela. *Learning to Win: Sports, Education, and Social Change in Twentieth-Century North Carolina*. Chapel Hill: The University of North Carolina Press, 2001.

Gutman, Bill. *Tales from the 1969–70 New York Knicks*. Champaign, IL: Sports Publishing, 2005.

Halberstam, David. *The Breaks of the Game*. New York: Hyperion, 1981.

Haskins, Don, with Dan Wetzel. *Glory Road: My Story of the 1966 NCAA Basketball Championship and How One Team Triumphed Against the Odds and Changed America Forever*. New York: Hyperion, 2006.

Haynes, Mike, and Dave Wohlfarth, eds. *Pride of the Plains: 50 Years of the Panhandle Sports Hall of Fame*. Amarillo, TX: Cenveo Publishing, 2008.

Hughes, Rich. *Netting Out Basketball 1936*. Overland Park, KS: Rich Hughes, 2011.

Johnson, Claude. *The Black Fives: The Epic Story of Basketball's Forgotten Era*. New York: Abrams Press, 2021.

Johnson, James W. *The Dandy Dons: Bill Russell, K. C. Jones, Phil Woolpert, and One of College Basketball's Greatest and Most Innovative Teams*. Lincoln: University of Nebraska Press, 2009.

Johnson, Scott Morrow. *Phog: The Most Influential Man in Basketball*. Lincoln: University of Nebraska Press, 2016.

Jordan, Michael. *For the Love of the Game: My Story*. New York: Crown Publishers, 1998.

———; photographs by Walter Iooss Jr., and edited by Mark Vancil. *Rare Air: Michael on Michael*. San Francisco: Collins Publishers, 1993.

Katz, Milton S. *Breaking Through: John B. McLendon, Basketball Legend and Civil Rights Pioneer*. Fayetteville: The University of Arkansas Press, 2007.

Kerkhoff, Blair. *Phog Allen: The Father of Basketball Coaching*. Indianapolis: Masters Press, 1996.

Kuska, Bob. *Hot Potato: How Washington and New York Gave Birth to Black Basketball and Changed America's Game Forever*. Charlottesville: University of Virginia Press, 2004.

Ladd, Tony, and James A. Mathisen. *Muscular Christianity: Evangelical Protestants and the Development of American Sport.* Grand Rapids, MI: BridgePoint Books, 1999.

Lattin, David "Big Daddy D." *Slam Dunk to Glory: The Amazing True Story of the 1966 NCAA Season and the Championship Game That Changed America Forever.* Lakeland, FL: White Stone Books, 2006.

Lyons, Robert S. *Palestra Pandemonium: A History of the Big Five.* Philadelphia: Temple University Press, 2002.

MacCambridge, Michael. *The Big Thing: How the 1970s Transformed Sports in America.* New York: Grand Central Publishing, 2023.

MacMullan, Jackie, Rafe Bartholomew, and Dan Klores. *Basketball: A Love Story.* New York: Broadway Books, 2018.

Mallozzi, Vincent M. *Asphalt Gods: An Oral History of the Rucker Tournament.* New York: Doubleday, 2003.

———. *Doc: The Rise and Rise of Julius Erving.* Hoboken, NJ: John Wiley & Sons, 2010.

Maraniss, Andrew. *Games of Deception: The True Story of the First U.S. Olympic Basketball Team at the 1936 Olympics in Hitler's Germany.* New York: Penguin Books, 2019.

———. *Strong Inside: Perry Wallace and the Collision of Race and Sports in the South.* Nashville: Vanderbilt University Press, 2014.

McLendon, John B. *Fast Break Basketball: Fundamentals and Fine Points.* West Nyack, NY: Parker Publishing Company, 1965.

Michener, James. *Sports in America.* New York: Random House, 1976.

Mosenson, Cecil. *It All Began with Wilt.* Mustang, OK: Tate Publishing, 2008.

Naismith, James. *Basketball: Its Origin and Development.* New York: Association Press, 1941.

———. *Rules for Basketball.* Springfield, MA: Springfield Printing and Binding Company, 1892.

Nocera, Joe, and Ben Strauss. *Indentured: The Inside Story of the Rebellion Against the NBA.* New York: Portfolio/Penguin, 2016.

Pearlman, Jeff. *Showtime: Magic, Kareem, Riley, and the Los Angeles Lakers Dynasty of the 1980s.* New York: Gotham Books, 2013.

Peeler, Tim. *Legends of N.C. State Basketball: Dick Dickey, Tommy Burleson, David Thompson, Jim Valvano, and Other Wolfpack Stars.* New York: Sports Publishing, 2004.

Peterson, Robert W. *Cages to Jump Shots: Pro Basketball's Early Years.* New York/Oxford: Oxford University Press, 1990.

Pluto, Terry. *Loose Balls: The Short, Wild Life of the American Basketball Association.* New York: Simon & Schuster, 1990.

Price, Asher. *Year of the Dunk: My Search for the History, Science, and Human Potential in Basketball's Most Dramatic Play.* New York: Crown Publishers, 2015.

Rains, Rob with Hellen Carpenter. *James Naismith: The Man Who Invented Basketball.* Philadelphia: Temple University Press, 2009.

Richman, David. *Wilt, Ike, & Me: A Personal Memoir of an American Dream and Beyond.* Philadelphia: Better Angels Publishing Company, 2018.

Rosen, Charley. *Scandals of '51: How the Gamblers Almost Killed College Basketball.* New York: Seven Stories Press, 1978.

———. *The Wizard of Odds: How Jack Molinas Almost Destroyed the Game of Basketball.* New York: Seven Stories Press, 2001.

Rosin, James. *Philly Hoops: The Sphas and Warriors.* Philadelphia: Autumn Road Publishers, 2003.

Roth, John. *The Encyclopedia of Duke Basketball.* Durham: Duke University Press, 2006.

Russell, Bill, and Taylor Branch. *Second Wind: Memoirs of an Opinionated Man.* New York: Random House, 1979.

———, with Bill McSweeny. *Go Up for Glory.* New York: Berkley, 1966.

———, with Alan Steinberg. *Red and Me: My Coach, My Lifelong Friend.* New York: HarperCollins, 2009.

Salzburg, Charles. *From Set Shot to Slam Dunk: The Glory Days of Basketball in the Words of Those Who Played It.* New York: E.P. Dutton, 1987.

Schaap, Jeremy. *Triumph: The Untold Story of Jesse Owens and Hitler's Olympics.* New York: Houghton Mifflin Harcourt, 2007.

Schumacher, Michael. *Mr. Basketball: George Mikan, the Minneapolis Lakers, and the Birth of the NBA.* New York: Bloomsbury, 2007.

Shelton, Ron. *The Church of Baseball: The Making of Bull Durham: Home Runs, Bad Calls, Crazy Fights, Big Swings, and a Hit.* New York: Alfred A. Knopf, 2022.

Sobel, Syl, and Jay Rosenstein. *Boxed Out of the NBA: Remembering the Eastern Professional League.* Lanham, MD: Rowman & Littlefield, 2021.

The Staff of the *Philadelphia Daily News*. *Philly Hoops: The Magic of Philadelphia Basketball.* Philadelphia: Camino Books, Inc., 2003.

Stark, Douglas, ed. *The James Naismith Reader: Basketball in His Own Words.* Lincoln: University of Nebraska Press, 2016.

Taylor, John. *The Rivalry: Bill Russell, Wilt Chamberlain, and the Golden Age of Basketball.* New York: Random House, 2005.

Telander, Rick. *Heaven Is a Playground.* New York: St. Martin's Press, 1976.

Thomas, Ron. *They Cleared the Lane: The NBA's Black Pioneers.* Lincoln: University of Nebraska Press, 2002.

Thompson, David with Sean Stormes and Marshall Terrill. *Skywalker.* Champaign, IL: Sports Publishing, 2003.

Valvano, Jim, and Curry Kirkpatrick. *Valvano: They Gave Me a Lifetime Contract, and Then They Declared Me Dead.* New York: Pocket Books, 1991.

West, Cornel. *Race Matters.* Boston: Beacon Press, 1993.

West, Jerry, and Jonathan Coleman. *West by West: My Charmed, Tormented Life.* New York: Little, Brown and Company, 2011.

Westhead, Paul. *The Speed Game: My Fast Times in Basketball.* Lincoln: University of Nebraska Press, 2020.

Wetzel, Dan, and Don Yaeger. *Sole Influence: Basketball, Corporate Greed, and the Corruption of America's Youth.* New York: Warner Books, 2000.

Wideman, John Edgar. *Brothers and Keepers.* New York: Holt, Rinehart and Winston, 1984.

———. *Hoop Roots: Playground Basketball, Love, and Race.* New York: Houghton Mifflin, 2001.

Williams, Pat, and Bill Lyon. *We Owed You One! The Uphill Struggle of the Philadelphia 76ers.* Wilmington, DE: TriMark Publishing, 1983.

Wolf, David. *Foul! The Connie Hawkins Story.* New York: Warner Books, 1972.

Wolff, Alexander, ed. *Basketball: Great Writing About America's Game.* New York: Library of America, 2018.

DOCUMENTARIES, FILMS, AND TELEVISION/STREAMING SERIES

expediTIously with Tip T. I. Harris, Spotify and Apple Podcasts, 2023.
First Take, ESPN, 2023.
First Things First, Fox Sports, 2023.
Goliath, Showtime, 2023.
Soul of the Game: The John McLendon Story, Intersport Television, 2021.
The VC Show with Vince Carter, ESPN, 2023.
White Men Can't Jump, 20th Century Fox, 1992.

JOURNAL, MAGAZINE, NEWSPAPER, AND ONLINE ARTICLES

Albergotti, Reed. "The Dunk That Made History." *The Wall Street Journal.* March 20, 2009.

Aldridge, David. "Ja Morant's Support System Needs to Step Up Now." TheAthletic.com. March 5, 2023.

Alexander, Chip. "Charles Develops His Game." *The News & Observer* (Raleigh, NC). February 7, 1984.

Alfano, Peter. "CBS Puts Over a Basketball Coup." *The New York Times.* November 22, 1983.

"All-Around Athlete." *The Arizona Republic.* January 12, 1947.

Amdur, Neil. "John McLendon, 84, Strategist in College and Pro Basketball." *The New York Times.* October 9, 1999.

Anderson, Dave. "Darrell Griffith: Doctor of Dunk." *The New York Times.* March 23, 1980.

Anderson, Kelli. "San Francisco Dons—In Their Own Style." *Sports Illustrated.* July 3, 2006.

Antonik, John. "WVU's Wells the First Woman to Dunk in a College Game." WVUSports.com. February 18, 2022.

Araton, Harvey. "Measuring Up to Chamberlain May Take More Than Stats." *The New York Times.* January 12, 2023.

Armstrong, Kevin. "Lorenzo Charles, Former Wolfpack NCAA Hero, Mourned by Entire State of North Carolina, Including Duke." *Daily News* (New York). July 5, 2011.

Atkin, Ross. "Houston's Style May Set a Trend—Will the Dunk Reign Supreme?" The Christian Science Monitor Service. April 10, 1983.

Baker, Chris. "Welcome to L.A." *Los Angeles Times.* July 2, 1995.

Ballenger, Bill. "A Young Wolf Finds His Teeth." *The Charlotte News.* January 15, 1973.

Baxley, Rodd. "N.C. State Basketball's David Thompson Honored with Statue, Lauded by Legends." *The Fayetteville Observer.* December 11, 2023.

Bechtel, Mark. "Magic vs. Bird: Reliving Basketball's Most Storied Rivalry 40 Years Later." *Sports Illustrated.* December 27, 2019.

Becker, Bill. "Alcindor, Who Has All the Shots, Seen Rising Above the Rim." *The New York Times*. March 30, 1967.

Beilue, Jon. "Hopes Are High for Movie, Hall of Fame Induction for Fortenberry and '36 Olympians." *Amarillo Globe-News*. September 14, 2017.

Bell, Jim. "Owens Earns Honor as 'Coach of Year.'" *Tulsa World*. December 29, 1968.

Benevento, Don. "Philadelphia Basketball Legend Welcomed Home." *Courier-Post* (Camden, NJ). March 19, 1991.

Benner, Bill. "'Dr. Dunk' Hillman in Slam Quarterfinals Test." *The Indianapolis Star*. February 13, 1977.

Bergera, Gary James. "This Time of Crisis: The Race-Based Anti-BYU Athletic Protests of 1968–71." *Utah Historical Quarterly*. No. 3, 2013.

Berkes, Howard. "Nazi Olympics Tangled Politics and Sport." National Public Radio. June 7, 2008.

"Bernard Dobbas Kills Mountain Lion with Club." *The Auburn Journal*. November 9, 1939.

Beschloss, Michael. "Naismith's Choices on Race, from Basketball's Beginnings." *The New York Times*. May 2, 2014.

Bibb, John. "Adolph and the Dunk." *The Tennessean*. April 2, 1976.

"The Big Surprise of 1955." *Sports Illustrated*. March 28, 1955.

Bilovsky, Frank. "Thirteen Years Ago at N.C. State, the Alley-Oop Began as an Errant Pass." *Democrat and Chronicle* (Rochester, NY). March 15, 1987.

Bishop, Greg. "Bedlam in Broadcasting: Remembering the Chaos of Julius Erving Slicing Up the Nuggets." *Sports Illustrated*. March 6, 2023.

Blackwell, Jon. "1900: Basketball's First Dynasty." *The Trentonian*. https://www.capital century.com/1900.html.

"Blindfolded, Crawley Wins Slam-Dunk Contest." Associated Press. January 18, 1999.

Bloom, Don. "Hillman Signs with Pacers, SF Says He Asked Too Much." *The Sacramento Bee*. April 15, 1971.

"Bob Kurland May Turn Pro." Associated Press. March 28, 1946.

"Bob Kurland Wore His Height Well." *Bartlesville Examiner-Enterprise*. October 2, 2013.

"Bogut Says Social Media Is Making Players Soft on Defense." NBA Australia. July 6, 2016.

Borden, Sam. "Before Wembanyama Hit the NBA Draft, There Was Frederic Weis." ESPN .com. June 24, 2023.

———. "For Frederic Weis, Knicks' Infamous Pick, Boos Began a Greater Struggle." *The New York Times*. July 14, 2015.

"Bouncing Back to a Golden Year." *The New York Times*. August 14, 1986.

Bradley, Mark. "Meet Earl 'The Goat' Manigault." *The Atlanta Journal-Constitution*. July 24, 1997.

Breen, Matt. "A Wilt Chamberlain Documentary Used Artificial Intelligence to Re-Create His Voice. The Family Is (Mostly) Thrilled to Hear Him Again." *The Philadelphia Inquirer*. July 14, 2023.

Brewer, Jerry. "When Did NBA Stars Become Too Cool to Dunk?" *The Washington Post*. February 18, 2023.

Broussard, Chris. "A Game Played Above the Rim, Above All Else." *The New York Times*. February 15, 2004.

Browning, Wilt. "Charles Is a Marked Man This Season." *The Greensboro Daily News*. March 24, 1983.

Brunson, Dennis. "Claflin's Morant Lives Up to Expectations." *The Item* (Sumter, SC). January 30, 1997.

Burgman, Grant. "Pittsburgh Pipers: The Forgotten Champions." *The Pitt News* (Pittsburgh, PA). November 8, 2017.

Burnes, Robert L. "Writer Who Has Watched the Best Picks Thorpe, Ruth, Louis as Tops." *St. Louis Globe-Democrat*. January 23, 1950.

Burnett, Zaron. "Why Did the NCAA Ban the Slam Dunk for Nine Years?" *MEL Magazine*. March 2022.

Busbee, Jay. "Dominique Wilkins Recalls Dueling with Michael Jordan at the 1988 Slam Dunk Contest." Yahoo! Sports. February 13, 2020.

Cacciola, Scott. "Ja Morant's Dunks Are Amazing. His Misses Are Even Better." *The New York Times*. August 3, 2020.

Caponi-Tabery, Gena. "Playing a Big Game, They Made a Huge Statement." *Austin American-Statesman*. January 24, 2006.

"Carlos, All Other Negro Athletes Hit San Jose State with Boycott Threat." Associated Press. November 26, 1968.

Carr, A. J. "State's High Wire Act." *The News & Observer* (Raleigh, NC). March 16, 1974.

Carry, Peter. "For Now, the Answer Is Not in the Stars." *Sports Illustrated*. September 20, 1971.

Carter, Aaron. "Wilt Chamberlain's Overbrook vs. West Philly Once Was the Most Anticipated High School Basketball Matchup." *The Philadelphia Inquirer*. January 27, 2023.

Cato, Tim. "Dunking Hurts: Why Players Hate—and Love—the NBA's Greatest Feat." TheAthletic.com. December 21, 2023.

"Cattleman Kills Lion with Club." Associated Press. November 8, 1939.

"CBS Dunk Contest Slammed." United Press International. June 5, 1977.

"Charles Charged." Associated Press. August 7, 1982.

"Charles to Serve 34-Hour Jail Term." Associated Press. August 10, 1982.

Christian, Darrell. "Will Purists Raise Basket to 12 Feet?" Associated Press. April 4, 1983.

Christian, Nichole M. "City Names Basketball Court to Honor the Goat Who Flew." *The New York Times*. May 26, 1998.

Clark, Christian. "What Became of Nuggets Star David Thompson After Injuries and Cocaine Derailed His Path to All-Time NBA Greatness." CPR News. September 11, 2019.

Clark, Kim. "Wherever Wilt Chamberlain Goes, He Finds Fans." *The Kansas City Star*. September 7, 1955.

Cobb, David. "A Single Highlight-Reel Dunk Defines Ja Morant Ahead of NBA Draft." *The Commercial Appeal* (Memphis, TN). June 17, 2019.

Cole, Milton. "In Game of Big Men, Bob Kurland Was Almost Too Big." *Daily Hampshire Gazette* (Northampton, MA). July 2, 1985.

Collins, Dick. "Dunk Rule Stuns Coaches." *Austin American*. March 30, 1967.

Connors, Bill. "'46 Cowboys Ready to Step into Spotlight Again." *Tulsa World*. February 20, 1996.

"Coogs Get Another Shot at Wolfpack." Associated Press. November 20, 1983.

Cory, Virgil. "Jack Ragland and Joe Fortenberry Quit National Champion Globes to Take Jobs with Phillips 66 at Bartlesville." *The Wichita Eagle.* September 11, 1936.

———. "Lanky Joe Fortenberry Answers the Charge That Universals and Globes Were Enemies in Berlin." *The Wichita Eagle.* September 9, 1936.

Coutros, Pete. "Wilt, Wilt, Who Gets Stilt?" *Daily News* (New York). March 20, 1955.

Crawford, Dakota. "Dr. Dunk, the Pacers' Often Forgotten Dunk Champion, Didn't Need Recognition." *The Indianapolis Star.* February 18, 2018.

Cronauer, Bill. "Putting the Dunk Back in Basketball." *St. Petersburg Times.* December 16, 1976.

Cross, Robert. "Bouncing Along with the Trotters." *Chicago Tribune.* January 30, 1977.

Cuddy, Jack. "'Raise the Hoop to 12 Feet,' Urges 'Phog' Allen, 'and Save Basketball from Those Glandular Goons.'" United Press International. December 2, 1942.

Curcio, Joe. "Pipers—Without Hawkins—Beat Chaps." *The Pittsburgh Press.* February 3, 1968.

Curti, Chuck. "Fifty Years after Their ABA Title, Pittsburgh Pipers Still Looking for Recognition." *Pittsburgh Tribune-Review.* April 21, 2018.

———. "Quotes, Anecdotes from Pittsburgh Pipers' 50th Reunion." *Pittsburgh Tribune-Review.* May 7, 2018.

Cushman, Tom. "Dunk Return, Higher Hoop?" *Philadelphia Daily News.* March 16, 1974.

Daley, Arthur. "AAU Boycotts 1936 Olympics Because of the Nazi Ban on Jews." *The New York Times.* November 21, 1933.

———. "Awesome Kansas Giants Reverse Basketball Layup Shot Process." *The New York Times.* March 10, 1936.

Dascenzo, Frank. "Thompson—Impossible to Describe." *The Durham Sun.* December 6, 1974.

Davy, Jimmy. "The Dunk's Grave Sinks Still Deeper." *The Tennessean.* March 27, 1976.

DeCock, Luke, Mandy Locke, and Caulton Tudor. "N.C. State Basketball Hero Could Inspire to the End." *The Charlotte Observer.* July 3, 2011.

Deford, Frank. "The Bouncing Ball." *Sports Illustrated.* December 3, 1973.

———. "The Ring Leader." *Sports Illustrated.* May 10, 1999.

Dell'Apa, Frank. "A Long Way from Dr. J." *The Boston Globe.* December 13, 1991.

Demirel, Evin. "The First Dunk." *Slam.* February 21, 2014.

Denberg, Jeff. "Hawks Take a Chance on Overweight Charles." *The Atlanta Journal-Constitution.* June 19, 1985.

DePaula, Nick. "The True Story of the 'Banned' Air Jordans." Yahoo! Sports. July 21, 2016.

Derrick, Mel. "'Dunk' Shot Ruled Illegal for College, High Schools." *The Charlotte Observer.* March 29, 1967.

Dick, Denny. "Joby's Tip Led Pacers to Darnell." *Indianapolis News.* December 2, 1971.

Dodds, Tracy. "The Men of '36." *Los Angeles Times.* July 27, 1984.

"Dons Trounce Texans; Test Utes Friday." United Press International. March 9, 1955.

Dopirak, Dustin. "Jordan vs. Dominique." *The Indianapolis Star.* February 15, 2024.

"The Dream Team of 1936." *Sports Illustrated.* July 22, 1996.

Duddy, James, and Owen Moritz. "A Hoop Hero and 5 Seized in Arms Raid." *Daily News* New York. July 8, 1977.

"Dunk Divides Cage Coaches." Associated Press. April 2, 1976.

Dwyer, Jim. "A Legend Returns, with Past Baggage." *Newsday.* June 24, 1991.

"'83 Legend Lorenzo Charles Dies in Crash." ESPN.com. June 28, 2011.

Elliott, Mal. "Original Dream Team Stole the Show in 1936." *The Wichita Eagle.* July 19, 1992.

Engellenner, Jon. "Barney Dobbas Had Larger-Than-Life Persona." *The Sacramento Bee.* July 11, 1996.

English, Reid. "CBS Makes a Quick Playoff Exit." *Statesman Journal* (Salem, OR). June 6, 1977.

Faraudo, Jeff. "DeJulio, 83, Who Spotted Russell for USF, Dies." *Oakland Tribune.* July 16, 2008.

Fitzpatrick, Frank. "At the Foul Line, Where Wilt's Myth and Reality Meet." *The Philadelphia Inquirer.* April 14, 2017.

———. "Doing Away with the Dunk: It's Hard to Believe the NCAA Once Outlawed It." *The Philadelphia Inquirer.* March 23, 2014.

Forde, Pat. "Kentucky vs. Texas Western, 30 Years Later." Gannett News Service. February 18, 1996.

Fowler, Scott. "Elon's Charlotte Smith Opens Up on Her Shot That Won the 1994 National Title for UNC." *The Charlotte Observer.* March 29, 2023.

———. "Wolfpack Great Thompson Talks Racism, Glory Days, and Whether He Can Still Dunk." *The Charlotte Observer.* July 12, 2020.

Frank, Stanley. "High Guy." *Collier's* magazine. March 17, 1945.

Freeman, Hal. "Chamberlain's 71 Sets Mark for Overbrook." *The Philadelphia Inquirer.* January 15, 1954.

Friend, Tom. "Old College Try." ESPN.com. February 9, 2010.

Garber, Greg. "Mother of Dunk Finally Getting Her Due." ESPN.com. July 22, 2009.

Garcia-Roberts, Gus, and Molly Hensley-Clancy. "In Memphis, Ja Morant's Summer of Trouble Went Unchecked by Authorities." *The Washington Post.* April 6, 2023.

Gardner, Hayes. "Wes Unseld Remembered as 'the Greatest Basketball Player to Ever Come Out of Kentucky.'" *Courier Journal* (Louisville, KY). June 2, 2020.

Gelke, Dick. "Roosevelt's Theme Is Erving and More." *Newsday.* March 14, 1968.

Gentile, Derek. "Recalling the Great Mikan." *The Berkshire Eagle.* June 11, 2005.

Giglio, J. P. "Mourners Say Charles a Hero on Court and Off." *The News & Observer.* July 3, 2011.

———and Chip Alexander. "Charles Remembered for More than Dunk." *The News & Observer.* June 29, 2011.

Glick, Shav. "Creating Their Own Fireworks." *Los Angeles Times.* May 10, 2004.

Goldman, Peter. "Gravity's Outlaw." *Sport.* March 1978.

Goldpaper, Sam. "Louisville's Griffith Is Dr. Dunk." *The New York Times.* February 21, 1980.

———. "Nets Get Erving from Squires for Carter, Cash, and . . ." *The New York Times.* August 1, 1973.

Goldstein, Joe. "Explosion II: The Molinas Period." ESPN.com. November 19, 2003.

Goldstein, Richard. "Bob Kurland, 88, Pioneer for Basketball's Big Men, Dies." *The New York Times*. September 30, 2013.

———. "Connie Hawkins, Electrifying NBA Forward Barred in His Prime, Dies at 75." *The New York Times*. October 7, 2017.

Good, Herb. "USF Whips La Salle for NCAA Title." *The Philadelphia Inquirer*. March 20, 1955.

Goodman, Irv. "The High School Kid Who Could Play Pro Right Now." *Sport*. March 1955.

Goudsouzian, Aram. "Bill Russell and the Basketball Revolution." *American Studies*. Fall/Winter 2006.

———. "Can Basketball Survive Chamberlain? The Kansas Years of Wilt the Stilt." *Kansas History*. Autumn 2005.

———. "The House That Russell Built: Bill Russell, the University of San Francisco, and the Winning Streak That Changed College Basketball." *California History*. Fall 2007.

"Grant Union's Aguirre Will Go on Boys' Club Cage Tour." *The Sacramento Bee*. February 2, 1952.

Gray, Ron. "Yank Cagers Cut Local 'Stars' Up." *Vancouver Sun*. February 7, 1952.

Greene, Jerry. "Trentons Can Help Us Deal with NBA Brawl." *Orlando Sentinel*. November 24, 2004.

Greer, Thom. "Dunk Slams Way into Cage Spotlight." *Chicago Sun-Times*. March 8, 1977.

Gregston, Gene. "Rogers Says Repeated Changes Hurting Game." *Fort Worth Star-Telegram*. March 25, 1955.

Grundy, Pamela. "A Position of Respect." *Southern Cultures*. Summer 2001.

Harbin, Tom. "Tar Heelia Producing Top-Grade Cage Talent." *Asheville Citizen-Times*. February 7, 1965.

Harris, Curtis M. "Basketball's Christian Origins." ProHoopsHistory.substack.com. January 19, 2020.

Harrison, Claude E. "Wilt Chamberlain Back at Kansas U." *The Philadelphia Tribune*. November 12, 1957.

Hauser, Thomas. "Thomas Hauser and Others Remember Dave Wolf at 75." *The Sweet Science*. August 20, 2018.

Hawley, Tom. "Dunk Contest Good for Some Laughs." *Wisconsin State Journal*. February 14, 1977.

Heckert, Druann Maria, and Amy Best. "Ugly Duckling to Swan: Labeling Theory and the Stigmatization of Red Hair." *Symbolic Interaction*. No. 4, 1997.

Heisel, Andrew. "The Plot to Kill the Slam Dunk." Vice.com. February 12, 2015.

Hensley-Clancy, Molly. "NBA Star Ja Morant Accused in Police Reports of Punching Teen, Making Threats." *The Washington Post*. March 1, 2023.

Herman, Jack. "When Seven-Foot Bob Kurland, All-America, First Reported for Practice at Jennings High." *St. Louis Globe-Democrat*. January 27, 1948.

Heufelder, Bill. "11,457 See Pros Trim New Orleans." *The Pittsburgh Press*. May 5, 1968.

———. "Pipers Fade, Lose 5th to New Orleans." *The Pittsburgh Press*. April 28, 1968.

Hofmann, Rich. "Mac McClung's Path Back to NBA: 30 Cities, 150 Teammates and a Dunk Contest." TheAthletic.com. February 15, 2023.

Hollinger, John. "Has NBA Offense Gotten Out of Control?" TheAthletic.com. January 29, 2024.

Huber, Robert. "Julius Erving Doesn't Want to Be a Hero Anymore." *Philadelphia* magazine. April 23, 2008.

Hunsinger Benbow, Dana. "Former Pacers' Star Darnell Hillman Is One Tough—Beloved—Youth Coach." *The Indianapolis Star.* March 25, 2019.

International News Service. "Cowboys, Razorbacks in Finals." March 24, 1945.

"Jack Inglis, Basketball Star, Is Victim of Spanish Flu." *The Carbondale Leader.* October 7, 1918.

"Jack Inglis, Troy Basketball Player, Dead of Pneumonia." *Pittston Gazette.* October 7, 1918.

Jacobs, Jeff. "Steitz Made His Mark as Father of Three." *Hartford Courant.* March 14, 2017.

Jacobson, Steve. "7-Footer Kurland, the First Very Big Man, Had Much in Common with Big Country." *Newsday.* April 2, 1995.

Jenkins, Sally. "NCAA Lost Its Teeth in Court in 1984, and No One's Been in Charge Since." *The Washington Post.* September 23, 2011.

Jeter, Fred. "VUU's Jackie Jackson of Harlem Globetrotters Fame Dies at 79." *Richmond Free Press.* May 10, 2019.

"Joe Fortenberry, Olympic Captain, 82." Associated Press. June 5, 1993.

Johnson, K. C. "Michael Jordan vs. Dominique Wilkins: An Oral History of the 1988 NBA Slam Dunk Contest." NBC Sports Chicago. February 11, 2020.

Jonze, Tim. "A Michael Jordan Slam Dunk from Above." *The Guardian* (New York and London). May 5, 2021.

J. S. "Dobbas Sinks 27 Points as Aggies Win." *Daily Democrat* (Woodland, CA). January 12, 1935.

Kang, Jay Caspian. "What the World Got Wrong About Kareem Abdul-Jabbar." *The New York Times Magazine.* September 17, 2015.

Keating, Thomas. "Hillman Wrapped in Bottle Shoppe." *The Indianapolis Star.* June 11, 1977.

Keech, Larry. "Charles Taking His Image to Court." *Greensboro Daily News.* November 19, 1983.

Keilman, John. "The Gadget Really Was a Slam-Dunk." *Chicago Tribune.* April 4, 2005.

Kerasotis, Peter. "Thompson Dunks Troubled Past." *Florida Today.* June 29, 1997.

Kindred, Dave. "Kurland-Mikan: The Start of Something Big." *The Washington Post.* December 9, 1982.

Kirkpatrick, Curry. "A Place in the Big-City Sun." *Sports Illustrated.* August 5, 1968.

———. "The Night They Drove Old Dixie Down." *Sports Illustrated.* April 1, 1991.

———. "They Run and They Gun—and They're a Mile High." *Sports Illustrated.* March 29, 1976.

Knafo, Saki. "He Changed the Game, but 'Nobody Knows Who He Is.'" *The New York Times.* February 18, 2022.

Knight, Joey. "Dereck Whittenburg Talks 'Survive and Advance' at Vitale Gala." *Tampa Bay Times.* May 11, 2019.

Kriegel, Mark. "Charles's Slam Heard Around the World." *Daily News* (New York). March 28, 1996.

Kritzer, Cy. "Is This Basketball—or Volleyball?" *Buffalo Evening News.* December 29, 1955.

"Kurland Leaves Tall Shadow." *Bartlesville Examiner-Enterprise.* October 1, 2013.

Lahnert, Lance. "Gold Again." *Amarillo Globe-News.* January 16, 2017.

Lake, Thomas. "A Letter to Michael Jordan." *Sports Illustrated.* August 14, 2012.

Lamm, David. "Wolfpack: Beautiful." *The Greensboro Record.* February 1, 1973.

Lapchick, Richard. "NBA Receives an A for Racial and Gender Hiring Practices." ESPN .com. August 8, 2023.

"Late Jack Inglis Was Great Athlete." *The North Adams Transcript.* October 9, 1918.

Lawrence, Mitch. "Syracuse Seeking Final Four." *Democrat and Chronicle* (Rochester, NY). April 7, 1983.

Leavy, Jane. "The Olympics Uproar." *The Washington Post.* June 22, 1980.

Lidz, Franz. "The ABA Was Short-Lived, but Its Impact on Basketball Is Eternal." *Smithsonian Magazine.* October 2017.

Lipsyte, Robert. "Go West, Young Man." *The New York Times.* May 4, 1965.

———. "The Long Odds and Big Dreams of the Goat." *The New York Times.* February 21, 1992.

Littwin, Mike. "Thompson Is No Longer Denver's Golden Nugget." *Los Angeles Times.* April 4, 1982.

Livingston, Bill. "76ers: Dunk Champions of the NBA." *The Philadelphia Inquirer.* November 23, 1976.

Lochner, Tom. "Eural McKelvey's Nicknames Were as Varied as His Arsenal of Hoop Shots." *West County Times.* July 13, 1997.

Lupica, Mike. "It's West, 125–124, but Doc's MVP." *Daily News* (New York). February 14, 1977.

MacGregor, Roy. "To Touch the Rock." *Ottawa Citizen.* October 17, 1995.

Mackey, Dick. "Slam-Dunk Contest a New Chance for McNeill." *The Kansas City Star.* February 18, 1977.

MacMullan, Jackie. "How the NBA Tapped into the Bird and Magic Machine." TheRinger .com. March 25, 2022.

Mallea, John R. "The Victorian Sporting Legacy." *McGill Journal of Education.* September 1, 1975.

Mallozzi, Vincent M. "Earl Manigault, 53, New York City Basketball Legend, Dies." *The New York Times.* May 16, 1998.

Markus, Don. "Charles Flexes His Muscles as a Senior." *The Record* (north New Jersey). December 23, 1984.

———. "Hesitant Terps Started Trend with a Super Bowl-Day Classic." *The Baltimore Sun.* February 4, 2018.

Martin, Charles. "The Color Line in Midwestern College Sports." *Indiana Magazine of History.* June 2002.

Martin, Douglas. "Lorenzo Charles Dies at 47; Made Winning Dunk in 1983 NCAA Title Game." *The New York Times.* June 28, 2011.

Martin, Gerald. "Down Lo, or on Wing, Charles Gets Job Done." *The News & Observer*. March 5, 1985.

Martin, Whitney. "Two Former Ogden Boosters to Play for Court Gonfalon." Associated Press. March 21, 1936.

Mazurkiewicz, Michal. "Muscular Christianity: Christian Roots of American Sports." *Zabawy i zabawki. Studia Antropologiczne*. 2018.

McCabe, Mick. "Marble, Mills Follow the Masters." *Detroit Free Press*. November 26, 1984.

McCallum, Jack. "In the Kingdom of the Solitary Man." *Sports Illustrated*. October 6, 1986.

———. "Losers Weepers." *Sports Illustrated*. March 8, 1999.

———. "The Top Dog of Dunk." *Sports Illustrated*. November 30, 1981.

McDermott, Barry. "Now You See Him, Now You Don't." *Sports Illustrated*. February 11, 1980.

McHugh, Roy. "Everything But Fans." *The Pittsburgh Press*. March 26, 1968.

McKie, Don. "A Gentle Giant Stirs Memories." *The Philadelphia Inquirer*. October 13, 1999.

McKnight, Michael. "Just Dunk." *Sports Illustrated*. June 1, 2015.

McLendon, John B. "More Than Just the Fellow with the Peach Baskets." *The New York Times*. October 27, 1996.

McLeod, Ken. "The Construction of Masculinity in African American Music and Sports." *American Music*. Summer 2009.

Meyer, Craig. "NBA Hall of Famer and Pittsburgh Legend Connie Hawkins Dies at 75." *Pittsburgh Post-Gazette*. October 7, 2017.

Miller, Glenn. "Sanibel's Kurland: Back-to-Back Titles." *The News-Press* (Fort Myers, FL). March 14, 1991.

Miller, Robin. "Dr. Dunk Turns on the Hep Pacer Crowds." *The Indianapolis Star*. February 13, 1972.

Minkoff, Randy. "Jordan Is Hot off the Court, Too." United Press International. October 20, 1985.

Morris, Ron. "How Thompson, Towe Pioneered the Alley-Oop." *The News & Observer*. February 26, 2016.

Morrow, Art. "7-Footer Grows Up." *The Philadelphia Inquirer*. December 21, 1944.

"N.C. State National Title Hero Charles Killed in Bus Crash." Associated Press. June 28, 2011.

Neal, Bill. "1968 Pittsburgh Pipers Celebrated, Appreciated During May 4–5 Reunion." *Pittsburgh Courier*. May 17, 2018.

Neel, Eric. "The Day the Dunk Was Born." ESPN.com. https://www.espn.com/espn/page2/story?page=neel/060217.

"Negroes Played Major Role in Recruiting Wilt 'The Stilt' Chamberlain for Kansas." *The Philadelphia Tribune*. January 26, 1957.

"New Rule to Outlaw Dunking in Basketball." United Press International. March 29, 1967.

Newell, Nat. "XBA Comes to Irmo High." *The State* (Columbia, SC). Jun 21, 2002.

———. "XBA Reunites Irmo Grads McKie, Orange." *The State* (Columbia, SC). July 25, 2002.

O'Connell, Robert. "Ja Morant's Night at a Denver Strip Club Could Cost Him $39 Million." *The Wall Street Journal*. March 17, 2023.

———. "The Unstoppable Move That's Taking the NBA by Storm." *The Wall Street Journal*. February 14, 2024.

O'Connor, Ian. "A Fallen King Revisits His Realm." *The New York Times*. June 16, 1989.

O'Neill, Dana. "Ed Steitz's 3-Point Dream Lives On." ESPN.com. November 3, 2011.

———. "What's the Lifespan of a Ghost? Forty Years After Its Miracle Run, N.C. State Is Trying to Find Out." TheAthletic.com. March 6, 2023.

"Opinions on Erving Deal." *Newsday*. October 31, 1976.

Oriard, Michael. "Why Football Injuries Remain a Part of the Game." *The New York Times*. November 20, 1983.

Ostler, Scott. "The Leaping Legends of Basketball." *Los Angeles Times*. February 12, 1989.

Overpeck, Keith F. "Slam-Bang . . . CBS to Stage NBA One-on-One Dunkoffs." *Courier-Journal* (Louisville, KY). January 12, 1977.

Owen, Howard. "The Dunk." *Richmond Times-Dispatch*. November 20, 1983.

Papanek, John. "Strutting Their Stuffs." *Sports Illustrated*. February 9, 1976.

Patterson, Donald W. "Alley-Oop!" *News & Record* (Greensboro, NC). March 5, 1998.

Patton, Kevin. "Ja Morant Is the Latest, Greatest in Murray State's History of Hoops Success." *The Gleaner* (Henderson, KY). March 9, 2019.

Pennington, Enos. "Today's Game Isn't What Inventor Planned." Scripps Howard News Service. November 21, 1987.

"Phog Allen Sees Big Argument for Loftier Baskets." United Press International. January 15, 1944.

Planos, Josh. "Ja Morant Would Like Your Attention." FiveThirtyEight.com. February 14, 2019.

Politi, Steve. "Perfect Stuffing for the Holidays." *The News & Observer* (Raleigh). December 3, 1994.

———. "Smith Jams! 'Just Me and the Goal.'" *The News & Observer* (Raleigh). December 5, 1994.

Pompey, Keith. "Sixers' Mac McClung Wins NBA Slam Dunk Contest and Captures Hearts with All-Time Performance." *The Philadelphia Inquirer*. February 18, 2023.

Posnanski, Joe. "Dunk a Shattering Experience." *The Kansas City Star*. November 28, 2004.

Price, S. L. "Oh, Brother." *Sports Illustrated*. June 8, 1999.

Pruett, John. "Interview with Ben Jobe." *The Huntsville Times*. March 10, 2008.

Putz, Paul. "Muscular Christianity and Moral Formation Through Sports." Blogs.baylor.edu. January 31, 2022.

Rains, Rob. "James Naismith Wouldn't Raise the Basketball Rim." *The New York Times*. May 20, 2013.

Rains, Sally Tippett. "Hellen Carpenter, Granddaughter of James Naismith—Inventor of Basketball—Remembered as Humanitarian, Author, and Hostess." StlSportsPage.com. April 27, 2021.

Ribler, Les. "Chamberlain Gets Record 90 Pts. as Overbrook Routs Roxborough." *The Philadelphia Inquirer*. February 18, 1955.

Riches, Sam. "Vince Carter and the Slam Dunk's Day of Reckoning." *The Atlantic*. November 16, 2017.

Robinson, Jackie. "Jackie Robinson Tells His Story." *Brooklyn Eagle*. August 16, 1949.

Rogers, Thomas. "Edward Steitz, 69, an Authority on the Rules of Basketball, Dies." *The New York Times*. May 22, 1990.

"The Role of the S.S. *Manhattan* in Olympic History." *Asbury Park Press*. September 29, 2016.

Rosaforte, Jim. "The Class of the Class of '84." *The Fort Lauderdale News*. October 22, 1984.

Rosen, Byron. "Thompson About to Be Highest Paid in NBA." *The Washington Post*. April 19, 1978.

Rosner, Dave. "N.C. State, Charles Miss Washburn." *Newsday*. December 30, 1984.

———. "N.C. State's Charles Tough to Overlook." *Newsday*. December 29, 1984.

"Russell Played Here in 1952." *The Bellingham Herald*. March 27, 1955.

Ryan, Bob. "Bill Russell Was Unparalleled on the Basketball Court, Uncompromising Off It." *The Boston Globe*. August 5, 2022.

———. "The Show Is Jordan's—but Celtics Steal It." *The Boston Globe*. April 21, 1986.

Sakamoto, Bob. "Jordan Will Miss 6 Weeks." *Chicago Tribune*. November 5, 1985.

Sandlin, Blake. "From Tee to Ja: Morant Finishing What His Father Started." *The Murray State News*. February 22, 2018.

———. "Making Morant: Ja Morant's Ascent from Small Town Kid to Big Stage Star." *The Murray State News*. March 1, 2019.

Sandomir, Richard. "NBC and NBA Agree to $750 Million Pact." *The New York Times*. April 29, 1993.

"Says Inglis Was Best of 'Em All." *The Wilkes-Barre Record*. March 6, 1923.

Schmitz, Brian. "Bob Kurland Is the Grand-Daddy of the Dunk." *Orlando Sentinel*. February 19, 2012.

Schreeder, Jack. "Can Tragic Story Have a Happy Ending with Utah Stars?" *The Salt Lake Tribune*. August 29, 1971.

Shapiro, Leonard. "A Basketball Idol Falls." *The Washington Post*. February 23, 1972.

Shefski, Bill. "Wrong Shot Banned?" *Philadelphia Daily News*. March 31, 1967.

Silary, Ted. "The Time Wilt Took On 'Nova." *Philadelphia Daily News*. October 14, 1999.

Slotnik, Daniel E. "Ben Jobe, Southern University Basketball Coach, Dies at 84." *The New York Times*. March 16, 2017.

Smith, Red. "Arthur Daley, Sports Columnist, Dies." *The New York Times*. January 4, 1974.

Snider, Steve. "Dons' Bill Russell Could Revolutionize Basketball." United Press International. March 23, 1955.

Solotaroff, Ivan. "Sitting on the Rim with Earl Manigault." *The Village Voice*. October 16, 1990.

"Sonic Takes a Fall." *The New York Times*. March 13, 1984.

Spencer, Frank. "Bigtime Basketball in a Little School." *Winston-Salem Journal*. February 17, 1965.

"Sports Insider." *Boca Raton News*. March 23, 1991.

Starner, Tom. "In a League of His Own." *Sports Illustrated*. July 29, 1991.

Steptoe, Sonja. "Meet an Ageless Wonder." *Sports Illustrated*. December 24, 1990.

Telander, Rick. "Da Stadium." *Sports Illustrated*. June 1, 1992.

———. "He's Bigger than He Looks." *Sports Illustrated*. November 29, 1982.

Terrell, Roy. "Even the Loss of K. C. Jones May Not Cost San Francisco the NCAA Title—But It May Make the Dons' Job Tougher." *Sports Illustrated*. January 23, 1956.

Thomas, Ben. "Exciting 'Dunk Shot' Returns to Collegiate Scene Next Year." Associated Press. April 1, 1976.

Thomas, Bob. "Legend Wooden Spells It Out." *The Washington Post*. October 8, 2000.

"Thompson Denies Drug Problem." Associated Press. June 30, 1982.

Tramel, Barry. "1945 Aggies Changed Map of Basketball." *The Oklahoman*. June 4, 1999.

Trubiano, Ernie. "Manigault Survived Early Life with Drugs." Knight-Ridder Newspapers. February 6, 1988.

Tudor, Carlton. "She Missed Lorenzo's Famous Shot." *The News & Observer*. June 28, 2011.

"TV Networks Pit Colleges Against Pros." Associated Press. December 31, 1976.

Uitti, Jacob. "The History of the Slam Dunk: From Outlawed Move to Beloved Highlight." *The Guardian* (New York and London). February 17, 2023.

Valenti, John. "'The Goat' Comes Home a Survivor." *Newsday*. August 12, 1986.

Vecsey, Peter. "A Junkie Wins a New Day on Court." *Daily News* (New York). September 2, 1971.

———. "U. Mass Soph Has Gift of Grab." *The New York Daily News*. March 12, 1970.

Verdon, Joe. "Who Really Taught Kareem Abdul-Jabbar His Hook Shot?" TheAthletic.com. March 2, 2023.

Vogt, Tom. "Dr. J Still Dunk King." *The Columbian* (Vancouver, WA). June 12, 1977.

Wallace, Ava. "Country Star." *The Washington Post*. March 1, 2018.

"Walter Byers, the First Executive Director of the NCAA, Dies at 93." Associated Press. May 28, 2015.

Washington, Jesse. "Holcombe Rucker for the Basketball Hall of Fame." ESPN.com. September 8, 2015.

———. "I Was Wrong for Saying Mac McClung Was in the Dunk Contest Because He's White." Andscape.com. February 20, 2023.

Weber, Bruce. "Darry Dawkins, Lovable NBA Figure and Fierce Dunker, Dies at 58." *The New York Times*. August 27, 2015.

Weiner, Natalie. "How Viral Dunkers Can Revolutionize Women's Basketball." Bleacher Report. September 29, 2017.

Weintraub, Robert. "Jamfest for the Ages." ESPN.com. https://www.espn.com/espn/eticket/story?page=jamfest83&redirected=true.

Wertheim, Jon. "Canadian Club, Neat. American Success Story, on the Rocks." *Sports Illustrated*. January 29, 2021.

Whicker, Mark. "David Thompson: His Finest Hour." *The Chapel Hill Newspaper*. January 16, 1973.

———. "Dawk Is Gone, but Lovetron Lives On." *Philadelphia Daily News*. September 8, 1982.

———. "Story of All-Black Starting 5 Beating All-White Kentucky Stands on Its Own." *The Orange County Register*. January 13, 2008.

White, Gordon S. "NCAA Title Basketball Sold to CBS for $48 Million." *The New York Times*. March 5, 1981.

Whiteside, Larry. "David Thompson: People Expect Him to Do Everything, and So Far He Has." *The Boston Globe.* November 21, 1976.

Wik, Dave. "Basketball Rules Group Tried, but Failed to Stop Russell." *The Daily Palo Alto Times.* March 10, 1956.

Wile, Otis. "Cowboys Riding on to New York for Title Game." *The Daily Oklahoman.* March 26, 1945.

Williams, Doug. "In 1974, N.C. State Stood Atop Hoops World." ESPN.com. April 2, 2013.

Winn, Luke. "The Freshman." *Sports Illustrated.* October 14, 2013.

Wittry, Andy. "The Story Behind the First Known Dunk in College Basketball History." NCAA.com. December 15, 2021.

Woike, Dan. "Brent Barry, One of Three L.A.-Based Players to Win Slam Dunk Contest, Revisits 1996 Triumph." *Los Angeles Times.* February 16, 2018.

Wolf, Dave. "Connie Hawkins: The Unjust Exile of a Superstar." *Life.* May 16, 1969.

Wood, Jeremy. "Ja Morant, Murray State's High-Flying Star, Is No Longer College Hoops's Best Kept Secret." *Sports Illustrated.* January 23, 2018.

"Woolpert Says Basketball Better Game 20 Years Ago." Associated Press. April 3, 1955.

Yip, Sam. "Nate Robinson: 'I'm Still Looking for a Kidney to This Day.'" HoopsHype .com. February 14, 2024.

Young, Dennis. "Bill Russell's 66-Year-Old University of San Francisco High Jump Record May Never Be Broken." *San Francisco Chronicle.* August 10, 2022.

Young, Dick. "Dons Win 35th; Oust HC, 67–51; UCLA Final Foe." *Daily News* (New York). December 29, 1955.

Young, Jabari. "NBA Star Ja Morant and His Mom Have a Mantra: 'Be a Billionaire by 30.'" Forbes.com. December 25, 2022.

Young, Masco. "They're Talking About." *The Louisiana Weekly.* March 18, 1961.

INTERVIEWS

Malik Beasley

Barry Beckham

Zac Boardman

Neal Bradley

Mel Brodsky

Fritz Byers

Celeste Carpenter Cox

Rick Coxto

Sylvia Crawley

Joel Embiid

Julius Erving

Beth Fortenberry

Oliver Fortenberry

Trish Fortenberry

Barry Galman

Theresa Grentz

William Gutman

Laura Dorsey Harris

Shawn Hawkins

Sonny Hill

Mo Howard

Walter Iooss

Stan James

Bobby Jones

Paige Kadish

Coby Karl

Aubrey Keeling

Rocky Kurland

Vince Lackner

Carl Lacy

David Lattin

Mac McClung

Greg McKelvey

Cozell McQueen

Bill Melchionni

DeAnthony Melton

Malcolm Moran

Ja Morant

Ronnie "Tee" Morant

Daryl Morey

Ernie Myers

Massillion Myers

John Nash
Bill Neal
Sally Fortenberry
  Nibbelink
Lucas Nichols
Ian O'Connor
Steve Prohm
Rob Rains
Dave Ramey
Barbara Rintala
Glenn "Doc" Rivers
Renee Robinson
Kenny Roth

Blake Sandlin
Garry Saunders
Leon Saunders
Ron Shelton
Brady M. Smith
Charlotte Smith
Jordan Smith
Ivan Solotaroff
Doug Stark
Bob Steitz
Steve Steitz
Lindy Suiter
Rick Telander

Sonny Vaccaro
Steve Vacendak
Peter Vecsey
Anthony "Spud" Webb
Dick "Hoops" Weiss
Mark Whicker
Dereck Whittenburg
Dominique Wilkins
Pat Williams
Dave Winder
Paul Woolpert
Ed Wright
John Wright

INDEX

ABOUT THE AUTHOR

Bob Zilahy

MIKE SIELSKI is the author of four books, including *The Rise: Kobe Bryant and the Pursuit of Immortality*. A columnist for *The Philadelphia Inquirer*, he was formerly a reporter at *The Wall Street Journal*, and his work has been anthologized three times in *The Best American Sports Writing* and *The Year's Best Sports Writing*. He lives in Bucks County, Pennsylvania, with his wife and two sons.